DICTI

OF

BANKING

BUSINESS DICTIONARY SERIES

DICTIONARY OF BUSINESS AND MANAGEMENT
Jerry M. Rosenberg
DICTIONARY OF BANKING
Jerry M. Rosenberg
DICTIONARY OF INVESTING
Jerry M. Rosenberg

OTHER BOOKS BY THE AUTHOR

Automation, Manpower and Education (Random House)

The Computer Prophets (Macmillan)

The Death of Privacy: Do Government and Industrial Computers Threaten Our Personal Freedom? (Random House)

Inside the Wall Street Journal: The History and Power of Dow Jones & Company and America's Most Influential Newspaper (Macmillan)

Dictionary of Artificial Intelligence and Robotics (John Wiley)

The New Europe: An A to Z Compendium on the European Community (Bureau of National Affairs)

Dictionary of Business Acronyms, Initials, and Abbreviations (McGraw-Hill)

Dictionary of Wall Street Acronyms, Initials, and Abbreviations (McGraw-Hill)

Dictionary of Information Technology and Computer Acronyms, Initials and Abbreviations (McGraw-Hill)

The New American Community: The U.S. Response to the European and Asian Economic Challenge (Praeger)

DICTIONARY
OF
BANKING

Jerry M. Rosenberg

**Professor, Graduate School
of Management, and
School of Business
RUTGERS UNIVERSITY**

Business Dictionary Series

John Wiley & Sons, Inc.

New York · Chichester · Brisbane · Toronto · Singapore

In recognition of the importance of preserving what has been written, it is a policy of John Wiley & Sons, Inc., to have books of enduring value printed on acid-free paper, and we exert our best efforts to that end.

This publication is designed to provide accurate and authoritative information in regard to the subject matter covered. It is sold with the understanding that the publisher is not engaged in rendering legal, accounting, or other professional service. If legal advice or other expert assistance is required, the services of a competent professional person should be sought. From a *Declaration of Principles jointly adopted by a Committee of the American Bar Association and a Committee of Publishers.*

Library of Congress Cataloging-in-Publication Data:

Rosenberg, Jerry Martin.
    Dictionary of banking / by Jerry M. Rosenberg.
        p.   cm. — (business dictionary series)
    ISBN 0-471-57435-X (cloth) ISBN 0-471-57436-8 (paper)
    1. Banks and banking—Dictionaries.   I. Title.   II. Series.
HG151.R66   1992
332.1'03—dc20   92-7419

Printed in the United States of America

10 9 8 7 6 5 4 3 2 1

To Lauren
with love

PREFACE

The upheaval in the banking industry, accompanied by new regulations has, since 1985 when the last edition of this work appeared, generated a significant outflow of new terminology.

Bank failures, global shifts in banking strategy, plans for single currency and unified banking within the European Community, and a search for currency convertibility in Eastern Europe and the former Soviet Union, all combine to create some confusion along with the expansion of concepts and phrases.

With this new edition, I have included the most current words in the banking industry, readjusted older ones, eliminated now obsolete concepts, and in general, attempted to present the user with the most up-to-date glossary of banking and related terminology available.

No dictionary can be the exclusive product of one person's effort. Even when written by one individual, such a work requires the tapping of many sources, which is especially true of this book. By the very nature of the fields included, I have had to rely on the able and extensive efforts of others.

When I have quoted a definition from another copyrighted source, a number in brackets appears at the end of the definition. This number indicates the primary reference used in defining the term which is identified in the "References" portion of the dictionary. When no reference source is shown following a term, this suggests that I have not deliberately quoted the definition from any copyrighted source. Any apparent similarity to existing, unreleased definitions in these cases is purely accidental and the result of the limitations of language.

Much assistance has come indirectly from authors of books, journal articles, and reference materials. They are too numerous to be named here. Various organizations have aided me directly by providing informative source materials. Some government agencies and not-for-profit associations have provided a considerable amount of usable information.

On a more personal level, I thank the various individuals whom I used as a sounding board to clarify my ideas and approach; they offered valuable suggestions and encouraged me to go on with the project.

Without the confidence of Stephen Kippur, Senior Vice President of John Wiley & Sons and my staunch supporter for more than a decade, Karl Weber, former editor and now Associate Publisher, and my present editor Neal Maillet, this dictionary would never have appeared. Lastly, but always there is my wife Ellen, daughters Liz and Lauren, and son-in-law Bob, who collectively continue to lend their reinforcement and share my interest in the meaning and usage of words. Once again, I look forward to hearing from readers with suggestions, both for changes and for future entries.

JERRY M. ROSENBERG

New York, New York

CONTENTS

INTRODUCTION

This dictionary is a practical guide and reference tool for proper handling of the many banking and financial problems and questions that arise in business every day. It provides a deeper understanding of operations, methods, and practices in the rapidly changing fields of banking and finance.

This work of approximately 7,500 entries has been prepared with the hope that awareness of the accepted meanings of terms may enhance the process of sharing information and ideas. Though it cannot eliminate the need for the user to determine how a writer or speaker treats a word, such a dictionary shows what usages exist. It should reduce arguments about words and assist in stabilizing terminology. Most important, it should aid people in saying and writing just what they intend with greater clarity.

A word can take on different meanings in different contexts. There may be as many meanings as there are areas of specialty. A goal of this dictionary is to be broad and to establish core definitions that represent the variety of individual meanings. My purpose is to enhance parsimony and clearness in the communication process within the banking and financial fields.

Many terms are used in different ways. I have tried to unite them without bias of giving one advantage or dominance over another. Whenever possible (without creating a controversy), I have stated the connection among multiple usages.

Commonly used symbols, acronyms, and abbreviations are given. Foreign words and phrases are included only if they have become an integral part of our English vocabulary.

Other dictionaries that deal with a similar subject tend to define their task rather narrowly, whereas this work purports to reach throughout all departments within banks and financial institutions by acknowledging that the sum of an organization is greater than any of its individual parts—the result, an all-inclusive dictionary of banking and financial terms.

The broad base in the banking and financial fields necessitated inclusion of terms within this dictionary from accounting, banking, brokerage, capital structure, capitalization, collections, commercial banking, commodities markets, computer systems, credit, credit unions, financial institutions, financial law, financial management, financial planning, financial reports, foreign trade, funding, government regulations and agencies, import-export, insurance, investments, lending, methods of financing, manpower and human resources, money concepts, mortgages, organization, personal finance, public finance, savings and loan associations, savings banks, securities markets, services, sources of bank and financial information, systems, transfers, and trusts.

ORGANIZATION

This is a defining work rather than a compilation of facts. The line is not easy to draw because in the final analysis meanings are based on facts. Consequently, factual information is used where necessary to make a term more easily understood.

All terms are presented in the language of those who use them. The level of complexity needed for a definition will vary with the user; one person's complexity is another's precise and parsimonious statement. Several meanings are sometimes given—relatively simple for the layman, more developed and technical for the specialist.

I have organized the dictionary to provide information easily and rapidly. Keeping in mind two categories of user—the experienced person who demands precise information about a particular word, and the newcomer, support member, teacher, or student who seeks general explanations—I have in most cases supplied both general and specialized entries to make this dictionary an unusually useful reference source.

FORMAT

Alphabetization.   Words are presented alphabetically. Compound terms are placed where the reader is most likely to look for them. They are entered under their most distinctive component, usually nouns. Should you fail to locate a word where you initially look for it, turn to a variant spelling, a synonym, or a different word of the compound term.

Entries containing mutual concepts are usually grouped for comparison. They are then given in inverted order; that is, the expected order of words is reversed to allow the major word of the phrase to appear at the beginning of the term. These entries precede those that are given in the expected order. The terms are alphabetized up to the first comma and then by words following the comma, thus establishing clusters of related terms.

Headings.   The currently popular term is usually given as the principal entry, with other terms cross-referenced to it. Some terms have been included for historical significance, even though they are not presently in common usage.

Cross-References.   Cross-references go from the general to the specific. Occasionally, "see" references from the specific to the general are used to inform the user of words related to particular entries. "See" references to presently accepted terminology are made wherever possible. The use of "Cf." suggests words to be compared with the original entry.

Synonyms.   The word "synonymous" following a definition does not imply that the term is *exactly* equivalent to the principal entry under which it appears. Usually the term only approximates the primary sense of the original entry.

Disciplines.   Many words are given multiple definitions based on their utilization in various fields of activity. The definition with the widest application is given first, with the remaining definitions listed by area of specialty (identified in boldface italic type). Since the areas may overlap, the reader should examine *all* multiple definitions.

A: see *account.*

AA: see *active account.*

ABA:
(1) see *American Bankers Association.*
(2) see *American Bankers Association number.*

ABA Transit Code: see *American Bankers Association number.*

abeyance: a temporary suspension of title to property before the correct owner is determined. See *cloud on title.*

ability to pay: the ability of the bank or financial organization's management to meet the financial demands of a union. This capacity depends on the financial condition of the institution and is often disputed.

abrasion: weight loss in coins that results from wear in circulation.

absolute title: a title without any conditions. An absolute title is usually critical to the granting of a mortgage by a bank.

absorption account: see *adjunct account.*

abstraction of bank funds: laws dealing with criminal offenses in the banking field. For example, embezzlement, abstraction, or willful misapplication of bank funds are misdemeanors and punishable by fine up to $5,000 and/or imprisonment for five years.

abstract of title: an attorney's prepared statement tracing the history of the ownership of real property to determine the present title. See *deed, encumbrance, search, title deed, title insurance.*

abutting: joining or adjacent; contiguous to another property. This variable is clearly identified in the granting of a bank mortgage.

AC: see *account current.*

accelerated remainder: property that passes to the remainderman through the failure of the income or preceding beneficiary. [105]

acceleration clause:
(1) the statement that a debt must

be paid in total in the event of default of any of its covenants.

(2) a clause included in the body of a contract, stipulating that the entire balance shall become due immediately and payable in the event of a breach of certain other conditions of the contract, such as insolvency or the debtor's failure to pay taxes on the mortgaged property.

acceptability: an attitude toward money resulting in its acceptance as a medium of exchange in the marketplace. See *eligible paper, rediscount.*

acceptance: a time draft (bill of exchange) on the face of which the drawee has written "accepted" over his signature. The date and place payable are also indicated. The person accepting the draft is known as the *acceptor.* See *bank acceptance, draft.*

acceptance credit: commercial banks and foreign banking institutions are able to participate in the acceptance practice to assist in financing import-export and domestic transactions by establishing an acceptance credit with a bank. See *bank acceptance, letter of credit.*

acceptance for honor: the receiving of a draft or bill of exchange by another party when collection has been rejected by the drawee and protest for nonacceptance has been claimed. Cf. *notice of dishonor.*

acceptance liability: a bank's full liability that has been accepted in handling bills drawn on it by customers for financing domestic, import, or export business. Banks are required by law to keep a record of the total of the liability by such acceptances in an account called liability on account of acceptances. See *acceptance credit, acceptance line, letter of credit.*

acceptance liability ledger: a ledger listing the bills accepted for each bank customer entered under an account containing his name, including name and address of customer, line, date, letter of credit number, acceptance number, expiration date, bill amount, total amount accepted or expired, and payment date. See *acceptance liability.*

acceptance line: the maximum limit in monies that a bank commits itself to accept for a single client.

acceptance maturity tickler: an accounting where acceptances are listed in order of maturity dates so that the amount of daily maturities can be grasped quickly. One page is usually given to the maturities for each day. See *tickler.*

acceptance register: a record containing details on all bills accepted by a bank for its depositors. Listed by date, these entries include date of acceptance, bank's acceptance number, name of bank representative giving authorization, signature of representative, customer's number of bill, date, tenor, maturity, drawee, payee, amount, list of document collected, affixed original or duplicates, number, and credit date.

acceptance supra protest: following a protest, the payment of a bill to preserve the reputation or credit of the drawer or endorser.

accepted bill: see *acceptance.*

accepted credit card: any credit card that the cardholder has requested or applied for and received, or has signed, used, or authorized another person to use for the purpose of obtaining money, property, labor, or services on credit. [105]

accepted debit card (or other means of access): a card, code, or other means to a consumer's account to initiate electronic fund transfers (e.g., transfer money between accounts or obtaining money, property, labor, or services). [105]

accepting house: a member of the London Accepting House Committee; there are 17 such firms, normally regarded as the most prestigious of the merchant banks.

acceptor: the drawee of a note for acceptance, who upon signing the form, agrees to pay a draft or bill when due.

accession: elevation to a higher office within the bank.

access right: the right of an owner of property or another person with the owner's approval to enter, enjoy, or leave the property without obstruction. If the property abuts on a public way, this is called a direct access right. If there is other property intervening between the owned property and the public way, the right is known as an *easement right.*

accommodation: historically, the lending of currency by a person who has it to another who has need of it, without collateral. More popularly, the lending of a person's honor or credit, without any consideration, to enable another to obtain borrowed money.

accommodation check: a check drawn by an association on its account with a bank, payable to a third party named by the saver making the withdrawal. [59]

accommodation endorsement: the signature or endorsement of a note or draft solely for the purpose of inducing a bank to lend money to a borrower whose personal credit is not substantial enough to warrant a loan.

accommodation endorser: a person who endorses a negotiable instrument for the accommodation of another person or parties, having no ownership right but simply guaranteeing the fulfillment of the contract to subsequent holders of the instrument. See *endorsement, endorser.*

accommodation note: any note that has received an accommodation endorsement.

accommodation paper: a promissory note, endorsed by an individual(s), allowing the original signer of the note to receive bank credit; thus the second or other signer(s) accept the guarantee of credit.

accommodation party: one who signs a note as maker, drawer, acceptor, or endorser without receiving value, although remaining totally liable for the purpose of lending the credit worthiness of his or her name to another person. See *accommodation paper.*

account: a record of all the transactions and the date of each, affecting a particular phase of a bank or financial institution, expressed in debits and credits, evaluated in money, and showing the current balance, if any. See *bank account.*

accountabilities: assets, liabilities, items held in trust, and the like, for which an individual, organization, or other legal entity renders an accounting. For example, when bank officials give an accounting of the disbursed funds entrusted to their care, the items are referred to as accountabilities.

account activity: all transactions on individual or group accounts, including, for example, debts, credits, and status changes.

account analysis: the process of determining and explaining the profit or loss on any account by means of systematic procedures.

account conversion: changing a person's account from one bank card plan to another (e.g., from a merchant's to a bank card plan or from one bank to another). [105]

account current: a statement posting the debits and credits of a depositor and the balance at the end of the accounting period or cycle billing time.

account history: the payment history of an account over a specified period of time, including the number of times the account was past due or over limit. [105]

account hold: a warning placed on a savings, loan, or other account to indicate the need for special handling. [59]

account in balance: an account where the debit and credit footings are equal.

accounting: the art, science, interpretation, and organized method of recording all transactions affecting the financial condition of a given business or organization.

account inquiry: used to identify the capability of accessing account information for such matters as demand deposit account, savings account, NOW account, line-of-credit, credit card, or other personal accounts. Often with this capability there is the ability to update temporarily or "memo post" the account balance and status. [105]

account in trust: an account opened by an individual to be held in trust and maintained for the benefit of another. In the absence of a legally constituted trust fund, withdrawals from the account are subject to the approval of the individual who has established the account. See *Totten trust.*

account number: the numerical identification given to an account in a given institution or business, such numerical identification being a part of and in direct harmony with the whole system of numerical description given to the accounts as a whole that exist in that institution or business. Cf. *American Bankers Association number.*

account reconciliation plan: a program using the auxiliary On-Us field on MICR checks to give high-volume accounts a list and the sum of paid and/or outstanding checks in numerical serial sequence and to assist in the balance of the bank's statement to the customer's check register.

account reconciliation: a bookkeeping service offered to some bank service customers to aid them in balancing their accounts. This service includes numerical sorting of checks, itemization of outstanding checks, and/or the actual balancing of the account. [105]

account representative: an individual responsible for resolving mail and telephone inquiries for bank card customers (or others). [105]

accounts current: see *account current.*

accounts receivable acquisition: the taking over by the bank of outstand-

ing balances on charge accounts formerly carried by a merchant or other financing agency. [105]

account status report: listing of all cardholder accounts on which there has been activity within a specified period of time. [105]

account transfer: see *account conversion.*

accretion: addition of principal or interest to a fund over a period of time resulting from a plan of accumulation. Cf. *amortization.*

accrue(d):
(1) to gain or profit by.
(2) to accumulate, grow, or add in an orderly fashion (e.g., interest accrues on invested funds).

accrued interest receivable: interest earned by a bank but not yet collected.

accumulated income: that portion of the income from a trust which is retained in the account. [105]

accumulated interest: unpaid interest payments that are past due.

accumulation:
(1) the opposite of *amortization;* a percentage added to life insurance benefits as a form of reward for continuous renewal.
(2) adding income from dividends, interest, and other sources to the principal amount of a fund, and the treatment of such additions as capital.

accumulation distribution: the amount of income earned by a trust in a previous year which is distributed to a beneficiary and is subject to the income tax throwback rules.

accumulative: see *cumulative.*

ACH: see *automated clearinghouse.*

acid test ratio: a credit barometer used by lending institutions; in-

dicates the ability of a business enterprise to meet its current obligations. The formula used to determine the ratio is

$$\frac{cash + receivables + marketable\ securities}{current\ liabilities}$$

Usually a 1:1 ratio is considered to be satisfactory.

Ack.:
(1) acknowledge.
(2) see *acknowledgment.*

acknowledgment:
(1) on a document, a signature that has received certification from an authorized person.
(2) a written notification that an item, now received, is available for its immediate payment.
(3) a statement that a proper document has been submitted.

Acpt.:
(1) accept.
(2) see *acceptance.*

acquiring bank: a bank, in interchange, which maintains the merchant relationship and receives all transactions. [105]

acquisition cost: monies paid in order to obtain property title prior to the granting of a mortgage.

acquisition program: advertising campaign, solicitation, or promotion designed to attract consumers to apply for a bank card. [105]

acquittance: a document giving written evidence of the discharge of, or freedom from, a debt or financial obligation.

action to quiet title: the legal process by which any person claiming an interest or estate in real property not in the actual possession of another may maintain a suit in equity against another who claims an adverse interest or estate therein for determining such conflicting or adverse claims, interests, or estates. [105]

active account: an account in which bank deposits or withdrawals are frequent.

active bad debt account: an account charged off but judged to be collectible at a later date. [55]

active corporation: an organization that maintains a system for operating property or administering its financial affairs.

active money: currency in circulation.

active partner: a partner of an organization who participates actively in the firm's operations for the benefit of all associates.

active trust: a trust where the trustee has a specific role to perform, as contrasted with a passive, bare, dry, or naked trust.

activity:

(1) a sign that a record in a bank's file has moved or has been referred to.

(2) any data resulting in use or modification of the data in a bank or financial institution's master file.

activity charge: a service charge imposed on checking account depositors by banks for check or deposit activity, where the average balances maintained are not enough to compensate for the cost of handling the items. See *checking account*.

activity ratio: the number of active accounts expressed as a percentage of total accounts. Calculated by dividing the number of active accounts by the number of total accounts in the cardholder file. [105]

acts of bankruptcy: any act listed under Section 3 of the National Bankruptcy Act, the most common being the inability to settle debts of not less than $1000 as they mature and voluntarily appearing in a bankruptcy court or undergoing involuntary bankruptcy where unpaid creditors petition the bankruptcy court. See *bankruptcy*.

actual: any physical commodity.

actual cash value: the cost of repairing or replacing damaged property with other of like kind and quality in the same physical condition; commonly defined as replacement cost less depreciation.

actual value: the price that property commands when sold on the open market.

actuarial: related to a bank's insurance mathematics and the application of statistics.

actuary: an individual, often holding a professional degree, whose primary functions include determining rates and rating systems, determining reserves against future liabilities for corporate and rate-making purposes, and designing and interpreting experience systems.

ACUs: see *Asian Currency Units*.

ACV: see *actual cash value*.

AD:

(1) see *after date*.

(2) anno Domini (in the year of our Lord).

(3) ante diem (before the day).

(4) see *availability date*.

ADB:

(1) see *African Development Bank*.

(2) see *Asian Development Bank*.

ad damnum clause: a clause in a plaintiff's complaint or statement that makes the demand for damages and declares the monies involved.

add-on charge: a method, no longer permissible, of advertising an interest rate on installment loans that understates the true interest rate. [78]

add-on interest: a method of calculating interest payments where a percentage of the desired principal is used to calculate the interest cost. Interest cost is then added to the principal to calculate the total amount to be repaid by the borrower. [105]

address:
(1) general: the location of a customer.
(2) banking: the location of a mortgaged structure or property.

adequate notice: a printed notice to a cardholder which sets forth the facts clearly and conspicuously, so that a person against whom it is to operate could reasonably be expected to have noticed it and understood its meaning. [105]

ADIBOR: Abu Dhabi Interbank Offered Rate. See *LIBOR.*

Adj.: see *adjustment.*

adjacent property: property near to or in the immediate vicinity of the insured property which may increase the hazard of loss. [56]

adjoining property: property that touches in some part the insured property. As distinguished from *adjacent property.* [56]

adjunct account: an account that adds to another existing account, represented by transfers from another account (e.g., the balances of related accounts are combined when preparing a financial statement). Synonymous with *absorption account.*

adjustable mortgage rate: see *variable-rate mortgages.*

adjustable peg: a system permitting changes in the par rate of foreign exchange after a country has had long-run disequilibrium in its balance of payments. It also allows for short-run variations within a narrow range of a few percentage points around the par value.

adjustable-rate mortgages (ARMs): variable-rate instruments, with initial rates below conventional fixed-rate loans.

adjustable rate preferred stock: a preference share which carries a floating dividend rate, adjusted periodically and generally linked to the rate on U.S. Treasury securities. [109]

adjusted bank balance of cash: the balance indicated on the statement from the bank plus or minus appropriate adjustments, such as for unrecorded deposits or outstanding checks, to reconcile the bank's balance with the correct cash balance.

adjusted book balance of cash: the balance indicated in the firm's account for cash in bank plus or minus appropriate adjustments, such as for notes collected by a bank or bank service charges, to reconcile the account balance with the correct cash balance.

adjusted capital funds: used in determining a bank's capital adequacy ratios—the change in book total of capital funds indicating more precise availability of capital cushion to risk assets—for establishing the risk asset ratio.

adjusted CD rate: the rate paid on a CD adjusted for reserve costs and FDIC insurance costs representing an attempt to measure the costs of a bank's funds.

adjusted credit proxy: see *credit proxy.*

adjusted gross estate: the value of an estate after all allowable deductions have reduced the gross estate, but before federal estate taxes. [34]

adjusted monetary base (AMB): a measure that is intended to isolate the effects of Federal Reserve actions that affect the money stock in a single summary measure. See *reserve adjustment magnitude.* [79]

adjusted trial balance: the merger of the trial balance columns of the work sheet with the adjustment columns. This balance represents the trial balance that could be obtained if it were prepared right after the adjusting entries are posted.

adjuster: an individual who reviews a bank customer's complaint concerning service or accuracy, with the authority to find an appropriate remedy.

adjusting entries: bookkeeping entries that are made after the trial balance has been prepared, but before the closing entries. The adjusting entries are necessary to make the income and expense accounts consistent with the accrual method of accounting. [105]

adjustment: a change in an account to correct an incorrect entry or for some other sound reason.

adjustment mortgage: any mortgage that has been released out of a reorganization.

administrator:
(1) general: a key executive in an organization.
(2) banking: a qualified individual or bank appointed by a court of law to manage and distribute the estate of a person who died intestate (without leaving a will) or

leaving a will that fails to name an executor. See *executor, letter of administration.*

ADR: see *American Depository Receipt.*

ad referendum: indicating that even though a contract has been signed, specific issues remain to be considered.

ad valorem taxes: real estate taxes determined by the value of the property.

advance:
(1) a price increase.
(2) a loan.
(3) a payment on account made prior to the due date.
(4) a rise in value or cost.

advance commitment: a written contract calling for the sale of a specified amount of mortgages (or mortgage-backed securities) at a given price or yield within a specified time. [105]

adverse claim: as applied to a bank account, a claim to ownership by a person other than the one in whose name the account has been entered. [39]

adverse possession: acquiring of property by a person who does not have title, or who has a defective title to it.

advice book: a statement of incoming and outgoing advices. See *advices.*

advice department: a department within the bank that processes advices. See *advices.*

advice fate item: see *wire fate item.*

advices: connotes several types of forms used in the banking field. Generally speaking, an advice is a form of letter that relates or acknowledges a certain activity or result with regard to a depositor's relations with a bank. Examples include credit advice, debit advice, advice of payment, and advice of execution. In commercial transactions, information on a business transaction such as a shipment of goods. [10]

advised line of credit: a credit facility whose terms and conditions are confirmed to the customer by the bank. [110]

advising bank: in documentary credit business, denotes the bank which informs the beneficiary of the credit that the credit has been opened. [111]

advisory funds: funds placed with a bank to invest at its own discretion on the customer's behalf.

AE: see *accommodation endorsement.*

A&F: August and February (semiannual interest payments).

AfDB: see *African Development Bank.*

affiant: one who makes an affidavit.

affidavit: a written, notarized, dated, and sworn statement of the facts pertaining to a financial transaction or civil event. Such a statement must show the name and address of the affiant, be signed by that person, and bear the signature of the attesting official (e.g., a notary).

affidavit of claim: the form required when filing a claim. In general, it contains the information on which the claim is based.

Affil.: see *affiliate.*

affiliate: a legal term described in the Banking Act of 1933, pertaining to any organization which a bank owns or controls by stock holdings, or which the bank's shareholders possess, or whose officers are also directors of the bank.

affirmative action: positive steps taken by banks and other financial organizations to remedy imbalances in their employment of members of minority groups.

afghani: monetary unit of Afghanistan.

AFH: see *acceptance for honor.*

African Development Bank (ADB): formed in 1964 with an objective to help provide development capital for Africa. The headquarters is at Abidjan, Ivory Coast.

AFT: see *automatic fund transfers.*

after-acquired clause: a section of the mortgage stating that any additional property which the mortgagor acquires after the mortgage is drawn will also be used as security for the loan.

after-acquired property: property acquired by a corporation subsequent to the execution of a mortgage or by a testator subsequent to the making of his or her will. [37]

after date: in bills of exchange and notes, the stated maturity of the instrument.

AG: silver (from *argentum*).

agency: used to describe certain types of accounts in trust institutions. The main distinguishing characteristic of an agency is that the title to the property does not pass to the trust institution but remains in the name of the owner of the property, who is known as the principal. [32]

agency bank: an organization used by foreign banks to enter the U.S. market; unable to accept deposits or extend loans in its own name but instead serves as agent for the parent bank.

agency bill: bills drawn on, and accepted by, the London branches of banks whose headquarters are located in other countries.

agent: an individual authorized by a bank or financial institution to act in behalf of another person, the principal. Banks are also appointed by individuals to act as their agents.

agent bank:

(1) a bank acting for a foreign bank.

(2) in the Eurocredit market, a bank appointed by other banks within the syndicate to handle the administration of the loan. The agent is usually a lead bank, but the agent functions starts with the signing of the loan when the lead bank function terminates. [83]

aggregate: any total (e.g., the gross national product; the sum of monthly sales).

aggregate balance: the calculated accumulation of account balances during the statement period. Used to determine the *average daily balance.* [31]

aggregate risk: full exposure of a bank to a customer for both spot and forward contracts. Cf. *marginal risk.*

agio:

(1) a premium paid for the exchange of one nation's currency for that of another's. Cf. *disagio.*

(2) the sum given above a nominal value, as in "the agio of exchange."

(3) the rate of exchange among differing countries.

agreement corporation: a state-chartered corporation that has agreed to operate as if it were organized under Section 25 of the Federal Reserve Act and has agreed to be subject to Federal Reserve Regulation K. They are restricted, in general, to international banking operations. Banks must apply to the Federal Reserve for permission to acquire stock in an agreement corporation. [202]

agreement for deed: a contract describing additional property payments and conditions; the deed will be delivered and title will pass after fulfillment of these terms.

agricultural loans: loans to farmers not secured by real estate. [40]

agricultural paper: notes and acceptances resulting from transactions dealing with farming and ranching, as distinguished from traditional commercial or industrial activities. See *Federal Intermediate Credit Banks, Federal Loan Bank.*

Agt.: see *agent.*

AI: see *accumulated interest.*

AIB: see *American Institute of Banking.*

Aj.: see *adjustment.*

AJOJ: April, July, October, January, (quarterly interest payments or dividends).

a/k/a: "also known as" (e.g., John Doe a/k/a J. Doe).

Aldrich-Vreeland Act: a forerunner of the Federal Reserve Act. Congress in 1908 passed legislation as a temporary relief measure until such time as new banking rules could be formulated.

alienate: the transfer of title to property.

alienation: the transfer of interest and property title to another person or organization. See *involuntary alienation, voluntary alienation.*

alienation clause: a form of acceleration clause that requires full payment of the mortgage note upon the transfer of title of the mortgaged property either through sale or some other means. [105]

all-in-one program: a bank's program in which the customer, if approved, is set up with a checking account, bank card account, instant cash, courtesy card, free personal checks, and traveler's checks. A monthly fee is charged. [105]

allotment ledger: a subsidiary ledger that contains an account for each allotment, showing the amount allotted, expenditures, encumbrances, the net balance, and other related information. See *appropriation ledger.* [49]

allotment notice: a document completed by an investment banker or syndicate manager which states the amount and related information or price and time of payment for securities and which is transmitted to the subscriber. It can be for the full amount of securities asked for by the subscriber, or less.

allowance: a reserve, or money set aside, for bad debts or for depreciation.

allowance for loan losses: a valuation allowance established and maintained by charges against operating income to provide a balance for absorbing possible losses in a bank's loan portfolio. [201]

alloy: base metal or metals combined with gold or silver to create a coin with superior durability. Today most coins are base-metal coins.

All-Savers certificates: a tax break under the Economic Recovery Tax Act of 1981 to encourage savings, the law created this instrument designed basically to benefit savings and loan associations rather than investors. Under the act, thrift institutions were able to offer a new, one-year Treasury note yield for a little more than 10 percent at current interest rates. What made the new certificate attractive was that interest income up to $1000 ($2000 on a joint return) was exempt from federal income tax. Now defunct.

alteration: any change involving an erasure or rewriting in the date, amount, or payee of a check or other negotiable instrument. In accounting records, necessary alterations are best made by crossing out the unwanted figure, leaving it legible, and writing the correct one above or below the original.

altered check: check on which the date, payee, or amount has been changed or erased. A bank is responsible for paying a check only as it is originally drawn; consequently, it may refuse to pay a check that has been altered.

alternate account: an account in the name of two or more persons, any of whom may draw against the account without further authority from the others. See *joint account; survivorship account.* [50]

alternate depositors: holders of a joint account; a deposit account made out in the names of husband and wife or of two partners which is payable to either or to the survivor is a joint account.

alternative mortgage instruments (AMIs): one of three alternatives to the traditional fixed-rate mortgage. See *graduated-payment mortgages, reverse-annuity mortgage, variable-rate mortgage.*

alternative mortgages: see *graduated-payment mortgages, shared-appreciation mortgage.*

alternative payee: one of two parties to whom an account or negotiable instrument, other bill, or draft is payable. Payment to either removes the payor of that extent of obligation to both or either. In a joint account in the name of a spouse, the financial organization may pay either as holder of the draft, passbook, or other financial instrument.

alternative pricing: when a borrower is given a choice of getting a loan tied to the prime, or some spread over the rate on the lender's certificates of deposit.

American Bankers Association (ABA): the national organization of banking formed in 1875 to "promote the general welfare and usefulness of banks and financial institutions." The association consists of 35 working groups, 4 divisions, 7 commissions, and a number of councils and committees.

American Bankers Association (ABA) number: a unit in the numerical coding system originated by the American Bankers Association for the easy identification of banks and to aid in sorting checks for their proper and ultimate destinations. Used principally on checks, the ABA number is usually placed in the upper right-hand corner of the check after the drawee bank's name.

American Depository Receipt: a form similar to a stock certificate which is registered in the holder's name. The certificate represents a certain number of shares in an alien corporation. Such shares are held by an alien bank that serves as the agent for a domestic commercial bank which has released the depository receipt.

American Institute of Banking (AIB): the educational section of the American Bankers Association, organized in 1900 to provide educational opportunity in banking for bank people. The institute's activities are carried on through numerous chapters and study groups in many cities and towns. In addition to its regular classes, the institute conducts correspondence courses. Membership is open only to employees and officers of ABA member institutions. [10]

American Savings and Loan Institute: see *Institute of Financial Education.*

American terms: an exchange rate expressed as a number of currency units per dollar. [106]

AMIs: see *alternative mortgage instruments.*

amortisement: synonymous with *amortization.*

amortization:
(1) the gradual reduction of a debt by means of equal periodic payments sufficient to meet current interest and to liquidate the debt at maturity. When the debt involves real property, the periodic payments often include a sum sufficient to pay taxes and insurance on the property.
(2) an attempt to liquidate a future obligation slowly by making charges against a capital account or by adding monies to cover the debt.

amortization fund: the sum of money accumulated periodically for the payment of a debt.

amortization loan: long-term loan permitted by the Federal Farm Loan Act where the principal is eliminated or amortized during the time the loan is made. See *amortized mortgage loan.*

amortization of debt discount: non-cash expenditures charged on a company's income statement to offset, over the life of a bond issue, the difference between the proceeds of bonds sold at a discount and the par value payable at maturity. [105]

amortization of discount on funded debt: a charge to income each fiscal period for a proportion of the discount and expense on funded debt obligations applicable to that period. The proportion is determined according to a rule, the uniform application of which through the interval between the date of sale and date of maturity will extinguish the discount and expense on funded debt. However, the accounting company may, at its option, charge to profit and loss all or any portion of discount and expense remaining unextinguished at any time. [18]

amortization payments: synonymous with *installment payments.*

amortization schedule: a table showing the amounts of principal and interest due at regular intervals and the unpaid principal balance of the loan after each payment is made. [105]

amortize:
(1) to write off a portion or all of the cost of an asset; to retire debt over a period of time.
(2) to discharge a debt in periodic payments until the total, including the interest, has been paid.

amortized mortgage loan: a mortgage loan that provides for repayment within a specified time by means of regular payments at stated intervals (usually monthly, quarterly, or semiannually) to reduce the principal amount of the loan and to cover interest as it is due. [44]

amount of interest: principal sum deposited for the purpose of earning interest. [12]

amount financed: the amount lent or financed exclusive of finance charges; total of payments less the finance charge. [55]

AN: see *account number.*

analysis files: in bank examination terms, those files containing the papers of examiners during the general examination. Upon completion of the examination, materials of continuing interest are transferred to a permanent file. [105]

analysis paper: paper used to analyze the trial balance and to gather information for the profit and loss statement and the balance sheet.

ancillary administration: see *domiciliary administration.*

ancillary letters testamentary: letters subordinate or auxiliary to letters testamentary, as, for example, those issued in one jurisdiction for probate of property owned by a nonresident decedent. [37]

ancillary receiver: a person appointed to assist a receiver. Usually, the receiver is handling a foreign corporation (one located outside the state) and the ancillary receiver aids in the liquidation and handles the claims within his or her own domestic state reporting to and taking guidance from the receiver who is in the foreign state. See *receiver, receivership.*

ancillary trustee: see *domiciliary trustee.*

ANFM: August, November, February, May (quarterly interest payments or dividends).

annual percentage rate (APR): the cost of credit on a yearly basis expressed as a percentage. Synonymous with *true annual rate of interest.* [1]

antedated check: a check that is dated prior to the date on which it is issued—that is, delivered or mailed to the payee. For example, if a check dated August 12 is not issued until August 17, it is an *antedated check.*

anticipated acceptance: an acceptance that has been paid prior to the specified terms of payment.

anticipated balance: the bank account balance projected through the end of the interest or dividend period, assuming that no additional deposit or withdrawal transactions occur.

anticipated interest: the amount of interest projected as earnings on bank accounts, assuming that no deposits or withdrawals occur before the end of the current interest period. This figure is updated after each deposit or withdrawal activity.

anticipation: payment of an account before the actual due date, thus permitting a discount.

anticipation, right of: the privilege given the mortgagor, by a provision in the mortgage instruments, to pay all or any portion of the outstanding balance of the obligation prior to its due date without penalty. [44]

anticipatory breach: the informing of the seller by a buyer before the closing of title that the buyer plans to terminate any involvement in the transaction.

any-quantity rate: a transportation rate applicable to any quantity of a commodity shipped.

A&O: April and October (semiannual interest payments).

AO: account of.

AP: see *authority to purchase.*

appellant: the party who makes a motion for an appeal from one jurisdiction or court to another.

application for guaranteed loan: bank's application to FmHA to question an FmHA loan guarantee. [105]

application-for-loan form: a printed form used by most financial institutions which contains a prospective borrower's request for a loan. [51]

application holder: container placed at the point of sale or throughout bank lobbies to display cardholder application (e.g., "Take One" box). [105]

application of funds statement: constructed from balance sheets to two periods, the statement allows an analysis of the changes that have evolved during the period that was chosen.

apportionment:
(1) dividing a unit into proportionate parts; the proper allocation of receipts and expenses between income and principal.
(2) involves the question of how much each of two or more insurance policies will contribute to the loss sustained by a covered risk. The decision of distribution is the apportionment.

appraisal: the setting of a value or evaluation of a specific piece of personal or real property, or the property of another as a whole.

appraisal fee: a charge for estimating the value of collateral being offered as security. [78]

appraisal report: a written report of the factors considered in arriving at a valuation of a particular piece of property. [61]

appraise: to determine the cost, quality, or value of an item (e.g., to appraise the value of one's house). Also used to appraise the adequacy and effectiveness of systems and procedures.

appraised value: an estimate of property value reached by an appraiser. [105]

appraiser: a person who makes appraisals.

appraising: synonymous with *valuation.*

appreciation rate: the index figure used against the actual or estimated cost of property in computing its cost of reproduction, new as of a different date or under different conditions of a higher price level. [62]

appropriation: an authorized sum of money set aside to pay certain known or anticipated costs of a given item or service.

appropriation ledger: a subsidiary ledger containing an account with each appropriation. Each account usually shows the amount originally appropriated, transfers to or from the appropriation charged against the appropriation, the net balance, and other related information. If allotments are made and a separate ledger is maintained for them, each account in the appropriation ledger usually shows the amount appropriated, transfers to or from the appropriation, the amount allotted, and the unallotted balance. See also *allotment ledger.* [49]

approval ratio: number of cardholder applications approved, expressed as a percentage of total applications received; calculated by dividing the number of approved applications for a specified time period by the total number of applications processed within the same time period. [105]

appurtenances: rights and interest that attach to and pass with the land.

APR: see *annual percentage rate.*

Arab African Bank: founded in 1964 and headquartered in Cairo; serves as a financial and economic link between the Arab and African countries.

Arab Bank for Economic Development in Africa: headquartered in Khartoum, Sudan; founded in 1973.

Arab International Bank: founded in 1971 and headquartered in Cairo; assists in the financing of development and of foreign trade, particularly the member states and other Arab states.

arbitrage: the simultaneous purchase and sale of mortgages, future contracts, or mortgage-backed securities in different markets to profit from price differences.

arbitrage house: a financial institution, such as a foreign exchange dealer or private banker, conducting business in arbitrage.

arbitrager (arbitrageur): an individual who engages in the activity of arbitrage.

arbitragist: synonymous with *arbitrager.*

arbitration of exchange: when prices of bills of exchange payable in foreign currency vary throughout financial centers in the world. Consequently, an individual from country A may find it profitable to purchase a bill of exchange from country B for payment in still another country.

archmonetarist: a supporter of Milton Friedman's monetary theory that changes in growth of money supply operate on the economy with such a long time lag that it is impossible for the authorities to know at any one moment what policy should be.

Arcru: a unit of account first used in 1974; based on the movement of 12 Arab currencies against the U.S. dollar.

arrange for the extension of credit (or for a lease of personal property): to provide or offer to provide consumer credit or a lease that is or will be extended by another person under a business or other relationship pursuant to which the person arranging such credit or lease (1) receives or will receive a fee, compensation, or other consideration for such service; or (2) has knowledge of the credit or lease terms and participates in the preparation of the contract documents required in connection with the extension of credit or the lease. [105]

arrears:
(1) a real or contingent obligation remaining unpaid at the date of maturity. Frequently used in connection with installment notes, mortgages, rent, and other obligations due and payable on a certain specified date.
(2) monies due but unpaid.

article eight currency: a senior currency according to the International Monetary Fund; should be convertible and free from controls.

Article 4—Uniform Commercial Code: governs checks and other negotiable instruments during bank collection and payment. [105]

Article 3—Uniform Commercial Code: governs the rights and duties of parties to commercial paper. [105]

AsDB: see *Asian Development Bank.*

Asian Clearing Union: a joint arrangement for settling international payments imbalances between Bangladesh, Burma, India, Iran, Nepal, Pakistan, and Sri Lanka.

Asian Currency Units (ACUs): the separate accounting entities by which the Asiadollar deposit market was created. The market emerged from a Bank of America proposal. ACUs totaled over $42 billion in early 1980.

Asian Development Bank (ADB): established in 1966 to help provide development capital for Asia. Headquartered in Manila.

Asian dollars: U.S. dollar bank deposits traded outside the United States.

ASKI system: an exchange control system under which payment for imported goods is made in marked funds usable only to purchase goods of the importing country. The term is the abbreviation of the German for "foreigners" special accounts for domestic payments.

as-of-adjustments: a correction to a bank's figure for reserves. If an error in accounting is discovered, or there was a telecommunications breakdown, a retrospective 'as of' adjustment is made to the bank's reserve figures. [112]

assay: a test of content, composition, and purity, often carried out in an assayer's office, on metals, usually gold and silver.

assemblage: the act of bringing two or more individuals or things to form an aggregate whole; specifically, the cost or estimated cost of assembling two or more parcels of land under a single ownership and unit of utility over the normal cost or current market prices of the parcels held individually. [62]

assembling land: the combining of nearby or contiguous properties to form one tract.

assess: to determine the value of something, or to fix its value for tax purposes.

assessed value: the official record of a tax assessed and collected; the tax roll value assigned to property.

assessment:

(1) a charge made against property for the purpose of levying a tax.

(2) any levy on members of a corporation for purposes of raising capital.

assessment ratio: the ratio of the assessed value of property to the full or true property value. Full value may be defined as fair market value at the bid side of the market, less a reasonable allowance for sales and other expenses. [105]

assessment roll:

(1) in the case of real property the official list containing the legal description of each parcel of property and its assessed valuation. The name and address of the last known owner are also usually shown.

(2) in the case of personal property, the assessment roll is the official list containing the name and address of the owner, a description of the personal property, and its assessed value. [49]

asset:

(1) anything owned by an individual or business that has commercial or exchange value. Assets may consist of specific property or claims against others, in contract to obligations due others. See *balance sheet, tangible assets.*

(2) uses of bank funds—cash, security investments, loans, and fixed assets. [105]

asset and liability statement: a balance sheet.

asset card: synonymous with *debit card.*

asset coverage: *direct*—the extent to which net assets (after all prior claims) cover a specific senior obligation, whether bank loans, debentures, or preferred stock. It may be expressed in either dollar, percentage, or ratio terms. *Overall*—the ratio of total assets to the sum of all prior obligations including that of the specific issue under consideration taken at liquidating value. [30]

asset currency: bank notes that are not secured by any particular assets but by the general assets of the issuing bank. Some countries have such characteristics. Today, more popularly referred to as *general asset currency.* See also *Baltimore method.*

assign: to transfer to another. A person to whom property is assigned. [76]

assignability: the capacity of property to be transferred to another person or organization.

assigned account: an account, usually receivable, which has been assigned to a bank as security for a loan by a borrower. In theory, the bank takes possession of the account pledged. In actual practice, however, so as not to jeopardize the relationship between the borrower and his customer (whose account has been pledged), the bank will allow the account to be paid by the customer in the normal manner, and will rely upon the integrity of the borrower to apply this payment against the loan balance. [31]

assigned book account: see *assigned account.*

assigned in blank: the space on a transfer-of-ownership document for placing the new owner's name. Often street certificates are assigned in blank where no name appears on the certificate.

assignment:
(1) banking: the transfer in writing by one individual to another of title of property.
(2) law: a transfer in writing of the legal right in a policy to another party. See *assignment in blank.*

assignment, lease: transferring leasehold interest to another person or group.

assignment, mortgage: transferring a mortgage to another person or group.

assignment for the benefit of creditors: a person or firm's action to transfer legal title to property to a trustee who has been authorized to administer and liquidate the property and make a distribution to creditors. See also *National Bankruptcy Act of 1898.*

assignment in blank: see *assigned in blank.*

assignment of leases: additional security often taken in connection with mortgages of commercial properties. [22]

assignment of mortgage: the written instrument evidencing an association's transfer of a loan obligation from the original borrower to a third person. [59]

assignment of rents: a written document that transfers to a mortgagee on default the owner's right to collect rents. [59]

assignment to creditors: the transfer of property in trust or for the benefit of creditors. [76]

assignor: an individual who assigns or transfers a claim, right, or property. See *assigned in blank, assignment, assignment for the benefit of creditors.*

Assmt.: see *assessment.*

associated banks: banks that are associated through membership in a clearinghouse association.

Associated Credit Bureaus of America, Inc.: membership organization of credit bureaus and collection service departments throughout the nation. Facilitates interbureau credit reporting by means of a *coupon system.* [41]

associate member: a bank that participates in a credit plan administered by another bank or group of banks. [105]

Association Cambiste Internationale: the international organization of foreign exchange dealers, consisting of national Forex clubs affiliated throughout the world; headquartered in Paris.

association (ABA) number: a numerical coding system originated by the ABA to facilitate the sorting and processing of checks. Each bank is assigned a unique identifying number, made of two parts separated by a hyphen. The first part of the number identifies the state, city, or territory in which the bank is located, and the second part identifies the bank itself. [105]

Asst. Cash.: assistant cashier.

assumable mortgage: a home mortgage where the buyer takes over the seller's original, below-market-rate mortgage.

assumption: bank loan payments accepted by a party other than the original maker.

assumption of debt: taking on another's debt. [61]

assumption of mortgage: accepting a property title that has an existing mortgage with personal liability for all payments by another.

AT: see *absolute title.*

ATM: see *automated teller machine.*

ATS: see *automatic transfer service accounts.*

attached account: an account against which a court order has been issued, permitting disbursement of the balance only with the consent of the court. See *frozen account.*

attached ledger: the book or ledger in which records of attached accounts are segregated and kept.

attachment: the legal proceeding following a court's action whereby a plaintiff acquires a lien on a defendant's property as security for payment of a judgment that the plaintiff can recover. Cf. *judgment lien.*

attachment ledger: see *attached ledger.*

attention party: in EFTS, the person or department within the receiving bank whose attention should be drawn to the message. [105]

attestation: the act of bearing witness or giving authenticity to a document by signing as a witness to the signature of another. See *notary public.*

attestation clause: the clause of a document containing the formal declaration of the act of witnessing; in the case of a will, the clause immediately following the signature of the testator and usually beginning "Signed, sealed, published, and declared by the said . . . ." [105]

attesting witness: one who testifies to the authenticity of a document, as the attesting witness to a will.

at thirty days sight: where the drawee is permitted 30 days' time on a time draft from the date of acceptance in which to pay the paper.

AU: gold (from *arum*).

Aud.:
(1) see *audit.*
(2) see *auditor.*

audit:
(1) inspection of a firm's books; a final statement of account.
(2) periodic or continuous verification of the stated assets and liabilities of a company or other organization. See *bank examination.*

audit comment: a situation that is noted by the auditors and reported to the department manager but which may not be reported to the senior management of the bank. [105]

audited voucher: a voucher that has been examined and approved for payment.

audit function: periodic or continuous verification of the bank's assets and liabilities. This function is performed by the auditor. The auditor is appointed by the board of directors and is responsible for the carrying out of this verification. Among the assets and liabilities more regularly verified are cash, loans, collateral for loans, and savings and checking accounts. Verification may consist of a physical count of the assets as reflected by the general ledger or a listing of the balances, as shown on each savings or checking account, with a proof of the total as shown on the general ledger. Direct verification may also be made with borrowers or depositors. [10]

auditor: a person qualified to conduct an audit. Qualification is defined by each state. See *audit, bank examiner, certified public accountant.*

auditor's certificate: a statement signed by an auditor in which the auditor states that he or she has examined the financial statements, the system of internal control, the accounting records, and supporting evidence in accordance with generally accepted auditing standards and in which the auditor expresses his or her opinion, based on such examination, regarding the financial condition of a unit or any of its enterprises, the results from operations, and any facts that he or she has investigated in his or her professional capacity.

audit report: the report prepared by an auditor covering the audit or investigation made by him or her. As a rule, the report should include a statement of the scope of the audit, a summary of findings, recommendations, a certificate, financial statements, and, sometimes, statistical tables. [49]

austral: monetary unit of the Argentines.

authenticated copy: a copy of an instrument on which an attestation is made in the manner required by law by an official authorized to make such certification, as by the certification and seal of a specified public official. [37]

authentication: the verification of a document as truthful, genuine, or valid.

authority to purchase: used in Far Eastern trade, a substitute for a commercial *letter of credit;* this instrument permits the bank to which it is directed to purchase drafts drawn on an importer rather than on a bank. See *letter of credit.*

authorization: the issuance of approval, by or on behalf of the card issuer, to complete a transaction for a merchant or another affiliate. [105]

authorization center: a credit-card centralized office that has records of the cardholder's account with an issuer bank. If sufficient credit is there, the purchase is authorized.

authorization code: number assigned by the bank to a merchant sale or cash advance which has received specific approval. The code is used as proof that the transaction has been properly authorized. [105]

authorization department: department responsible for providing telephone approval for purchases and cash advances. [105]

authorization number: see *authorization code.*

authorization request: a request for approval, by or on behalf of the card issuer, for a financial transaction. [105]

authorization reversal: a nonmonetary transaction issued to reverse a previous authorization and which increases the account's available credit by the amount of the authorization. [105]

authorized dealer: banks allowed by their regulating body to deal in foreign exchange. [84]

authorized settlement bank: a bank in the United States that clears cash items, either directly or indirectly, through the U.S. Federal Reserve System; and which has been empowered by a Visa International Clearing Member to prepare and/or honor clearing drafts for the settlement of interchange. [105]

automated clearinghouse (ACH): a computerized facility used by member depository institutions to process (i.e., combine, sort, and distribute) payment orders in machine-readable form (computer tapes or punched cards).

automated teller: see *unattended banking terminal.*

automated teller machine (ATM): a machine capable of processing a variety of transactions between a depository institution and its customers. These functions might include accepting deposits, providing withdrawals, transferring funds between accounts, and accepting instructions to pay third parties in the transaction. An ATM may or may not be on-line to a computer system and may be located on or off the premises of a depository institution. Placement in certain locations may permit customer access 7 days a week, 24 hours a day. See *Bellevue Project, cash dispenser, debit card, Customer-Bank Communication Terminal.*

automatic bill payment: payment by one check to a number of creditors or direct payment by the bank for specified recurring bills. [105]

automatic charge back: a transaction that does not meet the conditions for acceptance by the banks as set forth in the merchant agreement. [105]

automatic currency: see *elasticity.*

automatic deposit plan: a savings account deposit plan whereby the customer arranges for checks, such as Social Security payments and stock dividends, to be sent directly to his association for deposit to his savings account. [59]

automatic fund transfer: a regulation by the Federal Reserve Board and the Federal Deposit Insurance Corporation permitting a financial institution to move funds from a depositor's savings account to his checking account upon specific request.

automatic guarantee: a provision of the Veterans Administration under which it will guarantee with prior approval a mortgage loan made by a supervised lender. [59]

automatic standard: a monetary standard (the best example is gold standard) where the amount and value of money is consciously managed˙ but is the result of the working of demand and supply for the precious metal or foreign currency that follows upon differences in trading volume between nations.

automatic transfer between accounts: a deposit service that authorizes periodic transfer of funds between accounts. [105]

automatic transfer of funds: movement of funds between accounts at prearranged times, according to a prespecified agreement between a bank and a customer.

automatic transfer service (ATS) accounts: effective November 1, 1978, commercial banks began offering interest-paying checking accounts. Automatic transfer service accounts allow a bank saver to keep funds in a 5 percent passbook account, allowing the bank to shift a predetermined amount into a checking account periodically. See *negotiable order of withdrawal.*

AV: see *actual value.*

availability clause: see *currency availability clause.*

availability date: the date on which checks payable at out-of-town banks are considered to be collected and available for customers withdrawal; determined by the geographical location of the drawee bank, in relation to time and distance from the sending bank. Recently, local banks were included, and volume is replacing distance.

availability schedule: a list indicating the time that must elapse before deposited checks can be considered to be converted into usable funds. [105]

available assets: a person's or firm's assets that may be readily sold to meet a need. Such assets would usually not be mortgaged or pledged.

available balance: the book balance less any hold, uncollected funds, and restrictions against an account. [31]

available credit: the difference between the credit limit assigned to a cardholder account and the present balance, including authorization outstanding, of that account. See *open to buy.* [105]

aval: payment of a bill of exchange or promissory note that has been guaranteed by the signature of a third person appearing on the bill. Used extensively in Europe.

average balance:
(1) the sum of the daily balances in an account during a month divided by the number of days in that month.
(2) a high average balance for an account, indicating a more profitable account than another with a lower average balance.

average book: lender's record, as in a bank, showing differing averages, such as the average balance or average loan, by each customer, which are posted and often entered into the computer to aid management in future planning.

average collected balance: the average collected balance of a depositor's account is usually determined on a monthly basis. It is arrived at by adding the daily balances of the account, and deducting the sum of the float, or uncollected items, from the formal total, and dividing the remainder by the number of days in the month. [10]

average collection period: the ratio of (1) the total accounts receivable at any date multiplied by 365 to (2) net credit sales for the year.

average daily balance: the average amount of money that a customer keeps on deposit; determined by adding the daily balances of an account for a given length of time and dividing the total by the number of days covered.

average daily float: that portion of a customer's balance said to consist of deposited checks that are in the process of collection. The average daily float is deducted from the average book balance for purposes of account analysis. [105]

average life: the average maturity of a borrowing after taking into account repayments or sinking-fund provisions.

average loan file: see *average book.*

average outstanding balance: the averaged balance outstanding on all cardholder accounts within a specified time period; calculated by dividing the total outstanding by the number of accounts with balances. [105]

average ticket, average sale: the averaged dollar amount of sales drafts received by a bank during a specific period; can be calculated by adding the dollar totals of all sales drafts received (within a specified time period) and dividing the total by the number of sales drafts received (within the same period). Cash advances can be so identified also. [105]

average yield: in Great Britain, the average of all the yields implied by the prices bid for U.S. Treasury bills at the Bank of England tender.

avulsion: any shift of land from one property to another caused by forces of nature without change in ownership.

B: the monetary base.

BA: see *bank acceptance.*

backdating: placing on a statement a date prior to the date on which it was drawn up.

back door: another name for the U.S. Treasury.

back-end processing: a bank with an EFT network, perhaps an ATM network, that has each device attached directly to its proprietary data processing facility. At the same time, the bank participates in a shared ATM network with other banks where their customers can access other ATMs. The distinction is how those ATMs may be attached in the network environment. For transaction activity all on-us items, or items conducted by the owning bank at their ATM by their customer, will be processed at their data center. This is back-end processing for the network. Their customers accessing other ATMs in shared network would receive authorization from the same bank data center but through machines that could be attached at the front end. The back-end arrangement involves proprietary authorization of proprietary activity without passing the data through the shared network. Thus a back-end processor looks at and authorizes its own customers for its own customers at its own ATMs while participating in a large network. [105]

back office crunch (crush): a delay in daily operations, often resulting from a pileup of unprocessed work.

back-to-back:
(1) operations where a loan is made in one currency in one nation against a loan in another currency in another nation.
(2) credit opened by a bank on the strength of another credit. [85]

back-to-back letters of credit: two letters of credit with identical documentary requirements, except for a difference in the price of merchandise as shown by the invoice and the draft. [105]

BACS: see *Bankers' Automated Clearing House.*

bad debt: amount due on an open account that has been proved to be uncollectible; any uncollectible receivable.

bad debt expense: the cost of uncollectible accounts receivable. In most companies, bad debt expense is debited for the estimated amount uncollectible, and allowance for uncollectible accounts is credited.

bad debt recovery: money collected on a bad debt account. [55]

bad debts collected: amounts earlier written off as uncollectible that are subsequently collected.

bad debt writeoff: a customer's account that is removed from the books when payment appears unlikely.

bad faith: the intent to mislead or deceive (mala fides). It does not include misleading by an honest, inadvertent, or uncalled-for misstatement.

bad money: see *good money.*

bad news: slang, any bill for money owed.

baht: monetary unit of Thailand.

BAI: see *Bank Administration Institute.*

bailee: a person who acts as a receiver for personal property.

bailee receipt: the receipt presented to a bank holding title to goods by a bailee, a customer of the bank who is allowed to sell them for the amount of the owning bank.

bailor: an individual who delivers personal property for possession to another.

Bal.: see *balance.*

balance: the amount standing to the credit of a customer's account, representing the amount he is entitled to withdraw. The difference between total debits and credits, whether against or in favor of a bank at the clearinghouse. [31]

balance as a whole: a form of proof method employed in banks, usually in the bookkeeping department. A control total is established for several books or ledgers. Each bookkeeper processes work by posting to his or her accounts. At the end of the posting run, several bookkeepers will add their combined totals, and will *balance as a whole* to the control total for their group of ledgers. [10]

balanced budget: a budget in which forward expenditures for a set period are matched by expected revenues for the same period.

balance des paiements courants: French term for *current account* of the balance of payments.

balance due: the total amount needed to equalize the debit and credit sum of an account; the amount you owe.

balance of account: the net amount of the total debits and total credits posted to a given account. Balances are of three types: *zero balance,* indicating that total debits and total credits are equal; *debit balance,* indicating an excess of total debits over total credits; and *credit balance,* indicating an excess of total credits over debits, at a given time.

balance of payments (b.o.p.): a statement identifying all financial transaction of a country and its population with the other nations of the world. Cf. *dollar shortage.*

balance-of-payments table: a summary of transactions (loans, investments, repayments, donations, and other transfer of funds) in a given time period, published by the Department of Commerce. [105]

balance of trade: the difference between a country's imports and exports over a set period.

balance owing: the amount outstanding. [105]

balance sheet: an itemized statement listing the total assets and the total liabilities of a given business to portray its net worth at a given moment in time.

balance sheet audit: an examination of a statement of financial condition as of a given date, usually at the end of the normal accounting period. [49]

balance sheet equation: the equation stating that the total of assets equals the total of liabilities plus net worth (ownership).

balance slip: an itemized list made daily of coin and paper money to verify the correctness of a cash register audit tape strip.

balances with domestic banks: the total amounts that reporting member banks have on deposit in other commercial banks. [40]

balance transfer: the process of forwarding the balance from an old to a new ledger sheet. All or part of the old ledger becomes a statement of account which will be sent to a customer. [31]

balancing: the ultimate act of bringing two sets of related figures into agreement. As in proof work—the total of deposits being in agreement with the totals of all items making up the deposits—this is "balance" in banking parlance. All work in banks must be in balance, all debits equaling all credits. Minor errors that develop from large volumes are carried into "difference" or "suspense" accounts until uncovered by audits or until customers' discrepancies are reported and located. Adjustments are then made, and the difference account properly adjusted. [10]

balancing the account: determining the balance of an account, writing it on the smaller side, totaling and ruling the account, and bringing the balance into the new section of the account below the double lines.

balboa: monetary unit of Panama.

balloon: a lump-sum payment a home borrower owes after expiration of a home loan payable to the loaning bank. See *buy down, roll over.*

balloon loan: a loan on which small payments are made during the term of the obligation.

balloon mortgage: a mortgage that allows for payments that do not completely amortize the loan at the time of termination. As a result, the final payment is larger than any single payment made previously.

balloon note: a promissory note requiring only a small payment during the initial loan period, which is then offset by larger payments made before the date of maturity.

balloon payment: a large extra payment that may be charged at the end of a loan or lease. [1]

Baltimore method: a formula for appraising corner lots in which the lot is determined to be worth the value of the inside lots on each of its sides.

Banco Centroamericano de Integracion Economica (BCIE): founded in 1960, the BCIE's headquarters are in Honduras. Functions are to finance the economic development and integration of Central America.

band: under the Bretton Woods agreement, the range within which a currency is permitted to move.

banded currency: paper money that has been sorted, counted, and banded in separate denominations. [59]

bank: an organization, normally a corporation, chartered by the state or federal government, the principal functions of which are: (a) to receive demand and time deposits, honor instruments drawn against them, and pay interest on them as permitted by law; (b) to discount notes, make loans, and invest in government or other securities; (c) to collect checks, drafts, notes, and so on; (d) to issue drafts and cashier's checks; (e) to certify depositor's checks; and (f) when authorized by a chartering government, to act in a fiduciary capacity. See *branch banking, commercial bank, correspondent bank, country bank, drive-in banking, Federal Reserve Bank, group banking, independent bank, industrial bank, insured bank, investment banking, member bank, mortgage banker, multiple banking, mutual savings bank, national bank, private bank, savings bank, state bank, trust company.*

bankable bill: a document that can be discounted at a bank.

bankable paper: paper that meets the credit standards for acceptance or endorsement by a bank. This paper is called *bank paper.* See also *bankable bill.*

bank acceptance: signed by a bank, any accepted bill of exchange or draft.

bank accommodation: a short-term bank loan to a customer, either on the individual's own note or on the endorsement of another's note owed to him or her.

bank account: a financial relationship created in the name of a business or individual. There are a variety of such accounts, including time accounts; demand accounts; and single name, multiname, joint, or trustee accounts. Minimum balance and payment of interest will vary. See specific types of accounts.

Bank Act, Canada: passed in December, 1980 in Toronto, Canada, the size of any foreign-owned banking operation was limited to 8 percent of the domestic assets of all banks. The act automatically terminates in 10 years unless revised or extended.

Bank Administration Institute (BAI): an organization of bank officials, the purpose of which is to formulate and encourage the use of standard auditing and operating procedures for the common good of all banks. BAI, founded in 1924, was previously called the National Association of Bank Auditors and Comptroller (NABAC). [105]

BankAmericard Service Exchange: see *BASE.*

bank bailout bill: see *Savings industry bill.*

bank balance: the funds in a depositor's account after all deposits have been added to the previous balance and the depositor's checks and services charges have been subtracted.

bank bill: see *bank note.*

bank book: a passbook used by banks to list entries such as interest, deposits, and withdrawals for a customer. In ordinary situations, the customer retains the book as a permanent record.

bankbooks: a bank's records of the status of other banks' deposits with it and vice versa. The term *bankbook* is sometimes used in lieu of *passbook.* [31]

bank branch: an office that is physically separated from a bank's main office, but which offers banking services. [105]

bank by mail: a banking service offered by most institutions, where a customer can perform his or her transactions through the mail. [105]

bank call: a request for a bank's balance sheet for a specified date, made by government statement.

bank card: see *bank credit card.*

bank card association: a group of banks formed either for the purpose of sponsoring a single identity (i.e., Visa or MasterCard); or a group of banks formed to jointly operate a credit or debit card plan through common processing and administrative facilities. [105]

bank certificate of deposit: see *certificate of deposit.*

bank charge plans: a relatively new and important development in the general field of consumer credit. Usually a copyrighted plan brought to a community by a bank or private organization under charter or franchise for providing a complete credit service, including credit authorization, billing, and collection of 30-day accounts for representative stores. Most banks charge 5 percent or less of total credit sales for their service. [41]

bank charter: a document of incorporation issued by the state or fed-

eral government giving a group of individuals the right to establish a bank.

bank check: a check drawn by a bank on itself and signed by an authorized officer. Savings banks do not usually draw such checks. Synonymous with *cashier's check, officer's check, treasurer's check.* [39]

bank clearing:
(1) banking: bank items sent by member banks to a local clearinghouse for collection.
(2) finance: the total volume of dollars on all items that are exchanged among members of a local clearinghouse(s).

bank clubs: to cope with possible bankruptcies and near-failures, lending institutions are attempting, through the formation of a group of creditors, to administer the orderly liquidation or rehabilitation of their shakiest borrowers.

bank credit: credit created by commercial banks through the media of loans and discounts granted with or without collateral. The amount of credit so extended is controlled in part by the rediscount rates established by the Federal Reserve Board.

bank credit card: a credit card issued by a bank, enabling the borrower to buy goods and services or obtain a cash loan from banks honoring that card. [78]

bank credit proxy: an average deposit liability (including demand and time deposits and individuals, businesses, and agencies) of member banks. The information is available each day to the Federal Reserve Banks and is used as a relative correlation of the loans and investments of member banks. The latter figure is not available daily.

bank currency: see *bank note.*

bank debits: the sum total of all debits drawn against deposited funds of individuals, partnerships, corporations, and other legal entities during a given period—usually reported by banks daily.

bank deposit: the placing of valuables, including money, in a bank for safekeeping.

Bank Deposit Insurance Act of 1934: federal legislation, to protect depositors, extended to June 1935 for bank deposit insurance originally established by the Banking Act of 1933. This act eventually led to the creation of a permanent deposit insurance program in 1935.

bank deregulation: see *Depository Institutions Deregulation Committee.*

bank directors: selected by the stockholders of a bank from among their own number, directors are responsible to the stockholders for profitable management and to government supervisory authority for operation of the bank according to law and sound banking principles. [50]

bank discount: a charge, often expressed as a percent of the face amount of the commercial paper or personal note, which is imposed by a bank for payment prior to the note's maturity.

bank draft: a check drawn by one bank against funds deposited to its account in another bank.

bank-eligible issues: issues of U.S. Treasury obligations eligible for immediate purchase by commercial banks—mainly those due or callable within 10 years. [67]

bank endorsement: an endorsement stamped on the back of items passing through the bank. This endorsement is stamped either by a hand stamp or by endorsing machines. Banks either endorse or identify all items taken in through the teller's window or deposited through the mail, except "on us" checks cashed or items coming into the bank from clearinghouse exchanges or in cash letters. Banks in larger cities may use endorsing equipment whereby they can delete a portion of the bank endorsement, and show only the date and ABA transit number of the bank sending in the item. In this way, these banks can identify any item as to the bank which sent it to them. Bank endorsements contain the following legend: "Pay to the order of any bank, banker, or trust company. All prior endorsements guaranteed." The endorsement will show the date, the bank's name in full, and the bank's transit number, usually in two places. Bank endorsements are very important to all bankers, in that they provide a means of tracing items through the collection channels of the banking system. See *examine for bank endorsement, return item.* [10]

banker's acceptance: bill of exchange drawn on or accepted by a bank to pay specific bills for one of its customers when the bills become due.

Bankers' Automated Clearing House (BACS): the U.K. system of electronic funds transfer operated by the clearing banks. It handles routine, standard payments presubmitted by the members of the system. BACS was founded in 1968 and by 1983 600 million items were cleared through the system. [117]

banker's bank: a central bank. In the United States, one of the 12 Federal Reserve District Banks.

banker's bill: a bill of exchange drawn by an exporter on the importer's bank. [105]

banker's blanket bond: see *bond.*

banker's draft: a draft payable on demand and drawn by or on behalf of a bank upon itself. [85]

banker's lien: see *lien.*

banker's payment: an order or draft drawn by one bank in favor of another bank.

banker's pool: a combination of prominent financial and banking interests during the 1929 market break to support key issues. It failed in its effort to stabilize the market.

banker's shares: shares issued to an investment banker which frequently in the past could control or manipulate the firm because of voting features which the banker's shares had compared to the lack of vote or fractional vote of other shares, such as Class A stock.

bank examination: an examination made by representatives of a federal or state bank supervisory authority to make certain that a bank is solvent and is operating in conformity with banking laws and sound banking principles. [50]

bank examiner: person who, as the representative of a federal or state bank supervisory authority, examines the banks under its jurisdiction with respect to their financial condition, management, and policies. [31]

bank exchanges: checks, notes, drafts, and so on, that are collected through a clearinghouse system.

bank failure: the closing of a bank, either temporarily or permanently, resulting from financial difficulties.

bank for cooperatives: see *Farm Credit Administration.*

Bank for International Settlements (BIS): established in 1930, this organization was designed to foster cooperation among world central banks, to seek opportunities for development of financial activity among governments, and to serve as an agent involving the transfer of payments. BIS is located in Basel, Switzerland.

bank-guaranteed bond funds: portfolios of bonds unconditionally guaranteed against default by a major bank because the bank has agreed to buy any of the underlying securities in the portfolio at face value on six days' notice.

bank holding company: in general usage, any company that owns or controls one or more banks. However, a bank holding company as defined in the Bank Holding Company Act of 1956 is one that controls two or more banks. Such companies must register with the Board of Governors of the Federal Reserve System and are commonly referred to as registered bank holding companies. See entries under *Bank Holding Company Act.*

Bank Holding Company Act of 1956: applied to any corporation controlling 25 percent or more of the voting shares of at least two banks, or otherwise controlling the election of a majority of the directors of two or more banks. The law formulated standards for the formation of bank holding companies. These companies were strictly limited to the business of banking, managing banks, and providing services to affiliated banks. See *Bank Holding Company Act Amendments of 1966, 1970.* [64]

Bank Holding Company Act Amendments of 1966: established uniform standards for bank agencies and the court in evaluating the legality of bank holding company acquisitions. See *Bank Holding Company Act of 1956, Bank Holding Company Act Amendments of 1970.* [64]

Bank Holding Company Act Amendments of 1970: ended the exemption from the Bank Holding Company Act that one-bank holding companies had enjoyed since 1956. This last amendment clearly regulated the ownership of bank shares and limited bank holding company entries into activities related only to the business of banking. See *Bank Holding Company Act of 1956, Bank Holding Company Act Amendments of 1966.* [64]

bank holiday: a day on which banks are closed.

bank identification: a series of digits used to identify a particular bank. [105]

Bank Identification Number (BIN): a series or group of digits used to identify card-issuing banks, bank card associations, or interchange groups. [105]

Banking Act of 1933: the first major piece of banking legislation during the Roosevelt administration; it led to significant changes in banking laws (see, e.g., *bank credit, branch banking, insurance*). See also *Federal Deposit Insurance Corporation.*

Banking Act of 1935: federal legislation amending the Banking Act of 1933, the Federal Reserve Act, and other banking regulations, to make these laws more specific.

banking business: primarily the business of receiving funds on deposit and making loans. [10]

banking department (government): that part of a federal or state agency concerned with the enforcement of the respective banking code.

banking house: a structure used by a bank in its regular functions of banking.

banking power: the strength of investing possessed by a bank as determined by the bank's excess reserves.

"banking school" principle: a principle developed in England in the nineteenth century; maintains that under a purely metallic currency a gain or loss of gold from abroad would not automatically result in a corresponding increase or decrease of currency in circulation and thus influence the price level, but might instead change the amount of gold in hoards. The banking school also maintained that under a mixed currency of gold and convertible paper notes, the amount of paper notes in circulation was adequately adjusted to the needs of business by the processes of competitive banking. Cf. *"currency school" principle.*

banking syndicate: a group of banks created for the purpose of underwriting and selling of an issue of securities.

banking system: the type, structure, and method of operation of a state or country's banks.

banking time off: a reward practice of permitting workers to build up time-off credits for such things as good performance or attendance. Employees then receive the time off in addition to the regular vacation time granted by the organization because of seniority.

bank insolvency: where a bank's capital is impaired and the appropriate authorities decide to close and/or liquidate the bank.

Bank Insurance Fund: see *BIF.*

bank loan: any money borrowed from a bank for the purposes of business investment.

Bank Merger Act: federal legislation of 1960, amended in 1966, identifying the legal responsibilities resulting from bank mergers. See also entries under *Bank Holding Company Act.*

bank money: deposits (promises by a bank to pay) created by a bank when it is required to have on hand in reserves only a fraction of its total deposits.

bank money order: see *money order.*

bank note: a promissory note released by an authorized bank that is payable on demand to the bearer and can be used as cash. Such notes, as established by law, are redeemable as money and are considered to be full legal tender. Synonymous with *bank bill* or *bank currency.*

bank number: see *American Bankers Association number.*

bank of circulation: see *bank of issue.*

bank of deposit: usually associated with commercial banks that accept deposits subject to demand check withdrawal.

bank of discount: banks, usually commercial, that offer credit on acceptances, bills of exchange, and notes.

When Federal Reserve Banks engage in discounting, it is properly called *rediscounting* because the notes have already been discounted by the borrowing commercial bank.

bank of issue: any bank that is legally permitted to issue money (e.g., bank notes).

Bank of the United States: now defunct, a quasi-public bank, formed under a congressional charter, which through a central office and various branches issued bank notes and served as a depository for federal funds and as a fiduciary agent for the government.

bank overdraft: an amount owed to a bank by a customer on his or her account, resulting from payment of checks for an amount in excess of the drawer's balance. The bank levies a charge based on the amount overdrawn and calculated on a day-to-day basis, establishing a fixed limit that the customer may withdraw.

bank paper: paper showing acceptance or endorsement by a bank; paper that meets the credit standards for acceptance or bank endorsement.

bank passbook: a small book given to the customer by a bank to record deposits and withdrawals.

bank post remittance: the conversion into cash or a money form of a foreign bill of exchange, and subsequent mailing of the latter to the payee.

bank premises: book value of building and equipment. [40]

bank rate:
(1) the rate of discount established by the national bank of a country for rediscounting of eligible paper.

(2) the rate charged by the national bank of a country on advances on specific collateral to banks.

bank reconciliation: see *reconciliation.*

bank reference: the name of the bank with which a firm has an account, presented to another firm as a reference so that its credit position can be assessed.

bank regulation: the formulation and issuance by authorized agencies of specific rules or regulations, under governing law, for the conduct and structure of banking. [200]

bank release: a document from a bank after it has been paid or given an acceptance on a bill of exchange, thereby permitting the purchaser of items involved to take delivery, although the rights of other parties may need to be satisfied before the items are released for delivery, and in any case customs clearance must be arranged in due course.

bank reserves: commercial banks that are members of the Federal Reserve System are required to hold a proportion of their deposit liabilities in the form of reserves with the Federal Reserve District Bank or till cash. Nonmember state banks only have to fulfill the requirements of their state's banking laws.

bank return: a statement of a check clearinghouse.

bankroll: slang, to support with money any project managed by others.

bank run: a series of unusually large withdrawals made on a bank out of fear that the bank may run out of funds.

bankrupt: a person, corporation, or other legal entity which, being unable to meet its financial obligations, has been declared by a decree of the court to be insolvent, and whose property becomes liable to administration under the Bankruptcy Reform Act of 1978. See *insolvent.*

bankruptcy: the conditions under which the financial position of an individual, corporation, or other legal entity are such as to cause actual or legal insolvency. Two types are: (a) *involuntary bankruptcy*—one or more creditors of an insolvent debtor file a petition having the debtor declared a bankrupt; and (b) *voluntary bankruptcy*—the debtor files a petition claiming inability to meet debts and willingness to be declared a bankrupt. A court adjudges and declares a debtor a bankrupt. See *Bankruptcy Reform Act of 1978. National Bankruptcy Act of 1898.*

Bankruptcy Act: see *National Bankruptcy Act of 1898.*

Bankruptcy Reform Act of 1978: taking effect on October 1, 1978, the first complete overhaul of bankruptcy statutes in 75 years. Some major provisions are: (a) a consolidation of the three sections of the old law that dealt with business reorganizations—in effect, a restructuring to permit a company to return to fiscal soundness—into a new, streamlined Chapter 11; (b) various new tactical weapons for business creditors, one of which may allow them, in certain instances, to file their own reorganization plans for a company; (c) new federal exemptions for consumers that may allow them to keep more property after bankruptcy than they could under state laws unless the states take contrary action; and

(d) a new procedure that will allow small businesses to pay off their debts gradually under a proceeding similar to a reorganization. See *bankruptcy.*

Bankruptcy Tax Act of 1980: federal legislation that went into effect on January 1, 1981. In part, the law says that a company that buys back its own bonds at a discount price must pay income tax on the spread between the face value of the bonds, or the original sales price, and the discount repurchase price. See also *solvent debtor section.*

Bank Secrecy Act of 1970: federal legislation compelling banks to keep records of all customer transactions and to report any financial dealings involving more than $10,000 to the U.S. Treasury Department. The government contends that the records are the bank's business records and are not owned by the depositor.

bank securities: commercial bank offerings include convertible or nonconvertible capital debentures, convertible or nonconvertible preferred stock, and common stock.

bank service charge: a monthly charge made by a bank when the depositor's balance is less than a fixed sum in order to compensate the bank for the cost of handling a small account.

Banks for Cooperatives: a system of 12 banks scattered over the United States under the supervision of the Farm Credit Administration (FCA) to extend credit to farmer cooperatives.

bank stamp: a bank's endorsement placed on the back side of a check, note, or other negotiable instru-ment with an endorsement machine or rubber stamp.

bank statement:
(1) banking: a statement of a customer's account periodically rendered by the bank. It shows all deposits made and all checks paid and other debits posted during the period, usually one month, as well as the current balance; the customer's canceled checks may or may not be enclosed.
(2) banking: a bank's financial statement.

bank supervision: concern of financial regulators with the safety and soundness of individual banks, involving the general and continuous oversight of the activities of this industry to ensure that banks are operated prudently and in accordance with applicable statutes and regulations. [200]

bank term loan: a loan terminating in a year or more. At times used instead of a long-term bond issue, especially during periods of high interest rates.

bank-to-bank information: in EFTS, miscellaneous information pertaining to the transfer, including information specifying for which bank(s) the information is intended. [105]

Bank Wire System: a private, computerized message system administered for and by participating banks, through the facilities of Western Union. The system links about 250 banks in about 75 cities. Like the Fedwire, the Bank Wire transmits funds and transfers information, but also relays data concerning loan participations, bond closings, payment for securities, borrowing of federal funds, and balances in company accounts.

banque d'affaires: a French bank involved in long-term financing and in the ownership of companies, usually industrial firms. Synonymous with *merchant bank.*

Banque de France: the central bank of France, created by Napoleon Bonaparte in 1800.

Banque Française du Commerce Exterieure (BFCE): French quasi-government bank providing export finance at medium or long term. [118]

Ban Ser Corp: formed in 1974 to service insurance plans offered by savings banks to their employees, depositors, and/or mortgagors. Ban Ser does not handle general lines of insurance or service claims. Rather, it acts as liaison between savings banking and the insurance industry in developing new insurance plans to meet savings banks' changing needs and in monitoring existing plans for pricing, service, and standards of coverage. Ban Ser offers a complete insurance consulting service for thrift institutions. [8]

bar: one million sterling on the interbank market.

barren money: currency that does not earn interest or other forms of income.

barter: the direct exchange of one item for another without the transfer of money.

barter agreement: an agreement between two nations providing for the exchange of given quantities or values of specified commodities.

BASE (BankAmericard Service Exchange): the national authorization and electronic draft inter-change network used to process BankAmericard credit transactions. [36]

BASE central: the Visa U.S.A. operations center, which provides BASE I and II and central computer services. [105]

Basel Agreement: signed in 1967 between Great Britain and the major nations of the West, this agreement determined the repayment of advances for funds given to the United Kingdom during its sterling crisis. The agreement is important since it represents the first time that a nation agreed to a dollar guarantee on its debt to other nations.

BASE I: a data processing network of Visa U.S.A. capable of providing message processing, authorization services, and file services. [105]

Base I activity file: a file, maintained at BASE central, containing a record of account numbers that have had authorization approval responses generated by BASE I within a four-day period. [105]

BASE I exception file: a file, maintained at BASE central, which contains those cardholder account numbers for which authorization responses have been predetermined by the issuer. [105]

BASE I user: an authorizing member who, through a terminal or computer device, connects to BASE I for authorization and other services. (BASE I users include those affiliates who are so identified on their interchange data forms and all U.S. affiliates.) [105]

BASE II: an electronic draft data transmission system owned by Visa U.S.A. for the exchange of draft data by Visa U.S.A. and Visa International Clearing Members, including all BASE II equipment, software, processes, techniques, programs, and information provided by Visa U.S.A. and used in connection with the system. [105]

BASE II request: a request sent through BASE II for a copy of a specific sales draft retained at another bank card center. [105]

BASE II sales draft: purchase identified by a reference number which begins with "4." [105]

base-year analysis: a method of analysis of financial statements, whereby the figures for each of a series of years are compared to those of a common base year. [105]

basic balance: the sum of the balance-of-payments current account plus long-term capital movements.

basic IS-LM Model: see *IS-LM model.*

basic rating: standard classification under the numerical system for selection of risks. [12]

basic reserve position: developed to gauge pressure on a single money market bank or the entire group, by measuring the amount of residual borrowing in the federal funds market or from the Federal Reserve needed to cover requirements. [203]

basic yield: a concept similar to pure interest, that is, the annual rate of return in percent on a risk-free investment such as a long-term U.S. government bond. See also *pure interest.*

Basle Agreement: an informal agreement made in 1961 at the central bankers' monthly meeting to cooperate in the foreign exchange markets.

Basle Concordat: a 1975 agreement between the central banks, within the BIS framework, on supervisory matters.

batch: a group of deposits, or a group of other items, which are proved in one operation. See *block.* [39]

batch number: a number assigned to a batch of items processed in the proof department. The number is placed in the account number field of the batch ticket and on the rear of the remainder of the items in the batch.

batch proof: a system for proving deposits, usually performed in the following sequence: (a) deposits are assembled in groups of various sizes; (b) deposit tickets are sorted into one group; (c) checks are sorted into several classifications, such as clearings, transit, and bookkeeping; (d) cash release tickets are sorted according to teller; (e) deposit tickets, checks, and cash release tickets are listed on a "batch" or "block" sheet in their respective columns; and (f) the total of the deposit and other credits should equal the recapitulation of the checks and debits. [10]

batch sheet: a proof sheet used in the batch proof system. The batch sheet is arranged in columns for deposits, various classifications of checks and other debits, and cash release tickets. After sorting, all items in the batch are listed in their respective columns, the totals recapped and proved. The batch sheet then becomes a permanent record of the bank, and is used by bank auditors to check any errors arising from transactions. [10]

batch system: see *batch proof.*

batch ticket: when used in an MICR system, the batch ticket is a control document encoded with the total amount of a batch and identified by a special transaction code. The batch ticket can also contain such encoded information as batch number, source number, and/or proof machine number. This ticket accompanies the items from the proof department to the document processing center. [31]

BD: see *bill discounted.*

B/E: see *bill of exchange.*

bearer: any person holding a negotiable instrument.

bearer certificate: a certificate that is not filled out in the name of a particular person. Since these certificates are negotiable without endorsement, they should always be kept in a safe place.

bearer check: a check payable to cash or to the bearer rather than to a specific party. [59]

bearer instrument: a negotiable instrument payable on demand to the individual who holds the instrument. Title passes by delivery without endorsement.

bearer paper: in dealing with negotiable instruments, an instrument is called *bearer paper* when it is payable to bearer (i.e., the person having possession of it). Ownership of such a document is transferred by delivery, no indorsement being needed. If the person who originally issued the paper placed it in bearer form, it cannot thereafter receive a special indorsement. Cf. *order paper.*

bear squeeze: a strategy by central banks which know that uncovered bears have sold their currency short. By temporarily bidding up the currency until the time comes for the bears to deliver the currency they had contracted to sell, the central bank forces the bears to take a loss.

Bellevue Project: a banking program of study and implementation leading to the Bellevue Exchange, an automated teller facility in Bellevue, Washington, available to the customers of a group of cooperating thrift institutions on a shared basis and has become a model for other banks.

below par: at a discount; less than face amount.

below the line: the classification applied to an out-of-the-ordinary revenue or expense, or an extraordinary and material nonrecurring item that requires a separate grouping in a company's balance sheet or income statement. [105]

benchmark reserves: reserve funds, representing a specified percentage of savings deposits, that all savings association members of the Federal Savings and Loan Insurance Corporation must hold. [59]

beneficial interest (owner): an individual, not the true owner of property, who enjoys all or part of the benefits to it, by reason of a trust or private arrangement.

beneficiary identifier: a code that uniquely identifies the beneficiary to the beneficiary's bank. [105]

beneficiary identifier type: a code that specifies the type of beneficiary identifier used. [105]

beneficiary method of payment: specifies how payment is to be made to the beneficiary. [105]

beneficiary's bank: a bank that acts as the financial agent for the beneficiary of a transfer. [105]

beneficiary's bank advice charges: information specifying who to charge for advising the beneficiary's bank and how to apply those charges. [105]

beneficiary's bank advice identifier: information used in contacting the beneficiary's bank in order to send an advice (e.g., phone number, cable address). [105]

beneficiary's bank advice instruction: additional information which pertains to notification of the beneficiary's bank (e.g., bank's name, hours of availability). [105]

beneficiary's bank advice method: a code that specifies the method to be used to notify the beneficiary's bank that the account has been credited or that the funds are available (e.g., phone, letter, wire). [105]

beneficiary's bank identifier: a code that uniquely identifies the beneficiary's bank. [105]

beneficiary's bank identifier type: a code that specifies the type of identifier used for the beneficiary's bank. [105]

beneficiary's bank name and address: identifies the beneficiary's bank by name and optionally, the beneficiary's bank's postal address. [105]

beneficiary type: a code that specifies whether the beneficiary is a bank or a nonbank. [105]

benefit:
(1) a gain or advantage received by an individual; that which fulfills a need.
(2) the amount of indemnity to be regularly paid.

bequeath: to offer personal property in a will.

bequest: a gift of personal property made by a testator. See *legacy.*

Bernard rule: a rule for appraising a corner lot. First, the property is appraised as if it were an inside lot fronting on a side street; it is then taken as an inside lot on the main street. The value placed on the corner lot is the total of the two appraisals.

best bid: the highest price a person is willing to pay for something offered for sale. This bid is the relevant one used in determining the market for a security.

betterment: an improvement made to property that increases its value more than would ordinary repair or maintenance work.

BFCE: see *Banque Française du commerce exterieure.*

BH: see *bank holiday.*

biannual: occurring twice a year. [61]

Bibor: Bahrain InterBank Offered Rate.

BIF: Bank Insurance Fund. The new name for the Federal Deposit Insurance Corporation's fund that insures bank deposits up to $100,000. Its assets are currently $14 billion, considered too low. A new law increases bank premiums in replenish the fund. FDIC cannot commingle BIF and SAIF funds. See *Savings industry bill.*

big figure: used by foreign exchange dealers to denote the first three digits of an exchange rate.

Big Five:
(1) the five largest credit card companies: American Express, Carte Blanche, Diners Club, MasterCard, and Visa (BankAmericard).
(2) the five largest commercial banks of the United Kingdom: Midland Bank Ltd., Barclay's Bank Ltd., Lloyd's Bank Ltd.,

National Provincial Bank Ltd., and Westminster Bank Ltd.

big George: slang, a quarter (25 cents).

big one: slang, $1000, usually a $1000 bill.

bilateral agreement: an agreement made between two persons or two groups.

bilateral clearing: an international trade system to economize on the use of scarce foreign exchange by routing all payments through a central bank instead of with foreign trade banks or their equivalent demanding that the nations involved be required exactly to balance their mutual trade every year.

bilateral contract: an agreement containing promises, with each party serving as a promisor or promisee.

bilateralism: an international policy having as its object the achievement of particular balances of trade between two nations by means of discriminatory tariff, exchange, or other controls. The initiative is usually taken by the country having an "unfavorable" balance of trade. Extensive bilateralism results in a shift of international trade away from channels that would result from the principle of comparative advantage.

bilateral monopoly: exists when there is only one purchaser for an item or service and the creation of the supply is controlled by one seller.

bilateral payments agreement: an agreement between two countries or their central banks to channel all or specified settlements between themselves through special accounts, normally subject to a reciprocal credit margin (swing). Arrangements of this nature usu-

ally imply that the use of convertible foreign currencies or gold between the partner countries is avoided except when the credit margin is exceeded or net balances are settled. [42]

bill:
(1) an invoice of charges for services or a product.
(2) paper currency.

bill broker: any financial dealer in bills of exchange.

bill check: a payment system in which a debtor, on receipt of an invoice or statement, authorizes the creditor to obtain payment directly from the debtor's deposit account.

bill discounted: a promissory note or bill of exchange from which a bank deducts its interest in advance.

billed escrow: the amount of escrow payment that represents a total of the regular escrow payment plus arrears or minus prepaid escrow amounts.

billed principal: the amount of principal payment that represents a total of the normal principal amount plus any arrears.

biller: a person trained in operation of bookkeeping or billing machines and responsible for posting all debit and credit transactions to a group of individual customers' accounts. [41]

bill for payment: an instrument given to a debtor or representative for the purpose of being paid, as differentiated from one that was presented for acceptance.

billing: the process of submitting invoices or bills.

billing cycle: time interval, often a month, between regular periodic billing statement dates. [78]

billing date: the month, day, and year when a periodic or monthly statement is generated, and when calculations for appropriate finance charges, minimum payment due, and new balance have been performed. [105]

billing-only account: a bank card account set up with no cards being issued on the account. [105]

bill of credit:
(1) an individual's written request to a bank asking for the delivery of money to the bearer on the credit or account of the writer.
(2) used as if it were a state's currency. Article 1 of the U.S. Constitution forbids the states to issue their own currency.

bill of exchange: instructions from one party to another party to pay a third party following completion of an assignment. See *commercial set.*

bill of sale:
(1) a written agreement by whose terms the ownership of goods is transferred or assigned to another person.
(2) a formal written agreement by which one person transfers to another his or her rights, interest, and title in specified property. It is considered to be sufficient warranty of the seller's title to the property and his or her right to sell; it need not be recorded as a deed for real property.

bill payment: checkless system for paying recurring bills through one authorization statement to a financial institution. Automated clearinghouses are used by financial institutions to make necessary debits and credits. [105]

bills discounted: bills of exchange, notes, and acceptances that a bank has discounted for its customers.

bills discounted overdue: bills, notes acceptances, and similar obligations that have passed their due date or matured and are as yet unpaid. Representing past due accounts of doubtful value, they are segregated from other assets.

bills of credit: an obsolete term found in the U.S. Constitution for paper money issued by the government.

bills payable:
(1) a comprehensive term that includes all notes and trade acceptances that are owed by a business to trade creditors and must be paid by the business at maturity.
(2) the sum of money that a member bank has borrowed, on its own collateral note, from a Federal Reserve Bank.

bimetallism: a double standard of metals used in coins. The ratio of content and weight must be specified in terms of, for example, gold and silver. Cf. *monometallism, parallel standard, real money.*

BIN: see *Bank Identification Number.*

binder:
(1) a legal agreement issued either by an agent or by a company, to provide temporary insurance until a policy can be written. It usually contains a definite time limit, is in writing, and clearly designates the company in which the risk is bound the amount, the perils insured against, and the type of insurance.
(2) an initially written agreement, with a valuable consideration given as evidence of good faith by the offerer to purchase property.

(3) any temporary agreement obligating the several parties to the contract.

binding signature: a legally acceptable signature. One which when affixed to a legal document makes that document valid and enforceable. [55]

bind the bargain: see *earnest money.*

birr: monetary unit of Ethiopia.

BIS: see *Bank for International Settlements.*

Bk.: see *bank.*

Bkg.: banking.

Bks.: see *book(s).*

B&L ASSN: see *building and loan association.*

black light: a signature verification method whereby an ultraviolet ink signature is placed on a depositor's passbook. The signature of the customer can be verified on other items by comparing it to the ultraviolet signature, which shows up when placed under black light. [105]

black list: in international trade, a list of individuals and firms of another country with whom the domestic nation forbids commerce by its nationals.

black market: buying or selling of products and commodities, or engaging in exchange of foreign currencies in violation of government restrictions.

Bland-Allison Act: federal legislation of 1878 authorizing limited governmental purchase and coinage of silver; also permitted the issuance of silver certificates secured by silver in amounts equal to the face value of the certificates.

blank bill: a bill of exchange with the payee's name not appearing.

blank check: a bank form that has been signed, although the amount payable or the name of the payee has been left out.

blank endorsement: the signature or endorsement of a person or firm on an instrument such as a note or check making it payable to the bearer and therefore negotiable without restrictions.

blanket loan: a loan made to a developer or contractor for a number of individual properties. [59]

blanket mortgage: a mortgage covering all the property of a corporation and given to secure a single debt.

blank indorsement: the placing of one's name on a negotiable instrument without any qualification. Synonymous with *general indorsement.*

blasted: slang, a person without money.

blended credit: financial credit extended on the basis of more than one source of funding.

blind entry: a bookkeeping entry stating only the accounts and the amounts debited and credited, but not giving other data or accounting factors essential to an accurate record.

blip: slang, a nickel (5 cents).

block: a bundle of checks deposited for credit with a bank, along with their relative deposit slips.

blockage: designating the administration of an account as subject to U.S. Treasury control because of enemy or suspected enemy interest. A discount from the established market for which a large block of stock of a single corporation would have to be sold if the entire holding were placed on the market at a given date (a term used in connection with federal estate tax). [37]

block busting: the unethical real estate practice of creating fear by renting or selling units in a neighborhood to families of a religion or race different from that of the current residents, thus exploiting the prejudices and emotions of property owners so that they will sell their homes at reduced prices.

blocked accounts: in time of war the president of the United States issues directives to financial institutions to suspend payment of the accounts of enemy nationals of or individuals inhabiting occupied countries in the sphere of enemy influence. These funds may be released only by executive order, or by license under certain conditions. This action was taken in 1979 during the Iranian crisis.

blocked currency: currency, the conversion of which into another foreign currency is prohibited by law. [105]

block system: see *batch proof.*

blotter: a book of accounts or a journal used for entering the first or temporary list of transactions or occurrences. Cf. *daily reports.*

BN: see *bank note.*

boa: a proposed system of jointly floated currencies whose exchange rates are allowed to fluctuate against each other within limits that are wider than in the snake. See *snake system.*

Board of Governors: the seven-member governing body of the Federal Reserve System.

board of managers: in some states, the board of trustees of a mutual savings bank. [39]

board of trustees: the body in a mutual savings bank which manages the institution, establishes the policies under which it is to be operated, appoints the officers, and the like. [39]

bobtail statement: an abbreviated statement prepared for holders of demand deposit accounts. [105]

BOC:

(1) see *back office crunch.*

(2) see *breach of contract.*

"body": see *corpus.*

boffo: slang, $1.

boff out: slang, to lose one's money.

BOG: see *Board of Governors.*

bogus: false, counterfeit, nonexistent, or fraudulent. Bogus money is counterfeit currency; a bogus check is written on nonexistent account or bank.

boilerplate legends: long stereotyped provisions contained in a document, such as a deposit slip or contract, usually in very small print. [105]

bolivar: monetary unit of Venezuela.

boliviano: monetary unit of Bolivia.

bona fide: "in good faith" (Latin); with honest intent. Cf. *mala fides.*

bona fide purchaser: an individual who buys property in good faith, without notice of any defect in the title, and for a valuable consideration.

bona vacentia: describing property of which there is no apparent owner nor claimant (e.g., property in the hands of a liquidator after a firm has been dissolved).

bond:

(1) an interest-bearing certificate of debt, usually issued in series, by which the issuer obligates itself to pay the principal amount at a specified time, usually five years

or more after date of issue, and to pay interest periodically, usually semiannually. Bonds may be distinguished from promissory notes or other evidences of debt because of their formal execution under seal, and because a bank has certified that their issue has been authorized by the board of directors of a corporation or other governing body. Corporate bonds are usually secured by a lien against certain specified property.

(2) an instrument used as proof of a debt, usually secured by a mortgage. See other entries under *bond.* [5]

(3) a promise, under seal (i.e., closed from view by the public) to pay money.

(4) the obligation to answer for the debt of another person.

bond, banker's blanket: business insurance coverage guaranteeing banks against loss due to dishonest, fraudulent, or employee criminal activity. This bond insures against loss resulting from robbery, larceny, burglary, theft, holdup, misplacement, and other unexplained disappearances.

bond, borrowed: to meet specific requirements, banks and other financial institutions borrow bonds. Banks borrow bonds to comply with collateral requirements of governmental agencies, whereas brokers borrow bonds to make delivery on short sales.

bond, bulldog: a bond issued by a foreign borrower in the U.K. bond market.

bond, honor: a consumer-size certificate of deposit with denominations as low as $5.00, many banks promoted these bonds and told purchasers that they were merely honor-bound to report the interest on their tax returns. The Internal Revenue Service moved swiftly to eliminate this irregularity.

bond, mortgage: a bond that has as an underlying security a mortgage on all properties of the issuing corporation.

bond, municipal: a bond issued by a state or a political subdivision (county, city, town, village, etc.). Also, a bond issued by a state agency or authority. In general, interest paid on municipal bonds is exempt from federal income taxes and state and local taxes in the state of issue.

bond, municipal revenue: banks now may underwrite a few kinds of revenue bonds, which are obligations backed not by city or state tax revenues, but by revenue produced by the facilities that are financed—for example, a housing project. Banks want to be permitted to underwrite more kinds of revenue bonds. In addition, the Comptroller of the Currency is seeking to determine the legality of municipal revenue bonds underwriting, under which banks offer, in effect, to repurchase the bonds at par within five years. This recent activity in banking is testing the Glass-Steagall Act. See *Glass-Steagall Act.*

bond, obligation: a bond authorized by a mortgagor that is larger than the original mortgage amount. A personal obligation is created to safeguard the lender against any costs that may develop over the amount of the mortgage.

bond, open-end: a mortgage bond of an issue that has no limit on the number or quantity of bonds that can be issued under the mortgage. However, some relationship is often required of the number and quantity of bonds to the value of the property that has been mortgaged.

bond, optional payment: a bond that gives the holder the choice to receive payment of interest or principal or both in the currency of one or more foreign countries, as well as in domestic funds. [37]

bond, real estate: a bond secured by a mortgage or trust conveyance of real estate.

bond, Samurai: foreign bond denominated in yen and issued in Japan.

Bond, Savings (U.S.): Series EE, introduced at the start of 1980, replaced the highly popular Series E bonds. These new bonds are available in face-value denominations of $50, $75, up to $10,000, and are sold at one-half their face value. EE bonds pay varying interest rates—as much as one percent at six-month intervals if market conditions warrant. Presently, the maturity on Series EE bonds is eight years, down from nine years, effectively boosting the rate on those bonds to 9 percent. The rate on HH bonds is 8.5 percent. HH bonds are bought at face value, pay interest semiannually, and mature in 10 years. In 1982 a variable-interest-rate U.S. Savings Bond was approved. The investment yield on these bonds was increased to a level equal to 85 percent of the yield on five-year Treasury securities when held five years.

bonus: an additional dividend paid to savers who have met all the requirements of a special savings account contract.

bonus account: a savings account that earns interest at a bonus rate if the customer makes regular deposits to the account, leaves a specified amount on deposit for a specified term, or fulfills other conditions of the account contract. [59]

boodle:
(1) money received through corruption in public activities.
(2) counterfeit money.

book account: synonymous with *open account.*

book credit: items shown on a ledger accounts representing commitments of firms and individuals which are not secured by notes or other security.

booked: bookkeeping entries connected with a given transaction being entered in a nation other than where the transaction takes place; often done to lessen tax liability.

book-entry: one form in which Treasury and certain government agency securities are held. Book-entry form consists of an entry on the records of the U.S. Treasury Department, a Federal Reserve Bank, or a financial institution. [200]

bookkeeper: a person who makes entries on the general ledger of a business.

bookkeeping: the art, practice, or labor involved in the systematic recording of the transactions affecting a business.

bookkeeping cycle: the full bookkeeping process discharged in a fiscal period, including journalizing, posting, preparing a trial balance, and preparing financial statements.

bookkeeping department: a department of a bank where the records of all depositors' checking accounts are posted and kept. In the larger banks, there may be found several bookkeeping departments, such as commercial, corporation accounts, special checking, general ledger, bank ledger, foreign accounts, stock transfer, and trust bookkeeping. [10]

bookkeeping equation: a one-line summary of a balance sheet. The basic equation is assets = liabilities + proprietorship.

book liability: the amount at which securities issued or assumed by the carrier and other liability items are recorded in the accounts of the carrier. [18]

book of final entry: a book to which information is transferred from a book or original entry.

book of original entry: the record in which transactions are formally recorded for the first time, such as the cash journal, check register, or general journal. Where machine bookkeeping is used, it may happen that one transaction is recorded simultaneously in several records, one of which may be regarded as the book of original entry. [49]

book of secondary entry: ledger; not books of original entry (i.e., journals).

book-runner: a Euromarket term for the bank house that plays a central part in organizing the syndicate which is making the loan or buying the bond issue. [128]

books:
(1) journals, ledgers, or other records containing a firm's accounts.
(2) the record kept by a specialist in a particular security of all orders that were not executed

because they were limited to a price other than the one prevailing in the market.

book sort: a method of sorting checks and deposits into the books within the bookkeeping department's alphabetical breakdown by a rough sort (i.e., all items going to the A-B-C-D book or ledger are rough-sorted into this four-letter breakdown).

book transfer: a transfer of funds between two accounts, both on the books of the bank executing the transaction. [105]

book yield: the yield on a portfolio when it is valued at its book value.

borrow: to receive something from another, with the understanding that the item is to be returned.

borrowed funds: all direct or indirect nondeposit liabilities. Borrowings may be accomplished through the use of promissory notes, purchase of federal funds, bills payable, mortgages payable, due bills, securities borrowed, customer paper rediscounted, and assets sold with the bank's endorsement. [105]

borrowed reserves: discounts and advances from Federal Reserve Banks; mainly advances secured by U.S. government securities or eligible paper. [72]

borrower: one who borrows cash or buys something on time.

borrowing power: the ability to secure a loan from an individual or firm such as a bank.

borrowings: the amount borrowed by reporting member banks; the breakdown shows the amounts borrowed from the Federal Reserve Banks, and from others—mostly other commercial banks. [40]

Boston interest: ordinary interest computed by using a 30-day month rather than the exact number of days in a month. Cf. *New York interest.*

BOT: see *board of trustees.*

bottomry: a loan secured by a lien on a vessel. The contract of bottomry is in the nature of a mortgage. If the carrier is lost, the debt is canceled.

bounce: slang, the failure of a check to fulfill payment for an item or service.

box: short for *safe deposit box* where valuables are kept.

BR: depository institutions' borrowing from the Federal Reserve. [81]

BRA: see *Bankruptcy Reform Act of 1978.*

bracket: groupings determined by underwriting amounts in a new issue or loan.

branch banking: any banking system where there are few parent institutions, each having branches operating over a large geographic area. Some states have authorized the concept of branch banking under strict regulation. Federal control is maintained by the Board of Governors of the Federal Reserve System and the Office of Comptroller of the Currency.

branch clearing account: a general ledger account that reflects the flow of debit and credit items between community offices or administrative units. [105]

branch expense: cost of activities performed by bank branches on behalf of the bank credit card operation, such as receiving payments and merchant deposits and issuing cash advances. [105]

branch pickup: method of distributing new bank cards to cardholders whereby cardholders are notified that their new bank cards are being held for them at a specified branch and asked to visit that branch to obtain their new cards. [105]

brassage: the charge made by a government for producing coins from bullion. See *seignorage.*

breach of contract: not fulfilling one's part in an agreement; breaking a promise to carry out one's contractual responsibility.

bread: slang, money.

break:
(1) a second chance or another opportunity.
(2) a discount.
(3) in a Eurocredit, a clause which passes on to a borrower the risk that certain events may curtail the lender's activity or close the Eurocurrency market. Cf. *disaster clause.*

breakage: the fractional pennies due either party resulting from percentage calculations (e.g., when the decimal shows itself to be 0.5 or more, an added point is entered).

breakdown: an itemized listing of all activity occurring on an individual cardholder account. [105]

Bretton Woods Agreement of 1944: articles of agreement adopted by the international monetary conference of 44 nations which met at Bretton Woods, New Hampshire. The International Monetary Fund and the International Bank for Reconstruction and Development were created. The fund's major responsibility is to maintain orderly currency practices in international trade, while the bank's function is to facilitate extension of long-term investments for productive purposes. Periodic meetings are held at Bretton Woods to amend the original agreement.

brick: a package of new currency which is banded with steel straps, the straps being sealed at the joining points. New currency is shipped from the Federal Reserve Bank by this method of packaging. [10]

bridge financing: emergency financing whereby a short- or medium-term loan is secured to meet a debt obligation or to await favorable conditions for a longer-term loan.

bridge loan: synonymous with *swing loan.*

bridging loan: see *swing loan.*

broadcast system: syndicating Eurocredits whereby a bank (or banks) receive a mandate to provide the funds and then offer participation in the loan, more or less indiscriminately, to other banks, by letter or telex.

broken period: a forward foreign exchange arrangement which is not for a standard maturity period.

broker:
(1) a person who prepares contracts with third parties on behalf of the broker's principal.
(2) a specialist who represents buyers of property and liability insurance and deals with either agents or companies in arranging for the coverage required by the customer. The broker is licensed by the state or states in which he or she conducts business.
(3) a state-licensed individual who acts as middleman in property transactions between a buyer and seller.

brokerage: the business of a broker. [62]

brokered deposits: deposits which the reporting bank receives from bro-

kers or dealers for the account of others either directly or ultimately; include both those in which the entire beneficial interest in a given deposit instrument issued by the bank is held by a single depositor and those in which the broker sells participations in a given bank instrument to one or more investors. [202]

broker's line: the direct telephone line between a bank's dealing room and a broker's office.

broker's loan rate: the rate charged by U.S. banks to their stock-broker customers for lendings against the pledge of U.S. government securities. Because of the first-class collateral the loan rate is normally well below price—up to 1 percent. [129]

brown Abe: slang, a penny.

BS: see *balance sheet.*

buck: slang, one dollar.

budget loan: a mortgage loan that requires a proportionate amount of tax, insurance, and assessment to be held in escrow, in addition to interest and principal payments.

buffering: a fraud scheme for bank cards containing usage information. It consists of copying and storing magnetic stripe information, using the card, and restoring the original information. Synonymous with *refreshing.*

building and loan association: a cooperative or stock society for the saving, accumulation, and lending of money. Deposits in an institution of this kind may be represented by shares issued in the name of the depositor. [31]

building loan: a mortgage loan made to finance the construction of a building. It is advanced in stages as the construction work progresses. See *construction loan.* [39]

building societies: a British term for *public deposits* where a high interest rate is given to attract funds to finance home loans and property purchases. Similar to savings and loan associations in the United States.

bulk cash: rolled or bagged coins or banded currency. [105]

bulk filing: the filing of canceled customer checks and/or debit/credit transactions in a bulk of mass file and not by individual account number. Such items filed in a bulk manner are not returned to the customer at the time the account statement is rendered. Items are retrieved only upon request. [105]

bulk transfer: the transfer of more than 50 accounts from one branch office to one or more other branch offices in a one-week period. [55]

"bullet": a borrowing that is not to be repaid gradually but in a lump sum at the end of its term. [89]

bulletproof: slang, any document with no loopholes.

bullion: usually gold or silver, formed in ingots or bars, for use as a coin.

bullionism:
(1) the monetary policy of mercantilism that called for direct regulation of transactions in foreign exchange and in precious metals in order to maintain a favorable balance in the home country. Cf. *mercantilism.*
(2) followers of the monetary theories of the Bullion Report (England 1810).

Bundesbank: established in 1875, the central bank of West Germany, located in Frankfurt.

bundle: slang, a large amount of money.

bundle of rights: the legal rights that go with property ownership: the rights to sell, lease, build, mortgage, improve, and so on.

B-unit: a large trading unit whose value varies from day to day. It is composed of equal proportions of different currencies: American dollar, German mark, French franc, Swiss franc, and British pound. [105]

business day: any day on which the offices of the consumer's financial institution involved in an electronic fund transfer are open to the public for carrying on substantially all of its business functions. [105]

business ethics: socially accepted rules of behavior that place pressure on business executives to maintain a high sense of values and to be honest and fair in their dealings with the public.

business index (indices): a time series that presents economic data (i.e., the Federal Reserve Board's Index of Industrial Production).

business trust: an unincorporated business organization in which title to the property is given to trustees to hold, manage, or sell. This structure is sometimes employed when a parcel of land is divided, improved, or sold. Has been referred to as a *Massachusetts trust* or *common law trust.*

buy:
(1) the quality of a purchase (e.g., a good buy).
(2) to acquire ownership of something in exchange for a monetary consideration.

buy down: a builder pays the bank a lump sum of money in advance to reduce the monthly interest charges on the mortgage. See *balloon, roll over.*

buyer credit: paying an exporter promptly by the overseas importer, who obtains the needed funds by means of a loan from a bank; the payment is usually made directly by a bank to an exporter.

buying rate: the publicized quotation for buying such things as foreign exchange, commodities, and bills of exchange which a bank or other buyer employs to inform the trader of his desire to buy.

by tale: see *tale.*

C:
(1) see *cash.*
(2) see *cent.*
(3) the currency component of money. [81]

C$: Canadian dollar.
(1) see *capital account.*
(2) see *chartered accountant.*
(3) see *custodian account.*

cabbage: slang, paper money, banknotes, or other funds.

cable: slang, the dollar/sterling spot exchange rate.

cable rate: the charge for a cable transfer, contrasted with the check (demand draft) rate, and the rate for 30-, 60-, and 90-day bills of exchange. The cable rate is at all times higher than the check rate. See *check rate.*

cadastre: the official inventory of the real property in a community, the cadastre is used for determining taxes and its appraised value.

caeteris paribus: latin for "other things being equal." The usual assumption in economic theory under which only a few phenomena are permitted to vary at one time; to facilitate tracing the effects of the variations.

call: to demand payment of a loan secured by collateral because of failure by a borrower to comply with the terms of the loan.

callable: that which must be paid on request, as a loan.

call-back: the act of reading back posting media to the postings, or checks making up a list to the listing of the items. One person reads the amounts to another person, who is checking the "run" for accuracy. Call-backs are often made when a balance or settlement is not accomplished, the call back being one form of proving the accuracy of a run of items. [10]

call loan: a loan payable on request.

call money: currency lent by banks, usually to stock exchange brokers, for which payment can be demanded at any time.

call report: agencies such as the Comptroller of the Currency and Federal Reserve Banks require periodic status reports from banks under their jurisdiction. The precise date is not given in advance so as to minimize manipulation of the information.

cambism: engaging in the sale of foreign monies.

cambist:
(1) an individual who buys and sells foreign currencies.

(2) a handbook in which foreign country funds are converted into currency tables of the country for which the handbook is issued.

cambistry: the study of exchange of foreign currencies, with emphasis on identifying the least expensive procedure for remitting to a foreign nation.

Cambridge equation: see *cash balance equation (exchange form).*

Can.: see *cancellation.*

Canadian Bank Act: see *Bank Act, Canada.*

Canc.: see *cancellation.*

cancel: to mark or perforate; make void. [61]

canceled checks: checks that have been paid and charged to the depositor's account; then stamped or perforated with the date of the payment and the drawee bank's name or clearinghouse number. These checks are retained in the files of the bank until a statement of the depositor's account is sent to him or her. [31]

canceling machine: a machine used for canceling checks; passbooks; and other records in a bank. [10]

cancellation: the annulment or rendering void of any bank instrument upon payment; the termination of a policy or bond before its expiration, by either the bank or other party. Almost invariably, the contract states the type of notice necessary before cancellation becomes effective.

cancellation clause: a provision giving one or both parties the right to cancel the agreement in the event of a specified occurrence.

"cannibalism": in banking; occurs when customers transfer funds from passbook and other low-

yielding accounts into accounts that carry interest rates at close to money market levels.

canons of taxation: the principles advanced by Adam Smith that taxes (a) should be in proportion to revenue received, (b) should be certain and not arbitrary, (c) should be levied at a time convenient for taxpayers, and (d) should cost as little as possible to collect.

canvass: to call on prospective customers in person or by telephone to sell banking services to determine interest or gather information.

Cap.:
(1) see *capital.*
(2) see *capitalization.*

capacity:
(1) the largest amount of insurance a bank will accept on one risk.
(2) one of the three elements of credit.
(3) competency or legal authority.

capital:
(1) *general:* the amount invested in a venture. See *equity.*
(2) *banking:* describes a long-term debt plus owners' equity.

capital account: an account maintained in the name of the owner or owners of a business and indicating his or their equity in that business—usually at the close of the last accounting period.

capital adequacy rules: federal regulations that require large banks to maintain capital equal to a certain percentage of their assets, which consist principally of loans.

capital and surplus: found in a condensed statement of a bank's condition showing the bank's financial status. The two accounts, capital and surplus, are brought together because the surplus account of a bank corresponds to capital surplus, and pays no dividends.

capital appreciation: an increase or other appreciation in a capital asset's value.

capital asset pricing model (CAPM): a model used to estimate the required rate of return (discount rate) for an asset. It is based on the notion that the required rate of return equals the risk-free interest rate plus a beta-related risk premium.

capital assets: a collective term that includes all fixed assets, consisting of furniture and fixtures, land, buildings, machinery, and so on: as differentiated from property consumed; that is, property that yields income or reduces expenses.

capital budget: a budget that itemizes expenditures to be used for building and for purchasing capital goods, and which identifies the source of the funds required to meet the expenditures.

capital cost: the cost of improvements extending the useful life of property and/or adding to its value.

capital employed: capital used in business, referring to net assets, but often includes loans and overdrafts.

capital expenditures budget: the estimate of cash expenditures for new equipment purchases or for other fixed assets during a future fiscal period.

capital flight: a large transfer of money from one nation to another as a hedge against poor economic or political conditions.

capital formation: the development or expansion of capital goods as a result of savings.

capital gain or loss: the difference (gain or loss) between the market or book value at purchase or other acquisition and the value realized from the sale or disposition of a capital asset. The 1986 Tax Reform Act ended preferential treatment and gains were taxed at a top rate of 28 percent for individuals beginning in 1987. See also *Tax Reform Act of 1986.*

capital intensive: characterized by the need to use additional capital to increase productivity or profits.

capitalism: an economic system based on freedoms of ownership, production, exchange, acquisition, work, movement, and open competition.

capitalization:
(1) the sum of all monies invested in a firm by the owner or owners; total liabilities.
(2) the method of appraising property by deducting the estimated normal expenses from the amount of income the property is expected to yield. The resulting net profit does not necessarily represent the actual property value.

capitalize:
(1) to classify a cost as a long-term investment item instead of a charge to current operations.
(2) to divide income by an interest rate to obtain principal.

capitalized cost: the original cost of an asset plus the net charges incurred to prepare or complete it for its stated use.

capital loan: a loan that cannot be repaid without disposing of capital assets, in contrast to a loan, for example, to purchase merchandise, the sale of which will provide funds to repay the loan. [50]

capital movements: the shifts in indebtedness and in gold stocks serving as balancing items when determining the international payments of a nation.

capital net worth: the total assets of a business less the liabilities.

capital outlay: expenditures for the acquisition of or addition to fixed assets; included are amounts for replacements and major alterations but not for repair. Cf. *operating expense.*

capital paid in: the amount paid in for Federal Reserve Bank stock owned by member banks. [40]

capital readjustments: any fundamental, voluntary changes in the capital structure of a firm, involving the modification of the debt.

capital rent: the price paid for the use of improvements permanently affixed to land.

capital requirement: the total monetary investment needed to create and operate any business.

capital resources: resources of a fixed or permanent character, such as land and buildings, which cannot ordinarily be used to meet expenditures. [49]

capital risk: a risk created when a bank has to pay out funds to a counterpart in the deal without knowing whether the counterpart is able to meet its side of the bargain.

capital sum: the original amount of an estate, fund, mortgage, bond, or other financial dealing, together with accrued sums not yet recognized as income.

CAPM: see *capital asset pricing model.*

card-activated nite drop: a separate machine device used for deposits (primarily commercial) after normal banking hours. This device can be attached to the electronics controlling an ATM at the same location. The plastic card can be coded to allow a special transaction which can activate the device, thus allowing a deposit and providing a receipt for the customer. [105]

card base: the total number of plastic cards outstanding by an issuing institution. This can be expressed as a percentage of the total personal deposit account base. [105]

card carrier: see *card mailer.*

cardholder: any person to whom a credit card is issued for personal, family, household, agricultural, business, or commercial purposes. [105]

cardholder account: record kept by the bank on each account for which a card has been issued. [105]

cardholder accounting: the position of debits, credits, adjustments, and payments to cardholder accounts for the purpose of accounting and reporting to the cardholder. [105]

cardholder agreement: written understanding stating the terms and conditions of card usage and payment by the cardholder. [105]

cardholder bank: the bank that has issued a bank card to an individual. The term is frequently used in conjunction with the intercharge arrangements to identify the card or issuing bank. [105]

cardholder base: the total number of cardholder accounts belonging to a specific bank. [105]

cardholder history file: record containing historical data on each cardholder account; minimum information: current balance, credit limit, high credit, and delinquency experience. [105]

cardholder master file: a record of all cardholder accounts. [105]

cardholder profile: describing the demographics of a bank's cardholder base or a survey panel of that base. [105]

cardholder statement: the billing summary produced and mailed at specific intervals, usually monthly. [105]

card imprint: printing appearing on a sales draft, credit voucher, or cash advance draft. A mechanical device (imprinter) is used to produce the imprint. It includes the embossed characters of the credit card and the merchant or bank name and identification numbers. [105]

card issuer:
(1) the financial institution that authorizes the issuance of a card for which the institution; or its agent, carries the liability for the use of the card. The issuer retains full authority over the use of the card by the person to whom the card is issued.
(2) any bank or organization that issues, or causes to be issued, bank cards to those who apply for them. [105]

card mailer: a carrier used in mailing to the cardholder a card which may contain specific instructions for the cardholder regarding the card use.

card network: the geographic area in which the cards issued by a particular institution have some matter of acceptability. [105]

card pick-up: an order to have outside agencies, merchants, or bank personnel pick up a credit card that is being misused. [105]

card reissue: process of preparing and distributing bank cards to cardholders whose cards have expired or will expire in the near future. [105]

card security number (CSN): a hidden or difficult-to-reproduce number on or in the plastic of a card for fraud deterrence purposes. [105]

Carey Street: British term for *bankruptcy.*

Caribbean Development Bank (CDB): created in 1970; headquartered in Barbados; to finance economic development and integration in the Caribbean.

carrier: the bank's insurance department that writes and fulfills the conditions of the insurance policy.

carry:
(1) to enter or post.
(2) the interest cost of financing the holding of securities.
(3) to provide the difference between a partial down payment and the total price of a product or service.

carry forward: to transfer the balance of an account from one balance sheet to another.

carrying charge:
(1) the continuing cost of owning or holding any property or items.
(2) the amount of charges added to the price of a service to compensate for deferred payment.

carrying value: the value of a fixed asset remaining after its accumulated depreciation reserve has been deducted from its original depreciable cost. [49]

carryover funds: monies authorized in a particular budgetary period which an administrative agency can encumber and then spend in a succeeding budgetary period.

carte a memoire: a credit card developed in France which has an integrated circuit that enables a user to record more than 100 transactions on the card, updating the balance each time without the need to communicate with a central computer. See *"smart" credit cards.*

case note: slang, a $1 bill.

case of need: when an exporter draws a bill on a foreign importer, he or she gives instructions "Refer to XYZ Co. in case of need." XYZ Co. is usually an agent or subsidiary, with power to act, or merely serves as a source of advice. Should something go wrong, the bank collecting the bill proceeds to contact the agent.

Cash.: see *cashier.*

cash: an all-embracing term associated with any business transaction involving the handling of currency and coins.

cash account: a cash basis account, where all purchases are completely paid for.

cash advance: cash loan obtained by a cardholder through presentation of his or her credit card at a bank office, or by mail request. [105]

cash advance balance: that portion of the total balance representing any unpaid portion of cash advance loans previously issued. [105]

cash advance draft: a document executed by a cardholder that shows a cash advance obtained through using a bank card. [105]

cash advance reimbursement fee: a fee paid or received as compensation for granting a cash advance to a cardholder. [105]

cash assets: assets described on a financial statement represented by actual cash on hand, and the total of bank deposits.

cash audit: an examination of cash transactions during a given time period to determine whether all received cash has been documented.

cash balance: all cash on hand.

cash balance equation (exchange form): in monetary theory, the cash balance equation is $P = M/KT$, where P is the average price level of T, M the quantity of money, T the total business transactions, and K the fraction of receipts held in idle cash and hence $1/V$ in the Fisher equation. Synonymous with *Cambridge equation.*

cash basis: the system of accounting under which revenues are accounted for only when received in cash, and expenditures are accounted for only when paid. [49]

cashbook: a book of original entry where the cash receipts journal and the cash payments journal are put together, forming one book.

cash bus: a cabinet on wheels where tellers store cash in the teller's cage or wicket during the day. This cabinet has sufficient room for the cash till and also storage under lock and key for packaged specie money that may be required for making change in large orders. The teller wheels the cash bus into the vault after balancing the cash at the end of the day. [10]

cash credit: the British custom of allowing check overdrafts to a specified amount.

cash credit discount: in installment cash credit, the discount is the charge for the credit service which is deducted from the total amount of the loan before the borrower receives the balance in cash. [55]

cash dispenser: a machine capable of giving out cash representing a withdrawal from a deposit account or an extension of credit. Synonymous with *ATM, cashomat.* See also *unattended banking terminal.*

cash dividend: declared dividends payable in cash, usually by check.

cash earnings: the profits or net income of an organization. These earnings include all depreciation and amortization accruals.

cashed check: check accepted by a bank in exchange for cash. Usually such an item can be identified by a teller's stamp or cash-out symbol. [31]

cashier: a bank's officer or representative responsible for the custody of the bank's assets, and whose signature is required on official documents.

cashier's account: the ledger account of a bank that is primarily used to record cashier's checks.

cashier's check: a bank's own check signed by a cashier, becoming a direct obligation of the bank. Upon issue to a customer, it becomes a loan and a debit in the cashier's account. It differs from a certified check in that it is drawn against the funds of the bank itself, not against the funds found in a specific depositor's account. Cf. *certified check, register(ed) check.* Synonymous with *official check, treasurer's check.*

cash in vault: coin and currency actually held by the banks on their own premises. [40]

cash items: items listed in a firm's statement that are the equivalent of cash, such as bank deposits, government bonds, and marketable securities.

cash letter: a transit check with listing tapes, transmitting items from one bank to another for collection. Frequently, the items contained in the cash letter are grouped into several batches with a listing tape attached to each batch. The totals are recapped on the transmittal form letter. Generally, these are associated with mail deposits received from other banks. [31]

cash letter of credit: a letter addressed by a bank to its correspondent bank to make available to the party named in the letter, funds up to a specified amount within certain time limitations. The sum named in the letter is deposited with the bank before the letter is issued, hence the designation *cash letter of credit.* [10]

cash loan: see *policy loan.*

cash management: payment and collection services to corporate customers to speed collection to receivables, control payments, and efficiently manage cash. [105]

cash management account (CMA): a bank-type development of Merrill Lynch in partnership with Bank One of Ohio, based in Columbus, where affluent clients are offered a Visa credit card and checking to draw against their investment balances. The account was initially offered in 206 of Merrill Lynch's 382 offices in the United States.

Cash Management Bill: U.S. Treasury bills introduced in 1975 to raise funds quickly for a short period; ranging from 9 to 20 days to maturity, with notice of their offering given up to 10 days ahead. All payment must be made in federal funds.

cash on hand: cash drawer money, vault cash, and demand deposits in commercial banks or regional Federal Home Loan Banks. [59]

cash over: a general ledger account to which tellers' cash overages are credited. See *cash over and short.* [10]

cash over and short: the difference between the cash on hand and the balance of the cash account or cashbook. When the cash on hand is over the balance of the cash account or cashbook, the cash is over; when less than that of the balance, the cash is short.

cash paid receipt: receipt given to a customer when making a bank card payment in cash. It contains the community office number, date of payment, and teller's initials. [105]

cash payment: a payment made by cash at a community office. [105]

cash payments journal: a special journal in which all cash payments, and only cash payments, are entered.

cash position: the percentage of cash to the total net assets; the net amount after the deduction of current liabilities.

cash ratio:
(1) the ratio of cash and related assets to liabilities.
(2) the ratio of cash to total deposit liabilities.
(3) in Great Britain, deposits required by the Bank of England.

cash receipts journal: a special journal in which all cash receipts, and only cash receipts, are entered.

cash register: a machine used to provide an immediate record of every cash transaction by having a convenient place for sorting and keeping the funds used in daily transactions.

cash register totals: daily totals for all transactions; including cash sales, charge sales, receipts on account, and so on.

cash release ticket: a slip either handwritten or machine printed by which a teller charges himself for the amount of cash on a deposit. [10]

cash report: a statement, prepared on a daily basis, showing the cash position of the organization for each day.

cash reserve:
(1) requirements for banks to maintain a sufficient portion of deposits as required by federal law.
(2) funds readily available to be converted into cash in an emergency. See entries under *liquid.*

cash short: a general ledger account to which tellers' cash shortages are charged. [10]

cash statement: a classified summary of cash receipts and disbursements.

cash substitution ticket: see *cash release ticket.*

cash surrender value: the sum total of money paid by a bank upon cancellation of its life insurance policy.

cash ticket: a slip or ticket used as a substitute for cash included in a deposit. The teller verifies and retains the cash, recording the amount on the cash ticket. [31]

cash till: a tray built with compartment bins to help tellers sort and have ready for easy access the various denominations of currency. [10]

cash with fiscal agent: deposits with fiscal agents, such as commercial banks, for the payment of matured bonds and interest. [49]

casting: slang, any coin.

cast up: to add up a total, as "to cast up an account."

casual forecasting: predictions on the future activity of bank products or services which can be made if enough data have been collected to determine the "cause" of success or failure. [105]

CATS: see *Certificate of Accrual on Treasury Stocks.*

CBCT: see *Customer-Bank Communication Terminal.*

CBCT ruling: an interpretive ruling by the Comptroller of the Currency (May 19, 1975) stating that CBCTs do not constitute branches and permitting national banks, without regard to state branching law, to establish these facilities on a proprietary basis within 50 miles of a branch and outside that 50-mile radius only with an offer to share with other institutions. [105]

CC:
(1) see *cancellation clause.*
(2) see *cashier's check.*

CCA: see *Credit Control Act of 1969.*

CCCS: see *Consumer Credit Counseling Services.*

CD: see *certificate of deposit.*

CDR: see *Continental Depositary Receipt.*

CE: see *cash earnings.*

cent: the coin of lowest worth in the United States, equal to one-hundredth of a dollar ($0.01).

center: an affiliate's location(s) for the operation of its bank card program or a center location providing identical processing services (e.g., authorization, interchange) for more than one affiliate. [105]

Center for Financial Studies, Inc.: organized in 1977, this Connecticut nonprofit corporation directs the operation of the Center for Financial Studies on the campus of Fairfield University. The center is a joint undertaking by the university and the savings bank industry. Funds to construct the center were raised through a subscrip-

tion by National Association of Mutual Savings Banks member savings banks. Upon completion of the center in late 1979, most of NAMSB's education programs were transferred there. [8]

Central American Bank for Economic Integration: see *Banco Centroamericano de Integracion Economica.*

Central American Clearing House: created in 1961 to establish a multilateral mechanism for clearing international payments between the Central American central banks.

central bank:
(1) a banker's bank. See *banker's bank.*
(2) a bank holding the main body of bank reserves of a nation and the prime reservoir of credit (e.g., Bank of England, Bank of France).

central information file (CIF): in most banks, a ledger record of the bank services used by its customers, indicating in which office or offices the business is handled. [10]

central liability: the grouping together on one record of all liabilities of a borrower, such as loans both direct and indirect, consumer credit, letters of credit, guarantees, and other accommodations. The purpose of this record is to prevent overextensions of credit to the borrower, show what is currently due from him, and provide a history of his borrowing. [10]

central proof: a system for effecting economy of operation by centralizing all proof and distributing functions in a single department of a bank. See *proof department.* [31]

central rate: a rate established under a temporary regime (based on an International Monetary Fund executive board decision of December 18, 1974) by a country which temporarily does not maintain rates based on a par value in accordance with the relevant fund rules but does maintain transactions in its territories. Central rates are in certain respects treated as par values, and the concept was introduced primarily to allow fund members who, prior to August 15, 1971, had an effective par value to base their exchange rates on a stable rate subject to specified margin requirements during the period when the par value of the U.S. dollar was not effective. The temporary regime provides for the possibility of margins of $2^1/4$ percent either side of the central rate. After the change in the par value of the U.S. dollar on May 8, 1974, a number of countries have replaced their central rates with new par values. [42]

Central Reserve Cities: established by the National Bank Act, New York City and Chicago are central reserve cities. See *reserve city bank.*

central reserve city bank: a member bank in New York City or Chicago that held legal reserves of state banks. Presently, this specialized treatment has largely disappeared.

century: slang, a $100 bill.

Cert.: see *certificate.*

certificate:

(1) a form of paper money, issued against silver or gold deposited in the U.S. Treasury.

(2) any written or printed document of truth that can be used as proof of a fact.

certificate account: a savings account containing a fixed amount of funds deposited for a fixed term. The customer is charged a penalty for premature withdrawal, but is paid interest at a rate higher than that on passbook accounts if the deposit remains untouched for the full term. See also *savings certificate.* [59]

certificate check: see *certified check.*

Certificate of Accrual on Treasury Stocks (CATS): created in 1982, effectively, a zero-coupon Treasury bond. An investment bank creating the CATS purchases treasury securities and deposits them with a bank or trustee. It then issues receipts against each coupon and principal repayment the treasury is scheduled to make. The receipts are then sold for the present value of the payments they evidence, creating a series of zero-coupon treasury bonds, maturing on each coupon and principal repayment date.

certificate of claim: a contingent promise of the Federal Housing Administration to reimburse an insured mortgagee for certain costs incurred during foreclosure of an insured mortgage provided the proceeds from the sale of the property acquired are sufficient to cover those costs. [44]

certificate of deposit (CD): a negotiable, nonnegotiable, or transferable receipt payable to the depositor for funds deposited with a bank, usually interest bearing. See also *certificate of deposit (demand), certificate of deposit (time), variable interest plus.*

certificate of deposit (demand): a negotiable or transferable receipt issued for funds deposited with a bank and payable on demand to the holder. These receipts do not bear interest and are used principally by contractors and others as a guarantee of performance of a contract or as evidence of good faith when submitting a bid. They may also be used as collateral.

certificate of deposit (time): a negotiable or transferable receipt for funds deposited with a bank, payable to the holder at some specified date (not less than 30 days after issuance) and bearing interest.

certificate of indebtedness:
(1) a short-term note issued by a governmental agency, describing the current debt.
(2) an unsecured promissory note, the holder having a general creditor's recourse against general assets.

certificate of lender and loan applicant: bank's certification to FmHA that it would not make a loan to an applicant without the FmHA loan guarantee. [105]

certificate of manufacturer: in foreign trade, a statement signed by an exporter that goods ordered by the importer have been finished and set aside for shipment. This document is used with a letter of credit for the benefit of the exporter.

certificate of no defense: when a mortgage is sold, the certificate signed by the borrower that identifies the mortgage indebtedness.

certificate of occupancy: a permit issued by a building department verifying that the work meets the local zoning ordinances and the structure ready for occupancy.

certificate of origin: a certificate declaring that goods purchased from a foreign country have indeed been produced in that country and not another.

certificate of ownership: see *proprietorship certificate.*

certificate of release: a certificate signed by the lender indicating that a mortgage has been fully paid and all debts satisfied.

certificate of title: a title company certification that the seller possesses sound, marketable, and/or insurance title to the property. If a title company issues this certificate and a defect is identified at a later time, the title company will indemnify the holder. See *title insurance.*

certificates: U.S. paper money circulated in the form of a receipt for silver or gold coins. The U.S. silver certificates are the best known. The redemption privilege was revoked by Congress on June 14, 1968. [27]

certificates of debt: certificates indicating that a loan or some other form of debts remains to be paid.

certification: an assurance by a bank that the drawer of a check has sufficient funds on deposit to cover payment on the check and that monies have been set aside to meet the incoming obligation. *Certification* is usually stamped across the face of the check. See also *cross check.*

certification department: that part of a bank where certification tellers process checks and record which checks are certified.

certification teller: a teller whose duty is to certify or accept checks or depositors. In large banks this may be his or her only duty, but in smaller banks it is usually combined with others. [10]

certified check: the check of a depositor drawn on a bank; the face of the check bears the word "accepted" or "certified," with the date and signature of a bank official or authorized clerk. The check then becomes an obligation of the bank, and regulations require that the amount of the check be immediately charged against the depositor's account. Cf. *cashier's check.*

certified public accountant (CPA): an accountant who has been certified by the state as having met that state's requirements of age, education, experience, and technical qualifications. Not all who practice accounting are certified.

cestui: a beneficiary of a trust.

cestui que trust: French adaption of a Latin phrase designating the person for whose benefit a trust has been established.

ceteris paribus: the assumption that the values of all variables and parameters other than those being analyzed are constant.

CH: see *clearinghouse.*

chain banking: a form of multiple-office banking under which a minimum of three independently incorporated banks are controlled by one or more individuals. Cf. *branch banking.*

chain of title: the succession of conveyances from some accepted starting point from which the present holder of real property derives his title. [62]

Chairman of the Office of Savings Associations: the new head regulator of the savings and loan industry, replacing the Federal Home Loan Bank Board.

chancellor of the exchequer: the person in the United Kingdom in charge of the receipts and payments of the government. A function similar to the Secretary of the Treasury in the United States.

Chandler Act: passed by Congress in 1938, this act revised the federal law on financial reorganization of corporations, including bankruptcy.

change: money returned following a purchase, when a larger sum of money was given than was required (e.g., on a sale purchase of $0.98, a $1.00 handout returns $0.02 in change).

CHAPS: see *Clearing House Automated Payments Systems.*

Chapter 11: see *Bankruptcy Reform Act of 1978.*

charge:
(1) a cost or expense allotted to a specific account.
(2) to purchase for credit without making an immediate payment; usually to be paid following billing.

charge account banking: permits consumers to arrange a line of credit with a bank or lending institution; usable to make purchases in many participating establishments. The plan may provide simply a 30-day charge account or installment payment service. [28]

charge back: a transaction that the cardholder bank returns either to its own merchant or to the merchant bank because the transaction fails to meet certain established criteria. [105]

charge-back rules: the rules governing the right of a card-issuing bank to charge back to the signing merchant bank sales made that do not conform to agreed-on standards. [105]

charge notice: see *debit memo.*

charge off: to treat as a loss; to designate as an expense an amount originally recorded as an asset. Cf. *write-off.*

charge-out: designates the release of debits or credits to other departments for further handling. Before such items are released, their package totals are recorded on a charge-out sheet. Later, the totals are included in the final proof. [31]

charge ticket: that written memorandum which a bookkeeper uses as a guide in posting a debit item to an account. Synonymous with *debit ticket.* [31]

charge wire: see *reverse money transfer.*

chartered accountant (CA):   in the United Kingdom, Canada, and Australia, a certified accountant.

chartered banks: banks that operate under a government and state charter as opposed to private banks. [27]

Chartered Life Underwriter (CLU): the professional designation awarded by the American College of Life Underwriters to those who have completed the prescribed series of examinations and have satisfied the organization's experience requirement.

chattel: derived from "cattle." All property that is not real property. A structure on real property is a chattel real; movable properties (e.g., automobiles) are chattels personal. See *replevin;* cf. *chose(s) in action, goods and services;* synonymous with *personal property.*

chattel, personal: any item of movable property besides real estate. [62]

chattel, real: an interest in land, such as a leasehold, which is less than a freehold estate. See *tenancy at sufferance, tenancy at will, tenancy for years.* [32]

chattel mortgage: an instrument prepared by a debtor (the mortgagor) transferring a chattel's interest to a creditor (mortgagee) for the purposes of providing security for a debt. If the debt is not paid, the mortgagee can sell the chattel and use the monies received to satisfy the debt outstanding.

chattel mortgage agreement: a legal agreement with a purchase of merchandise on an installment basis. Provides that the buyer accepts title to goods on delivery but gives the seller a mortgage on such merchandise that may be foreclosed under certain conditions and by prescribed legal procedure. [41]

chattel mortgage method: a method of obtaining a security interest in a dealer's inventory using a separate mortgage for each transaction. [105]

chattel personal: an article of personal property; to be distinguished from an interest in real property. [105]

chattel real: a nonfreehold interest in real property. The principal types are leases regardless of their length and estates at will.

cheap money: money that is available at relatively low rates of interest.

check:

(1) a process for determining accuracy.

(2) the Federal Reserve Board defines a check as follows: "a draft or order upon a bank or banking house purporting to be drawn upon a deposit of funds, for the payment of a certain sum on money to a certain person therein named, or to his order, or to bearer, and payable instantly on demand."

checkable: that which can be withdrawn against a checking account, such as checkable bank deposits.

check authorization/verification: an inquiry process undertaken to reduce the risk of accepting a fraudulent check or a check written for an amount that exceeds the account balance. Check authorization systems may be provided and maintained by the party accepting the check, by a financial institution, or by a third party engaged in such a business. These systems may be designed to access bank records directly or may rely on secondary data sources. In some systems, check approval is accompanied by a guarantee of payment.

checkbook: a book containing blank checks furnished by banks to depositors to permit them to withdraw funds from their checking accounts. A customer may keep a complete record of his or her deposits, withdrawals, and balance, by means of stubs or a register book. [31]

checkbook money: synonymous with *deposit currency.*

check bouncer: slang, an individual who writes checks against nonexistent bank accounts or against accounts with insufficient funds to cover the check.

check bouncing protection: a service provided to customers where a line of credit is associated with their checking accounts. Checks written on insufficient checking account deposits are paid, for a fee, by drawing automatically on this credit line. [105]

check clearing: the movement of checks from the banks where they are deposited back to those on which they are written, and funds movement in the opposite direction. This process results in credits to the accounts of the banks of deposit and corresponding debits to the accounts of the paying bank. The Federal Reserve operates a nationwide check-clearing system, though many checks are cleared by private sector arrangements. [1]

check credit: a bank service whereby a customer is granted a certain amount of credit, draws checks against this credit at times, and repays the bank periodically.

check credit plan: a type of installment loan plan normally used in conjunction with a customer's regular checking account in a commercial bank, including a revolving line of credit combined with personal checking privileges; the line of credit may be drawn upon as needed by the individual and repaid in monthly installments. [105]

check currency: demand deposits generated by a bank loan that is subject to withdrawal by check as opposed to coin or paper money.

check desk: that section of a bookkeeping department through which all incoming and outgoing debit and credit items pass. It assembles and controls all final proof figures for the bookkeeping department. The term is also applied to a proof department for incoming and outgoing items. [10]

check files: the files in which all paid and canceled checks are stored until they are ready to be returned to the depositors with their statements. Check files may simply be drawers in a bookkeeper's desk, or in large banks a section of the bookkeeping department charged with the responsibility of filing checks and providing them with the statements before mailing. [10]

check filing: the process of placing canceled checks in storage to facilitate the periodic mailing of customers' statements. [31]

check guarantee: a term that identifies a service provided through a plastic card that guarantees payment up to the defined limit, when the merchant follows proper steps in accepting the check. [105]

check guarantee services: a bank service that guarantees payment of a check to merchants and banks. [105]

checking account: a demand account subject to withdrawal by check of funds on deposit.

check-kiting scheme: where several bank accounts are played off against one another to avoid bouncing any checks and to gain, in effect, interest-free loans.

checkless banking: describes a banking system in which checks are not required for monetary exchange; funds are transferred electronically. [105]

checkless society: describes the predicted absence or need for checks as a medium for transferring funds. The realization of this futuristic concept will come about with the universal usage of bank credit cards, widespread adoption of common machine languages, the ability of financial and commercial concerns of all types and sizes to communicate on-line and in real-time processing, and a complete program for automatic transfer of funds within a bank or between cooperating banks. The depositor's universal bank credit card will authorize debits to his or her account for purchases and services which he or she is presently paying for with a check. Settlements between all banks, to accommodate payments of their customers, are also made automatically. [10]

checklist: an adding machine list of a depositor's checks that are to be charged to his checking account. The number of checks used to make a list varies with the individual bank. The number of checks attached to a list is usually indicated on the list to be used for account analysis. The object of a list is to cut down on the number of items posted to a depositor's account, since only the total of the list appears on the depositor's statement. [10]

check number: the sequential numbers located in the top righthand corner of customer checks. Check numbers are used for the customer's recordkeeping purposes. [105]

check on us: checks drawn on a bank and presented to it for deposit or payment. [50]

checkout: when a block does not prove and the difference is not located by verifying the addition of the deposit tickets and comparing the check amounts with the listings, it is necessary to resort to a checkout. This consists of matching each item shown on the deposit tickets with a similar amount appearing on the block listing tapes, which will establish that the depositor has done one of the following: included a check without listing it, listed a check but failed to include it, or listed a check incorrectly. [31]

check processing: the internal receiving, recording, and perhaps the redistribution of checks written by customers of the institution or deposited by such customers and drawn on another institution. This includes the traditional posting, or recording, of the check in the individual customer's account, the microfilming, and the balancing of all such items received. [105]

check-protecting equipment: machines that prevent a change in the check amount or in the name of the payee.

check rate: the basic rate for foreign exchange trades, used to calculate all other rates. Synonymous with *demand rate.*

check register: the form of the cash payments journal used with a voucher system.

check requisition: a written request made to the accounting department of a firm for the preparation of a check. [59]

check-routing symbol: a device to facilitate the handling and routing of transit items through banks that remit at par all over the United States. The check-routing symbol is the denominator of a fraction, the numerator being the ABA transit number. The entire fraction is located in the upper right-hand corner of a check. The check-routing symbol is composed of three or four digits. The first digit in a denominator of three figures or the first two digits in a denominator of four figures identify the Federal Reserve District (1–12) in which the drawee bank is located. The next to the last digit designates the Federal Reserve Bank head office or branch through which the item should be cleared and also any special clearing arrangement. (The head office is indicated by the number 1. Branches, if any, arranged alphabetically, are indicated by numbers 2 to 5. Numbers 6 to 9 are used to designate special collection arrangements.) The last digit shows whether the item is acceptable for immediate or deferred credit. [10]

check safekeeping: see *free check storage account.*

check serial number: the magnetic characters imprinted in the auxiliary On-Us field. These figures correspond to the number on each check used by the maker as identification. See *account reconcilement.* [31]

check services: a service that provides the customer with a method of paying specialized bills with a bank card. [105]

check stub: that portion of a check form kept permanently in a checkbook as a record of the check that is attached to it.

check trading: selling bank checks to a customer, who is expected to repay the amount of the check plus interest in installments.

check truncation: the conversion of information on a check into electronic impulses after a check enters the processing system. It is called truncation because the physical processing of the check is cut short. See *truncation.* [105]

check verification: used to identify the capability of verifying demand deposit account balances via a terminal. This may be used as a prelude to a point-of-sale system. [105]

check verification guarantee: systems providing retail merchants with varying degree of insurance against bad check losses by (a) verifying the authenticity of the check and/or its presenter, or (b) guaranteeing payments of the check by the bank. [33]

checkwriter: the device used to imprint the amount of a check on its face, in order to make alteration difficult. [105]

cheque: *check* in French or British English.

chicken feed: slang, small amount of money; small change.

chief clerk: usually a junior officer or a senior clerk whose duties consist of handling various transactions of an important nature, such as notary work, protests, wire transfers, and technical negotiable instruments. In branch banking, the chief clerk is a junior officer who is charged with the supervision of personnel and the general operations of the branch. [10]

Chinese Wall: a policy barrier between the trust department and the rest of the bank designed to stop the flow of information to prevent use by the trust department of any material inside information, which may come into the possession of other bank departments, in making investment decisions. [105]

CHIPS: see *Clearing House Interbank Payment Systems.*

chisel: slang, borrowing money with the expectation of not paying.

chose: anything that is personal property. [37]

chose(s) in action: a right to, but not possession of, funds or property; the actual taking possession may result from some other event. The right may be enforced by a court ruling and may cover debts, mortgages, negotiable instruments, insurance policies, and warrants. See *chose.*

chose(s) in possession: tangible personal property in actual possession (e.g., an automobile), as contrasted with a *chose in action.* See *chose;* cf. *corporeal property.*

Chq.: see *cheque.*

Christmas Club account: a savings account whereby a customer deposits a specified sum each week in order to accumulate a lump sum for Christmas expenditures. [31]

CI: see *compounded interest.*

Cincotta-Conklin Bill of 1976: a New York state law permitting state savings banks and savings and loan associations to offer checking accounts like commercial banks, but at no cost.

cipher-proof: a method of balancing whereby certain figures are automatically subtracted from a control total. If the balance results in zero, it is proved that all figures were added and listed correctly. Sometimes referred to as zero balance. [32]

circuity of action: when a bill of exchange is returned to the person who has already signed it, he or she may renegotiate it, but this person has no claim against individuals signing the bill between the time he or she initially signed it and its return to him or her.

circular letter of credit: a document, frequently issued by a bank, that is not addressed to any particular agency or bank. The issuing bank accepts drafts on it when they are within the terms of the letter.

circulating medium: money; any form of exchange that is accepted without endorsement.

circulation:
(1) the total value of the issued bank notes of a bank that are in use, as distinguished from those being held in the bank's reserve.
(2) the total of all currency in use at a given period. See *velocity of circulation.*

circulation statement: published monthly by the U.S. Treasury Department showing amounts of currency outstanding and in circulation, currency by denominations and coin, and the comparative sums of money in use.

circumfiduciation: the shifting of certificates of deposit money to other investments.

city bond: see *bond, municipal.*

city collection department: a department in a bank which handles the collection of items payable within a city, and receives and collects these items by messenger. As a general rule, those items which cannot be collected through the local clearinghouse owing to their being drawn on nonmembers, or drafts with documents attached which require special handling, pass through this department. [10]

city items: negotiable items, notes, and checks that are drawn upon individuals or institutions located in the same local or city in which they were deposited.

Ck.: see *check.*

CL:
(1) see *call loan.*
(2) see *cash letter.*

claim: a demand by an individual or a corporation to recover, under a policy of insurance, for loss that is covered by that policy.

claim against estate: a demand made upon the estate to do or to forebear

some act as a matter of duty. A common example would be the claim submitted by a creditor for a debt owed him or her by the decedent at the time of his or her death. [37]

claims reported by U.S. banks (long-term): long-term claims reported by U.S. banks represent commercial bank loans to foreigners. These loans may go to private business, individuals, or foreign governments. A large part of these comprise loans for foreign corporations, including loans to finance ship mortgages, U.S. exports, plant expansion, and to refinance debts outstanding. A loan is considered long-term if its repayment schedule is for more than one year. The flow in the opposite direction appears in long-term liabilities reported by U.S. banks. [73]

claims reported by U.S. banks (short-term): short-term claims include loans extended to foreigners with a maturity of less than one year. Loans to foreign banks for the purpose of financing general trade transactions on foreign accounts and short-term bank claims in foreign currencies that represent correspondent balances held in the bank's own account abroad are included. Nonbank claims such as outstanding collections held in the bank's custody or short-term investments in foreign money market assets are also included. [73]

claims reported by U.S. residents other than banks (long-term): those claims reported by private business firms resulting from their export transactions. These claims assume various forms. A common example is "supplier's credit." This is the long-term financing extended to a foreigner by a U.S. corporation in order that it may sell its product abroad. Long-term loans made to foreigners by insurance companies are also included. [73]

claims reported by U.S. residents other than banks (short-term): includes those claims reported by U.S. brokerage houses. These claims may be in the form of a cash account held by the broker. Also included are other short-term financial assets held abroad such as the unused proceeds of loan flotations by U.S. corporations in foreign capital markets. [73]

class:
(1) to place in ranks or divisions.
(2) a category of employees in the schedule of group insurance, denoting the amounts of coverage for which the members of the class are eligible.

classified loan: a loan made by a bank to a customer and subsequently criticized by examiners as being substandard.

classified property tax: the descriptions of properties by owners for the purpose of setting assessment with respect to market value and tax rates.

classified taxation: a tax structure in which real property is categorized by function, with differing tax rates applied to each class. In such situations, some classes are excluded from paying any tax.

clean credit: any letter of credit from a bank against which the foreign seller can draw a bill without documentary support. This credit is available only to firms having the best credit reputation.

clean float: see *floating currency.*

clean letter of credit: a letter of credit that does not demand such documents as bills of lading as a condition of acceptance by a bank. Such letters are issued only to prime risks.

clean payment: payment not encumbered by documents. [105]

clear:
(1) to make a profit or gain.
(2) having passed through or having been collected by a clearinghouse. See also *clearing and settlement.*
(3) free from encumbrance.

clearance:
(1) an act of clearing.
(2) the adjustment of debits and credits in a clearinghouse.

clearing agreement:
(1) an agreement between two or more nations to buy and sell goods and service among themselves according to a specified rate of exchange.
(2) any local, national, or international plan for the periodic mutual exchange by banks of charges against them by others in the plan and the settlement of adverse balances.

clearing and settlement: the process whereby checks or other records of financial or point-of-sale transactions are moved (physically or electronically) from the point at which they were originated to the organization (bank, thrift institution, or other agency) that keeps the accounts for, and expects to collect from and account to, the responsible payor. The settlement process completes the internal financial transactions among the (possibly) many parties involved in the clearing operation.

clearing bank: bank that has been designated by an interchange agreement to be the settlement bank for bank card transactions. [105]

clearing checks: the return of checks to the bank on which they were drawn for payment.

clearing credit: the total amount of checks presented by a clearinghouse bank drawn on the other participating banks. [105]

clearing debit: the total amount of checks presented to a clearinghouse bank by the other participating banks. [105]

clearinghouse: an association of banks in a city, created to facilitate the clearing of checks, drafts, notes, or other items among the members. It also formulates policies and rules for the mutual welfare of all members.

clearinghouse agent: a bank that is a clearinghouse member and which accepts checks of another bank, not a member, for settlement through the clearinghouse. Synonymous with *redemption agent.*

clearinghouse association: a voluntary association of banks within the same city that has been established to facilitate the daily exchange of checks, drafts, and notes among its members and to settle balances caused by these exchanges.

Clearing House Automated Payments Systems (CHAPS): the central United Kingdom money transfer mechanism for larger payments. CHAPS consists of a network of linked computers operated by the U.K. clearing banks. [133]

clearinghouse balance: the sum of the debit and credit totals or balances at the end of the banking day.

clearinghouse certificate: prior to the formation of the Federal Reserve System, debit balances resulting from clearinghouse exchanges were settled in gold. In times of financial stress, member banks pooled their securities with the clearinghouse, to be used for the settlement of balances in lieu of gold. Clearinghouse certificates were issued against this pool of securities by the manager of the clearinghouse association to settle the exchange balances of debtor banks whose own resources were inadequate. The New York Clearing House Association resorted to the use of clearinghouse certificates 10 times in its history, the first being at the outbreak of the Civil War in 1861. [10]

clearinghouse exchanges: synonymous with *exchanges.*

clearinghouse funds:

(1) monies within the banking system that are transferable from bank to bank through the Federal Reserve System. Federal funds are available on a daily basis, whereas clearinghouse funds require three days to clear.

(2) funds used to settle transactions on which there is a one-day float. [105]

Clearing House Interbank Payment Systems (CHIPS): an automated clearing facility operated by the New York Clearing House Association which processes international funds transfers among its members. CHIPS is a system that moves dollars between 100 New York financial institutions—mostly major U.S. banks, branches of foreign banks, and Edge Act subsidiaries of out-of-state banks. See *Edge Act.*

clearinghouse statement: released by large clearinghouse association, a weekly report showing the surplus, capital, undivided profits, average net demand deposits, and average time deposits of its member banks.

clearing member: a member of a clearinghouse who is also an exchange member. Since not all exchange members are members of a clearinghouse, they clear their transactions with a clearing member.

clearing member bank: a bank, though not a member of the Federal Reserve System, permitted to collect its out-of-town checks via the Federal Reserve check-collecting system. By maintaining a balance with the Federal Reserve Bank in their district a bank may be allowed to become a clearing member.

clearings: the incoming cash letters of items which must be proved, sorted, returned if necessary, and for which settlement must be made. [31]

clear title: synonymous with *good title, just title,* and *marketable title.*

Clifford trust: a ten-year trust to reduce income taxes by diverting the income from property placed in trust from the grantor to a beneficiary, usually a member of the grantor's family in a lower income tax bracket. At the end of the trust period of ten years or more, the trust property reverts to the grantor. Synonymous with *ten-year trust.*

CLOC: see *clear letter of credit.*

clock stamp: a mechanical or electric time recording device for imprinting upon an inserted document the time of arrival, and frequently the date upon which the item was received or transmitted. Such devices are frequently used in safe deposit and security deposit vaults. [10]

close:
(1) to transfer the balances of revenue and expense accounts at the end of an accounting period (e.g., close the books).
(2) to sign legal papers indicating that the property has formally changed ownership.
(3) to conclude a sale or agreement.

closed account: an account with equal debits and credits.

closed mortgage: a mortgage that cannot be paid off until maturity occurs.

closing account: an account in which various ledger accounts are merged for summary and ultimate transfer to a final statement.

closing agreement: any final or definitive agreement. Used particularly to refer to final settlement of income tax liability and to real estate deals.

closing a mortgage loan: the consummation of a loan transaction in which all appropriate papers are signed and delivered to the lender, the making of the mortgage becomes a completed transaction, and the proceeds of the mortgage loan are disbursed by the lender to the borrower or upon the borrower's order. [44]

closing charges: the expenses or costs incurred in the sale, transfer, or pledging of property, such as recording fees and title examination fees, which must be provided for and distributed between the parties upon the consummation of the transaction. [44]

closing costs: the expenses incurred by sellers and buyers in the transfer of real estate ownership (e.g., attorney's fee, title insurance, survey charge, recording deed and mortgage). See *Real Estate Settlement Procedures Act.*

closing entries: journal entries made at the end of an accounting period to close (bring to zero balance) all revenue, expense, and other temporary accounts.

closing statement: an accounting of funds in a real estate sale.

closing the ledger: recording the closing entries in the general journal, posting them to the ledger, and ruling and balancing the ledger accounts.

closing (or passing) title: the formal exchange of money and documents when real estate is transferred from one owner to another. See *objection to title, paper title, presumptive title, quiet title suit, title defect.*

cloud on title: any claim or existing shortcoming that interferes with the title to real property. See *abeyance, curing title;* cf. *marketable title, perfect title.*

"club":
(1) a grouping of nations involved in a financial arrangement, often an LDC debt rescheduling. Cf. *Paris Club.*
(2) a Euromarket term for a loan syndication technique, where various responsibilities are carried out by the lead bank and comanagers. Fees are reduced using this approach. [91]

club account: the popularity of the Christmas Club account has led banks to open other types of club accounts on the same basis. It is a convenient method of saving small amounts regularly for a definite purpose. Popular names for the newer club accounts are "budget savings," "vacation club," "travel club," and "all purpose club." Many depositors are using these club accounts to accumulate savings for annual premiums on life insurance, taxes, and vacations. [10]

CM:
(1) see *call money.*
(2) see *cheap money.*

CMA: see *cash management account.*

Cmm.: see *commission.*

Cncld.: see *cancel.*

Cnl.:
(1) see *cancel.*
(2) see *cancellation.*

C note: slang, a $100 bill.

coassignee: a person or company to whom some property right has been assigned jointly with another person or company.

COC: see *Comptroller of the Currency.*

code of accounts: a chart of accounts classified by digits referring to account types. [105]

cofinancing: financing a nation in parallel by institutions such as the International Monetary Fund, the World Bank, and commercial banks. May include situations where commercial lendings are made with cross-default clauses relating to IMF or World Bank loans. Default on the latter is taken as default on the commercial loans. [92]

cognovit note: a form of note (legal evidence of indebtedness) which is both a promissory note and chattel mortgage. The borrower, within the wording of the instrument, waives his or her right of action to the chattel property in case of his or her default in any payments agreed to in the transaction. [10]

COI: see *certificate of indebtedness.*

coin: a piece of stamped metal authorized by a government for use as currency; specie.

coin-counting machine: a machine used in banks to count accurately and swiftly large volumes of specie, or coins. The machine has a hopper into which are fed all denominations of coins. The machine is regulated to sort out coins from the smallest size (dime) to the largest (half dollar). The coins are automatically counted as they are sorted, one denomination at a time, and are then packaged in coin wrappers. [10]

coining rate: the mint ratio.

coin pack: a technique of roll-wrapping a cylindrical stack of disks such as coins.

Coll.: see *collection.*

collateral heir: a person not in the direct line of the decedent from whom he inherits real property, as, for example, a nephew of the decedent who receives a share of his uncle's estate. See *heirs.* [37]

collateralized loan: a loan granted a customer upon the pledge of liquid assets or illiquid assets. Should the borrower be unable to repay, the lender sells the collateral.

collateral loan: a loan obtained by the pledge of title to personal property. See *hypothecated account.*

collateral mortgage: a document used in connection with a loan which effects a lien on real estate, where the purpose of the loan is not for the purchase of the property offered as security. [105]

collateral mortgage bonds: collateral trust bonds that have been secured by a deposit of mortgage bonds.

collateral note: a promissory note secured by the pledge of specific property. [50]

collateral pledge: the agreement under which a third party pledges a savings account or other property as additional security for the lender's mortgage-secured advance of funds by check and extending credit. [59]

collateral security: property security, as distinguished from personal security.

collateral value: the estimate of value of the thing put up as security for a loan made by a lender. With securities and commodities, the lender is usually restricted in his or her valuation by rules of an appropriate agency, such as the exchange or Federal Reserve Board.

collected funds: cash or checks deposited in the bank which have been presented for payment and for which payment has actually been received. [105]

collectible: that which can be converted into cash. Synonymous with *liquid.*

collecting bank: a bank that collects payment on the bill sent by a remitting bank. [85]

collection:
(1) presentation for payment of an obligation and the payment thereof.
(2) the getting of money for presentation of a draft or check for payment at the bank on which it was drawn, or presentation of any item for deposit at the place at which it is payable. See *float, value date.*

collection activity: process of contacting delinquent cardholders either by mail or by phone in an effort to obtain payment. [105]

collection agent: a person or bank that handles checks, drafts, coupons, and related items for another person or bank with the purpose of trying to collect such instruments.

collection analyst: a person in the collection division of the credit office, responsible for determining status and subsequent collection procedure of customers' past-due accounts. [41]

collection charge: a bank's charge made for the collection of checks, coupons, drafts, notes, and acceptances that have been drawn on the bank, corporations, or persons out of the location of the sending bank. See also *exchange charge.*

collection clerk: a bank representative involved in the collection of checks, drafts, and other items drawn on out-of-town points.

collection correspondent: a person in the collection division of a credit office, responsible for handling collection matters by mail. [41]

collection cycle: the activity taking place between the extension of credit and the receipt of payment.

collection department: the department that handles checks, drafts, coupons, and other items received form a depositor with instructions to credit his or her account after final payment has been received. In large cities, the collection department is usually divided into four sections (i.e., city collection, country collection, coupon collection, and foreign collection). [10]

collection expense: all expenses incurred in the collection of notes, drafts, or accounts.

collection item: items (drafts, notes, acceptances, etc.) received for collection and credited to a depositor's account after final payment. Collection items are usually subject to special instructions regarding delivery of documents when attached, protest, and so on, and in most banks are subject to a special fee for handling called a collection charge. Synonymous with *collection.* [31]

collection ledger: a ledger that is part of the bookkeeping records of a bank transit unit showing the holding charges to other banks for checks and items while in transit or in the process of being collected. Synonymous with *float ledger.*

collection letter: a letter of transmittal containing special handling instructions which accompanies items to be handled for collection and credit after payment. [31]

collection manager: supervisor of the collection division of the credit office. Usually (although not always) responsible to the credit manager. Handles all collection matters. [41]

collection percentage: the amount collected during a given period, usually one month, expressed as a percentage against the total amount owed by all customers at the beginning of a period. [41]

collection period:
(1) the period of time that it takes such items as checks and notes to clear.
(2) the collection period of accounts receivable used by credit men as one measurement of their efficiency. [4]

collection ratio: the ratio of receivables (accounts, interest, and notes) to net sales, indicating the efficiency of an enterprise in the collection of its customers' accounts.

collection reminder: reminder to customer that payment or payments are past due. Can be printed, typed, or in the form of a statement or sticker insert. [41]

collection teller: a teller whose regular duty is the handling of collections. [10]

collective ownership: possession of an item in common, with no particular part of proportion assigned to anyone.

collective reserve unit (CRU): an international currency or unit of money for use along with currencies in the reserves of banks around the world.

Coll. L.: see *collection letter.*

colon: monetary unit of Costa Rica and El Salvador.

colorable title: a claim to ownership supported by some facts or circumstances tending to support the claim.

color of title: an appearance of title founded upon a written instrument which, if valid, conveys title.

columnar journal: a journal having special columns for the classification of transactions.

comaker: an individual who signs the note of another person as support for the credit of the primary maker. See *unsecured loan.*

comanager: in a Euroloan, the lender ranking next to the lead manager.

combined cash journal and daily financial statement: bookkeeping forms for use in accounting systems that omit the use of a ledger.

come across: slang, to pay money owed.

Com'l. Ppr.: see *commercial paper.*

commerce: trade between states and nations.

commercial accounts: in general, a checking account; a bank account established for the purpose of enabling the depositor (usually a business person) to draw checks against the balance maintained. See *checking account.*

commercial agency: an organization that offers facilities in the field of credit and collections.

commercial and industrial loans: loans for business purposes except those secured by real estate. [40]

commercial bank: an organization chartered either by the Comptroller of the Currency and known as a national bank or chartered by the state in which it will conduct the business of banking. A commercial bank generally specializes in demand deposits and commercial loans. See also other entries under *bank.*

commercial bank, eligible: a U.S. commercial bank or other financial institution (such as an Edge Act Corporation) or a branch or agency of a foreign bank that is subject to regular examination by state or federal banking authorities and is approved by Eximbank. [11]

commercial bank participation: the share of the financed portion lent by one or more commercial banks or similar institutions in transactions in which Eximbank is also a lender. [11]

commercial bar: a brick, or bar of precious metal, usually gold or silver, used in the arts and industry area, as distinguished from one created for monetary use, (i.e., a jeweler's bar, which is usually smaller than the bar used for monetary purposes).

commercial bills: bills of exchange resulting from a commercial business transaction as contrasted with noncommercial bills (i.e., banker's bills).

commercial borrowing:
(1) loans made to retailers and wholesalers, as differentiated from those loans to made to manufacturers.
(2) loans made to private individuals (i.e., personal loans, car loans), as differentiated from loans made to companies.

commercial lending: loans to businesses to meet short- or long-term needs. [105]

commercial letter of credit: an instrument by which a bank lends its credit to a customer to enable him to finance the purchase of goods. Addressed to the seller, it authorizes him to draw drafts on the bank under the terms stated in the letter. [50]

commercial loan: commercial loans are principally loans made to businesses for the financing of inventory purchases and the movement of goods, as distinguished from personal loans or consumer credit loans. Commercial loans are short-term loans or acceptances (time drafts accepted). See also *loan.* [10]

commercial mortgage: a loan secured by real estate, and for which the real estate is used or zoned for business purposes or multiunit dwellings, or is part of a real estate investment portfolio. [105]

commercial overhead: those expenses of a business other than materials, direct labor, manufacturing expense, and income taxes.

The principal categories are selling, administration, financial, and staff functions.

commercial paper:
(1) any notes, drafts, checks, or deposit certificates used in a business.
(2) in 1978 the Bankers Trust Company sold several issues of clients' commercial paper—short-term IOU's issued by corporations. The securities industry has tried unsuccessfully to get the Federal Reserve Board to prohibit that sale on grounds that it violated the Glass-Steagall Act, which separates commercial from investment banking. See *Glass-Steagall Act of 1933.*

commercial-paper house: principals and dealers who purchase commercial paper at one rate and attempt to sell it at another.

commercial paper names: established borrowers who are frequently in the commercial paper market.

commercial property: property to be used for business purposes, as contrasted with residential, agricultural, or industrial functions.

commercial report: see *credit report.*

commercial teller: an employee whose prime function is paying and receiving funds for bank customers.

commercial year: a business year; unlike the calendar year, it consists of 12 months of 30 days each, totaling 360 days.

commingled accounts: when several bank trust department accounts are managed as one account to take advantage of economies available to large investments, the accounts are referred to collectively as a commingled account. Banks may not sell shares to the public that would increase the size of these accounts and make them, in effect, open-ended investment companies or mutual funds. A recent Supreme Court decision, however, allows bank holding companies to advise, sponsor, and organize closed-end investment companies, which sell only a certain number of shares that are then traded in the open market like common stocks. Commingled accounts are testing the validity of the Glass-Steagall Act. See *Glass-Steagall Act of 1933.*

commingled fund: a common fund in which the funds of several accounts are mixed. [37]

commingled investment fund: a bank-operated trust fund in which accounts of individual customers are commingled and lose their identity. Each customer, in effect, owns a share of the entire fund. Such a fund differs only in detail from a mutual fund. [74]

commission:

(1) the amount paid to an agent, which may be an individual, a broker, or a financial institution, for consummating a transaction involving sale or purchase of assets or services. Cf. *override.*

(2) agents and brokers are usually compensated by being allowed to retain a certain percentage of the premiums they produce, known as a commission.

commissioner of banking: a state's banking department manager who regulates the state chartered banks in his state. In some states, known as *superintendent of banking.*

commitment: an advance agreement to perform in the future such as by an association to provide funds for a mortgage loan. [59]

commitment and disclosure statement: a written acknowledgment by a lender, required under the Truth-in-Lending Act, in which the lender stipulates under what conditions funds will be lent to the applicant. [105]

commitment fee: a fee charged when a bank has granted an overdraft or term loan which is not being fully used. [93]

commitment fee (loan): any fee paid by a potential borrower to a lender for the lender's promise to lend money at a specified rate and within a given time in the future. [105]

committee for incompetent: an individual or a trust institution appointed by a court to care for the property or the person (or both) of an incompetent; similar to a guardian, conservator, or curator. [32]

Committee on Uniform Securities Identification Procedures: see *CUSIP.*

commodity rate: the rate of interest charged by banks on notes, drafts, bills of exchange, and other related documents issued on stable commodities.

commodity reserve theory: a monetary theory under which money would be convertible into one commodity at a specified rate or the commodity convertible into money at the same rate at the option of the holder of either the money or the commodity. One variation of the theory substitutes a bundle of staple commodities for one commodity alone.

commodity standard: a suggested monetary system that proposes to substitute a commodity or commodities for the precious metal or other base of a currency.

commodity theory of money: the claim that the value of money is determined by the value of the commodity of which is composed or which it represents.

common disaster clause: a clause added to a life insurance policy to instruct the bank in paying the proceeds of policies when the insured and the named beneficiary die in the same disaster.

common language for consumer credit: a standardized system of terminology and abbreviations for reporting the payment habits of credit users, developed by the Associated Credit Bureaus, Inc. [105]

common law trust: see *business trust.*

common machine language (MICR): the common machine language for mechanized check handling is a specially designed group of 10 Arabic numbers and four special symbols printed in magnetic ink in designated field locations along the bottom edge of a check. The Bank Management Commission of the American Bankers Association, in their 1959 publication number 147, stated the original intention of the MICR program as follows: "The concept of the Common Machine Language, of course, is for the amount to be encoded by the first bank receiving the item for collection. This would permit all further handling in intermediate and paying banks to be primarily mechanical, resulting in tremendous economies in the banking system." This quotation assumes that eventually all banks will at least have their transit number routing symbol encoded on their checks,

regardless of whether they intend to use equipment that will read the magnetic ink characters or not.

common property: land generally, or a tract of land, considered as the property of the public in which all persons enjoy equal rights; a legal term signifying an incorporeal hereditament consisting of a right of one person in the land of another, as common of estovers, of pasture, of piscary, property not owned by individuals or government, but by groups, tribes, or in formal villages. [62]

common trust fund: a fund maintained by a bank or a trust company exclusively for the collective investment and reinvestment of money contributed to the fund by the bank or trust company in its capacity as trustee, executor, administrator, or guardian and in conformity with the rules and regulations of the Board of Governors of the Federal Reserve System pertaining to the collective investment of trust funds by national banks, as well as with the statutes and regulations (if any) of the several states. [37]

communication system:
(1) the means by which instructions and information pass from one bank to another. These include telex, cable, and mail in communications.
(2) in EFTS, a service that moves messages among subscribers, including funds transfer transactions, that are subject to settlement by other means. [105]

community bank trust department: a trust department holding less than $100 million in trust assets. A community bank holds less than $100 million in deposits. [25]

community property: property that is owned jointly by a husband and wife by fact of their marriage. The state laws vary, but in states were community property applies, a husband and wife are considered to share equally in all of each other's property that is acquired during the marriage and in any income received or increase in value occurring during the marriage.

Community Reinvestment Act (CRA) Statement: a description available for public inspection at each bank office indicating, on a map, the communities served by that office and the types of credit the bank is prepared to extend within the communities served. [78]

company check: a check drawn by a corporation, partnership, or other business entity on its account with a bank.

comparative balance sheet: a balance sheet showing information for more than one fiscal period.

comparative profit and loss statement: a profit and loss statement showing information for more than one fiscal period.

comparative reports: financial reports giving the figures for more than one fiscal period.

comparative statement: the income, expense, profit and loss, balance sheet, or other financial statement of the same concern for two or more consecutive years that are analyzed to determine the increase or decrease in their component items, frequently for credit purposes. [10]

comparisons: the exchange of information between a broker and his bank or between two brokers to verify that each party's records of collateral held against loan are valid and in agreement. If there is disagreement, the parties can rapidly track down any difference.

comparison shopping:
(1) evaluation of a lender's annual percentage rate (APR), which tells the borrower the relative cost of credit, against the APRs quoted by other lenders. See *annual percentage rate.* [78]
(2) an investor who compares certificates of deposits or other rates at several banks.

compensated dollar: a monetary unit where the gold content is periodically changed to retain the purchasing power level with some commodity index.

compensating balance: the lowest percentage of a line of credit that the customer of a bank is expected to maintain at all times.

compensating depreciation: a depreciation system dealing with the problem of fluctuating prices for the items being depreciated.

compensating payment: the sum of money just offsetting a given change in price or market condition.

compensation financing: see *compensatory official financing.*

compensation trading: when an exporter agrees to accept part-payment in items from the purchaser's nation in lieu of cash.

compensatory balance: the balance a borrower from a bank is required by the bank to keep in his or her account.

compensatory principle of money: the claim that the ratio between the mint and market values of two metals in a bimetallic monetary system will be maintained through normal operation of the forces of supply and demand.

compensatory principles of bimetallism: the principles applying when the currency of a nation is redeemable for fixed amounts of either gold or silver at the option of the currency holder. The principles is that the ratio between gold and silver established by the government will prevail in the free market by withdrawals from the mint or deliveries to the mint, according to the market price of one metal relative to the other is higher or lower, respectively, than that prevailing in the market for that metal.

competitive bid: the awarding of a new stock issue to the highest bidder. In most cases, this nonnegotiated bid is made by investment banking groups.

Competitive Equality Banking Act, The (1987): allows the Federal Savings and Loan Insurance Corporation, which insures deposits in 3,200 institutions, to borrow up to $10.8 billion over three years to close weak savings and loans or subsidize their takeover by healthier ones. The law also requires banks to clear consumers' checks more quickly, and bans creation of new limited-service banks.

competitive price: a price determined in the market by the bargaining of a number of buyers and sellers, each acting separately and without sufficient power to manipulate the market.

competitive profile: a resource containing a list of the bank's major competitors, growth comparisons of deposits and loan volume, product mixes, and service comparisons. [105]

completed transaction: a sale property that has closed. In this transaction all legal and financial aspects are identified, and title to the property has transferred from seller to buyer.

complete special audit: a complete audit of some particular phase of a governmental unit's activities, such as sinking fund transactions or a complete audit for all of a governmental unit's transactions for a shorter or longer period of time than the usual audit period. [49]

complete trust: a trust in which the trustee in not required to distribute income currently, or distribute amounts other than income, or make a charitable contribution. [37]

complex trust: see *simple trust.*

compliance examinations: specially designed examinations given by the three federal bank regulatory agencies. These examinations include procedures and standards, adopted by those agencies which will, for the first time, subject banks to a comprehensive review of their compliance with federal and state consumer credit statutes and regulations. [105]

compliance inspection report: a report given to a lender by a designated compliance inspector, indicating whether or not construction or repairs have complied to conditions established by a prior inspection. [105]

composite check: a listing of payments to be made from an account, sent by the owner of the account to his or her depository institution with instructions to effect the payments and debit the account for the total amount. The payments are transmitted by the depository institution to the creditors for subsequent deposit by them in their respective accounts.

composite commodity standard: a monetary system concept where the value of the monetary unit is defined in terms of a selected number of commodities (composite commodity unit) instead of in terms of one or more precious metals.

composite inventory: data accumulation on bank customers, including the most pertinent information that can be obtained about them.

composite rate depreciation: a single depreciation rate to be applied against the total of depreciable assets or a group of such assets; based on an average of the rates applicable to individual items with some weighting of the relative importance of the several items.

composition: agreement between a borrower in financial difficulty and a lender, allowing the borrower to eliminate debt by paying only a portion of the total amount owed the lender. [78]

composition settlement: a creditor's acceptance of an amount smaller than that which he or she is legally entitled to from a debtor. By doing this the creditor waives any right to the full amount.

compound: to add interest to principal at time intervals for the purpose of establishing a new basis for subsequent interest computations.

compounded: indicating the frequency with which interest is computed and added to the principal to arrive at a new actual balance.

compounded interest: interest created by the periodic addition of simple interest to principal, the new base thus established being the principal

for the computation of additional interest.

compound-interest method of depreciation: taking the initial cost of a capital asset, deducting the expected salvage value at the time it is expected to be discarded and spreading the difference in equal installments per unit of time over the estimated life of the asset but then reducing the depreciation charge for each period by the amount of interest that such a charge would earn from the period of the charge to the time of discard.

compounding: the evaluation of how a certain interest rate will cause a certain present dollar amount to grow in the future.

compounding period: the time span for which interest is calculated.

Compt.: see comptroller.

comptroller: an executive officer whose job embraces the audit functions of the business.

Comptroller of the Currency (COC): a federal office created in 1863 to oversee the chartering and regulation of national banks.

comptroller's call: the Comptroller of the Currency may "call" upon all national banks to submit a complete financial report of their activities at any given date. Reports must, according to law, be submitted at his call at least three times a year. These "called reports" must also be published in all local newspapers in the town nearest to the bank. [10]

concentration account: a deposit account to which funds from other accounts held in the same name are periodically transferred. [105]

concentration banking: a cash management technique in which customers are instructed to mail their payments to a regional collection center, rather than to a firm's home office, in order to speed their collection.

condensed balance sheet: a balance sheet where the details have been removed to give an easy, though accurate, reading of the assets, liabilities, and capital of the corporation. See *balance sheet.*

condensed statement: a financial statement grouping minor details together so that the statement can be more easily studied by the general public.

conditional commitment for guarantee: FmHA's notice to a bank that the loan for which the bank is requesting a guarantee is approved for guarantee, subject to the conditions set forth in the commitment. [105]

conditional endorsement: an endorsement describing and imposing conditions upon a transferee. The instrument can still be negotiated within the terms of the condition, but the person who has made the conditional endorsement has the right to the proceeds of the instrument if the conditions are not fulfilled.

conditional indorsement: see *conditional endorsement.*

conditional sales: sales under a payment contract where title remains with the seller until final payment is made, but the property is transferred to the buyer at once. [28]

conditional sales contract: document used in installment sales credit arrangements, which withhold ownership title from the buyer until the loan has been paid in full. [78]

condition of weekly reporting member banks: the Federal Reserve System release showing the changes in the reporting banks each week. These financial data, in part, show the changes in banks which represent more than half the banking resources of the United States.

condominium: individual ownership of a portion of a building that has other units similarly owned. Owners hold a deed and title. Owners pay taxes independently of other owners and can sell, lease, or otherwise dispose of the portion that the individual owns. Common areas, including halls, elevators, and so on, are jointly owned by the other tenants. See *lease-purchase agreement.*

condominium conversion: changing rental units into condominiums, where the buyer gets title to a specified unit plus a proportionate interest in common areas. See *condominium.*

confirmation: an assurance of title by the conveyance of an estate or right from one to another, by which a voidable estate is made sure or valid, or at times increased.

confirmed letter of credit: a foreign bank wishing to issue a letter of credit to a local concern may request a local bank in the city in which the beneficiary is located to confirm this credit to the beneficiary. The purpose of this confirmation is to lend the prestige and responsibility of the local bank to the transaction because the status of the foreign bank may be unknown to the beneficiary. The confirming bank assumes responsibility for the payment of all drafts drawn under the credit and usually charges a fee for doing so. [10]

confiscation: the seizure of private property, without compensation, usually by a governmental agency. Cf. *expropriation.*

conformed copy: a copy of an original document with the signature, seal, and other such features being typed or otherwise noted. [37]

conforming mortgage loan: a mortgage loan that conforms to regularity limits such as loan-to-value ratio, term, and other characteristics. [59]

congeneric: meaning "of the same kind," this term has been used to designate one-bank holding companies that have diversified into areas beyond the traditional bounds of banking, but within the financial field. This term distinguishes them from the conglomerates, which are corporations that include business enterprises of all descriptions. [74]

consent to pledge: a legal document signed by a party who owns a particular asset, which gives permission for another party to pledge that asset as security for a loan. [105]

consent trust: a trust in which the consent of the settlor or some designated person is required before specified action by the trustee. [37]

consequential damage: the impairment of value which does not arise as an immediate result of an act, but as an incidental result of it. The impairment of value to private property caused by the acts of public bodies or caused by the acts of neighboring property owners.

The term "consequential damage" applies only in the event no part of land is actually taken. The damage resulting from the taking of a fraction of the whole, that is, over and above the loss reflected in the value of the land actually taken, is commonly known as *severance damage.* [62]

conservator: a court-appointed official responsible for the protection of the interests on an estate.

Consid.: see *consideration.*

consideration:
(1) synonymous with *premium.*
(2) a requirement of valid contracts according to which all parties must provide something of value. Cf. *nudum pactum.*

consignment ledger: a subsidiary ledger containing individual accounts with consignors.

consolidated mortgage: when two or more firms, each holding a mortgage on property, combine, and then the consolidated organization takes out a mortgage, the latter mortgage is referred to as a consolidated mortgage.

consolidation loan: combines several debts into one loan, usually to reduce the annual percentage rate or the dollar amount of payments made each month, by extending them over a longer period of time. [78]

consolidation of bills: the borrowing of a lump sum of money for the payment of past-due bills; the money borrowed is then repaid in installments. [41]

consortium bank: a bank whose shareholders consist of a group of other banks.

constant-dollar estimates: an estimate that removes the effects of price changes from statistical series reported in dollar terms.

constant dollars: the actual prices of a previous year or the average of actual prices of a previous period of years.

constant factor: the periodic amount of principal and interest that is required to retire a loan.

constant payment: a fixed or invariable payment, a continually recurring payment. [62]

constant ratio: a method of comparing mortgage amortization (principal and interest) on an annual basis to the original amount of the mortgage. Expressed as a percentage. Synonymous with *mortgage constant.*

constant yield rate: an installment finance method where a rate is computed on the total note as in the true discount rate for a contract of 12 monthly payments only.

construction loan: funds extended on the security of real property for the purpose of constructing or improving a building. [39]

consumer: any person who uses goods and services.

Consumer Checking Account Equity Act: allows (a) members' banks and FDIC-insured nonmember banks to continue to provide automatic transfers from savings to checking accounts; (b) NOW accounts are permitted nationwide December 31, 1980 at all depository institutions for individuals and nonprofit organizations; (c) federally insured credit unions were authorized to offer share draft accounts; (d) federal deposit insurance at commercial banks, savings banks, savings and loan associations and credit unions was increased to $100,000 per account; (e) federal credit unions could make residential real estate loans on residential cooperatives. [203]

consumer credit: credit extended by a bank to a borrower for the specific purpose of financing the purchase of a household appliance, alteration, or improvement, a piece of equipment, or other personal needs. This form of credit is generally extended to individuals rather than to business executives.

Consumer Credit Counseling Services (CCCS): a unit of the Federal Home Loan Bank System. CCCS specializes in working with people who are overextended with debts and need to make arrangements with local creditors.

Consumer Credit Protection Act of 1968: see *Truth in Lending Act of 1968.*

consumer debentures: investment notes sold directly to the public by a financial institution. These notes are much like the certificates of deposit sold by banks and savings and loans. Unlike banks selling notes, these notes can be sold anywhere, at any interest rate determined to be found competitive by the institution.

Consumer Protection Act: see *Truth in Lending Act of 1968.*

consumer sale disclosure statement: a form presented by a dealer giving essential details on financing charges relative to a purchase on an installment plan. This is required under the Consumer Credit Protection (Truth-in-Lending) Act.

consummation: a defined term under Regulation Z, meaning the actual time that a contractual relationship is created between borrower and lender, irrespective of the time of performance of a particular transaction. Depending upon the state law of contracts governing a particular association, consummation may occur at the time a loan is closed, at the time a lender accepts (as distinct from receives) a borrower's loan application, or at the time a firm commitment is given to make a loan. See *Regulation Z*. [59]

consumption loan: a loan whose proceeds are used for personal purposes.

Cont.: see *contract*.

contemporaneous reserve accounting (CRA): a one-day lag allowing member banks of the Federal Reserve to calculate their required reserves and reserves held as vault cash for a week before making the final adjustments to their reserve balances on Wednesdays. This system is "contemporaneous" because, except for the one-day lag, assets and liabilities used in calculating reserves and required reserves are those of the same week. See *lagged reserve accounting*.

contest of a will: an attempt by legal process to prevent the probate of a will or the distribution of property according to the will. [37]

Continental Depositary Receipt (CDR): issued by several Dutch banks; made out in bearer form, permitting trade in United States, United Kingdom, and Japanese registered company share on the Amsterdam Stock Exchange, which permits only trading in bearer shares.

continental rate: the rate charged in Europe for foreign exchange and on bills of exchange.

contingent executor: an executor named in a will whose capacity as executor is dependent upon the action or nonaction of the principal executor. [37]

contingent interest: the right to property that depends for "vesting" or realization on the coming of some future uncertain occurrence. Cf. *vested interest*.

contingent trustee: a trustee whose appointment is dependent upon the failure to act of the original or a successor trustee. [37]

continuing account: a running or open book account where settlements are made regularly (e.g., 30 to 60 days).

continuing guaranty: a form given to a bank by a person to guarantee repayment of a loan to another party. This guaranty promises payment by the guarantor in the event of default by the borrower, and is so worded that it may apply to a current loan, or to one made at a later date. The guaranty may or may not pledge collateral as security for the loan. [10]

continuous audit: an audit where the detailed work is carried out continuously or at short, regular periods throughout the fiscal year, usually at the shortest intervals (weekly, monthly) when subsidiary records are closed and made available for audit in controllable form.

continuous compounding: compound interest where the compounding period is every instant of time.

contocurrent account: used in West Germany and parts of Switzerland to identify what is called in the United States a checking account.

contra: means that an account has an offsetting credit or debit entry. [59]

contrabalance: a balance in an account which is the opposite of the normal balance of that account (e.g., an accounts receivable account with a credit balance; such a balance if correctly shown as a liability). Asset valuation accounts, such as bad debt reserve, are contrabalances to the asset.

contract: an agreement between two or more persons, as established by law, and by which rights are acquired by one or more parties to specific acts or forebearance from acts on the part of others.

contract, breach of: see *breach of contract.*

contract account: general term describing a long-term credit arrangement for purchase of specific items described in the contract. Usually includes a service or carrying charge. See *chattel mortgage agreement, conditional sales contract.*

contract for deed: a written agreement between the seller and buyer of a piece of property, whereby the buyer receives title to the property only after making a determined number of monthly payments; also called an *installment contract* or *land contract.* [59]

contract of guarantee (line of credit): FmHA issues this to the lender testifying to its agreement to guarantee the bank's loan. [105]

contract of sale: a written document whereby an owner agrees to convey title to a property when the purchaser has completed paying for the property under the terms of the contract. [59]

contract payable: sums due on contracts. [49]

contract sale: a sale of real estate in which the seller retains title to the property until the buyer has made the required number of monthly payments. [59]

contracts in foreign currency: agreements to buy and sell an amount of one currency for another at an agreed rate of exchange. [105]

contribution:
(1) something given, such as time or money.
(2) the bank's payment of, or obligation to pay, all or part of a loss.

contribution margin: the excess of total revenue over total variable cost.

control: a system under which all transactions or balances of a given type are included in a single total, so that the accuracy of their recording may be proved. [50]

control account: an account in the general ledger used to carry the total of several subsidiary accounts. Whenever any subsidiary account is affected, the same will be reflected in the control account total. Control accounts are also used as "total" accounts, controlling the accounts within a "book" or "ledger" in the bookkeeping department and the savings department. [10]

control card: a card which indicates the total dollar amount on deposit and the total number of accounts in a single ledger. Control cards are debited and credited according to each day's transactions and are used as a basis of proof when trial balances are taken. In addition to the control card for each ledger or section, there is a master control card for each unit, or for the bank as a whole. [39]

controlled account: where the principal authorizes the broker, with a power of attorney, to exercise his or her own discretion in the purchasing and selling of securities or commodities.

controlled inflation: an economic situation that causes monetary and fiscal experts to urge creation or inflationary conditions, usually be increasing the supply of money in order to pull the economy out of a recession or deflation period into prosperity.

controller: see *comptroller.*

controlling account: an account, usually kept in the general ledger, which receives the aggregate of the debit and of the credit postings to a number of identical, similar, or related accounts called subsidiary accounts so that its balance equals the aggregate of the balance in these accounts. [49]

controlling records: a class of financial records within a bank composed of the controlling books or accounts of the bank. See *controlling account.*

controls: approaches by regulatory agencies to keep the economy in a healthy position. In most cases, governmental agencies act, by creating rules, to monitor the condition of the nation's economy.

conventional fixed-rate mortgage: a mortgage with a fixed term, fixed rate, and fixed monthly payments which is fully paid off within 30 years or less. It is a mortgage without government insurance or guarantee. See also *conventional loan.* [66]

conventional loan: a mortgage loan, usually granted by a bank or loan association. The loan is based on real estate as security rather than being guaranteed by an agency of the government. This loan has a fixed interest rate and fixed payments for the life of the loan. See also *conventional fixed-rate mortgage.*

conversion: the process of changing from one system or one type of equipment to another.

conversion rate: an exchange rate from foreign to U.S. currency. [105]

conversion value: value created by changing from one state, character, form, or use to another. [62]

convertibility: ease of exchanging one currency for that of another nation or for gold. See *soft currency.*

convertible currencies: includes the U.S. Treasury and Federal Reserve holdings of foreign currencies that are counted as part of official U.S. reserve assets. [11]

convertible money: money that can be exchanged at par for the standard or legal money.

convertible wraparound mortgage: see *CWM.*

conveyance: a written statement called a deed, whereby ownership of property is passed from one person or organization to another.

conveyancing: the act of transferring title to real property.

cooperative: anything owned jointly to the same end.

cooperative apartment: dwelling units in a multidwelling complex in which each owner has an interest in the entire complex and a lease on his or her own apartment, although he or she does not own the apartment as in the case of a condominium. [105]

cooperative bank: a term given in some states to an institution that operates as a savings and loan association. See *savings and loan association.* [39]

cooperative central bank: a state-chartered mutual institution in Massachusetts to which all state savings associations (called cooperative banks) in Massachusetts must belong; it insures the savings accounts held by members and serves as a central credit facility. [59]

co-ownership: synonymous with *multiple ownership.*

cordoba: monetary unit of Nicaragua.

Corp.: see *corporation.*

corporate agent: trust companies act as agents for corporations, governments, and municipalities for various transactions. In each case, a fee is charged for the particular service rendered. [10]

Corporate Bankruptcy Act: see *National Bankruptcy Act of 1898.*

corporate-bond unit trusts: similar to GNMA trust units, but without monthly return of principal. Yield is close to a point less. See *Government National Mortgage Association.*

corporate depositary: a trust institution serving as the depositary of funds or other property. See also *depositary, depository.* [37]

corporate fiduciary: a trust institution functioning in a fiduciary capacity, such as an administrator, trustee, executor, or guardian.

corporate indenture: an agreement made by a bank to act as an intermediary between a corporation making a public bond offering and the purchasers of the bonds. The bank agrees to act as a trustee by protecting the interest of the lenders (bondholders). [105]

corporate resolution: a document given to a bank by a corporation defining the authority vested in each of its officers who may sign and otherwise conduct the business of the corporation with the bank. Corporate resolutions usually are given with or without borrowing powers. These powers are granted by the board of directors of the firm. [10]

corporate surplus: as of the date of the balance sheet, the equity in the assets not offset by the capitalization, current or deferred liabilities, or unadjusted credits. It includes appropriations for additions to property, for retirement of funded debt, reserves for sinking and other funds, and other appropriations not specifically invested. [18]

corporate trustee: a trust institution serving as a trustee. [37]

corporation:
(1) *general:* an organization having purposefulness, declared social benefit, derived powers, legal entity, permanence, and limited liability.
(2) *law:* individuals created by law as a legal entity, vested with powers and ability to contract, own, control, convey property, and discharge business within the boundaries of the powers granted.

corporation account: a checking or savings account owned by a corporation and established in accordance with a resolution adopted by its board of directors.

corporation charter: a document issued by the state or federal government giving a group of persons the right to act as a legal person in the conduct of an enterprise and specifying at least some of the conditions of operation.

corporators: the group which in certain states elects the trustees of a mutual savings bank. The number of corporators is not limited, and the group is self-perpetuating. [39]

corporeal: pertaining to a right or group of rights of a visible and tangible nature. [62]

corporeal heraditament: tangible property that can be inherited.

corporeal property: real or personal property having form or structure (e.g., house, furniture, land, fixtures). Cf. *chose(s) in possession.*

corpus: a term used in trust companies and trust accounting to describe all the property in a trust, also referred to as the "body" of the trust. A corpus may consist of real estate, stocks, bonds, and other personal property, cash in the form of bank accounts, and any items that the donor may wish to have included. [10]

correction: any price reaction within the market leading to an adjustment by as much as one-third to two-thirds of the previous gain.

correction voucher: a form used by tellers to facilitate the correction of any errors made in the recording of transactions on electronic data-processing equipment. [59]

correlation: a relationship or dependence. Reflecting the principle that two things or variables are so related that change in one is accompanied by a corresponding or parallel change in the other.

correspondency system: the origination and administration of mortgage loans for investors by independent loan correspondents. [22]

correspondent bank: a bank that is the depository for another bank. The correspondent bank accepts all deposits in the form of cash letters and collects items for its bank depositor.

corset: a strategy whereby the more money that banks accumulate for lending over six months, the bigger the deposits with a central bank will have to be.

cosigner: synonymous with *comaker.*

cost accounting: a branch of accounting dealing with the classification, recording, allocation, summarization, and reporting of current and prospective costs. It provides the means by which management can control manufacturing costs.

cost approach to value: a method of estimating the value of real property by deducting depreciation from the cost of replacement and adding the value of the land to the remainder. See *appraisal.*

cost ledger: a subsidiary record wherein each project, job, production center, process, operation, product, or service is given a separate account where all items entering into its cost are posted in the required detail. Such accounts should be so arranged and kept that the results shown in them may be reconciled with and verified by a control account or in the general books. [49]

cost of funds: interest (dividends) paid or accrued on savings, Federal Home Loan Bank advances, and other borrowed money during a period as a percent of average savings and borrowings.

cost of money:

(1) *bank card:* the expense, expressed as an annual percentage,

which is charged by the bank to a credit card operation for the use of funds.

(2) *lending:* a calculated figure that considers the respective costs of the several sources of bank funds to establish a cost that must be covered by a bank's rate structure on loans. [105]

cost of occupancy: the periodic expenditure of money necessary to occupy a property, exclusive of the expenses directly attributable to the conduct of a business. [6]

cost of reproduction: the cost of replacing a building as of any given date (usually current). [59]

cost records: all ledgers, supporting records, schedules, reports, invoices, vouchers, and other records and documents reflecting the cost of projects, jobs, production centers, processes, operations, products, or services, or the cost of any of the component parts thereof. [49]

cotrustee: a person, trust organization, or bank permitted to provide trust functions, acting with another as a trustee.

counter cash: that part of the actual cash of a bank kept by the tellers in their cages. [31]

counter check: a form of check provided by a bank for the convenience of the depositor. A counter check may be cashed only by the drawer personally. [50]

counter deposits: a deposit presented at the teller's window by a customer. Other forms include deposits by mail, clearings, collections, or internal sources. [31]

countererror: in accounting, an error (over or short) that is offset by an error of equal amount, thus creating a balance which is correct without disclosing that two or more of the transactions apparently proved are actually in error. [31]

counterfeit: imitation or fraudulent money.

counterfeit card:

(1) device or instrument that has been printed, embossed, or encoded like a bank card, but which is not a card because it is not authorized by an issuer.

(2) a card that has been validly issued by an issuer and which has been changed without the authorization of the issuer. [105]

counter item: any item accepted or originated at the bank teller window as contrasted with those received by mail, clearings, or from internal departments. [10]

counterpart monies: local currency equivalents of dollar assistance given to nations by the United States following World War II that are in turn used to purchase U.S. goods or services. Cf. *tied loan.*

countersignature:

(1) the signature of a licensed agent or representative on a policy, which is necessary to validate the contract.

(2) a signature added to a document to authenticate it. Cf. *attestation.*

countervailing credit: see *back-to-back.*

country bank: a national or state bank that is not located in a Federal Reserve city. Country banks' legal reserve requirements are usually less than for large city banks.

country check: a transit check; an item drawn on an out-of-town bank; a check drawn upon a bank out of a central reserve or reserve city.

country club billing: a billing system in which the account statement is accompanied by copies of original invoices. [36]

country code: a three-digit code to identify uniquely the country to which the transaction data generated by the card should be routed. [105]

country collections: all items that are being sent outside the city in which the sending bank is located. A banker will speak of "city collection," which are items drawn on banks and business houses upon whom drafts are to be collected within the city of the bank's location; and "country collections," which are sent out of the city to the bank's correspondents for collection and payment. [10]

country item: see *country collections.*

coupon account: type of credit extension whereby books of coupons having a stated value are sold on an installment payment basis. Coupons are used in issuing stores as cash. Payment for the coupon book is stretched over a period of time. Coupon accounts are generally used for credit customers of limited responsibility, and whose buying must be closely controlled. [41]

coupon book: a set of payment cards or computer cards that the borrower returns to the association one at a time with regular loan repayments, or with deposits for savings accounts such as a club account. [59]

coupon collection: being negotiable, coupons are collectable like any other negotiable instrument. The owner of the bond from which

the coupon was clipped signs a "certificate of ownership" and attaches the coupon to this certificate. It is then either cashed by the bank, or deposited by the depositor as a credit to his or her account. Coupons are collected by banks under special transit letters which require considerably more description than is required for check collections. [10]

coupon collection teller: the person in a coupon collection department who processes coupons presented for payment.

coupon envelope: a special envelope provided by a bank for the deposit of interest payments on loans. [105]

coupon ledger: the ledger used by a bank or trust company to record the receipt of monies in order to pay coupons, disbursements for their redemption when presented for payment, and the number of coupons paid.

coupon-paying department: found within a bank or trust company, a department chosen as paying agent by corporations and others to pay matured coupons and bonds.

coupon payment form: a form sent to a credit bureau after an inquiry has been made by telephone. The proper coupon is attached to it. [76]

coupon payments account: to show the total coupon checks outstanding, a bank or trust company will create a general ledger account to identify coupon redemption payments.

coupon rate: the interest rate specified on interest coupons attached to a bond. Synonymous with *nominal interest rate.* [49]

coupon shell: used in certain localities to describe the envelope in which maturing coupons are enclosed for collection. [10]

coupon system: see *Associated Credit Bureaus of America, Inc.*

coupon teller: a bank teller responsible for controlling the redemption of matured coupons that have been presented for payment.

coupon transmittal form: a form used to request a credit report by mail. The proper coupon is attached to it. [76]

court account: accounts that require court accountings and approval in their normal conduct. Probate, guardianship, conservatorship, and testamentary trust accounts are the most common. [37]

court trust: a trust coming under the immediate supervision of the court such as a trust by order of court or, in some states, a trust under will. [37]

covenant: a contract pertaining to an undertaking, a promise, or an agreement to do or forbear from doing that which has legal validity and is legally enforceable.

covered arbitrage: arbitrage between financial instruments dominated in differing currencies, using forward cover to eliminate exchange risk.

covered margin: the interest rate margin between two instruments denominated in differing currencies, after taking account of the cost of forward cover.

cover payment: an arrangement by which a correspondent bank is reimbursed for payment made in accordance with instructions of the sending bank. [105]

coverture: the legal status of a married person. [105]

CP: see *commercial paper.*

CPA: see *certified public accountant.*

CQ respondent bank: banks that have exchanged authorized signature lists, and/or engage in an exchange of services, and/or have an account or accounts with each other. [105]

Cr.:
(1) see *credit.*
(2) see *creditor.*

CR: see *cash reserve.*

CRA: see *contemporaneous reserve accounting.*

crash: a sudden and disastrous drop in business activity, prices, security values, and so on, as occurred in October of 1929.

crawling peg: foreign exchange rates that permit the par value of a country's currency to change automatically by small increments, upward or downward, if in actual daily trading on the foreign exchange markets the price in terms of other monies persists on the floor or ceiling of the established range for a given period.

creampuff sale: an expression suggesting that real property is easily sold.

creative financing: any of various home mortgage arrangements to make buying more affordable.

creator: a trustor or settlor; a person who creates a trust by will or a voluntary trust.

Cred.:
(1) see *credit.*
(2) see *creditor.*

Crediscope: a more objective system of reporting trade data from creditor's ledgers. It was introduced in 1977. [76]

credit:
(1) an entry recorded on the right side of a ledger. Cf. *debit.*
(2) funds remaining in a bank account. See also *bank credit.*
(3) sales or purchases that are accompanied by a promise to pay later.

credit acceptance: notification to a customer that his or her credit application has been accepted and an account is now available for his or her use. [41]

credit adjustment: a correction issued and posted to a cardholder account which reduces the balance of the account. [105]

credit agency: firms that provide credit and collection information.

credit analyst: an expert who determines by examining a person's present and past activities whether the person has earned credit. [41]

credit application: a form filled out by a borrower wanting credit, or an interview, which seeks information about an applicant regarding residence, employment, income, and existing debt. [78]

credit approval department: that aspect or department of a bank card operation which is responsible for the processing of new cardholder applications to determine if the applications are approved or declined. May include the responsibility for limit control. [105]

credit association: a group of local retail credit granters forming a dues-paying association. In most cases the local association with 10 or more members is a unit of the National Retail Credit Association. Usually known as the Retail Credit Association. [41]

credit authorization/verification: an inquiry process undertaken to reduce the risk of credit fraud or of extending credit in excess of an imposed credit limit.

credit balance: see *balance of account.*

credit bank: synonymous with *commercial bank.*

credit barometrics: financial ratios applied to balance sheets and profit and loss statements that aid in credit analysis.

credit bill: a bill of exchange where the debtor has arranged in advance for credit with the drawee.

credit bureau: an agency holding central files of data on consumers in a given trade area. These bureaus collect personal data, data on paying habits of individuals, and so on, and make impartial reports for credit granters.

credit card: a card issued by an organization entitling the bearer to credit at its establishments (e.g., Exxon's credit card used at gas stations). There are single-purpose cards issued by a specific firm, multipurpose cards (e.g., American Express, Carte Blanche), and bank cards (e.g., MasterCard and Visa).

credit card center: the physical facility where credit card operations are conducted. [105]

Credit Card Issuance Act: federal regulation, which became effective in October 1970, that regulates the issuance of credit cards and the extent of a cardholder's liability in case a card is used without permission. [105]

credit clearing: see *credit interchange.*

credit company:
(1) a commercial credit organization.

(2) a firm that operates as a factor and takes paper subject to recourse rather than without recourse.

credit contract: a written statement showing how, when, and how much you will pay for goods and services.

credit control: any policy purporting to expand or contract credit, such a policy being applied by governments, banks, a central banking organization, or other agencies.

Credit Control Act of 1969: federal legislation giving the Federal Reserve System standby authority to control the price and allocation of credit if authorized by the president, one that has never been invoked. Expired June 30, 1982.

credit criteria: the standards applied to cardholder applications or to previous account records in order to determine approval or rejection of the application for the issuance of a credit card, the establishment of a line of credit, or the increase of a line of credit. [105]

credit currency: currency that does not have full convertibility into standard money. Synonymous with *fiduciary money (or standard).*

credit decline: notification to a customer that his or her credit application has not been accepted.

credit de mobilisation de creances commerciales: French for short-term bank lendings in the form of discounted bills of exchange backed by underlying trade debt.

credit department:
(1) in a nonbank the department of a company that establishes lines of credit for various customers and authorizes the extension of credit. In addition, most mercantile credit

departments also have responsibility for the collection of the accounts.
(2) a department in a bank where credit information is obtained, assembled, and retained for reference purposes. Credit applications for loans are presented to this department by a loan officer. The credit department gathers all available information on the customer, and prepares it for the confidential use of the loan officer. Based on the findings of the credit departments, which will make an analysis of the credit information, the loan officer is in a position to make a decision as to whether the loan application should be rejected. The credit department also obtains information and answers credit inquiries for its bank correspondents, who may have a business transaction pending that will involve credit knowledge on a local business. [10]

credit entry: an entry placed on the right-hand side of an account.

Creditexport: a nonprofit-making consortium of Belgian commercial banks and other public and private financial institutions to fund medium- and long-term export credit.

credit facilities: a business system set up to offer credit services to those who possess personal or business credit. [28]

credit file: an assembly of facts and opinions which indicates the financial resources of an individual (or an enterprise), his or her character, and his or her record of performance, especially toward financial obligations. [44]

credit folder: synonymous with *credit file.*

credit footing of an account: the columnar total written at the foot of the credit money column in an account.

credit history: a continuing record of a borrower's debt commitments and how well these have been honored. [78]

credit information: information on a person, company, or subject made available to a credit analyst.

credit instrument: a written guarantee to pay, which serves the purpose of money in consummating commercial exchanges, although actual money or bank notes are not used.

credit interchange: the sharing among suppliers of data shown by the ledger about accounts.

credit interchange bureau: an organization that serves as a clearinghouse for its members credit requests.

credit interviewer: an individual who secures from a credit applicant needed data for establishing worthy credit.

credit investigation: an inquiry made by a lender to verify data given in a credit application or to investigate other aspects the creditor believes to be relevant to credit worthiness. See *acid test ratio.*

credit letter: another title for a cash letter. See *cash letter.* [10]

credit life insurance: synonymous with *mortgage life insurance.*

credit limit: amount, established with or without agreement of the customer, to which credit purchases may be authorized. [41]

credit line: see *line of credit.*

credit losses: the money lost by a finance company or other credit-granting institution when a debt is not paid. This loss may be increased by the cost of collection activities before the debt is finally written off as uncollectable. [55]

credit manager: individual responsible for the credit function of a credit card plan, including the approval of new applications and the establishment and/or increase of credit lines. [105]

credit mechanism: see *credit facilities.*

credit memo:
(1) a posting medium authorizing the credit to a specified account of a certain named amount that bears the complete description of the transaction, the date, and the signature of the party responsible for the authorization of the credit.
(2) a detailed memorandum forwarded from one party or firm to another, granting credit for returned merchandise, some omission, overpayment, or other cause. [10]

credit money: fiduciary money that is not completely backed by a precious metal.

creditor: one who is due money from another. Synonymous with *lender.* See *guaranty.*

creditors: those to whom one owes an obligation (usually financial). [28]

creditor's bill: a proceeding commenced by one or more unpaid creditors petitioning a court of equity to appoint a receiver to manage the affairs of a debtor who is not meeting his or her obligations.

creditor's position: that portion of the market price of a property which is represented by or can be obtained through a first mortgage. [62]

credit party: the party to be credited or paid by the receiving bank. [105]

credit proxy: the sum of member bank deposits plus nondeposit items. Often referred to as adjusted credit proxy.

credit rating:
(1) the amount, type, and form of credit, if any, which a bank estimates can be extended to an applicant for credit.
(2) an estimate of the credit and responsibility assigned to mercantile and other establishments by credit investigating organizations.

credit rating book: the list of established credit users in a region together with a code letter showing general credit rating.

credit record: a complete and permanent record of your credit performance. [41]

credit report: a confidential report made by an independent individual or organization that has investigated the financial standing, reputation, and record of an applicant for insurance.

credit reporting agencies: organizations structured to supply to business and industry the information they need to reach credit, sales, financial, and general management decisions.

credit risk: the risk assumed for the possible nonpayment of credit extended.

credit sales department: recommended by the National Retail Credit Association to designate the place where credit and collection functions are carried on. [41]

credit scoring system: a statistical measure used to rate credit applicants on the basis of various factors relevant to credit worthiness. [78]

credit service charge: the charge made for the use of credit facilities. [28]

credit side: the right-hand side of an account.

credit slip: document showing the return of merchandise by a cardholder to a merchant, or other refund made by the merchant to the cardholder. A copy of this document is used by the bank to credit the cardholder's account. Synonymous with *credit voucher and refund slip.*

credit standing: one's present credit worthiness as determined by his or her past credit performance. [28]

credit system: a creditor may use a demonstrably and statistically sound, empirically derived credit system obtained from another person, or may obtain credit experience from which such a system may be developed. [105]

credit terms: specification of the terms for the payment of a credit obligation.

credit ticket: a bank bookkeeping memorandum or posting medium on which the transaction leading to a credit entry in a ledger account is described in detail. [31]

credit transaction: every aspect of an applicant's dealings with a creditor regarding an application for, or an existing extension of, credit. [105]

credit transfer: a voucher giving bookkeeper authority to credit an account according to instructions on the voucher. Cf. *debit transfer.*

credit transfer system: a computer system which will make available collected funds already in a customer's account to an account maintained by the retailer. [105]

credit union: a cooperative financial organization established within and listed to a specific group of people. See *Federal Credit Union, share draft.*

credit voucher: synonymous with *credit slip.*

credit worthy (credit worthiness): receiving a favorable credit rating; an individual or business is thereby entitled to use the credit facilities of the organization(s) who requested the information. See *open credit.*

"cremation": the act of destroying by fire certain records of the bank. The legal counsel of the bank advises the bank which records and documents may be destroyed, as a result of having outrun the statute of limitations according to the laws of the state in which the bank is operating. The term also applies to the destruction by fire of certain bonds and coupons that have been redeemed by a bank acting as fiscal agent for the issuing corporation or governmental agency. The cremation of paid securities is by agreement between the bank and the issuing agency. [10]

Crime of 1873: in 1873 the coinage laws were revised and the standard silver dollar was omitted (i.e., silver was demonetized). this was done because very little silver had come to the mint after 1834 since the market value of silver was higher than the price paid by the Treasury. The law was later called the "Crime of '73."

crime of receiving: receiving, possessing, concealing, storing, bartering, selling, or disposing of any property, money, or other thing of value

with the knowledge that it has been stolen. [59]

cross bill: see *redraft.*

cross-border lending: lending of funds by a U.S. bank to less-developed countries.

cross check: the placing of two diagonal lines across the front of a check and the addition of a term or series of words to determine the negotiability of the check such as to one's banker if his name is inserted between the lines. Rarely used in the United States, but found in parts of Europe and Latin America.

cross-currency exposure: when a firm's debt servicing requirements in a currency are not covered by its revenue-generating capabilities in that currency.

cross-default clause: a loan agreement clause stating that default on any other loans to the borrower will be regarded as default on this one.

crossfoot: to add figures horizontally across columns. [43]

crossrate: the determination of the rate of exchange of two foreign currencies by using the rate of exchange of each currency in a third nation's currency.

cross remainders: dispositive provisions of a will or trust agreement wherein there is provision that surviving life beneficiaries shall be entitled to receive or share in the income of the deceased beneficiary. [105]

CRU: see *collective reserve unit.*

crunch: an economic squeeze; a crisis created by some financial pressure.

cruzeiro: monetary unit of Brazil.

CSN: see *card security number.*

C-speck: slang, a $100 bill.

Csv.: see *cash surrender value.*

Ctfs.: see *certificate.*

Cts.: see *cent.*

CU: see *credit union.*

Culpeper Switch: a computerized Federal Reserve facility located in Culpeper, Virginia, which serves as a central relay point for messages transmitted electronically between Federal Reserve districts on the Fedwire. Messages moving billions of dollars of funds and securities daily are processed by Culpeper in electronically coded form. They originate in commercial banks, are sent to Reserve Banks, and then are transmitted to Culpeper, where they are switched to other Reserve Banks and, in turn, to other commercial banks. [1]

Cum.: see *cumulative.*

cumulative: an arrangement whereby a dividend or interest which, if not paid when due or received when due, is added to that which is to be paid in the future. [37]

curable depreciation: depreciated property that is still considered to be economically useful.

curator: an individual or a trust institution appointed by a court to care for the property of a minor or an incompetent person. In some states a curator is essentially the same as a temporary administrator or a temporary guardian. [37]

curing title: the removal of a claim from a title, to make it marketable.

Curr.: see *currency.*

currency: paper money and coin issued by a government or central bank, which circulates as a legal medium of exchange. [7]

currency availability clause: a Euromarket clause providing that banks can switch their lending to a different currency should the original currency be no longer available.

currency band: a carefully defined area within which a nation's money fluctuates on both sides of its official parity. Set at 2.25 percent each side of the parity at the 1971 Washington Smithsonian Agreement.

currency bloc: nations that use a common currency base; for example, the British sterling bloc exists for Great Britain and many of her present and former colonies.

currency cocktail: a unit of account based on a number of currencies.

currency code: code identifying the currency of the transaction amount (the three-letter ISO code is recommended). [105]

currency convertibility: the ability to exchange for gold, as well as for other currencies.

currency exchange (swap): a long-term exchange of currency between two firms in different nations.

currency parities: as agreed upon by members of the International Monetary Fund, funds of all of the world's major nations are set in relation to the U.S. dollar.

currency pouch: a zipper pouch in which a cashier places and locks the money from the cash drawer at time of closing the cash drawer. [55]

"currency school" principle: a principle developed in England in the nineteenth century, maintaining that under a purely metallic currency any loss of gold to foreign countries or the reserve would result automatically in a corresponding decrease or increase in currency in circulation and thus immediately influence the price level. Under a mixed currency of gold and convertible paper, the same effect would not occur automatically, but would be brought about only by regulation of the quantity of paper money to conform to the quantity of gold. This principle was essentially embodied in Peel's Bank Charter Act of 1844. Cf. *"banking school" principle.*

currency shipment: the responsibility of the Federal Reserve Bank and other large city banks to supply other banks with an appropriate quantity and quality of coins, paper money, and orders for the transfer of money.

currency transferability: the ability of a currency to be easily exchanged for another currency by any and all of its owners.

current: in budgeting and accounting, designates the operations of the present fiscal period as opposed to past or future periods. [49]

current account: a running account between two companies, reflecting the movement of cash, merchandise, and so on.

current account balance: the difference between the nation's total exports of goods, services, and transfers and its total imports of them. It excludes transactions in financial assets and liabilities. [1]

current and accrued assets: generally consists of items realizable or to be consumed within one year from the date of the balance sheet. Includes cash, working funds, and certain deposits, temporary cash investments, receivables, materials and supplies including fuel, and prepayments. [3]

current and accrued liabilities: generally consists of obligations incurred, accrued, or declared, including short-term borrowing, all of which are either due and payable, payable on demand or, in any event, contemplated to be paid within one year. [3]

current and collectable: money that flows or passes from hand to hand as a medium of exchange. [61]

curtesy: a husband's life interest in the property of his deceased spouse. Cf. *dower.*

cushion checking (credit): a check overdraft plan that is also an instant loan. When a check is issued in excess of the customer's account balance or a request is made to transfer from the customer's cash reserve to his or her checking account, a loan is made for up to 36 months plus a modest interest charge.

CUSIP: the American Bankers Association's Committee on Uniform Securities Identification Procedures that established alphabetical and numerical descriptions of securities traded on the exchanges and in over-the-counter markets.

custodian: a banking institution that holds in custody and safekeeping the securities and other assets of an investment company. [23]

custodian account: any financial account (i.e., bank, securities) created for a minor, as provided by state law.

custodianship: the relationship between a trust firm or bank where the bank controls the customer's property subject to the owner's instructions. To be differentiated from the safe depository function where the bank does not control the customers property but merely provided a place for safekeeping.

custody: the banking service that provides safekeeping for a customer's property under written agreement, and additionally calls for the bank to collect and pay out income, and to buy, sell, receive, and deliver securities when ordered by the principal to do so. [105]

custody account: one in which securities or other assets are held by a bank on behalf of a customer under a safekeeping arrangement. [202]

customer-bank communication terminal (CBCT): the name given to remote (i.e., not on bank premises) electronic devices through which customers may withdraw, deposit, or transfer funds from or to their checking or savings accounts. Cf. *automated teller machine.*

customer draft: see *sight draft.*

customer risk: see *credit risk.*

customer's acceptance liability: customers' liability on outstanding drafts and bills of exchange that have been accepted by a bank. This acceptance by the bank is referred to as a *banker's acceptance.* [201]

customer's ledger: a ledger that shows accounts receivable of each customer.

customers' liability: an account in a bank's general ledger as an offset to existing letters of credit that have not been paid but remain guaranteed. See *letter of credit.*

customhouse: the place for the payment of import duties in the United States and for the payment of import and export duties in other nations.

cut: an expression used in banks to denote the taking of a total of a pack of checks sorted and going to one destination. The term is most frequently used in banks equipped with proof machines. Since these machines can list a large number of checks on a tape, it has been found more convenient to "cut a tape" by taking totals at intervals of between 100 and 200 items per total. The term also is applied to canceling checks. [10]

cut notes: paper money issues that have been officially bisected or quartered and each portion given its own value, normally indicated by over-stamping. This has usually been an emergency measure due to a shortage of coins. [27]

cutoff: to effect better control over huge volumes of checks passing through the proof department in large banks, these banks have periodic "settlements" or "cutoffs" of work. Each cutoff is balanced and items are immediately released from the proof department after each settlement. This not only affords better control, but permits transit items to be mailed in several deliveries each business day. [10]

cut slip: a slip of paper upon which is imprinted or written the total of a particular "cut." The cut slips are retained and used to "settle" a proof machine when the settlement is made. [10]

cutthroat competition: intensive competition that may lead to the bankruptcy of a major competitor, allowing the survivor to raise prices considerably. See *rate war.*

CWM: convertible wraparound mortgage; a mortgage making it possible for builders to offer below-market, fixed-rate, fully amortized loans to home buyers during periods of high interest rates without requiring forfeiture of the builder's profit through interest rate buy-downs or subsidies.

Cy.: see *currency.*

cycle: the grouping of cardholder accounts to provide for a distribution of work load and easier account identification. [105]

cycle mailing: the practice adopted by a number of banks of dividing the depositors' accounts into groups termed "mailing cycles," and the mailing of the statements at stipulated intervals during the month. Proponents of this practice claim that it decreases the cost and confusion experienced when all statements for all depositors are mailed at the same time (usually at the end of the month). [10]

cycle period: a specific period of time during which both debit and credit transactions are accumulated for billing. [105]

cycle posting: the practice of dividing accounts to be posted into groups termed "cycles" and posting these accounts at stipulated intervals during the month. [10]

D:
(1) see *dollar.*
(2) checkable deposits of depository institutions. [81]

DA:
(1) see *depletion allowance.*
(2) see *dormant account.*

D/A: see *documents against acceptance.*

DAC: see *Development Assistance Committee.*

dace: slang, 2 cents.

D/A drafts: documents on acceptance. Time drafts (trade acceptances) payable at some time in the future. [105]

daily balancing: procedure by which all monetary transactions received within a given 24-hour period are balanced. [105]

daily interest account: a savings account that pays interest daily from the date of deposit to the date of withdrawal. [59]

daily reports: skeleton copies of insurance policies prepared for the agent and the bank, consisting of the declarations page and fill-in endorsements.

daily reserve calculation: a daily calculation to determine the "reserves" necessary to meet the "lawful reserve" requirements. See *lawful reserve.* [10]

daily statement: a daily transcript of the balances shown on the accounts in the bank's general ledger. [31]

daily transaction tape: in fully automated demand deposit accounting, the magnetic tape record of each day's debits and credits to all accounts, usually in account number sequence. [105]

Daily Treasury Statement: a listing of transactions that clear through the U.S. Treasurer's account. For each business day it reflects cash deposits, cash withdrawals, and the status of the Treasurer's account.

dalasi: monetary unit of Gambia.

damages:
(1) loss sustained to a person or his or her property.

(2) loss in value to remaining property when a portion of one's property is expropriated.

(3) money awarded by the court to the plaintiff to be paid by the defendant, as compensation for the plaintiff's loss.

Dansk Eksportfinansierungsfond (DEFC): Danish Export Credit Finance Corporation set up in 1975 by the Danish Central Bank and the commercial banking sector. It normally lends for 2 to 5 years at a preferential rate, but may lend for longer, especially to developing countries. [145]

date: the point in time, fixed by the year, month, and day, when an occurrence takes place. See also *effective date.*

date of acceptance: the date when a time draft is accepted, or honored.

date of draft: the date when a draft is drawn.

date of maturity: the date on which a debt must be paid. Usually applied to those debts evidenced by a written agreement, such as a note, bond, and so on.

date of payment of dividends: the date when declared dividends are to be paid.

date of the note: the date of issue.

date of trade: the day when an order to buy or sell is executed.

dating: a technique of extending credit beyond the time it was originally given. Often used as an inducement to dealers to place orders far in advance of the coming season.

day book: a record book in which all financial transactions are noted without regard to debit or credit. Later the journal entries are made from the day book. Sales checks,

petty cash slips, and other devices have largely replaced the day book.

daylight exposure: the total open position allowed to a bank's foreign exchange department during a business day.

daylight overdraft: occurs when a bank overdraws its reserve account during the day even if the account is replenished by the end of the day; a practice frowned upon by the Federal Reserve Board.

daylight overdrafts: loans that banks make to customers during the business day with the expectation they will be repaid by 5 P.M.

day points: used in connection with transit work and the general ledger in a bank. The term is applied to the number of days required to send transit letters to distant points geographically by the best means of transportation. Because of the adequacy of transportation today, banks average their availability for collection of transit items into one day, two days, and three days. When transit letters are sent out, the bank knows the number of days it will take to collect the items. On the day that collection should be accomplished, the totals of all transit letters scheduled for credit that day are transferred from a deferred account to the available asset account "due from banks." See also *due from banks.* [10]

days of grace: the reasonable length of time allowed, without suffering a loss or penalty, for postponed payment or for the presentment for payment of certain financial documents. See *grace period.*

day-to-day loans: synonymous with *call loan.*

day-to-day money: synonymous with *call money.*

day trust: see *passive trust.*

DD:

(1) see *demand draft.*

(2) see *due date.*

DDP: see *direct deposit of payroll.*

dead hand: used to indicate the continuing hold of a settlor or a testator, who has been dead for many years, upon living individuals or organizations that are confronted with conditions which the settlor or the testator could not have foreseen. [37]

dead pledge: an expression for a mortgage that is paid on time.

dead president: slang, a U.S. banknote; any piece of paper money.

dealer activities: a bank operating as a securities dealer by underwriting, trading, or selling securities. [105]

dealer financing: a dealer of commodities, such as household appliances, may make arrangements with a bank for the bank to finance the purchase of these appliances upon their sale by the dealer. The customers who purchase these items then become borrowers of the bank under "consumer credit" or "time sales" loans. The bank usually has the dealer endorse the notes of his customers as additional security for the loans, and has the dealer maintain reserves on each note with the bank as other security. These reserves are termed *dealer holdbacks* or *dealer reserves.* [10]

dealer holdbacks: see *dealer financing.*

dealer loan: see *dealer financing.*

dealer rebate: some portion of interest received by a bank on a dealer-financed loan, which is paid to the dealer for arranging the loan through the bank. [105]

dealer reserves: see *dealer financing.*

dear: costly; expensive; priced unusually high.

dear money:

(1) the presence of high interest rates. See *hard money (currency).*

(2) a situation created when loans are difficult to obtain because of the supply and demand for credit.

debase: to reduce the quality, purity, or content, or otherwise alter the accepted intrinsic value of the coinage of a realm.

debenture certificate:

(1) a document authorizing payment of money granted as a bounty to an exporter of some domestic items.

(2) a customhouse document authorizing a rebate on duties paid on imported items to be exported.

debit: any amount in dollars and cents that, when posted, will increase the balance of an asset or expense account and decrease the balance of a liability account. All asset and expense accounts normally have debit balances, and all liability, capital, and income accounts normally have credit balances. Cf. *credit.*

debit adjustment: a correction posted to a cardholder's account which is added to the balance owing. [105]

debit card: a cash machine automator and a check guarantee. A recent innovation permitting bank customers to withdraw cash at any hour from any affiliated automated teller machine in the country, and to make cashless purchases from funds on deposit without incurring revolving finance charges for credit.

debit column: the left-hand side of an account or journal column.

debit entry: an entry placed on the left-hand side of an account.

debit footing of an account: the columnar total written at the foot of the debit money column in an account.

debit in error: a paperless debit entry that has been posted to a customer's account and which he or she maintains was not properly authorized by him or her. The rules of automated clearinghouses provide that receiving banks must allow customers a specified time frame during which they may unilaterally revoke debits in error. Regulation E also spells out the corrective time requirements when this occurs. [105]

debit memo:
(1) a posting medium authorizing the debit to a specified account for a certain named amount which bears the complete description of the transaction, the date, and the signature of the party responsible for the authorization of the charge. (2) a detailed memorandum forwarded from one party or firm to another charging for some omitted charge, disallowed or improper payment, or other causes. [10]

debit party: the source of funds for a payment on the receiving bank's books. [105]

debit ticket: a bank bookkeeping memorandum or posting medium on which the transaction leading to a debit entry in a ledger account is described in detail. [50]

debit transfer: a voucher giving a bookkeeper authority to charge on account according to the instructions on the voucher. Opposite of *credit transfer*. [41]

debt: money, services, or materials owed to another person as the result of a previous agreement. See also *effective debt, funded debt, gross debt, total debt.*

debt discount: the difference between the proceeds of a loan and the face value of the note or bond, where the former is smaller. [105]

debtee: a creditor.

debt limit: a maximum amount of money that a state or local government can borrow; usually set by legislation of the state involved.

debt monetization: the process by which the national debt is used to increase currency in circulation. Essentially, this is carried out by the purchase of government bonds by the Federal Reserve System, thus releasing Federal Reserve notes into circulation. These purchases may be effected through member banks.

debtor: one who owes money to another.

debtor bank: a bank which, following check distribution in a clearinghouse, has fewer claims against other banks than the other banks have against it.

debtor nation: a country whose citizens, companies, and government owe more to foreign creditors than foreign debtors owe them.

debtor's position: that portion of the market price of property which is in excess of a prime first mortgage, or mortgagable interest; the equity holder's position. [62]

debt ratio: total debt divided by total assets.

debt service: interest payments and capital reduction on government, industrial, or other long-term bonds. See *debt service fund.*

debt service fund: a fund established to finance an account for the payment of interest and principal on all general obligation debt, serial and term, other than that payable exclusively from special assessments and revenue debt issued for and services by a governmental enterprise. [49]

debt service fund requirements: the amounts of revenue provided for a debt service fund so that all principal and interest payments can be made on schedule. [49]

debt-service ratio: payments made by a country to foreign debt as a percentage of the country's export earnings. [105]

debt service requirement: the amount of money required to pay the interest on outstanding debt, serial maturities of principal for serial bonds, and required contributions to a debt service fund for term bonds. [49]

debts written-off: see *credit losses.*

debt-to-net worth ratio: all liabilities divided by net value.

decal: emblem placed on merchant windows and doors to identify affiliation with a credit card plan. [105]

deceased account: a bank deposit account in the name of a deceased person. Upon notification of death, the bank segregates the decedent's account and withholds release of funds until a court of law authorizes payment to the legal heirs. See *frozen account.*

decedent estate account: a savings account held in the name of a deceased person. [59]

declaration:
(1) the full disclosure of items, property, or income, as with a customs declaration.
(2) a statement by an applicant for insurance, usually relative to underwriting information. Sometimes, this is copied into the policy.
(3) the first pleading in an action.

declaration of condominium ownership: a complex legal document with appropriate addenda which provides for qualifying a multiunit property for condominium development and sale in accordance with a local state's condominium act (law). [59]

declaration of trust: a written agreement that property to which one person holds title actually belongs to another person, for whose benefit the title is maintained. See *fiduciary, trust.*

declaratory judgment: a court's determination on a question of law, stating the parties' rights without ordering any action.

decree: the judge's conclusion in a suit in equity (e.g., an order that an agreement be put into effect immediately).

deduction: taking away, as from a sum or amount. Discount, rebate, method of reasoning. [61]

deed: a formal, written agreement of transfer, by which title to an estate or other real property is transmitted from one person to another. See *deed, quitclaim.*

deed, bond for: an executory contract for the sale of land, with title remaining with the grantor until the purchase price is paid; ordinarily binding on both parties. [6]

deed, committee: a deed employed when the property of a child or a person declared incompetent is conveyed. A court-approved committee is obtained before the transfer. See *deed, guardian.*

deed, executor's: a deed by a person named by the decedent in his will to manage and settle his estate. [6]

deed, general warranty: a deed stating that a grantor is giving the grantee good title, free of debt. The most secure of deeds, it guarantees that the grantor will defend the title against any claims. It is a deed in full covenant. See *perfect title.*

deed, guardian: a deed to convey the property of an infant or incompetent. See *deed.*

deed, mortgaged: a deed by way of mortgage which has the effect of a mortgage on the property conveyed and imposes a lien on the granted estate. [6]

deed, quitclaim: a document by which one's legal right to, title to, interest in, or claim to a specific property, or an estate held by oneself, or others, is forever relinquished to another; usually contains no warranty or statement against the claims that others might have in the property.

deed, special warranty: a deed in which the grantor defends property title against demands made by grantees, heirs, and other claimants. No other liability is assumed by the grantor. Trustees often use this deed when transferring title, and following a court decision, to convey tax titles.

deed, trust: a deed that establishes a trust. Generally, it conveys legal title to property to a trustee and states his authority and the conditions binding upon him in dealing with the property held in trust. Frequently, trust deeds are used to secure lenders against loss. In this respect, they are similar to mortgages. [62]

deed, trustee: a deed by a party who holds property in trust. [6]

deed absolute: synonymous with *deed given to secure a debt.*

deed description: a recitation of the legal boundaries of a parcel of land as contained in a deed of conveyance. [6]

deed given to secure a debt: a form of mortgage in which title to the property is handed over to the lender by the borrower as security for the repayment of a debt. Synonymous with *deed absolute.* [59]

deed in lieu of foreclosure: a mortgagor's way of presenting title to the mortgagee to prevent foreclosure of property.

deed of release: a deed that releases property from the lien of a mortgage.

deed of surrender: an instrument by which property is identified as an estate for life or an estate for years to a person who will receive it in reversion.

deed of trust: a deed that is placed in trust with a third party to ensure payment of the indebtedness or to assure that other conditions of the transaction are met. Upon satisfaction of the debt, the third party transmits the deed to the purchaser, freeing the third party from future responsibilities.

deed restrictions: provisions inserted in a deed limiting the use of the property conveyed by the deed. [44]

deemed transferor: the parent of the transferee of property who is more closely related to the grantor of the trust than the other parent of such transferee. Where neither parent is related to the grantor, the deemed transferor is the parent who has a "closer affinity to the grantor." [105]

defaced coins: coins that have been mutilated in some manner. [10]

default risk:
(1) the risk that the firm will not make specified contractual payments at the specified times.
(2) the possibility that interest or principal might not be paid on time and in the amount promised.
(3) the risk that the issuer of a bond will not meet promised payments.

DEFC: see *Dansk Eksportfinan-sierungsfond.*

defeasance: a clause that provides that performance of certain specified acts will render an instrument or contract void. [62]

defease: see *defeasance.*

defeasible: able to be annulled or made void.

defer: to delay payment to a future time. [78]

deferment charge: an additional charge on a precomputed loan which results in extending all fully unpaid installments one or more months and thus deferring the formal final interest maturity date. (This is similar to collecting interest only on a simple interest account for one month.) [55]

deferment short: the amount by which a payment is insufficient to pay the deferment charges being assessed on an account. [55]

deferred availability cash items: checks received for collection for which credit has not yet been given. The Reserve Banks credit the banks sending in the checks according to a time schedule based on the normal time required to collect payment on the checks. [40]

deferred credit: a credit that has been delayed in posting for a reason. A deferred credit may be a deposit that came into a bank after business hours and is therefore entered on the books the next business day.

deferred debits: accounts carried on the asset side of the balance sheet in which are recorded items being amortized as charges against income over a period of years (such as debit discount and expense) and items held in suspense pending final transfer or disposition (such as extraordinary property losses, clearing accounts (net), retirement or other work in progress, etc.). [3]

deferred expense: an asset that has been created through the payment of cash by an entity before the time it will obtain benefits from that payment. Basically synonymous with *prepaid expense.*

deferred interest:
(1) the delay in paying interest.
(2) the postponement in crediting out-of-town checks deposited by people holding interest-bearing balances for interest purposes until the required days pass to collect them.

deferred payments:
(1) mortgage allowances for postponement of interest payments. A type of installment plan.
(2) delayed payments postponed until a future time; usually against some future period.

deferred posting: the posting of items in the bookkeeping department on a delayed basis. All items received during one day's business are intersorted and posted on the next business day, as of the date received. [31]

deferred special assessments: special assessments that have been levied but are not yet due. [49]

deferring: in accounting, relieving the expense and/or income accounts of those portions of expenditures and receipts which are not yet actual expense or income, and diverting them to future accounting periods.

deficiency guarantee: a guarantee given to a lender, limited in amount to the deficiency suffered by the lender on realization of an asset in the event of the borrower's default.

deficiency judgment: a court order authorizing collection from a debtor of any part of a debt that remains unsatisfied after foreclosure and sale of collateral. [44]

deficit:
(1) the excess of liabilities over assets; the excess of obligations and expenditures affecting a given budget period which is in excess of the budget established for the period.
(2) indicating obligations or expenditures for items that are in excess of the amount allotted for those items in a financial budget.

deflation:
(1) a decline in the general price level, resulting in an increase in the purchasing power of money.
(2) the lessening of the amount of money in circulation.

deflator: a statistical device or divisor that removes the influence of some increase such as the changing value of currency.

defraud: to deprive an individual, by deceit, of some right; to cheat; to withhold improperly that which belongs to another.

defray: to pay; to carry an expense; for example, a court settlement may include an amount of money to defray the legal costs of the winning party.

Delaware Banking Law of 1981: a comprehensive Delaware law aimed at out-of-state banks that would grant them a wide range of credit powers, unavailable in most states. These powers include the ability to charge interest rates not subject to any legal ceiling, to raise interest rates retroactively, to charge variable interest rates, to levy unlimited fees for credit card usage and to foreclose on a home in the event of default for credit card debts. The law also includes a provision that would lower taxes. It would allow, for example, New York banks that relocate in Delaware and earn more than $30 million a year to be taxed at a rate of 2.7 percent, compared with 8.7 percent for those Delaware banks earning under $20 million and a rate of 25.8 percent for banks that remain in New York.

delegated authority: the authority of a commercial bank to commit Eximbank's guarantee for specified amounts and under certain conditions without prior approval from Eximbank. Delegated authority is available in the working capital guarantee program and the medium-term bank guarantee program and is conferred only through a separate delegated authority letter of agreement with Eximbank. [198]

delinquency: failure to pay a debt when due.

delinquency percentage: the percentage of either dollar amount or number of accounts that are past due;

calculated for dollar amount by dividing dollars delinquent by total dollars outstanding; calculated for number of accounts by dividing the number of accounts delinquent by the total number of active accounts. [105]

delinquency ratio: ratio of past due loans to total loans serviced. [105]

delinquent account: a cardholder account on which a payment or payments have not been made in accordance with the terms and conditions of the cardholder agreement. [105]

delinquent account receivable: a debt remaining unpaid after the due date. [43]

delinquent special assessments: special assessments remaining unpaid on and after the date on which a penalty for nonpayment is attached. [49]

delivery: the transfer of the possession of an item from one person to another.

Dem.: see *demand*.

demand:
(1) the willingness and capability to purchase goods or services.
(2) a request to call for payment, or for the carrying out of an obligation. See *sight draft*.
(3) a claim, or the assertion of a legal right.

demand deposit: a deposit on account in a commercial bank on which checks can be drawn and funds taken out without any advance notification. Demand deposits are the greatest part of our money supply.

demand deposit (adjusted): the total of customers' deposits in reporting member banks subject to immediate withdrawal (checking accounts), excluding interbank deposits and deposits of the U.S. government, less checks in the process of collection. [40]

demand deposits due from banks in the U.S.: balances that can be withdrawn without notice, including cash items in the process of collection which appear on a reporting bank's books as being owed to it by other depository institutions, including savings banks, U.S. branches and agencies of foreign banks, New York State Article XII investment companies, Edge Act and Agreement corporations, and U.S.-chartered foreign-owned banks, in the U.S., Puerto Rico, and U.S. dependencies and insular possessions. [203]

demand draft: a draft payable immediately upon sight or presentation to the drawee. Synonymous with *sight draft*. See *draft*. [31]

demand line of credit: the line of credit with a bank permitting a client to borrow on demand.

demand loan: a loan that has no fixed maturity date but is payable on demand of the bank making the loan. Demand loans can be "called" by a bank at any time payment is desired.

demand mortgage: a mortgage that may be called for payment on demand. [44]

demand note: a note or mortgage that can be demanded at any time for payment by the holder.

demand-pull inflation: an increase in the price level created by an abundance of money pursuing too few commodities. The demand for items is greater than the capability to produce or supply them.

demand rate: synonymous with *check rate*.

demand secured loan: a demand loan for which collateral is held as security by the lender. The value of the collateral must be at least equal to that of the loan. [105]

demand sterling: used in London and other English banks; sight bills of exchange drawn in pounds.

demonization (demonetization):
(1) the reduction in the number of government bonds and securities by a commercial bank, resulting in an increase in the value of deposit and paper currency, including federal reserve notes.
(2) the withdrawal of specified currency from circulation.

demonetarize: see *demonization.* [2]

demonstrative gift: a gift, by will, or a specified sum of money to be paid from a designated fund or asset; as a gift of $1,000 from a specified bank account. [37]

denial letter: FmHA's notice to a bank that it cannot guarantee a loan under the proposed conditions. [105]

denomination value: the face value of all currencies, coins, and securities.

de novo: slang, new banks.

Dep.:
(1) see *deposit.*
(2) see *depositary.*

Department of the Treasury, U.S.: a federal agency created in 1789 to impose and collect taxes and customs duties, to enforce revenue and fiscal laws, to disburse federal funds; to manage the public debt, and to coin and print money.

deployment: the distribution and placement of financial service terminals providing convenience to customers. This may occur in traditional market areas or new market areas. [105]

depo: short for *deposit.*

deposit: an amount of funds consisting of cash and/or checks, drafts, coupons, and other cash items that may be converted into cash upon collection. The deposit is given to a bank for the purpose of establishing and maintaining a credit balance.

deposit analysis: a process by which account deposits are analyzed to determine that portion of the deposit which must be considered float and cannot be immediately credited to an account. [105]

depositary: an individual or institution identified as one to be entrusted with something of value for safekeeping (e.g., a bank or trust company).

deposit banking: the activity of a commercial bank dealing with deposits, receiving checks on other banks, remitting on checks forwarded for the purpose of collection, and paying out deposits by check.

deposit book: a passbook of a customer of the bank showing the amounts of deposits made.

deposit ceiling rates of interest: maximum interest rates that can be paid on savings and time deposits at federally insured banks, savings and loan associations, and credit unions. Ceilings are established by the Federal Reserve Board, the Federal Deposit Insurance Corporation, the Federal Home Loan Bank Board, and the National Credit Union Administration. [1]

deposit correction slip: a form used to notify a depositor of an error made by the depositor. When the error is located, the bank makes

out a deposit correction slip showing what the error was and the corrected new balance of the deposit.
The depositor can then correct his
or her records accordingly. [10]

deposit creation multiplier: the dollars of lending generated by an independent increase of one dollar
in bank deposits.

deposit currency: checks and other
credit items deposited with a bank
as the equivalent of cash. Synonymous with *checkbook money.*

deposit date: the date on which paper is received by a bank from a
merchant. [105]

deposit envelope: an envelope used by
merchants to transport sales drafts
and credit vouchers to banks for
credit to their deposit accounts.
[105]

deposit function: the business of
receiving money on deposit for
safekeeping and convenience. This
function includes the receiving of
demand deposits subject to check
and the receiving of savings (time)
deposits at interest. [31]

deposit funds: funds established to
account for collection that either
are held in suspense temporarily
and later refunded or are paid into
some other fund of the government or held by the government
as banker or agent for others. Cf.
escrow.

deposit insurance: insurance to protect the depositor against bankruptcy of a bank or savings and loan
institution (see, e.g., *Federal Deposit Insurance Corporation*).

deposit interest rate: limits set by
the Federal Reserve System and
Federal Deposit Insurance Corporation on interest rates that commercial banks can declare on time

deposits. The bank is prohibited
from paying any interest rates on
demand deposits.

deposit liability: a bank's total liability to customers shown by all demand deposits, time deposits, certificates of deposit and so on.

deposit line: the approximate average
amount that a bank's customer usually maintains in a bank account.

deposit loan: loans that are made by
the banker crediting the borrower's
account with a "loan deposit" for
the sum of the loan. This is different from giving the borrower currency when granting a loan.

depositor: an individual, partnership,
business proprietorship, corporation, organization, or association
is termed a depositor when funds
have been placed in bank in the
name of the person or entity.

depository: a bank in which funds or
securities are deposited by others,
usually under the terms of a specific depository agreement. Also,
a bank in which government funds
are deposited or in which other
banks are permitted by law to
maintain required reserves. [50]

depository agreement: see *mortgage
certificate.*

**Depository Institutions Deregula-
tion and Monetary Control Act:**
legislation passed in the spring of
1980, the act committed the
government to deregulating the
banking system. It provided for
elimination of interest-rate controls (known as Regulation Q) for
banks and savings institutions
within six years, and it authorized
them to offer interest-bearing
NOW accounts beginning in
1981 anywhere in the country.
The act also wiped out all state

usury laws on home mortgages above $25,000. It also modernized the mortgage instrument by repealing dollar limits, permitting second mortgages, and eliminating lending-territory restrictions. See *graduated-payment mortgage, pledged-account mortgage, variable-rate mortgage.*

Depository Institutions Deregulation Committee (DIDC): charged with deregulating the banks and savings industry. Created by Congress in the spring of 1980, it has a panel of five voting members: the Federal Reserve Board chairman, the Treasury secretary, and the chairmen of the Federal Home Loan Bank Board, the Federal Deposit Insurance Corporation, and the National Credit Union Administration.

In June 1981, it approved a plan to phase out interest rate ceilings on deposits at banks and savings and loan associations during the following four years.

On August 1, 1981, current ceilings on 2½ year certificates were removed. Also on that date, interest rate ceilings were eliminated for accounts maturing in four years or more at banks or thrift institutions.

On August 1, 1982, ceilings were eliminated for accounts maturing in three years or more. Interest on deposits maturing in two to three years were tied to the rate on two-year Treasury securities. Thrift institutions were allowed to pay as much as the Treasury rate, whereas commercial banks were held to 0.25 percentage point less.

On August 1, 1983, ceilings were eliminated on accounts maturing in two years or more, and the rates for deposits maturing in one to two years were tied to the one-year Treasury rate, without any differential between bank and savings and loan rates.

On August 1, 1984, ceilings were eliminated on accounts maturing in one or two years, and the rates for deposits maturing in less than a year were tied to the comparable Treasury rate without a differential between bank and savings and loan rates.

On August 1, 1985, ceilings were removed from accounts that matured in less than one year, except for passbook savings accounts. The committee did not decide what to do about the passbook accounts, although controls on them ended April 1, 1986, under a law passed by Congress in 1980.

depository receipt: short for American depository receipt. See *American depository receipt.*

depository transfer draft: a preprinted, no-signature instrument used only to move funds from one account to another account in the same name at another bank. [105]

deposit receipt: in banks where tellers' machines are now used, the machine issues a printed receipt for the deposit made. This receipt does away with the pen-and-ink entry made in the passbook used by checking account depositors. The bank furnishes a folder in which the depositor keeps his deposit receipts until he has received his bank statement. After verifying his statement for accuracy of entry of all deposits, he can destroy the receipts, since he has been properly credited by the bank as evidenced on his statement. [10]

deposits in federal reserve banks: deposit accounts held as follows: (a) *member banks*—deposits of member banks, which are largely legal required reserves; (b) *U.S. Treasurer*—general or checking accounts of the Treasury; (c) *foreign*—balances of foreign governments and central banks; and (d) *other*—other deposits, includes those of nonmember banks maintained for check-clearing purposes. [40]

deposits in transit: deposits made by a company but not yet reflected on a bank statement.

deposit slip: an itemized memorandum of the cash and other funds which a customer (depository) presents to the receiving teller for credit to his or her account. [31]

deposit-taking company (DTC): a financial institution that can take deposits, make loans, discount bills, issue letters of credit, but cannot be called a bank. The concept originated in Hong Kong.

deposit ticket: a business form onto which a depositor itemizes all items that he or she wishes to deposit in a bank.

deposit warrant: a financial document prepared by a designated accounting or finance officer authorizing the treasurer of a governmental unit to accept for deposit sums of money collected by various departments and agencies of the governmental unit. [49]

depot: short for *deposit.*

depreciable: the state of any asset that is subject to depreciation. [105]

depreciable asset: property used in business or income production whose cost a taxpayer can recover as deductions from income over the useful life of the asset.

depreciable cost: the value of a fixed asset subject to depreciation. Sometimes this is the original cost, at other times, the original cost less an estimated salvage value.

depreciate: the process of reducing the book value of a fixed asset at periodic intervals to charge a portion of the assets' cost as an expense of the period in which it provides a service.

depreciated cost: cost less accumulated depreciation and less other valuation accounts, having the effect of reducing the original outlay to a recoverable cost; the book value of a fixed asset.

depreciated currency: resulting from the lowering in the exchange value of currency, funds not accepted at face or par value.

depreciation:
(1) normally, charges against earnings to write off the cost, less salvage value, of an asset over its estimated useful life. It is a bookkeeping entry and does not represent any cash outlay, nor are any funds earmarked for the purpose.
(2) a decline in the value of property.

depreciation book: accrued depreciation shown on books of account. [6]

depreciation of money: the fall in the value of the monetary unit measured in terms of goods and services which the unit will buy compared with a base point in time. Sometimes restricted to change of the metal content of the monetary unit.

depressed market: a situation created when prices of goods or services are unusually low.

depression: an economic condition: business activity is down over a long period, prices drop, purchasing power is greatly reduced, and unemployment is high.

Depression of the 1930s: the Great Depression, a severe economic crisis that afflicted the United States and also affected worldwide business, is thought to have begun with the collapse of the stock market in October 1929 and finally ended in the early 1940s, when defense spending for World War II strengthened the general economy.

Deregulation Act: see *Depository Institutions Deregulation and Monetary Control Act.*

dereliction: the intentional abandonment of property. "Derelict property" is any property forsaken or discarded in a way indicating that the owner has no further use or need of it.

derivative deposit: a deposit that is created when a person borrows money from a bank (e.g., deposit currency). A customer is lent a sum, not in money but by credit to his or her account, against which he or she may draw checks as required.

derogatory information: data received by a credit card issuer indicating that an applicant or cardholder has not paid his or her accounts with other creditors according to the required terms. [105]

descendant: one who is descended in a direct line from another, however remotely (child, grandchild, great-grandchild). [37]

descent: the passing of property, or title to the property, by inheritance, as contrasted with request or purchase.

description: items are sometimes described on the deposit ticket, by the teller or another clerk, as to the city or bank of payment. This provides a source reference record and assists in the calculation of uncollected funds. [31]

descriptive billing: a billing system in which an account statement is not accompanied by copies of original invoices. Instead, the statement contains sufficient detail to permit the customer to identify the nature, date, and amount of each transaction processed during the statement period. Cf. *country club billing.*

descriptive statement: a bank account statement that contains one or more described entries for which no separate item is enclosed. Bill check, preauthorized payments, and direct payroll deposits necessitate some form of descriptive statement unless a substitute enclosure document is produced by the bank. [105]

desk, the: the trading desk at the New York Federal Reserve Bank, through which open market purchases and sales of government securities are made. The desk maintains direct telephone communication with major government securities dealers. A "foreign desk" at the New York Reserve Bank conducts transactions in the foreign exchange market. See also *foreign exchange desk.* [1]

desterilizing gold: the issuance by the Treasury of gold certificates to the Federal Reserve System covering gold previously bought by the Treasury but against which the Treasury had not yet issued gold certificates. Cf. *sterilizing gold.*

detailed audit: an audit in which an examination is made of the system of internal control and of the details of all transactions and books of account, including subsidiary records and supporting documents, as to legality, mathematical accuracy, complete accountability, and application of accepted accounting principles for governmental units. [49]

details of payment: see *originator to beneficiary information.*

determination date: the latest day of the month on which savings may be deposited and still earn interest from the first day of the month; set by an association's board of directors, but usually the tenth day. [59]

detinue: a common law action to recover property.

deutsche mark: West Germany's currency, replacing the old Reichsmark in 1948.

devaluation: an action taken by the government to reduce the value of the domestic currency in terms of gold or foreign monies.

Development Assistance Committee (DAC): a committee of the Organization for Economic Cooperation and Development whose function is to encourage the flow of funds from member nations to the developing countries.

Development Finance Companies (DFCs): the financing of development finance companies by the World Bank commenced in 1950 with a loan of $2 million to the Development Bank of Ethiopia. By the end of fiscal 1975, bank lending to such intermediaries had reached almost $3 billion to 68 DFCs (including three regional DFCs serving the East Africa Community, Africa, and Latin America, respectively) in 44 countries and the three regions. See also *International Bank for Reconstruction and Development.* [16]

deviation:
(1) a rate or policy form differing from that published by a rating bureau.
(2) a measure of dispersion, calculated to be the difference between the particular number or item and the average, which is usually the arithmetic mean, or set of numbers or items.

devisen: German term for *foreign exchange.*

devises: French term for *foreign exchange.*

devolution: the passing of real estate title by hereditary succession.

DFCs: see *Development Finance Companies.*

diary: a record kept of maturity dates for notes, bonds, and other instruments. See *tickler.*

DIDC: see *Depository Institutions Deregulation Committee.*

dies non: Latin, a day on which no business can be transacted.

differences account: see *over and short account.*

digitizing machine: a bank machine that reproduces the signature of a customer (which is stored on a card previously signed by the customer) at the top of each check. Thus, when a customer actually countersigns a check for a cash advance, the two signatures can be corroborated.

dime: a 10-cent coin, valued at 10 percent of a U.S. dollar.

dinar: monetary unit of Abu Dhabi, Aden, Algeria, Bahrain, Iraq, Jordan, Kuwait, Libya, South Yemen (Aden), Tunisia, and Yugoslavia.

direct debit: a method of collection used for certain claims, generally those which are repeated over a period of time, under which the debtor gives his or her bank a standing authorization to debit his or her account on sight of the direct debit issued by a creditor. [105]

direct debt: the debt that a unit has incurred in its own name or assumed.

direct deposit of payroll (DDP): a payroll system in which employee earnings are deposited directly to the employee's account at a depository institution.

direct inquiry: generally speaking, an inquiry about a person's credit standing made by one firm to another. As distinct from an inquiry to a credit bureau. [41]

direct lease financing: a form of term debt financing for fixed assets. Leases are similar to loans from a credit viewpoint because of considerations of cash flow, credit history, management, and projections of future operations. [105]

direct liability: a debtor's obligation arising from money, goods, or services received by him or her from another.

direct loan: a loan made directly to a customer for which the customer applied in person or by mail; opposed to a "sales contract," where credit is advanced to a customer through the purchase of a conditional sales contract from a merchant. [55]

direct obligation: a drawer's obligation as the instrument maker, as contrasted with the indirect obligation of an endorser of the instrument.

directors' examination: the periodic examination of banks by their directors, a committee of the directors, or CPAs or other auditors on behalf of the directors. [201]

direct payroll deposit: an electronic system which permits a corporation to pay its employee without formally preparing checks. The data processor serving the corporation generates paperless credit entries representing deposits and delivers such entries to its bank on or before each payday. The bank, through processing, extracts those paperless entries which are for its own customers and credits the employee's personal account. In turn, it sends the remainder of the entries to the local automated clearinghouse and, in so doing, becomes the originating bank for these entries. The ACH processes the entries, makes settlement between the originating and receiving banks on payday, and transmits the entries to the appropriate receiving banks. The receiving bank posts the entries on or before payday and consequently reflects such items on the customer's periodic statements. [105]

direct reduction loan: a loan repayable in consecutive equal monthly payments of interest and principal sufficient to retire the debt within a definite period. "Direct" actually means that after the monthly interest payment has been taken out of the payment, the balance of the loan payment is applied directly to the reduction of the principal of the loan. [51]

direct reduction mortgage (DRM): a direct reduction mortgage is liquidated over the life of the mortgage in equal monthly payments. Each monthly payment consists of an amount to cover interest, reduction in principal, taxes, and insurance. The interest is computed on an outstanding principal balance monthly. As the principal balance is reduced, the amount of interest becomes less, thereby providing a larger portion of the monthly payment to be applied to the reduction of principal. As taxes and insurance are paid by the mortgagee (lending association), these disbursements are added to the principal balance. This procedure follows throughout the life of the mortgage. [10]

direct sendings: items that are drawn on a particular bank, and sent directly to that drawee bank by another bank, are known as direct sendings. This is to be distinguished from a transit letter, which may be sent to a "correspondent bank" and which contains items on many drawee banks within a certain area. [10]

direct verification: a method of bank audit whereby the auditor of a bank sends a request for the verification of the balances of deposits or loans as of a stated date to the depositors or borrowers. Verifications are returned directly to the auditor, confirming the correctness of balances or listing discrepancies. [10]

dirham: monetary unit of Morocco.

dirty: a foreign exchange float where the value of the currency is controlled by the authorities rather than the market.

Dis.: see *discount.*

disagio: the charge made for exchanging depreciated foreign monies. Cf. *agio.*

disaster clause: a Eurocredit loan agreement clause containing provisions for repayment of the loan if the Euromarket should disappear. Cf. *break.* [87]

Disb.: see *disbursement.*

disburse: to pay out money; to expend. [61]

disbursement: an actual payment of funds toward the full or partial settlement of an obligation.

disbursement schedule: a list or tabular statement of the amounts to be disbursed on specific dates in accordance with agreements entered into in a mortgage loan transaction. [44]

disbursement voucher: an order for making payments.

DISC: see *Domestic International Sales Corporation.*

discharge: the release of one party from meeting his or her obligation under a contract because parties other to the contract have failed to meet their obligation(s).

discharge of bankruptcy: an order that terminates bankruptcy proceedings, usually relieving the debtor of all legal responsibility for certain specified obligations. [76]

discharge of contract: the fulfillment of a contract's obligations.

discharge of lien: the recorded release of a lien when debt has been repaid. [78]

disclaimer: a document, or a clause in a document, that renounces or repudiates the liability of an otherwise responsible party in the event of (a) noncompliance by such other party to certain conditions described in the instrument, (b) named external conditions, or (c) losses incurred because of a discrepancy in the goods delivered and the weight or count made by the shipper.

discount:

(1) *finance:* the amount of money deducted from the face value of a note.

(2) *foreign exchange:* the relationship of one currency to another. For example, Canadian currency may be at a discount to U.S. currency.

discount charge: a finance charge deducted in advance. [78]

discount check: as determined by the New York Fed, the difference between the purchase price and the face value of a bill purchased from a Federal Reserve Bank.

discount clerk: a bank's representative working in the discount unit. Duties traditionally include the calculations of notes, acceptances and the maintenance of records of bills discounted.

discount corporation: any banking institution involved in the buying and discounting of trade and bankers' acceptance, commercial papers, bills of exchange, and so on.

discounted value: the present value of future payments due or receivable, computed on the basis of a given rate of interest. [12]

discounting: occurs when an institution lends money to a business with a customer's debt obligation to the firm as security on the loan.

discounting a note receivable: selling a note receivable to a bank or to someone else.

discount loan: a loan on which the interest and/or charges are deducted from the "face amount" of the loan at the time it is made. [55]

discount market: differing from the bank's discounts for its own clients, the open market for commercial papers and acceptances. This market deals with banks of the Federal Reserve System, other banks, discount and commercial-paper houses, dealers of notes, and so on.

discount on purchases: a cash discount taken by a buyer.

discount on sales: a cash discount granted by a seller.

discount rate: the Federal Reserve Bank's interest rate charged to member banks for loans. In most cases, higher interest rates lead to the lowering of security prices. See *easy money, prime interest (rate), tight money.*

discount register: a bank's book of original entry, in which a daily record is kept of all loan department transactions, such as loans made, payments received, and interest collected. [105]

discounts and advances: outstanding loans of the Federal Reserve Banks, primarily to member banks. [40]

discount tables: see *tables, discount.*

discount window: in 1980 a law was passed giving the Federal Reserve Board smoother control over the economy, requiring all banks and savings and loan associations to keep reserves behind checking-type deposits. One of the provisions of the law gives about 15,000 other banks and savings and loan associations the right to borrow from the Federal Reserve through its so-called discount window. It is felt by some analysts that this approach would hamper the Fed's ability to regulate the growth of reserves, the base for deposit and money creation.

discount yield: the ratio of the annualized discount to the par value. [107]

discretionary fund: discretionary income enlarged by the amount of new credit extensions, which also may be deemed spendable as a result of consumer decision relatively free of prior commitment or pressure of need. [48]

discretionary trust: a trust that entitles the beneficiary to use only so much of the income or principal as the trustee in its uncontrolled discretion shall see fit to give him or her to apply for his or her use.

Disct.: see *discount.*

dishonored: describes a negotiable instrument offered for acceptance of payment that is turned down or cannot be obtained. See *notice of dishonor.*

disinflation: the result of a strategy to reduce the general price level by increasing the purchasing power of money.

disintermediation: the taking of money out of interest-bearing time accounts (e.g., savings and commercial bank accounts) for reinvestment at higher rates for bonds and so on.

disinvestment: the reduction of capital goods.

disk: a circular metal plate with magnetic material on both sides, continuously rotated for reading in a computer network.

disk pack: a set of magnetic disks designed to be placed in a computer central processing unit for reading and writing.

dismiss:
(1) *general:* to release an employee.
(2) *law:* to dispose of a case without a trial. See *nolo contendere.*

dispatch earning: a saving in shipping costs arising from rapid unloading at the point of destination.

dispositive provisions: the provisions of a will or trust agreement relating to the disposition and distribution of the property in the estate or trust; to be distinguished from administrative provisions that relate to the handling of the property while it is in the hands of the executor or trustee. [37]

dispossess: to put an individual out of his or her property by force.

disseisin: the forcible expulsion of an owner from his or her land; the loss of property possession by claiming ownership. See *ejectment.*

dissent: the act of disagreeing. Thus, a widow's refusal to take the share provided for her in her husband's will and assertion of her rights under the law is known as her dissent from the will. See *dower.* [32]

Dist.: see *discount.*

distrain: to seize another's property as security for an obligation.

distress for rent: the taking of a tenant's personal property in payment of rent on real estate. See *general lien, landlord's warrant.*

distributable net income (DNI): all income generated by a trust, less all deductible expenses paid by a trust, whether charged against principal or income. [105]

distributes: a person to whom something is distributed; frequently applied to the recipient of personal property under intestacy; to be distinguished from "heir"—a person who inherits real property. [32]

distributing syndicate: investment bankers, brokerage houses, and so on, who form a joint venture to sell an issue of securities. See *distribution.*

distribution:

(1) the dividing up of something among several people or entities; the process of allocating income and expenses to the appropriate subsidiary accounts.

(2) the division of aggregate income of a community among its members.

(3) the apportionment by a court of the personal property of a deceased person among those entitled to receive the property according to the applicable statute of distribution.

distribution in kind: the distribution of the assets of an estate in their original form and not the cash value of the property. Stocks and bonds are generally distributed among those entitled to receive them instead of being converted into cash for the purpose of effecting distribution. [37]

distribution of certificate account maturities: legislation of 1978; Federal Home Loan Bank System members may not accept certificate deposits that would cause the aggregate amount of certificates maturing in any consecutive three-month period to exceed 30 percent of an association's savings ($100,000 certificates excepted). [51]

distributive share: the share of a person in the distribution of an estate. [37]

divergence indicator: an indicator purporting to measure which member currency of the European Monetary System diverges from its central parity against the European Currency Unit. [96]

dividend check: a negotiable instrument in the form of a check drawn on a depository bank of the corporation issuing the dividend. It is signed by the secretary of the corporation.

dividend reinvestment plans: a service in which the bank, as agent, automatically reinvests the customer's dividends in a security. [25]

division of labor: breaking a bank's job down into the smallest number of operations without jeopardizing performance.

Dix: slang, a $10 bill.

D&J: December and June (semiannual interest payments or dividends).

DL: see *demand loan.*

DM: see *deutsche mark.*

DMJS: December, March, June, September (quarterly interest payments or dividends).

DNI: see *distributable net income.*

dobra: monetary unit of San Tóme and Principe.

doctrine of asset shiftability: banks need not seek supplementary liquidity in its loan portfolio, as this liquidity is available through the shifting of nonloan assets (secondary reserves) to the open market. [105]

document:

(1) a form, voucher, or written evidence of a transaction.

(2) to instruct, as by citation of references.

(3) to substantiate, as by listing of authorities. [105]

documentary credit: when a bank, in behalf of its customer makes payment to (or to the order of) a third party (a beneficiary) or is to pay/accept/negotiate bills of exchange drawn by the beneficiary; or authorizes such payments to be made, or such drafts to be paid/accepted/ negotiated by another bank.

documented discount notes: commercial paper backed by a letter of credit from a bank stating that it will pay off the paper at maturity if the borrower does not. Such paper is often also referred to as LoC **(letter of credit)** paper. [129]

documents against acceptance: referring to domestic or foreign bills of exchange, notice that supporting statements will not be given to the drawee until acceptance of the bill.

documents against payment: referring to domestic or foreign bills of exchange, notice that supporting statements will not be given to the drawee until payment of the bill.

DOG: see *days of grace.*

dog: slang, a promissory note.

Dol.: see *dollar.*

dollar:

(1) monetary unit of the United States. Also the currency for Guam, the Marshall Islands, Puerto Rico, the Ryukyu Islands, Solomon Islands, and the Virgin Islands (U.S.).

(2) monetary unit of other nations, including Antigua, Australia, Bahamas, Barbados, Belize, British Honduras, Brunei, Canada, Dominica, Fiji, Grenada, Guiana, Guyana, Hong Kong, Jamaica, Kiribati, Liberia, Montserrat, Nauru, Nevis, New Guinea, New Zealand, Singapore, Somoa (British), St. Kitts, St. Lucia, St. Vincent, Taiwan, Trinidad and Tobago, Tuvalu, and Zimbabwe.

dollar acceptance: an acceptance or any bill of exchange drawn in a foreign nation or in the United States that is payable in dollars.

dollar control: guiding inventory by the amount of funds rather than by the number of physical items.

dollar credit: a letter of credit permitting drafts to be drawn in dollars.

dollar exchange: banker's acceptances and bills of exchange drawn overseas that are paid in the United States or around the world in dollars, or conversely drawn in the United States and paid overseas in dollars.

dollarize: to bring a foreign nation or its economy under the monetary power of the United States as through conversion into U.S. dollars or investment in the United States.

dollar-month computation: a method of computing earnings on savings accounts based on the premise that every dollar held in a savings account for one full year will earn the number of cents equivalent to the earnings rate. [59]

dollar shortage: a nation's lack of sufficient money to buy from the United States, caused by a steady favorable balance of payments for the United States.

dollar stabilization:

(1) acts by monetary authorities (i.e., the Federal Reserve Board, International Monetary Fund) to reduce the fluctuation of the international exchange value of the dollar.

(2) an idea of economist Irving Fischer that would result in a compensated dollar tied to commodities rather than gold.

domestic acceptance: any acceptance where the drawee and drawer are situated in the United States and consequently paid in this country.

domestic bill: any of several documents (i.e., sight or time drafts) drawn and payable within the same state.

domestic exchange: any check, draft, or acceptance drawn in one location and paid in another within the United States. Synonymous with *inland exchange;* cf. *foreign exchange.*

domiciliary administration: the settlement of the portion of a decendent's estate which is located in the state of his domicile; to be distinguished from "ancillary administration," which relates to property elsewhere than in the state of the decendent's domicile. [37]

domiciliary trustee: the trustee of that portion of a decendent's or settlor's property which is located in the state of his domicile; to be distinguished from "ancillary trustee," who administers property elsewhere than in the state of the decendent's or settlor's domicile. [37]

dominion: in transferring property from one to another, the separation by the transferor from all power over the property and passing such power to the transferee.

donative interest: an interest in property that is subject to gift. [37]

donee: one who receives a gift.

dong: monetary unit of Viet Nam.

donor: one who makes a gift.

donor (trust): a living person who creates a "voluntary trust." [10]

dormant account: an account that has had little or no activity for a period of time.

DOT:
(1) see *date of trade.*
(2) see *Department of the Treasury, U.S.*

double charge: a single purchase in which the cardholder was charged twice. [105]

double counting (entry): in bookkeeping, since every transaction is entered two times, counting the same quantity twice when evolving a total; procedure used in determining the gross national product.

double-declining-balance method of depreciation: spreading the initial cost of a capital asset over time by deducting in each period double the percentage recognized by the straight-line method and applying that double percentage to the undepreciated balance existing at the start of each period. No salvage value is used in the calculation.

double eagle: a U.S. $20 gold piece.

double financing: fraudulent action on the part of a dealer who submits a credit application and receives a loan for the same customer from two different banks. [105]

double liability: the liability of the stockholders of banks before banking legislation of the 1930s brought about the elimination of this feature for all national banks and most state banks. Under the double liability provision, the stockholders of a bank, in the event of its liquidation, were held legally responsible for an amount equal to the par value of their stock in addition to the amount of their original investment. [39]

double posting: the posting of a debit amount or a credit amount to two accounts.

double sawbuck: a $20 bill.

double standard: see *bimetallism.*

dough: slang, money or cash.

Douglas amendment: amendment to the Bank Holding Company Act of

1956 that prohibits bank holding companies from acquiring out-of-state banks unless laws of the host state specifically permit such entry. See *Bank Holding Company Act of 1956.*

dower: a right for life by a married woman in a portion of the land owned by her husband, which becomes vested upon his death. In some states, a wife owns one-third of her deceased husband's real estate. See *tenant in dower;* cf. *curtesy.*

down payment: money deposited as evidence of good faith for purchasing property upon contract signing.

downstream borrowing: the borrowing of money by a corporation through the use of the credit standing of its subsidiaries.

D/P: see *documents against payment.*

DR:
(1) see *daily reports.*
(2) see *discount rate.*

drachma: monetary unit of Greece.

draft: an order in writing signed by one party (the drawer) requesting a second party (the drawee) to make payment in lawful money at a determinable future time to a third party (the payee).

draft envelope: a wrapper used by merchants to transmit sales drafts and credit slips to the bank for credit to their deposit accounts. [105]

draft number: the sequential number printed on formsets. [105]

draw-down: drawing funds made available under a Eurocredit.

draw-down request: an instruction to reduce the balance of the sender's account with the receiver by a payment to the sender's account at another financial institution. [105]

drawee: any party expected to pay the sum listed on a check, draft, or bill of exchange.

drawee bank: the bank upon which a check is drawn. [7]

drawer: any party who draws a check, draft, or bill of exchange for the payment of funds.

drive-in banking: because of traffic congestion and lack of parking space, many banks now have tellers' windows facing the outside of the building, or separate outside booths, for the convenience of depositors. The bank customer drives up to a teller's window.

DRM: see *direct reduction mortgage.*

dry run: another name used by banks for the machine pay plan of journalizing the posting media before posting to the statement. See also *machine pay.* [10]

dry trust: see *passive trust.*

DTC: see *deposit-taking company.*

dual banking: some banks are chartered by the state in which they operate and others by the federal government. This allows for dual banking, where each independent component cooperates with the other to offer its clientele complete banking services.

dual billing and posting: posting a customer's purchases to ledger, as independent from the preparation of a bill for the customer.

dual currency account: an account kept by a bank with a bank in a foreign country in the foreign currency. [105]

dual dating: a practice of embossing two dates on the face of credit cards, the first date being the effective date and the second being the expiration date. [105]

dual exchange market: exists when the authorities operate two exchange markets, prescribing the use of one market for exchange transactions relating to specified types of underlying transactions and the use of the other permitted dealing in foreign exchange.

duality: effective in 1977, the ability of a single bank to be a card-issuing member of more than one credit card.

dual posting: see *double counting (entry)*.

dual savings plan: a plan whereby two separate operations are required to post a savings deposit or a withdrawal to an account.

dual system of banking: banks may choose to operate under either a federal or state charter. Regulations and requirements vary, depending on whether a bank is regulated by a state or the federal government. Regulations also vary among states. [33]

Du. Dat.: see *due date.*

due-bill-check: a due bill in the form of a check payable on the date of payment of a cash dividend, which prior to such date is considered a due bill for the amount of the dividend.

due date: the date on which on instrument of debt becomes payable; the maturity date.

due from: specifies an obligation owed to you. [105]

due from account: title given to bank asset accounts that represents its funds on deposit with a corresponding bank. [105]

due from balance: British term for *nostro account.*

due from banks: title of an asset account in the general ledger. Subsidiary accounts under this title include each account of funds that a bank has on deposit with other banks. Legal reserve funds and funds placed on deposit with correspondent banks are among these accounts. [31]

due from banks, collections: any contingent asset account within the bank's financial ledger showing the aggregate balances that are due from other banks.

due from Federal Reserve Bank: any asset account listed in a financial ledger of a member or clearing member bank showing the balance due from a Federal Reserve Bank. The figure shows the approximate cash reserve, as required by law, that is held with the Federal Reserve Bank.

due from Foreign Exchange Department: an asset account in the bank's financial statement showing the total funds within a foreign department for purposes of investment in foreign exchange activities.

due-on-sale: a clause in a conventional home mortgage stating that the balance of the existing mortgage must be paid to the lending bank when the home is sold by the owner.

due process of law: all actions of a court taken to ensure the rights of private individuals before the law; all legal steps to protect these rights. A court order to compel compliance with its wishes (e.g., a summons, issued to compel attendance in court).

due to: specifies an obligation owed by you. [105]

due to balance: British term for *vostro account.*

due to banks: the title of a liability account in the general ledger.

Includes subsidiary accounts of funds that one bank has on deposit with another bank. [31]

due to fiscal agent: amounts due to fiscal agents, such as commercial banks, for servicing a unit's maturing interest and principal payments on indebtedness. [49]

dun: to press for payment of a debt; to demand repeatedly what one is owed.

durability:
(1) the lasting quality of an item.
(2) money that can be used over an extended period or can be replaced at minimal cost.

duty card: synonymous with *tickler.*

EA: see *Edge Act.*

eagle: a U.S. $10 gold coin, first coined in 1795. The Treasury demanded the surrender of all gold coins in 1933.

earmarked gold: a treasury or stabilization fund; quantities of gold found in the fiduciary reserves of one nation's central bank for another nation's central bank.

earnest money: money given by a contracting party to another at the time of the signing of a contract to "bind the bargain"; this sum is forfeited by the donor if he or she fails to carry out the contract.

earning assets: loans and investments that together are the assets responsible for most of the bank's earnings. [67]

earnings assets: the loans and investments that, together, represent the source of most bank revenue. [105]

earnings credit: an offset to service charges on checking accounts, calculated on the basis of the average balance held in the account during the specified period. [105]

earnings statement: an analysis or presentation of the earnings of an enterprise in statement form. An income statement form is an earnings statement. [105]

easement right: see *access right.*

easy money: money that can be obtained at low interest rates and with relative ease as the result of sufficient supply of a bank's excess reserves.

EBIT: earnings before interest and taxes.

EC: see *European Community.*

Economic Recovery Tax Act of 1981 (ERTA): federal legislation, signed by President Reagan in August, 1981; includes the following provisions.

Tax rate cuts: (1981) credit of 1 1/4 percent against individual tax bills and 5 percent withholding rate reduction on October 1; (July 1982) tax rate reduction of 10 percent, followed by another in July 1983. By 1984, the top rate on $50,000 in earned income dropped from 49 percent to 38 percent; (1985) cost-of-living wage and salary increased offset by widening tax brackets, raising "zero bracket" at low end, boosting personal exemptions.

Unearned income and capital gains: (June 9, 1981) the maximum tax on capital gains realized a drop from 28 percent (gain after 60 percent exclusion taxed at 70 percent) to 20 percent (gain after 60 percent exclusion taxed at 50 percent). Minimum holding period for long-term capital gain remains 12 months. (1982) Top rate on dividends, interest, rents, and royalties dropped from 70 to 50 percent, equal to maximum tax on salary income.

Marriage tax offset: (1982) if both spouses work, a 5 percent deduction from the salary of the lower-paid partner, up to $1500; (1983) a 10 percent deduction, up to $3000.

Pension deductions: (1982) tax deductions for contributions to Individual Retirement Accounts raised to $2000 and the 15 percent limitation canceled. The IRA provision is extended to employees already covered by pensions. Voluntary thrift plans as well as separate IRA accounts qualify.

Interest deductions: (1981-1982) exempt interest income up to $1000 ($2000 joint return) on special "All-Savers" savings certificates was offered for one year only. A deduction of $750 ($1500 joint return) of public utility stock dividends was allowed if paid into a reinvestment plan; (1985) exclusion of 15 percent of savings interest, less interest paid on consumer (but not on mortgage) loans.

Estate and gift tax reductions: (1982-1986) progressive exclusion from taxation of the first $250,000 of estate up to the first $600,000 of estate; (1982) unlimited deduction for estate and gift transfers to a spouse; (1982) annual gifts excluded from taxation raised from $3000 to $10,000.

Stock option treatment: (1981) no tax at exercise on $100,000 per year in stock. Capital gains treatment on gain over option price at sale.

Depreciation and investment tax credits: (1981) accelerated depreciation rules and expanded tax credits for certain classes of real estate investment should shelter more income for investors. See also *All-Savers certificates, Tax Reform Act of 1984.*

economic rent: the estimated income a property should bring in the existing rental market. The economic rent can be either above or below the amount actually received. Cf. *rack rent.*

ECR:

(1) see *electronic cash register.*

(2) see *embossed character reader.*

ECU: the *European currency unit.*

Edge Act: recreated a dual banking system for foreign banks by establishing a new class of Federal charters for them. It also gives the Federal Reserve Board the right to impose reserve requirements on foreign banks. The 1978 International Banking Act restated the broad purpose of the Edge Act statute, in which Congress requires the Fed to revise any of its regulations that unnecessarily disadvantage American banks in the conduct of business. The act also allowed U.S. banks to open offices across state lines to assist in foreign trade financing. See *International Banking Act of 1978.*

edge corporation: a foreign banking organization structured in compliance with the Federal Reserve Act.

EEC: see *European Economic Community.*

effective annual yield: the return on an investment, expressed in terms of the equivalent simple interest rate. [105]

effective date:

(1) the date on which an insurance binder or policy goes into effect and from which time protection is provided.

(2) the date on which an agreement or contract goes into effect; the starting date.

effective debt: the total debt of a firm, including the major value of annual leases or other payments that are equivalent to interest charges.

effective exchange rate: any spot exchange rate actually paid or received by the public, including any taxes or subsidies on the exchange transaction as well as any applicable banking commissions. The articles of agreement envisage that all effective exchange rates shall be situated within permitted margins around par value. [42]

EFT: Electronic Funds Transfer.

EFTS: see *electronic funds transfer system.*

EI:

(1) see *exact interest.*

(2) see *ex-interest.*

EIB: see *Export-Import Bank.*

ejectment: the legal action brought to retain possession of property and to receive damage monies from the person who illegally retained it. See *right of possession, seisin;* cf. *landlord's warrant.*

ekuwele: monetary unit of Equatorial Guinea.

elastic currency: see *elasticity.*

elasticity: the ability of a bank to meet credit and currency demands during times of expansion and to reduce the availability of credit and currency during periods of over

expansion. See *Federal Reserve Notes.*

elastic money: currency or money supply that increases or decreases with the economy's needs. Elasticity is affected by decisions of monetary authorities or by making currency related to bank loans by the rediscount device.

electronic banking: banking transactions conducted via computerized systems, effecting efficiency and lower costs.

electronic cash register (ECR): a cash register in which electronic circuitry replaces electromechanical parts.

electronic funds transfer (EFT): see *electronic funds transfer system(s) (EFTS).*

Electronic Fund Transfer Act: passed by Congress in 1978, but the effective date of most of its provisions was delayed until May 10, 1980, to allow time for the federal bank regulatory agencies to develop a comprehensive set of implementing regulations. Essentially a consumer protection measure, the art requires financial institutions to disclose to new customers the terms and conditions of EFT services, including the consumer's liability for unauthorized transfers; and to describe the type and availability of EFT services offered, and the service charges. The law covers the consumer's right to receive documentation of transfers and to have errors corrected promptly; preauthorized transfer procedures; and the institution's liability if it fails to make or stop transfers. See *Regulation E.* [14]

electronic funds transfer system(s) (EFTS): a loose description of computerized systems that process financial transactions or process information about financial transactions, or effect an exchange of value between two parties. See *Bank Wire System, Fedwire, Hinky Dinky, paperless item processing system, pre-authorized payment, prestige card, service counter terminals.*

eligible acceptance: see *eligible paper.*

eligible bill: see *eligible paper.*

eligible borrower: a borrower who meets the eligibility standards set by FmHA for participation in its guaranteed loan programs. [105]

eligible commercial bank: see *commercial bank eligible.*

eligible commercial paper: a negotiable instrument, having met certain requirements, that is eligible for rediscounting at a special rate by member banks of the Federal Reserve System.

eligible investment: any income-producing investment that is considered to be a sound repository for the funds of savings banks and similar institutions.

eligible lender: FmHA will consider guaranteeing loans made by any federal or state chartered bank, Federal Land Bank, Production Credit Association, and other lending institutions approved by FmHA. [105]

eligible paper: instruments, securities, bills, and so on, accepted by a financial institution (i.e., a Federal Reserve Bank) for the purpose of rediscounting.

eligible stock: a stock in which banks, charitable organizations, trustees, and so on, may invest funds committed to their care.

emboss: a process of printing identifying data on a bank card in the form of raised impressions. [105]

embossed character reader (ECR): a device that reads embossed characters on a bank card. [105]

embossing: the mechanical raising of data from an otherwise flat surface of a bank card for subsequent automatic or manual reading. [105]

Emergency Banking Relief Act of 1933: federal legislation returning to the president World War I power relating to transactions in credit, currency, silver and gold, and foreign currencies, and the fixing of a $10,000 fine and 10 years of imprisonment for violators. Also authorized the president to fix regulations on Federal Reserve member banks.

Emergency Home Finance Act: federal legislation of 1970; created the Federal Home Loan Mortgage Corporation, under the Federal Home Loan Bank System, to provide a secondary market for conventional loans as well as Federal Housing Administration and Veterans Administration mortgages; extended from 20 to 30 years the period allowed for associations to accumulate Federal Savings and Loan Insurance Corporation-required reserves. [51]

emphyteutic lease: a perpetual lease whereby the owner of an uncultivated parcel has granted it to another in perpetuity or for a lengthy period on condition the leasee will improve the land.

EMS: see *European Monetary System.*

EMTS: electronic money transfer system.

EMU: see *European Monetary Union.*

encoder:

(1) a device capable of translating from one method of expression to another.

(2) the encoding process usually refers to inscribing or imprinting MICR characters on checks, deposits, or other bank documents. [105]

encoding: synonymous with *imprinting.*

encoding strip: on bank checks, the area in which magnetic ink will be deposited to represent characters; the clear band. [105]

encroachment:

(1) the gradual expansion of a low-value district into a higher economic residential section.

(2) the infringement of another's property without the owner's consent.

encumbered: property to which one has title, but against which a claim has been made or granted to another.

encumbrance (incumbrance):

(1) that which holds back or weighs down.

(2) a claim or interest in land or other property that although its value depreciates, does not prevent transfer or sale.

endorsement:

(1) a show of support, a verification.

(2) a signature written on the back of an instrument constitutes an endorsement. An endorsement is required on a negotiable instrument in order to transfer and pass title to another party, who becomes a "holder in due course." The endorser, in signing the endorsement, guarantees that he or she is the lawful owner of the instrument, knows of no infirmity in the instrument,

accepted it in good faith for the value received, and is a holder in due course and has the legal capacity to transfer title to another party in the normal course of business.

(3) also spelled *indorsement.*

endorsement date: the date appearing on the interchange advice and endorsed on paper by the clearing member first entering the paper into interchange. The date must be the same date as that on which the paper is mailed to the card issuer's clearing member. [105]

endorser: one who endorses; the person who transfers his or her title to an instrument to another by endorsement. Also spelled *indorser.*

endorsing: signing a check, note, or other financial instrument purporting to transfer it to another person.

endosser: French term for *to endorse.*

end sentinel: end-of-text character which signals the end of the message or of the information encoded on the magnetic strip on the bank card. [105]

enfeoff: to give a gift of ownership to property.

entail: to limit or curtail the succession to property by ordinary rules of inheritance. Cf. *primogeniture.*

entirety (estate by): the property of husband and wife passed on to the survivor on the death of one. The estate is called "entirety" because the law looks on the husband and wife as one.

Entree: a debit card produced by Visa (formerly BankAmericard).

Epunts: a European financing technique whereby the unit of account is a payment guarantee, the value of which is expressed in terms of gold, as are free-world currencies.

The unit is not a gold obligation itself but has a value based on gold. Each unit represents slightly less than nine-tenths of a gram of gold, the same as the basis of the value of the American dollar. The holder of a matured bond that is expressed in Epunts can request payment in any one of 17 currencies, irrespective of the kind of currency the holder used when he or she made the purchase. The name Epunts comes from the European Payments Union, formed in 1947 to facilitate currency exchange, to which 17 nations belonged. The union no longer exists.

Equ.: see *equity.*

equal dignity: a reference to mortgages or other legal obligations so that all have equal ranking to prevent one from taking precedence over another. See *parity clause;* cf. *first lien, overlying mortgage, second lien, subordinated interest, tacking, underlying mortgage.*

equalization fund: see *Exchange Stabilization Fund.*

equilibrium interest rate: the interest rate that keeps the price level constant. This rate coincides with the rate that keeps money incomes constant only in a stationary economy.

equitable charge: a charge on property imposed by and enforceable in a court of equity, as distinguished from a charge enforceable in a court of law. A conveyance of real property, absolute on its face but intended only as security for a loan, may constitute an equitable charge on the property. [105]

equitable conversion: permitting real property to be converted into personal property. Real property owned by a partnership is, for the purpose of the partnership, personal property, because to determine a partner's interest, the real property must be reduced to cash.

equitable mortgage: a written statement making certain property security for a debt.

equitable ownership: the estate or interest of a person who has a beneficial right in property, the legal ownership of which is in another person. For example, a beneficiary of a trust has an equitable estate or interest in the trust property. Cf. *legal partnership.* [37]

equitable right of redemption: a defaulted borrower's right to redeem his property, by full payment of the mortgage debt, up to the date of the mortgage foreclosure sale. [59]

equitable title: the right that exists in equity to secure total ownership to property when its title is in someone else's name.

equity:
(1) the value placed on the distribution of income.
(2) the difference between liens against property and the current market value.

equity conversion: synonymous with *reverse-annuity mortgage.*

equity income: net operating income less loan interest.

equity mortgage: home mortgage contract in which the lender reduces the interest rate by a certain percentage in return for the same percentage of profit when the borrower sells a home.

equity of redemption: see *equitable right of redemption.*

equity stake mortgage: low interest rates on a mortgage, one-third less on the average, in return for one-third of the profits when the property is sold.

equity transaction: a transaction resulting in an increase or decrease of net worth or involving the transfer between accounts making up the net worth.

error resolution: Regulation E outlines the requirement for error resolution and the liability and consequences for the bank and its customer. [105]

errors and omissions: insurance coverage for liability arising out of errors or omissions in the performance of professional services other than in the medical profession; applicable to such services as engineering, banking, accounting, insurance, and real estate.

ERTA: see *Economic Recovery Tax Act of 1981.*

escalator clause:

(1) provides for an adjustment of wages in accordance with such factors as cost of living, productivity, or material costs. Escalator clauses are designed to keep real wages reasonably stable during the term of a contract.

(2) provides for increased payments in the event of unforeseen occurrences (e.g., increased fuel or maintenance costs).

escheat: the reversion of property to the government when a person dies without leaving a will and has no heirs, or when the property is abandoned.

escheat law: pertaining to the reversion of land to the state by the failure of persons having legal title to hold the same.

escrow: a written agreement or instrument setting up for allocation funds or securities deposited by the giver or grantor to a third party (the escrow agent), for the eventual benefit of the second party (the grantee). The escrow agent holds the deposit until certain conditions have been met. The grantor can get the deposit back only if the grantee fails to comply with the terms of the contract, nor can the grantee receive the deposit until the conditions have been met. See also *billed escrow;* cf. *deposit funds.*

escrow agent: see *mortgage department.*

escrow agreement: an arrangement whereby two parties agree to place a sum of money in the hands of a third party for conditional delivery under specified circumstances.

escrow analysis: the periodic examination of escrow accounts by the mortgagee to verify that current monthly deposits are sufficient to provide the necessary funds to pay taxes, insurance, and other bills when they are due. [105]

escrow closing: a type of loan closing in which an escrow agent accepts the loan funds and mortgage from the lender, the down payment from the buyer, and the deed from the seller. [59]

escrow funds: as applied to mortgage loans, represents reserves established for the repayment of taxes and insurance when due. Reserves are collected monthly by the mortgagee as part of the regular payment. [31]

escrow officer: an officer of a financial institution designated as the escrow agent or the custodian of the funds, securities, deeds, and so on, deposited until their release by agreement upon the completion of the agreed-upon act. [10]

escudo: monetary unit of Azores, Cape Verde Islands, Guinea-Bissau, Madeira, Mozambique, Portugal, Portuguese East Africa, and Timor.

Est.: see *estate*.

estate:
(1) any right, title, or other interest in real or personal property.
(2) all assets owned by an individual at the time of his or her death. The estate includes all funds, personal effects, interests in business enterprises, titles to property (real estate and chattels), and evidence of ownership, such as stocks, bonds, and mortgages owned, and notes receivable.

estate account: an account in the name of the estate of a decedent, administered by the executor or administrator of the estate. [39]

estate at will: of indefinite duration; the estate allows the lessee possession as long as both lessor and lessee mutually agree to it.

estate in common: see *tenancy in common.*

estate in fee simple: the absolute right to ownership in real estate. [105]

estate in reversion: the remaining portion of an estate that the grantor retains after certain interests in it have been transferred to another.

estate in severalty: an estate held by one person only. No other party has any part of it.

estate in tail: see *entail.*

estate plan: a definite plan for the administration and disposition of one's property during one's lifetime and at one's death; usually set forth in a will and one or more trust agreements. [37]

estimated balance sheet: the estimate of assets, liabilities, and proprietorship at the end of a future fiscal period.

estimated gross national product: an estimation of the GNP based on the combined estimates of its four main components: consumer spending; spending by business firms; spending by local, state, and federal governments; and net foreign spending. [105]

estimated profit and loss statement: the estimate of income, expenses, and net profit for a future fiscal period.

estoppel certificate: an instrument indicating the unpaid principal balance of a mortgage plus the amount and rate of interest thereon.

et al.: (abbreviation of *et alii,* Latin) "and others" (who are specified elsewhere in the document.)

EURCO: see *European Composite Unit.*

Eurobank: a western European bank, especially one that receives deposits, makes loans, and extends credit in Eurocurrency. [204]

Eurobill of Exchange: a bill of exchange drawn and accepted in the usual fashion but expressed in foreign currency and accepted as being payable outside the country whose currency is being used.

Eurobond: a bond released by a U.S. or other non-European company for sale in Europe. In this market, corporations and governments issue medium-term securities, typically 10 to 15 years in length. See *Eurocredit sector.*

Euro-Canadian dollars: Canadian dollars dealt in the Euromarkets.

Eurocard: a European credit card developed by the West German banking system that is accepted in most western European countries.

Eurocheque: a credit card for purchasing goods in several western European countries.

Euroclear: a computerized settlement and depositary system for safe custody, delivery of, and payment for Eurobonds. It is owned by 120 banks and securities firms and managed by Morgan Guaranty. [155]

Eurocommercial paper: commercial paper issued in a Eurocurrency. See *Eurocurrency.*

Eurocredit: any lending made using Eurocurrency. See *Eurocurrency.* [87]

Eurocredit sector: a sector of the Euromarket, where banks function as long-term lenders by constantly rolling over short- and medium-term loans at rates that fluctuate with the cost of funds. See *Eurobond.*

Eurocurrency: monies of various nations deposited in European banks that are used in the European financial market. Synonymous with *Euromoney.*

Eurodollar collaterized certificates of deposits (CDs): certificates of deposit of at least $100,000 to foreign investors issued by federally chartered and Federal Savings and Loan Insurance Corporation-insured institutions.

Eurodollar deposits: bank deposits, generally bearing interest and made for a specific time period, that are denominated in dollars but are in banks outside the United States. [106]

Eurodollars: short-term, high quality source of funds to banks; deposits in foreign branches or banks denominated in dollars.

Euroequity: equity share denominated in a currency differing from that of the nation in which it is traded.

Eurofrancs: Swiss, Belgian, or French francs traded on the Eurocurrency markets.

Euroguilder notes: notes denominated in Euroguilders. [204]

Euroguilders: Dutch guilders traded in the Eurocurrency markets.

Euromarket (Euromart):
(1) see *Eurobond.*
(2) see *Eurocredit sector.*

Euromarks: Deutschmarks traded in the Eurocurrency market.

Euromoney: synonymous with *Eurocurrency.*

Euro-notes: with a syndicated Eurocredit, where the actual lending takes the form of short term bearer notes which can be re-sold, but the syndicate participants are committed to underwriting the initial purchases of the paper. [156]

European Bank for Reconstruction and Development: created on January 15, 1990 by the 12 member nations of the European Community. The Bank's purpose is to make loans to help rebuild the former Soviet-bloc economies. The Bank commenced operations in April 1991 and is located in London. Synonymous with *European Development Bank.*

European Community (E.C.): the three European communities, created by the 1957 Treaty of Rome, the European Coal and Steel Community, European Atomic Energy Community, and the European Economic Community, merged in

1965 to form the European Community. Presently composed of 12 western European nations of 350 million people.

European Composite Unit (EURCO): a nonofficial, private unit of account based on member currencies of the European Community; includes a quantity of each of the European Communities' currencies, in a proportion that reflects the importance of the country.

European currency band: see *snake system.*

European Currency Unit (ECU): money made up of nine European currencies: the Deutschemark, French franc, British pound, Italian lira, Belgian franc, Dutch guilder, Danish krone, Luxembourg franc, and Irish punt-plus 20 percent gold. Synonymous with *European Monetary Unit.*

European Economic Community (EEC): see *European Community.*

European Development Bank: synonymous with *European Bank for Reconstruction and Development.*

European Investment Bank: created by the Rome Treaty as a finance institution of the European Economic Community, this bank assists in financing projects within the Common Market.

European Monetary System (EMS): intended to move Europe toward closer economic integration and to avoid the disruptions in trade that can result from fluctuating currency values. France, West Germany, Belgium, Luxembourg, The Netherlands, Ireland, and Denmark all plan to prevent their currencies from rising or falling in value against each other any more than 2.5 percent. Italy will keep its lira from fluctuating against the other currencies by more than 6 percent. See *European Monetary Union.*

European Monetary Union (EMU): created on January 1, 1979, the union is Europe's response to U.S. monetary profligacy. Under EMU, currencies of member nations would rise together, rather than fluctuating separately. Founding members were Germany and France, but the expectation is that all nine Common Market members will join, with invitations going out to non-Common Market countries as well. See *European Monetary System.*

European Monetary Unit: synonymous with *European Currency Unit.*

Eurosterling: a sterling deposit acquired by a bank outside the United Kingdom.

Eurosyndicated loans: large bank credits, usually with maturities of 3 to 10 years granted by international bank syndicates put together on an ad hoc basis. Funds for the loans are drawn from the Euromarket. [204]

even keeling: the process of the Federal Reserve Banks keeping interest rates stable through infusion of currency into circulation at the time the Treasury is borrowing with government securities in the market.

evergreen credit: a revolving credit free of a maturity date, but giving the bank the opportunity, once each year, to convert into a term loan.

eviction: the depriving by due process of law land or property in keeping with the judgment of a court. See *disseisin, ejectment.*

Ex.: see *exchange.*

exact interest: interest compounded on a 365-days-per-year basis. See *compounded interest, ordinary interest, simple interest.*

Examination Objectives: a subsection in the Comptroller's Handbook describing, for each banking activity, the goal of primary importance to the examiner. Certain objectives determine the scope of specific areas of examination interest. Other objectives ensure compliance with laws, rules, and regulations. [105]

examination of title: the review of the chain of title on a piece of real estate as revealed by an abstract of title from the public records pertaining to the property. [105]

Examination Procedures: a subsection in the Comptroller's Handbook for each banking activity which includes the procedures that an examiner is required to perform. These procedures are supervisory in nature and help the examiner to accomplish the target objectives for each subject area. [105]

examine for bank endorsement: an act performed generally in a bank's proof department or bookkeeping department whereby clerks examine the backs of all checks to see that the bank which forwarded the items has properly endorsed them. The bank endorsement is very important because banks use it to trace the path of an item through the banks through which it has passed. The whole system of returning items for infirmity through the channels from which they came relies to a great extent upon clear, legible bank endorsements. [10]

examine for endorsements: an act performed to determine whether an item has been properly endorsed so as to complete its negotiability. Tellers, or clerks who receive the items from tellers, check endorsements so that the depositor of any item can be readily determined. It is the responsibility of bookkeepers to see that items are properly endorsed before they are paid by the bank. Many cases involving the negotiability of an instrument have arisen because of improper, incomplete, or faulty endorsements on the instrument. [10]

examine for missorts: bookkeepers are required to examine checks before posting them to determine that they are drawn on accounts in their particular ledger, or that they are actually drawn on the drawee bank. There are two types of missorts: checks sorted to the wrong ledger, or checks drawn on another bank where a depositor may maintain another account but is using a similar style of check. [10]

ex-ante saving: a form of planned saving which may be more or less than ex-ante investment (planned investment). Cf. *ex-post saving.*

exception item: item that cannot be paid by drawee bank for one reason or another, such as stop payment or insufficient funds. [105]

exception report: see *exceptions.*

exceptions: transactions, either monetary or nonmonetary, which fail to meet the parameters of the system: usually displayed periodically on a listing called an *exception report.* [105]

excess bank reserves: the deposits that a member bank has with the Federal Reserve Bank over and above the amount required to be on deposit there.

excess condemnation: in condemnation proceedings, taking more land or property than is truly required for the government project in question.

excess liquidity: banks with liquidity, cash, or cash instruments, over and above their normal requirements.

excess loan: an illegal bank loan made to one customer that is in excess of the maximum stated by law. Directors of banks approving such loans have been held by court decisions to be personally liable for the bank's losses.

excess reserves: designates the amount of funds held in reserve in excess of the legal minimum requirements, whether the funds are on deposit in a Federal Reserve Bank, in a bank approved as a depository, or in the cash reserve carried in its own vaults.

Exch.: see *exchange.*

exchange:
(1) an organization or place for carrying out business or settling accounts.
(2) the volume of monies available for use.

exchange bureau: a consumer reporting agency cooperatively maintained and operated by banks engaged in installment credit activities. [105]

exchange charge: has a variety of meanings. Sometimes it refers to a remittance charge, which is a charge that some banks deduct in paying checks drawn upon themselves when they are presented through the mails from out-of-town points for the service of remitting the proceeds to these distant points. The term may also refer to a charge for drafts on other cities or to a charge which banks make for collecting out-of-town items. Generally called *collection charges.* [50]

exchange controls: governmental restraints limiting the right to exchange the nation's currency into the currency of another country.

exchange current: the current rate of exchange.

exchange depreciation: the decline of a foreign currency or currencies which a currency experiences. This is usually created by a reduction in the base, such as gold, of the currency but can also be caused by other factors, such as monetary funds, stabilization, or government action.

Exchange Equalization Fund: the stabilization fund of the United Kingdom, originally created to help the British Treasury meet the problems that arose from the suspension of gold in 1931.

exchange jobber: a banker who buys foreign exchange in large amounts for resale at a margin to smaller banks or individuals.

exchange rate: refers to the price of one currency in relation to that of another.

exchanges: all checks, drafts, notes and other instruments that are presented to a clearinghouse for collection. Synonymous with *clearinghouse exchanges.*

Exchange Stabilization Fund: a department of the U.S. Treasury established in 1934 with the "profits" derived from the reduction in the gold content of the dollar for the purpose of stabilizing the foreign exchanges.

exchange value: the value of any good considered as the quantity of other things that will be given in exchange for it.

exchequer: that account of the Chancellor of the Exchequer of the United Kingdom used to handle the revenues and payments of the kingdom. This account is maintained in the Bank of England and parallels the U.S. Treasury Department's account in the 12 Federal Reserve Banks.

exclusion:
(1) any restriction or limitation.
(2) a provision of an insurance policy or bond referring to hazards, circumstances, or property not covered by the policy.

exculpatory clause: a clause that relieves the landlord of liability for personal injury to tenants as well as for property damages. The clause does not necessarily protect the landlord against liability to a third party.

executor: a party (person, bank, etc.) identified in a will to administer the estate upon the death of the maker of the will (the testator) and to dispose of it according to the wishes of the testator.

executor of an estate: the person appointed by a testator to execute his or her will or to see its provisions carried into effect after his or her decease. [76]

executory: until all parts of a contract are performed, the contract is said to be executory as to the part not performed.

executrix: a woman identified in a will to administer the estate upon the death of the maker of the will (the testator) and to dispose of it according to the wishes of the testator.

Eximbank (Ex-Im Bank): see *Export-Import Bank of the United States.*

Ex. Int.: see *ex-interest.*

ex-interest: having no interest. Synonymous with *flat.*

existing mortgage: a mortgage that is encumbering a property. After the property has been sold, the mortgage may or may not remain.

exotic: a currency in which a large international market does not exist.

expense account cards: a type of card issued to a cardholder which is used exclusively for that cardholder's business expenses.[105]

expense fund: a fund, required by law, held by a mutual savings bank or directors of a nonstock bank to ensure the financial stability of the bank at the time of its dealings with the public.

experience: the premium and loss record of an insured or of a class of coverage.

experience rating: a type of individual risk rating that, based on insured experience on the risk, measures the extent to which a particular risk deviates from the average of its class and reflects this deviation in the rate for the risk. See *basic rating,* cf. *judgment rates.*

expiration:
(1) termination, cessation.
(2) the date on which a policy will cease to be in effect, unless previously canceled.

expire: to arrive at the termination period of an agreement, contract, or other instrument.

expired account: an account on which the originally agreed period for payment has elapsed, but an unpaid balance remains due. [55]

expired card: a bank card that has passed its expiration date. [105]

explicit interest: the amount of money or goods paid on a loan.

Export-Financiering-Maatschappij: Dutch export finance company set up by the large commercial banks in 1951.

Export-Import Bank of Japan: a Japanese export credit financing institute established in 1950 which also administers government loans to developing countries within the framework of the official aid program; financed by capital issued by the government and by borrowing from a Trust Fund Bureau or by borrowing foreign exchange from commercial banks. It may not borrow from the Bank of Japan. [145]

Export-Import Bank of the United States (Eximbank) (Ex-Im Bank): this independent federal banking corporation, established in 1934, facilitates and aids in financing exports and imports and the exchange of commodities between the United States and foreign nations; it offers direct credit to borrowers outside the United States as well as export guarantees, export credit insurance, and discount loans.

ex-post saving: realized saving. If hoards are considered as constant, ex-post saving must equal ex post investment. Cf. *ex-ante saving.*

exposure: when a bank has lent funds (or engaged in foreign exchange dealing with) or invested in a company or country.

Express Company money orders: money orders, similar to postal and bank money orders.

expropriation: the act of taking private property for public purpose, or the modification of the right to private property by a sovereignty or any entity vested with the proper legal authority; for example, property under eminent domain is expropriated. Cf. *confiscation.*

Extd.: see *extended.*

extend(ed):
(1) to multiply the unit price by the quantity of units to ascertain the total cost on an invoice.
(2) to allow a period of time for the payment of a debt beyond the date originally set.
(3) describes a contractual obligation that has been prolonged beyond the originally stated date of maturity or termination.

extended fund facility: where the International Monetary Fund lend funds over a three-year period rather than the usual one-year period.

extension:
(1) moving the maturity date to a later time, resulting in prolongation of the terms of a loan.
(2) the granting of borrowing rights, or the permission to buy without immediate payment.
(3) a postponement by agreement of the parties of the time set for any legal procedure.

extension agreement: a written authorization by creditors involved in bankruptcy proceedings to postpone the due date of their bills, with the hope that the debtor will be able to improve his or her financial condition and honor the debts at a later time. [105]

extension fee: a charge made on an installment loan for postponing the due date of a payment. [105]

extension of credit: the granting of credit in any form. [105]

extension of mortgage: an agreement which prolongs the terms of a mortgage.

external bill: a bill of exchange drawn in one country but payable in another country. Cf. *foreign bill*.

external public debt: that part of the public debt owed to nonresident foreign creditors, made payable in the currency of the nation of the creditors, as to both interest and principal.

external security audit: a security audit conducted by an organization or individuals independent of the one being audited. [105]

extinguish: to wipe out, settle, or conclude, as with a debt or obligation.

F&A: February and August (semi-annual interest payments or dividends).

FA: see *face amount*.

FAC: Federal Advisory Council. A group of 12 advisors representing the 12 Federal Reserve districts, which meets several times a year to confer with the Board of Governors of the Federal Reserve System.

face amount: the principal sum involved in a contract. The actual amount payable by the company may be decreased by loans or increased by additional benefits payable under specified conditions or stated in a rider.

face of a note: the amount stated on a note. Synonymous with *principal*.

face value: the principal value of an instrument. It is on the face value that interest is computed on interest-bearing obligations such as notes and bonds. The legal entity issuing a note, bond, or other obligation contracts to repay the face value of the obligation at maturity.

facsimile signature: a mechanically imprinted signature placed on an instrument, check, bond, security, and the like. Although such signed checks are accepted as equal to hand-signed ones, banks usually have certain stipulations that must be met prior to honoring them.

factoring:
(1) a method commonly employed by an installment loan department of a bank for computing the amount of interest to be refunded or credited because a 12-month loan is being liquidated before maturity. It is also a method for accruing earned discount.
(2) selling accounts before their due date, usually at a discount.

factor, 78th: a method commonly employed by the installment loan and other departments of a bank for computing the amount of interest to be refunded or recredited when a 12-month loan is liquidated prior to maturity. Also, a method used for accruing earned discount. [10]

FAIR Certificate: *f*ree from tax *af*fordable, *i*nsured *r*ewarding; the 1981 Savings and Loan Association strategy with Congress to allow a savings certificate that would be free from federal income tax, offered in affordable denominations, insured by a federal agency, and pay a significant net turn. See *All-Savers certificates*.

Fair Credit Billing Act: an amendment to the federal Truth in Lending Law that protects charge account customers against billing errors by permitting credit card customers to use the same legal defenses against banks or other "third party" credit card companies that they previously could use against merchants.

Fair Credit Reporting Act of 1971: federal legislation giving the user of credit, the buyer of insurance, or the job applicant the right to learn the contents of his or her file at any credit bureau.

Fair Debt Collection Practices Act: an amendment to the Consumer Practices Act, signed by President Carter, its basic objective is to eliminate abusive and bitterly unfair debt collection practices, such as threats of financial ruin, loss of job or reputation, and late evening telephone calls. The law became effective in March 1978.

false pretense: any untrue statements or representations made with the intention of obtaining property or money.

Fannie Mae: see *Federal National Mortgage Association.*

Farm Bankruptcy Act of 1933: federal legislation that allowed farmers added time to pay off their debts. The provisions of the act expired in 1949.

Farm Credit Administration: the U.S. agency responsible for the cooperative farm credit system, providing long- and short-term aid to farmers.

Farmers Home Administration (FmHA): an agency of the federal government that makes, participates in, and insures loans for rural housing and other purposes. [59]

FASB8: Statement of Financial Accounting Standards No. 8; governs corporations' financial accounting and reporting for foreign currency transactions, and sets standards for foreign currency financial statements incorporated in the financial statements of a firm by consolidation, combination, or the equity method of accounting. [101]

Fas-Cash: a copyrighted system designed to expedite the handling of cash by the teller. Currency is precounted and strapped by the teller before banking hours. The currency is strapped in packages of from $2 through $9, and from $10 through $100. This permits the teller to select rapidly nearly any combination of precounted packages of currency, and he or she is required only to get the correct change from an automatic cashier. For example, a customer wants to cash a check for $38.75. The teller selects a $30 and an $8 package of currency and selects $0.75 from the automatic cashier. This is a very fast method of handling customers at the teller's window. [10]

fat snake: slang, a monetary union to create a European fixed system. See *European Monetary System, European Monetary Union.*

FC: see *fixed capital.*

FCRA: see *Fair Credit Reporting Act of 1971.*

FCU: see *Federal Credit Union.*

FDCPA: see *Fair Debt Collection Practices Act.*

FDIC: see *Federal Deposit Insurance Corporation.*

FE: see *foreign exchange.*

feature: the components of an item or service that yield a benefit.

FECOM: European Monetary Co-operation Fund.

Fed: slang, the Federal Reserve System.

Federal Advisory Council: a committee of the Federal Reserve System that advises the Board of Governors on major developments and activities.

Federal agency issues: interest-bearing obligations evidencing debt of the U.S. government agencies or departments. [105]

Federal Credit Union: a cooperative association organized under the Federal Credit Union Act for the purpose of accepting savings from people, making loans to them at low interest rates, and rendering other financial services to members.

federal debt limit: a limit imposed by law on the aggregate face amount of outstanding obligations issued, or guaranteed as to principal and interest, by the United States; guaranteed obligations held by the secretary of the Treasury are exempted.

federal deficit: a public or federal debt; the difference that exists between revenue and government expenditures.

Federal Deposit Insurance Corporation (FDIC): a government corporation that insures the deposits of all banks that are entitled to the benefits of insurance under the Federal Reserve Act. The FDIC was created through the Banking Act of 1933 and was affected by amendments of 1935. All national banks and all state banks that are members of the Federal Reserve System are required by law to be members of the FDIC. Mutual savings banks are also encouraged to join. In 1989, dissolved and replaced by the Bank Insurance Fund. See *BIF, Federal Home Loan Bank Agency, Savings industry bill.*

Federal Deposit Insurance Corporation Assessment: the annual premium, equal to $1/12$ of 1 percent of deposits, which FDIC member banks pay for insurance coverage. [105]

federal discount rate: the interest rate charged on federal funds. The interest is charged on a discount basis and is a key factor in determining the prime rate charged for commercial loans. [105]

Federal Financial Institutions Examination Council: see *Financial Institutions Regulatory and Interest Rate Control Act.*

Federal Financing Bank (FFB): established in 1973 to assist in financing U.S. government agencies; authorized to acquire any obligation that is issued, sold, or guaranteed by any Federal agency, except those of the Farm Credit System, the Federal Home Loan Banks, the Federal Home Loan Mortgage Corporation, and the Federal National Mortgage Association.

federal funds: funds available at a Federal Reserve Bank, including excess reserves of member banks and checks drawn in payment for purchases by the Federal Reserve Bank of government securities.

federal-funds market: the market in which excess bank reserves are borrowed and lent by federal banks.

federal funds payment/transfer: payment effected by check or wire transfer against a bank's account with a Federal Reserve Bank. [105]

federal funds purchased: short-term borrowing of reserves from another bank. [105]

federal funds rate: the interest rate charged on loans by banks that have excess reserve funds (above the level required by the Federal Reserve) to those banks with deficient reserves. The Fed funds rate is closely watched as an early warning indication of major changes in the national economy. See *legal reserve.* [33]

federal funds sold: temporary transfer of reserves to another bank. [105]

federal funds transactions: involve the reporting bank's lending (federal funds sold) or borrowing (federal funds purchased) of immediately available funds for one business day or under a continuing contract, regardless of the nature of the contract or of the collateral, if any. Due bills and borrowings from the Discount and Credit Department of a Federal Reserve Bank are excluded from federal funds. [202]

federal government securities: all obligations of the U.S. government. See *Treasury bill, Treasury note.*

Federal Home Bank: one of 11 regional banks established in 1932 to encourage local thrift and home financing during the Depression. The banks are owned jointly by various savings and loan associations. The Federal Home Loan Bank Board serves as a management body.

Federal Home Loan Bank System: a system established in 1932 to serve as a mortgage credit reserve system for home mortgage lending institutions. Members may obtain advances on home mortgage collateral and may borrow from home loan banks under certain conditions. [44]

Federal Home Loan Mortgage Corporation (FHLMC) (Freddie Mac): established in 1970, responsible for aiding the secondary residential mortgages sponsored by the Veterans Administration and Federal Housing Administration in addition to nongovernment protected residential mortgages.

Federal Housing Administration (FHA): the government agency that carries out the provisions of the National Housing Act, approved in June 1934. The FHA promotes the ownership of homes and also the renovation and remodeling of residences through government guaranteed loans to home owners.

Federal Housing Administration mortgage: a mortgage made in conformity with requirements of the National Housing Act and insured by the Federal Housing Administration. [22]

Federal Housing FHA Insured Loans: insured mortgages from private lending institutions to stimulate homeownership and rental opportunities to American families. Applicants who wish to participate in a single-family mortgage insurance program must apply to a HUD-approved mortgage lender, who then applies to HUD. Interest rates are set by the FHA on these loans. [66]

federal insurance reserve: a general loss reserve required to be established by a federal association under the rules and regulations of the

Federal Savings and Loan Insurance Corporation. [59]

Federal Intermediate Credit Banks (FICB): regional banks created by Congress to provide intermediate credit for ranchers and farmers by rediscounting the agricultural paper of financial institutions.

Federal Land Bank (FLB): supervised by the Farm Credit Association, one of 12 banks that offers long-term credit to farmers. Strictly speaking, the Land Banks are a competitor to thrifts. However, regulations limit their participation in housing loans to 15 percent of their total investments. Also, their money is limited to farmers and ranchers.

Federal Loan Bank: one of 12 district banks, originally established in 1916, to make available long-term mortgage loans, at equitable terms, to farmers to enable them to own their own farms. The Federal Loan Bank System is the largest holder of farm mortgages in the world.

Federal National Mortgage Association (FNMA): an independent agency, originally chartered in 1938 and reconstituted in 1954. Its major function is to purchase mortgages from banks, trust companies, mortgage companies, savings and loan associations, and insurance companies to help these institutions with their distribution of funds for home mortgages. Nicknamed *Fannie Mae.*

Federal Open Market Committee (FOMC): the Federal Reserve System's most important policy-making group, with responsibility for creating policy for the system's purchase and sale of government and other securities in the open market.

Federal Reserve Act: legislation signed by President Wilson on December 23, 1913, establishing the Federal Reserve System to manage the nation's money supply.

Federal Reserve agent: chairman of the board of a Federal Reserve District Bank (a Class "C" director) who is responsible for maintaining the collateral for all Federal Reserve notes held within his bank.

Federal Reserve Bank: one of 12 banks created by and operating under the Federal Reserve System. Each Federal Reserve Bank has nine directors. The banks and districts are listed under *banker's bank.*

Federal Reserve Bank account: as mandated by Federal Reserve regulations, the account kept by all member banks and clearing member banks with a Federal Reserve Bank in its district. It shows the cash balance due from a Reserve Bank to guarantee that the member bank has sufficient legal reserves on hand.

Federal Reserve Bank collections account: shows the sum of monies for out-of-town checks distributed for collection by a Federal Reserve check collection system that are not presently available in reserve but being collected.

Federal Reserve bank float: Federal Reserve Bank credit on uncollected deposits.

Federal Reserve bank note: U.S. paper money released prior to 1935 by Federal Reserve Banks and secured by U.S. bonds and Treasury notes authorized to be used for that purpose. These notes have been retired from circulation.

Federal Reserve Board: the seven-member governing body of the Federal Reserve System; the governors are appointed by the President, subject to Senate confirmation, for 14-year terms. Created in 1913 to regulate all national banks and state-chartered banks that are members of the Federal Reserve System, the board possesses jurisdiction over bank holding companies and also sets national money and credit policy.

Federal Reserve branch banks: see *banker's bank.*

Federal Reserve Bulletin: a monthly journal issued by the Board of Governors of the Federal Reserve System dealing with issues in banking and finance.

Federal Reserve Chart Book: a monthly and semiannual publication of the Board of Governors of the Federal Reserve System, presenting charts of interest to the financial community.

Federal Reserve check collection system: the system, established in 1916, by which the Fed accepts out-of-town checks from the banks at which they were deposited or cashed, routes the checks to drawees, and credits the sending bank. It handles over 60 million checks each business day.

Federal Reserve cities: see *Federal Reserve District Banks.*

Federal Reserve Communications System: see *FRCS-80.*

Federal Reserve credit: the sum of the Federal Reserve credit as measured by the supply that its banks have given to member bank

reserves. It is composed primarily of earning assets of the Federal Reserve Banks.

Federal Reserve currency: paper money issued by the Federal Reserve Banks that circulates as a legal medium of exchange and is legal tender.

Federal Reserve District Banks: there are 12 of these central banks, or "banker's banks." They are:

1st District	Boston
2nd District	New York
3rd District	Philadelphia
4th District	Cleveland
5th District	Richmond
6th District	Atlanta
7th District	Chicago
8th District	St. Louis
9th District	Minneapolis
10th District	Kansas City
11th District	Dallas
12th District	San Francisco

Federal Reserve float: checkbook money that for a period of time appears on the books of both the payor and payee due to the lag in the collection process. Federal Reserve float often arises during the Federal Reserve's check collection process. In order to promote an efficient payment mechanism with certainty as to the date funds become available, the Federal Reserve has employed the policy of crediting the reserve accounts of depository institutions depositing checks according to an availability schedule before the Federal Reserve is able to obtain payment from others. [200]

Federal Reserve notes: when certain areas require large volumes of currency, or in seasons of the year when the public demand for currency is very heavy, Federal Reserve Banks have the power under the Federal Reserve Act to issue notes. When the need for currency relaxes, Federal Reserve Banks retire these notes. Federal Reserve notes are issued to member banks through their respective Federal Reserve Banks in denominations of $1, $5, $10, $20, $50, $100, $500, $1000, $5000, and $10,000. Federal Reserve notes answer the need for an elastic currency with full legal tender status.

Federal Reserve notes of other banks: the total amount of Federal Reserve notes held by Reserve Banks other than the Reserve Bank that issued them. [40]

Federal Reserve Open Market Committee: a committee of the Federal Reserve System that has complete charge of open market operations, through which the Fed influences the growth of the nation's money supply. It includes the members of the Board of Governors of the Federal Reserve System and five representatives of the 12 Federal Reserve Banks. [33]

Federal Reserve oversight: to tighten their rules for dealing with multinational banks, the U.S. Congress adopted in 1991 a Federal Reserve proposal for policing foreign banks operating in the United States. The law provides that all foreign banks operating in the United States be subject to firm, consolidated supervision in their home country. The legislation gave the Fed new powers to gather financial and ownership information regarding such banks and clarified the Fed's power over these banks in the United States if they superseded state authority.

Federal Reserve requirements: the amount of money that member banks of the Federal Reserve system must hold in cash or on deposit with a Federal Reserve Bank, in order to back up their outstanding loans. The requirement is expressed as a percentage of outstanding loan volume. [105]

Federal Reserve routing symbol: see *American Bankers Association.*

Federal Reserve System: the title given to the central banking system of the United States as established by the Federal Reserve Act of 1913. The system regulates money supply, determines the legal reserve of member banks; oversees the mint, effects transfers of funds, promotes and facilitates the clearance and collection of checks, examines member banks, and discharges other functions. The Federal Reserve System consists of 12 Federal Reserve Banks, their 24 branches, and the national and state banks that are members of the system. All national banks are stockholding members of the Federal Reserve Bank of their district. Membership for state banks or trust companies is optional. See *Federal Reserve Board.* See also *banker's bank.* [31]

Federal Reserve Wire Network: see *Fedwire.*

Federals: items drawn on banks in a large city in which a Federal Reserve Bank is located, although the banks do not belong to the city's clearinghouse association.

Federal Savings and Loan Association: one of the associations established by the Home Owners' Loan Act of 1933, and amended in the

Home Owners' Loan Act of 1934, which brought existing and newly formed mutual savings banks and building and loan associations under a federal charter. See *Federal Savings and Loan Insurance Corporation.*

Federal Savings and Loan Insurance Corporation (FSLIC): an organization created in 1934 for the purpose of insuring the shares and accounts of all federal savings and loan associations and of such state-chartered savings and loan associations as apply for insurance and meet the requirements of the corporation. [39] See *Savings Association Insurance Fund, savings industry bill.*

Federal Savings Association: a savings association chartered and regulated by the Federal Home Loan Bank Board. [59]

fed funds: see *federal funds.*

Fed Funds Bill: see *Cash Management Bill.*

fed funds rate: the rate of interest payable on federal funds; considered the key short-term interest rate because it indicates the intentions of the government. [90]

Fed intervention hour: the period when the Fed typically enters the market to conduct its various open market operations, usually shortly before noon Eastern time.

Fed open-market operations: the Fed increases the supply of bank reserves by buying U.S. government securities, and reduces reserves by selling them. Temporary reserve injections are made through repurchase agreements (RPs), while temporary draining is accomplished through matched sale-purchase agreements (reverse RPs). Traders

and analysts analyze these operations to determine whether the Fed is making reserves more or less plentiful, resulting in lower or higher interest rates.

Fedwire: a communications network linking Federal Reserve Banks, branches, and member banks; used both to transfer funds and to transmit information. Cf. *Bank Wire System.*

fee:
(1) an inheritable estate in land. Cf. *fee simple estate, freehold.*
(2) a remuneration for services.

fee checking account: a type of checking account on which a fixed fee is charged for each check written or item deposited. This distinguishes it from the regular checking account plan, which sometimes requires a minimum balance and the service charge is computed on a measured activity analysis of the account. The fixed fee may be charged before any checks are written, in which case the book of blank checks is sold to the depositor. The fixed fee may be charged at the time the checks or deposits are posted to the account, in which case the bookkeeper posts the service charge immediately after posting the check or deposit to the account. [10]

fee simple estate: an absolute fee; an estate of inheritance without limitation. This form of estate is not qualified by any other interest and upon the owner's death passes unconditionally to the heirs.

fee tail: an estate limited to a person and the heirs of his or her body; fee tail male if male heirs, fee tail female if female heirs. In most states, estates in fee tail have been abolished, generally by converting them into fee simple estates. [105]

feoffment:
(1) the granting of a fee.
(2) the granting of land by the act of taking possession. See *enfeoff.*

FF.&C.: see *full faith and credit.*

FHA: see *Federal Housing Administration.*

FHB: see *Federal Home Bank.*

FHLBS: see *Federal Home Loan Bank System.*

FHLMC: see *Federal Home Loan Mortgage Corporation.*

fiat money: money circulated by government decree and having no precious metal backing. See *gold exchange standard;* cf. *full-bodied money, real money.*

fiat standard: see *managed money.*

FICB: see *Federal Intermediate Credit Banks.*

fictitious paper (spooks): fraudulent action on the part of a dealer whereby forged contracts in the names of mythical persons are sold to a bank. [105]

fictitious registration: a document issued by a country or state official to identify the exact ownership of a business, where the name of the business does not do so. [105]

Fid.: see *fiduciary.*

fiduciary: an individual, corporation, or association, such as a bank, to whom certain property is given to hold in trust, according to an applicable trust agreement. The property is to be utilized or invested for the benefit of the property owner to the best ability of the fiduciary. Administrators and executors of estates, and trustees of organizations, are common examples of fiduciaries. Investments of trust funds, are usually restricted by law.

fiduciary accounting:
(1) maintaining property accounts in the hands of a trustee, executor, or administrator.
(2) estate accounting.

fiduciary loan: an unsecured loan.

fiduciary money (or standard): currency not secured completely by any precious metal. Synonymous with *credit money.*

fiduciary service: a service performed by an individual or corporation acting in a trust capacity. A banking institution authorized to do a trust business may perform fiduciary services, for example, by acting as executor or administrator of estates, guardian of minors, and trustee under wills. [50]

fiduciary standard:
(1) a monetary system in which the monetary unit is defined in terms of paper money.
(2) a monetary system based on a precious metal and the coinage thereof, where the face value of the coins is very little more than a substance on which to stamp an arbitrary value.

field warehousing loan: a loan made on inventories held in field warehouses established on the premises of the borrower.

figure: slang, meaning "00" and denoting an exchange-rate level.

filing: giving public notice of a lender's assignment of collateral. The information is recorded with the appropriate governmental authority by presenting applicable documentation. [105]

filing fee: a charge made for the recording or official notation of documents required for evidencing a security interest or lien. [105]

fill or kill: slang, a request to execute an order immediately at the specified price or cancel it. [116]

final commitment: an authorization by Eximbank setting forth the terms of financing offered by Eximbank under the direct loan, financial guarantees, and engineering multiplier programs. Final commitments are issued after the foreign buyer has decided to contract with a U.S. supplier(s). A final commitment is usually preceded by a preliminary commitment. Cf. *preliminary commitment, purchase commitment.* [198]

finance:
(1) to raise money by sale of stock, bonds, or notes.
(2) describes the theory and practice of monetary credit, banking, and comprehensive promotion methods. This theory covers investment, speculation, credits, and securities.
(3) to raise money by taxation or bond issue, and to administer revenue and expenditures in a governmental organization. More recently, this activity has become known as *public finance.*

finance bill: any draft drawn by one bank on a foreign bank against securities retained by the overseas institution.

finance capitalism: the period in the United States from about 1865 to 1929 when industrial empires came into the possession of few bankers and investors.

finance charge: the cost of a loan in dollars and cents as required by the Truth in Lending Act. See *Truth in Lending Act of 1968.* [78]

finance company: any institution other than a bank that makes loans to businesses or individuals. See *sales finance company.*

finance lease: a lease transaction for a lessor's service is a financial one where the lessee assumes responsibilities, such as maintenance, taxes, insurance, and so on, related to the possession of the equipment. Finance leases are usually full-payout agreements.

financial accounting: recording and interpreting revenues, expenses, assets, and liabilities of a company. [105]

Financial Accounting Standards Board (FASB): an independent accounting organization formed in 1973, responsible for creating "generally accepted accounting principles." FASB is a self-regulatory organization whose impact is on accounting firms and practitioners.

Financial Accounting Standards No. 8: see *FASB8.*

Financial Center Development Act of 1981: legislation of the State of Delaware, the act has provisions designed to alter the state's banking and tax codes in order to convince out-of-state banks to establish subsidiaries in Delaware. The tax provision, replacing a flat 8.7 percent franchise tax on banks, calls for a regressive income tax on banks starting at 8.7 percent and declining to 2.7 percent for all income over $30 million. The bill also includes an elimination of interest rate ceilings on all consumer transactions; permission for banks to charge customers additional expenses, such as cash withdrawal fees and transaction fees, on top of interest costs; permission for a lender to foreclose on a borrower's home in the event of default, and an allowance for a retroactive raise in interest rates on credit card transactions.

financial counseling: expert advice given to a family with respect to money and credit management. [55]

financial expense: the interest expense on long-term debts.

financial institution: an institution that uses its funds chiefly to purchase financial assets (deposits, loans, bonds) as opposed to tangible property. Financial institutions can be classified according to the nature of the principal claims they issue: nondeposit intermediaries include, among others, life and property/casualty insurance companies and pension funds, whose claims are the policies they sell, or the promise to provide income after retirement; depositary intermediaries obtain funds mainly by accepting deposits from the public.

Financial Institutions Reform, Regulation and Enforcement Act (FIRREA): see *savings industry bill.*

Financial Institutions Regulatory and Interest Rate Control Act: federal legislation of 1978; modified authority to invest in state housing corporation obligations; increased Federal Savings and Loan Insurance Corporation insurance limits for IRA and Keogh accounts from $40,000 to $100,000; permitted FSLIC to issue cease-and-desist orders against associations, directors, officers, employees, and agents; authorized cease-and-desist orders against associations, holding companies, their subsidiaries, and service corporations; expanded criteria for removal of a director interlocks among depository institutions; created interagency Federal Bank Examination Council to encourage uniformity in financial institutions supervision; authorized Federal Home Loan Mortgage Corporation purchase of secured home improvement loan packages; amended Consumer Credit Protection Act establishing rights and responsibilities for electronic funds transfer; established procedural safeguards for dissemination of financial institution records to federal agencies; extended Regulation Q authority for rate control and rate differential until December 15, 1980. [51]

financial instrument: any written instrument having monetary value or evidencing a monetary transaction. [105]

financial intermediaries: organizations operating in money markets that permit buyers and sellers, borrowers, and lenders, to meet easily.

financial lease: long-term, noncancelable lease.

financial management:
(1) the function of making sure that funds are available in adequate amounts when needed.
(2) the function of raising and providing funds for capital purchases as well as for operating expenses. [105]

financial markets: the money and capital markets of the economy. The money markets buy and sell short-term credit instruments. The capital markets buy and sell long-term credit and equity instruments.

financial paper: accommodation paper, that is, a short-term loan not supported by a specific commercial transaction or transfer of goods. Cf. *commercial paper.*

financial ratios: the relationships that exist between various items appearing in balance sheets and income accounts and occasionally other items. These ratios are used to measure and evaluate the economic condition and operating effectiveness of a firm.

financial service terminal: an electronic device used in conducting activity for an EFT system. Such a device may be an ATM, POS terminal, or similar devices. The terminal accepts, through automatic or manual input, specific electronic instructions which it transmits to the authorizing data processor for proper response to the customer at the terminal. [105]

financial statement: any statement made by an individual, a proprietorship, a partnership, a corporation, an organization, or an association, regarding the financial status of the "legal entity."

Financial Times (of London): considered by professionals as one of the best English-language newspapers for business and financial news.

financing: involves the purchase of or advance of funds against paper arising from installment sales by a dealer. [105]

financing statement: the statement, filed by a creditor, giving a record of a security interest or lien on the debtor's assets. [105]

finder's fee:
(1) payment given to an individual for bringing together a buyer and seller.
(2) payment to someone for acquiring a potential buyer with a property. A fee is usually paid when the seller and the buyer conclude an arrangement.

fine:
(1) a penalty charged a violator by a government, court, or other authority for breaking a law or rule.
(2) a relatively low interest rate or margin, as when a loan is made at the finest rate.
(3) the purity of precious metals.

fine metal: the degree of purity of precious metals.

fineness: the degree of purity when speaking of gold or silver coin. United States coin was formerly nine-tenths fine or pure and one-tenth alloy.

fine tuning: the manipulation of discretionary monetary and fiscal policy to offset changes in the level of economic activity.

firm commitment:
(1) for loans, a lender's agreement to make a loan to a specific borrower on a specific property within a given time period. In the secondary market, a buyer's agreement to purchase loans under specified terms.
(2) FHA or MIC agreement to insure a loan on a specific property with a designated borrower. [105]

firming of interest rate: a period during which interest rates are rising and the supply of money tends to become less plentiful. [67]

firm order: a definite order that cannot be canceled. It may be written or verbal.

FIRREA: Financial Institutions Reform, Regulation and Enforcement Act. 1989 Federal legislation for bailing out the savings and loan industry. See *savings industry bill.*

first deed of trust: a deed of trust that is recorded first and is the first lien.

first lien: a first mortgage. Cf. *equal dignity.*

first mortgage: the mortgage on property that takes precedence over all other mortgages. A first lien. See also *prior lien, underlying mortgage.*

first notice day: first day on which transferable notices can be issued for delivery in a specified delivery month. [11]

first teller: the paying teller in a bank.

first-use notice: the announcement sent to a cardholder when a debit transaction is posted to an account for the first time. The purpose of this notice is to thank the cardholder for using his or her account and to act as a security measure if the bank card was never received by the cardholder of record. [105]

fiscal: relating to financial matters.

fiscal agency services: services performed by the Federal Reserve Banks for the U.S. government. These include maintaining accounts for the Treasury Department, paying checks drawn on the Treasury, and selling and redeeming Savings Bonds and other government securities. [1]

fiscal agent: a bank or trust company acting under a corporate trust agreement with a corporation. The bank or trust company may be appointed in the capacity of general treasurer of the corporation, or may be appointed to perform special functions as fiscal agent. The principal duties of a fiscal agent include the disbursement of funds for payment of dividends, redemption of bonds and coupons at maturity, and the payment of rents. [10]

fiscal monopoly: monopolization by a government of the manufacture and sale of certain commodities in general use for the purpose of getting revenue for the Treasury.

fiscal year (FY):
(1) *general:* a corporation's accounting year. It can be any 12 consecutive months (e.g., February 1 of one year through January 31 of the next). Most companies operate on a calendar year basis.
(2) *government:* the fiscal year of the U.S. government begins October 1. Before 1976 the government's FY began on July 1.

Fisher equation: in monetary theory, the Fisher equation is $PT = MV$, where P is the general price level, T the total volume of transactions, V the transactions velocity of money, and M the quantity of money.

"five and five" power: a noncumulative general power of the donee to appoint in each calendar year the greater of $5,000 or 5 percent of the value of the trust at the end of the year. [105]

five-case note: slang, a $5 bill.

five Cs of credit: a method of evaluating credit-worthiness, including character, capacity, capital, collateral, and conditions. [105]

five percent redemption fund: the amount of funds retained by all Federal Reserve Banks held on deposit with the U.S. Treasury.

five-spot: slang, a $5 bill.

fixed-balance bonus account: a savings account that pays earnings above the passbook rate if the balance in the account exceeds a specified minimum for a specified term. [59]

fixed credit line: synonymous with *irrevocable credit.*

fixed exchange rate: a concept within the European Monetary System, where all members except Britain maintain fixed exchange rates between their currencies, promoting monetary stability in Europe and throughout the world. See also *European Monetary System.*

fixed liabilities: all liabilities that will not mature within the ensuing fiscal period (e.g., mortgages due 20 years hence, bonds outstanding).

fixed rate: see *fixed exchange rate.*

fixed rate loan: a loan for a fixed period of time within a fixed interest rate for the life of the loan.

fixed-rate mortgage: a home mortgage with a fixed interest rate, usually long term; there are equal monthly payments of principal and interest until the debt is paid in full.

flagging an account: temporarily suspending activity on an account until brought up to date or for other relevant reason. See *rubricated account.*

flat: with no interest.

flatbed imprinter: a device that leaves an image of embossed characters from a credit card on all copies of a sales draft form set as a result of a manual horizontal movement of the imprinter head. [105]

flat broke: slang, penniless.

flat lease: synonymous with *straight lease.*

flat (rate) yield: see *interest yield.*

FLB:
(1) see *Federal Land Bank.*
(2) see *Federal Loan Bank.*

flexible exchange rates: where exchange rates of varying world currencies freely change in reaction to supply and demand conditions, free from governmental maneuvers to hold a fixed rate where one currency is exchanged for another.

flexible mortgage: there are two types. See *renegotiable-rate mortgage* and *variable-rate mortgage.*

flexible-payment mortgage: an interest-only type of loan for the first five years. Two major restrictions apply: each monthly payment must cover at least the interest due, and after five years, payments must be fully amortizing. A rarely used mortgage because it offers the home buyer only a slight reduction in monthly payments during the early years. See also *graduated-payment mortgage, pledged-account mortgage, reverse-annuity mortgage, rollover mortgage, variable-rate mortgage.*

flight of capital: the movement of capital, which has usually been converted into a liquid asset, from one place to another to avoid loss or to increase gain. See also *flight of the dollar.*

flight of the dollar: purchasing foreign securities with dollar exchange, to escape the adverse impact of inflation, deflation, or other economic condition.

flip mortgage: a graduate-payment scheme offered in some states.

float: the amount of funds in the process of collection represented by checks in the possession of one bank but drawn on other banks, either local or out of town. See *uncollected funds.*

floater: see *floating-rate CD* or *floating-rate note.*

floating charge: a business loan that is secured on assets rather than on a particular item. The lender has priority of repayment from the fund of assets that exist when a receiving order is made against the firm.

floating currency: one whose value in terms of foreign currency is not kept stable (on the basis of the par value or a fixed relationship to some other currency) but instead is allowed, without a multiplicity of exchange rates, to be determined (entirely or to some degree) by market forces. Even where a currency is floating, the authorities may influence its movements by official intervention; if such intervention is absent or minor, the expression *clean float* is sometimes used. [42]

floating debt: any short-term obligation; usually, the portion of the public debt held in Treasury bills or other short-term obligations.

floating exchange rate: fluctuation in the rate of exchange of a nation's currency when its value is no longer fixed in terms of gold or another national currency.

floating-rate CD (FRCD): a certificate of deposit whose coupon is variable and normally linked to the interbank money market rate. [105]

floating-rate note (FRN): used by banks to raise dollars for their Euromarket operations, a mixture of the rollover credit market with the Eurosecurities market. [102]

floating rates: the automatic determination of appropriate exchange rates by market forces, not a nation's reserve holdings. Nations that do not follow these rates are pressured into line; otherwise, they would see the value of their currency driven to unacceptably low levels or driven up to the point where no other nation would be able to purchase their goods.

float ledger: synonymous with *collection ledger.*

float one: slang, to cash a check or take a loan.

fluid savings: savings that have neither been spent nor invested.

FMAN: February, May, August, November (quarterly interest payments or dividends).

FmHA guaranteed loan: a loan made by a bank and guaranteed by FmHA against loss due to default by the borrower. [105]

FmHA insured loan: a loan made directly by FmHA to a borrower. FmHA also services this type of loan. [105]

FNMA: see *Federal National Mortgage Association.*

fold: slang, to go into bankruptcy.

folding money: slang, paper banknotes.

FOMC: see *Federal Open Market Committee.*

forbearance agreement: a verbal or written agreement providing that the association will delay exercising its rights (in the case of a mortgage loan, foreclosure) as long as the borrower performs certain agreed-upon actions. [59]

forced sale: the sale or loss of property when one does not wish to dispose of it, as in bankruptcy. Synonymous with *judicial sale.* See *involuntary alienation.*

for deposit only: a restriction to an endorsement, limiting the negotiability of a check. [105]

foreclose (foreclosure): a legal process whereby a mortgagor of a property is deprived of his or her interest therein, usually by means of a court-administered sale of the property. See *deed in lieu of foreclosure, referee's foreclosure deed;* cf. *mother hubbard clause;* see also *equity of redemption, shortcut foreclosure.*

foreign bank: any bank other than the subject bank. Items of other banks included with the bank's are considered to be on a "foreign bank." The term may also refer to a banking concern outside the continental limits of the United States. [31]

foreign bill: a bill drawn in one state and payable in another state or nation. Cf. *external bill.*

foreign bill of exchange:
(1) the system by which the balances arising out of transactions between countries are settled.
(2) the currency used in making the settlement. [50]
(3) a draft, directing that payment be made in a foreign currency.

foreign card: bank card issued by another bank. Synonymous with *out-of-area card* or *out-of-plan card.*

foreign check: a check drawn on a bank other than that to which it is presented for payment. [105]

foreign collections: bills of exchange that have either originated overseas and are import or incoming collections or those which are export or outgoing collections in that they are payable in another country.

foreign correspondent: a bank in another nation serving as agent for a U.S. bank maintaining sufficient balances.

foreign currency: the currency of any foreign country which is the authorized medium of circulation and the basis for record keeping in that country. Foreign currency is traded in by banks either by the actual handling of currency or checks, or by establishing balances in foreign currency with banks in those countries. [10]

foreign currency account: an account maintained in a foreign bank in the currency of the country in which the bank is located. Foreign currency accounts are also maintained by banks in the United States for depositors. When such accounts are kept, they usually represent that portion of the carrying bank's foreign currency account that is in excess of its contractual requirements. [10]

foreign department: a division of a company that carries out the needed functions for the company to engage in foreign operations of a business nature, such as exports, imports, and foreign exchange.

foreign deposits: those funds held in accounts in financial institutions outside the United States payable in the currency of the country in which the depository is located. [105]

foreign direct investments: the flow of foreign capital into U.S. business enterprise in which foreign residents have significant control. [73]

foreign draft: a draft drawn by a bank on a foreign correspondent bank. [105]

foreign drawings and remittances service: a service through which foreign exchange banks make their due from accounts available to their correspondents for use in arranging foreign exchange transfers. [105]

foreign exchange (F/X): instruments used for international payments (i.e., currency, checks, drafts, and bills of exchange).

foreign exchange broker: a person, company, or bank that engages in buying and selling foreign exchange, such as foreign currency or bills.

foreign exchange desk: the foreign exchange trading desk at the New York Federal Reserve Bank. The desk undertakes operations in the exchange markets for the account of the Federal Open Market Committee, as agent for the U.S. Treasury and as agent for foreign central banks. See also *desk, the.* [1]

foreign exchange markets: those in which the monies of different countries are exchanged. Foreign exchange holdings—sometimes referred to as foreign exchange—are holdings of current or liquid claims denominated in the currency of another country. [73]

foreign exchange position: see *FX position.*

foreign exchange rate: the price of one currency in terms of another.

foreign exchange risk: the risk of suffering losses because of adverse movement in exchange rates.

foreign exchange trading: the buying and selling of foreign currencies in relation to either U.S. dollars or other foreign currencies. [105]

foreign exchange transactions: the purchase or sale of one currency with another. Foreign exchanges rates refer to the number of units of one currency needed to purchase one unit of another, or the value of one currency in terms of another. [1]

foreign inquiry: an inquiry made to a credit bureau for information on a person or firm from an other-than-normal service area of the bureau. [41]

foreign items:
(1) transit items payable at an "out-of-town" bank.

(2) bills of exchange, checks, and drafts that are payable at a bank outside the jurisdiction of the U.S. government. [10]

foreign money: see *foreign currency.*

foreign trade financing: any of the payment methods used to settle transactions between individuals in different countries. [105]

foreign trade multiplier: the concept that fluctuations in exports and/or imports may lead to significant variations in national income.

foreign transaction: an interchange item or an international transaction either originating or routed to a point outside the United States or Canada. [105]

forex: short, for *foreign exchange.*

forfeit: a thing lost to its owner by way of penalty for some default or offense.

forfeiture: the automatic loss of cash, property, or rights, as punishment for failure to comply with legal provisions and as compensation for the resulting losses or damages.

Forg.: see *forgery.*

forged check: one on which the drawer's signature has been forged. [50]

forgery: false writing or alteration of an instrument to injure another person or with fraudulent intent to deceive (e.g., signing, without permission, another person's name on a check to obtain money from the bank).

forint: monetary unit of Hungary.

Fort Knox: a U.S. Army reservation in Kentucky where the U.S. government stores its gold bullion and the majority of the nation's gold, most of which is held as security for the gold certificate account of the Federal Reserve Banks.

FORTRAN: acronym for the formula translation system. A language primarily used to express computer programs by arithmetic formulas.

forward buying: the buying of an actual or spot commodity where delivery is for the future rather than as a current delivery.

forward commitment: an investor's agreement to make or purchase a mortgage loan on a specified future date. [22]

forward contract: a contract between a customer and a bank whereby each agree to deliver at a specified future date a certain amount in one currency in exchange for a certain amount in another currency at an agreed rate of exchange.

forward cover: an arrangement of a forward foreign exchange contract to protect a foreign currency buyer or seller from unexpected exchange rate fluctuations.

forward deal: an operation consisting of purchasing or selling foreign currencies with settlement to be made at a future date. [105]

forward exchange: a foreign bill of exchange purchased or sold at a stated price that is payable at a given date.

forward exchange rate: an exchange rate (price) agreed upon today that will be utilized on a specified date in the future.

forward exchange transaction: a purchase or sale of foreign currency for future delivery. Standard periods for forward contracts are one, three, and six months. [42]

forward-forward: a deal for a future date in an instrument maturing on a further forward date; the instrument is usually a certificate of deposit and the object may be to extend the term of the deal.

forwarding: carrying information from one page to another in an account or journal.

forward margin: the margin between today's price of a currency and the price at a future date.

forward rate: see *forward exchange rate.*

FRA: see *Federal Reserve Act.*

fractional currency: any currency that is smaller than a standard money unit (e.g., any coin worth less than $1).

fractional money: coins of smaller value, such as the half-dollar, quarter, dime, and nickel in the United States.

fractional reserve: under the U.S. commercial banking system, a bank is required by law to maintain only a portion of any deposit as reserves. The difference is then permitted to be lent to borrowers.

franc: monetary unit of Belgium, Benin, Burundi, Cameroons, Central African Empire, Chad, Comoros, Congo (Brazaville), Dahomey, Djibouti, France, French Somaliland, Gabon, Guadeloupe, Ivory Coast, Liechtenstein, Luxembourg, Madagascar, Malagasy, Mali, Martinique, Monaco, New Caledonia, New Hebrides Islands, Niger, Oceania, Réunion Island, Rwanda, Senegal, Switzerland, Tahiti, Togo, and Upper Volta.

franchise plan: bank card plan for which right-of-use has been granted by one bank or association to another for a fee. [105]

Franc zone: the currency zone grouping most former French West African colonies and French dependencies in the Pacific coordinated and assisted by the Banque de France.

franked income: in Great Britain, income that has already suffered corporation tax. [162]

franken: monetary unit of Liechtenstein.

fraud account: an account on which the credit card has been used by an individual other than the cardholder of record and without the knowledge or consent of the cardholder of record. Usually the result of a lost, stolen, or never-received credit card. [105]

fraud loss: losses (charge-offs) stemming from the fraudulent use of a bank card. [105]

fraudulent conveyance: conveyance of property entered into by a debtor with the objective of defrauding creditors.

Frazier-Lemke-Long Act: see *Farm Bankruptcy Act of 1933.*

FRB: see *Federal Reserve Bank.*

FRCD: see *floating-rate CD.*

FRCS-80: the communications network of the Federal Reserve which interconnects Federal Reserve Bank offices, the Board of Governors, depository institutions, and the Treasury. It is used for Fedwire transfers, transfers of U.S. securities, as well as for transfer of Federal Reserve administrative, supervisory, and monetary policy information. [200]

Freddie Mac: see *Federal Home Loan Mortgage Corporation.*

free and clear: the absence of any liens or other legal encumbrances on property.

free balance: the minimum balance that a commercial bank allows a checking account customer to maintain without being charged a service fee. The free balance varies by commercial bank.

free banking: the concept that any group of incorporators of a bank that can fulfill the standards should be given a charter. Since 1933 this concept has been changed where the need for the service must be shown.

free checking account: a service offered by banks where demand deposit customers do not pay a fee for the privilege of writing checks. [105]

free check storage account: an example of what the banking industry calls check safekeeping, or truncation. It is a process that cuts off the normal cycle of check flow—from check to payee to bank and back to the check-writer—before it is completed.

free coinage: the obligation of the U.S. government to accept for coinage unlimited quantities of a specified metal or metals under the law. Cf. *gratuitous coinage.*

freedom shares: U.S. savings notes sold from 1967 through the mid-1970s.

free gold: the amount of gold in the Treasury in excess of gold needed to meet gold certificates and other indebtedness due in gold.

freehold: the holding of a piece of land, an office, and so on, for life, or with the right to pass it on through inheritance.

free item: an item received by the processing bank which is not listed on the cash letter or deposit where it is enclosed. [105]

freely convertible currency: a currency that may be used by citizens and foreigners without restriction. [105]

free period: that extent of time for which no finance charges will be levied provided that payment in full is made. Usually, the time period between the billing date and 25 days from that date. [105]

free-period cost of funds: charge expressed as a percentage for funds used to finance outstandings from the time a merchant account is credited for sales deposited until finance charges thereon are billed to a cardholder. [105]

free reserves: a Federal Reserve Bank term describing the margin by which excess reserves exceed the bank's borrowings.

free silver: see *free coinage.*

free trade: trade among countries in the absence of policy restrictions that may interfere with its flow.

friendly counter: a newer trend in bank lobby design. The friendly counter is an open counter where depositors and customers of a bank may transact business with the teller. The counter has no grille work other than a gate that the teller may open for the depositor to pass large packages over the counter. The friendly counter has a ledge constructed over the counter. Forms, working supplies, and so on, are under this ledge, and are beyond the reach of persons who might try to perpetrate illegal acts in the bank. [10]

FRN: see *floating-rate note.*

front-end fees: fees payable at the beginning of a loan.

front-end finance: finance for the initial part of a contract or project; usually used in export finance referring to that part of a loan not covered by export credit insurance.

front-end loading: fees and other charges which are levied more heavily to begin with and then taper off.

frozen:
(1) not easily available.
(2) when the conversion of something of value into money is impossible, the thing is said to be frozen. Cf. *liquid.*

frozen account:
(1) an account on which payments have been suspended until a court order or legal process again makes the account available for withdrawal. The account of a deceased person is frozen pending the distribution by a court order grant to the new lawful owners of the account. See *deceased account, sequestered account;* cf. *blocked accounts.*
(2) where a dispute has arisen regarding the true ownership of an account, it is frozen to preserve the existing assets until legal action can determine the lawful owners of the asset.

frozen asset: any asset that cannot be used by its owner because of pending or ongoing legal action. The owner cannot use the asset; nor can he or she dispose of it until the process of the law has been completed and a decision passed down from the courts.

frozen credit: a loan, normally called and matured, but because of economic factors is recognized by a creditor that such a step would precipitate bankruptcy and thereby preclude any substantial payment. Consequently, such credits can be carried or extended with the hope of liquidation when the debtor has recovered. Synonymous with *frozen loan.*

frozen loan: synonymous with *frozen credit.*

frozen out: action of one party to a transaction preventing or forcing a withdrawal from that transaction by a second party. The second party in this situation is *frozen out.*

FRS: see *Federal Reserve System.*

FS: see *financial statement.*

FSLA: see *Federal Savings and Loan Association.*

FSLIC: see *Federal Savings and Loan Insurance Corporation.*

full-bodied money: gold; currency that is worth its face value as a commodity. Cf. *fiat money.*

full faith and credit: a pledge of the general taxing power for the payment of obligations.

full faith and credit debt: a municipality's debt that is a direct obligation of the municipality.

full liability: liability not shared with others.

full payment: the amount of money owed on a single account that, if paid, will reduce the account to a zero balance. [105]

full-payout lease: see *finance lease.*

full recourse: type of dealer financing whereby a dealer sells or assigns to a bank installment sales paper a dealer originates with an unconditional guaranty; should the purchaser become delinquent, the dealer accepts full responsibility for the paper. [105]

full-service bank: a commercial bank that is capable of meeting the total financial needs of the banking public. Because the charters of some financial institutions limit their activities, this term draws attention to the advantages enjoyed by customers of a commercial bank. Cf.

Hinky Dinky, multiple banking, one-stop banking.

functional cost analysis program: a study based on data submitted by individual banks to the Federal Reserve System to compare various totals and cost ratios. [105]

fund:

(1) an asset of any organization set aside for a particular purpose. Not to be confused with general fund.

(2) cash, securities, or other assets placed in the hands of a trustee or administrator to be expanded as defined by a formal agreement.

fund accounts: all accounts necessary to set forth the financial operations and financial condition of a fund. [49]

fundamental disequilibrium: an International Monetary Fund expression indicating a substantial and persisting variation between the par exchange rate of a national currency and its purchasing-power parity with the currencies of other countries.

fundamental product: offering to the market that is immediately recognized as what is being sold, such as a savings account. [105]

fund balance: the excess of the assets of a fund over its liabilities and reserves except in the case of funds subject to budgetary accounting where, prior to the end of a fiscal period, it represents the excess of the fund's assets and estimated revenues for the period over its liabilities, reserves, and appropriations for the period. [49]

funded debt:

(1) exists when the method of paying off the debt and its interest is determined for specific periods.

(2) usually, interest-bearing bonds of debentures of a company; may include long-term bank loans but does not include short loans or preferred or common stock. [20]

funded debts to net working capital: funded debts are all long-term obligations, as represented by mortgages, bonds, debentures, term loans, serial notes, and other types of liabilities maturing more than one year from the statement date. This ratio is obtained by dividing funded debt by net working capital. Analysts tend to compare funded debts with net working capital in determining whether or not long-term debts are in proper proportion. Ordinarily, this relationship should not exceed 100 percent. [4]

funded debt unmatured: unmatured debt (other than equipment obligations), maturing more than one year from date of issue. [18]

funded reserve: a reserve invested in earmarked interest-bearing securities.

fund group: a group of funds which are similar in purpose and character. For example, several special revenue funds constitute a fund group. [49]

funds: a sum of money or stock convertible to money, assets. [61]

funds management: the continual arrangement and rearrangement of a bank's balance sheet in an attempt to maximize profits, subject to having sufficient liquidity and making safe investments. [105]

future depreciation:
(1) that loss from present value which will occur in the future.
(2) sometimes used to indicate the future annual charge necessary to recapture the present building value over its economic life or the annual amount necessary to amortize total investment. [6]

future estate:
(1) an estate developed for the purpose of possession, to be taken at an identified later date or upon occurrence of a future event.
(2) a *nonpossessory estate.*

future exchange contract: a contract for the purchase or sale of foreign exchange to be delivered at a future date and at a rate determined in the present.

future sum: the money that a borrower agrees to repay for an obligation. It is the interest or discount, plus service or other charges, added to the total amount borrowed.

future worth: the equivalent value at a future date on time value of money.

FV: see *face value.*

F/X: see *foreign exchange.*

FX (foreign exchange) position: a bank's net holdings of any commitments in foreign exchange in any particular currency at any given point in time. [105]

FY: see *fiscal year.*

G: gold.

GA:
(1) see *general account.*
(2) see *gross asset.*

GAAP: generally accepted accounting principles. See *Financial Accounting Standards Board.*

gain: any benefit, profit, or advantage, as opposed to a loss.

gap analysis: a technique to measure interest rate sensitivity. [107]

gap management: the identification of those assets and liabilities that are interest sensitive. [105]

Garnet St. Germain Depository Institutions Act of 1982: instructs the Depository Institutions Deregulation Committee to authorize money market deposit accounts (MMDAs), requiring that the account be "directly equivalent to and competitive with money market mutual funds." In addition, it specified that the account have no minimum maturity and that it allowed up to three preauthorized or automatic transfers and three transfers to third parties (checks) per month. [98]

geets: slang, money, purchasing power.

gelt: slang, money.

general account: an account appearing in the bank's general ledger; all accounts other than those of depositors and depositories.

general audit: an audit that embraces all financial transactions and records and which is made regularly at the close of an accounting period. [49]

general banking law: the banking law of an individual state under which the banks organized in that state are authorized to do business. [50]

general deposit: funds of banking deposits that are combined in the bank, as differentiated from special deposits that are kept separately and for which the bank serves as a bailee.

general depository: any Federal Reserve member bank authorized to handle deposits of the Treasury.

general examination: a detailed examination of all national banks undertaken every two years by the Comptroller of the Currency. [105]

general indorsement: synonymous with *blank endorsement.*

general journal: an accounting record into which journal entries are made.

general ledger: the most important bank record. Every transaction that takes place in the bank during the business day is reflected through various departmental subsidiary records to the general ledger. See also *suspense account.*

general legacy: see *legacy.*

general lien: a lien against an individual but not against his real property. It gives the right to seize personal property until a debt has been paid. The asset involved does not have to be that which created the debt. See *distress for rent, vendor's lien.*

general mortgage: a mortgage covering all properties of a debtor and not restricted to one parcel.

general reserves: funds set aside for the sole purpose of covering possible losses. Includes the Federal Insurance Reserve, reserve for contingencies, and any reserve "locked up" for losses. [59]

generic identification: the association of a group of cardholders as a single unit, that is, cardholders of several banks belonging to the same association, such as Visa or MasterCharge cardholders.

generic product: the essential benefit the buyer expects to receive from the fundamental product. When a customer opens a checking account, he or she is not buying paper checks, but is buying a bill-paying convenience. [105]

Gen. Led.: see *general ledger*.

Gen. Mtge.: see *general mortgage*.

gen-saki: a Japanese short-term money market; a market for conditional bond sales. A market where securities firms sell or buy bonds, usually for two or three months, while simultaneously including an agreement to repurchase them.

gentlemen's agreement: an unsigned, unsecured contract based on the faith of the involved parties that each will perform.

genuine and valid: a term indicating the acceptability of a check that is completed properly and drawn against sufficient funds. [105]

GES: see *gold exchange standard*.

gestor: one who acts for another, in law. [61]

Giffin effect: the situation noted by Sir R. Giffin that a rise in the price of all goods will, in the case of the poor whose incomes do not increase, cause an increase in the quantity of staple items of food consumed despite the increase in their price in order to make the income cover the needs.

Ginnie Mae: see *Government National Mortgage Association (GNMA)*.

Ginnie Mae trusts: closed-end unit investment trusts made up of Ginnie Mae certificates. The cost is $1000 per unit with a sales charge of around 4 percent. The monthly payments cover earned interest and amortization—the same as having direct participation in Ginnie Mae certificates, which are available only in the larger denominations. See *Government National Mortgage Association*.

Ginnie Mae II: started in July 1983, similar to the original Ginnie Mae with other advantages. Lets originators join together to issue jumbo pools, which combine mortgages from different issuers into a single package, as well as continue to be sole issuers. There is only one central paying agent, the Chemical Bank, leading to greater efficiency in payments and transfers. Holders of Ginnie Mae II are paid on the twenty-fifth day of the month, in contrast to the fifteenth day of the month for the original Ginnie Mae; thereby the 10-day delay lowers the yield on the securities by about five points. See also *Ginnie Mae trusts*.

GIRO: developed in the banking system of Germany, the payment system in which a bank depositor instructs his or her bank to transfer funds from his account directly to creditor accounts and to advise the creditors of the transfer.

Glass-Steagall Act of 1933: a legislative safeguard designed to prevent commercial banks from engaging in investment banking activities; also authorized deposit insurance. In recent years, attempts have been made to change this act. After a long period of contentment with the restrictions, the banking industry, especially the American Bankers Association, has begun to test the limitations on several fronts, including commercial paper, commingled accounts, money market funds, municipal revenue bonds. See *bond, municipal revenue; commercial paper; commingled accounts; money market funds*.

GNMA. see *Government National Mortgage Association*.

GNMA certificate unit trusts: backed by government-guaranteed mortgages. Maturities of 12 years or less. Big brokerage houses sweep monthly checks for interest and returned principal from mortgage amortization into a market-rate money fund. Requires periodic reinvestment decision.

GNMA mortgage-backed securities: securities guaranteed by GNMA and issued primarily by mortgage bankers (but also by others approved by GNMA). The GNMA security is passthrough in nature, and the holder is protected by the "full faith and credit of the U.S. government." It is collateralized by FHA or VA mortgages. [105]

gnomes: financial and banking people involved in foreign exchange speculation. The term was coined by Great Britain's Labour ministers during the 1964 sterling crisis.

goldbrick speculation: buying real estate with the intention of making no improvements, just waiting to make a profit.

gold bullion standard: a monetary standard according to which (a) the national unit of currency is defined in terms of a stated gold weight, (b) gold is retained by the government in bars rather than coin, (c) there is no circulation of gold within the economy, and (d) gold is made available for purposes of industry and for international transactions of banks and treasuries.

gold certificate account: gold certificates on hand and due from the Treasury. The certificates, on hand and due from the Treasury, are backed 100 percent by gold owned by the U.S. government. They count as legal reserve, the minimum the Reserve Banks are required to maintain being 25 percent of their combined Federal Reserve note and deposit liabilities. (40)

gold clause: contract term defining a money debt in terms of a U.S. dollar of a specified weight and quality of gold.

gold clearance fund: today, known as the *Interdistrict Settlement Fund*.

gold coin standard: the monetary system in which gold bullion, as distinguished from gold coins, is the standard medium of exchange.

gold cover:
(1) the gold reserve of a state or international organization which is a reserve against its currency or similar obligations. See *Gold-Cover Repeal Act*.
(2) a legal requirement, now defunct, for U.S. Federal Reserve notes that a specific percentage of the value of an issue of paper currency must be backed by an actual gold reserve.

Gold-Cover Repeal Act: federal legislation of 1968 which repealed the requirement that the U.S. paper currency (Federal Reserve notes) be backed by a gold reserve of 25 percent of the value of currency outstanding, thereby freeing more than $10 billion in gold reserves for international exchange activities. See also *gold cover*.

gold currency system: a monetary system where currency and gold can be freely converted one into the other at established rates.

golden passbook: see *time deposit (open account)*.

gold exchange standard: an international monetary agreement according to which money consists of fiat national currencies that can be converted into gold at established price ratios.

gold fixing: in London, Paris, and Zurich, at 10:30 A.M. and again at 3:30 P.M., gold specialists or bank officials specializing in gold bullion activity determine the price for the metal.

gold hoarding: with the hope of guaranteeing the value of their money, people who convert their funds into gold bullion and hold on to it over an extended time period.

gold market: a foreign exchange market dealing in gold. [105]

Gold Pool: seven representatives of central banks of the United States, the United Kingdom, Belgium, Italy, Switzerland, the Netherlands, and the Federal Republic of Germany, who, operating through the Bank for International Settlements of Basle, seek to maintain equilibrium in the price of gold by purchasing and selling on the markets within certain minimum and maximum levels.

gold price: see *two-tier gold price*.

gold production: as listed by the *Federal Reserve Bulletin*, appearing monthly, the estimated gold production in countries of the free world.

Gold Reserve Act: federal legislation of 1934 authorizing the devaluation of the dollar in terms of gold by from 50 to 60 percent at the discretion of the president and ordered the acquisition by the Treasury of all gold held by the Federal Reserve Banks in return for gold certificates. Coinage of gold was abolished, as was the redemption of money in gold.

gold reserves: gold, retained by a nation's monetary agency, forming the backing of currency that the nation has issued.

gold settlement fund: the fund of gold certificates deposited by the 12 Federal Reserve Banks with the Interdistrict Fund of the Federal Reserve System and used for clearance of debits and credits of each Reserve Bank against the other 11 banks in order to save transportation of money between the banks.

gold standard: applied to a monetary agreement according to which all national currencies are backed 100 percent by gold and the gold is utilized for payments of foreign activity. Cf. *limping standard*.

gold stock: value of gold owned by the government. [40]

gold tranche position in International Monetary Fund: represents the amount that the United States can draw in foreign currencies virtually automatically from the International Monetary Fund if such borrowings are needed to finance a balance-of-payments deficit. The gold tranche itself is determined by the U.S. quota paid in gold minus the holdings of dollars by the fund in excess of the dollar portion of the U.S. quota. Transactions of the fund in a member country's currency are transactions in monetary reserves. When the fund sells dollars to other countries to enable them to finance their international payments, the net position of the United States in the fund is improved. An improvement in the net position in the gold tranche is similar to an increase in the reserve assets of the United States. On the other hand, when the United States buys other currencies from the fund, or when other countries use dollars to meet obligations to the fund, the net position of the United States in the fund is reduced. [73]

good faith: trust. [28]

good-faith check: the check that must be included with a bid on a bond sale. The bidding notice ordinarily provides that if the bonds are awarded to a syndicate that does not pick them up as agreed, the good-faith check will be held as liquidated damages. The good-faith checks of unsuccessful bidders are returned. [105]

good-fors: usually applied to emergency low-denomination notes, which state on the face that they are "good for" a specified amount. [27]

good money: if two kinds of money of equal nominal value are in circulation, the general public may prefer one over the other because of metal content and will tend to hoard the "good money" and spend the "bad money," driving the good money out of circulation. See *Gresham's Law*.

good title: synonymous with *just title, marketable title*.

gourde: monetary unit of Haiti.

government check: checks drawn on the Treasurer of the United States and collected through the Federal Reserve Banks. [105]

government depository: a bank that has been chosen to receive deposits of a government or its agency. Usually used to differentiate a bank designated as a depository for the U.S. government.

government deposits: funds of the U.S. government and its agencies which are required to be placed in depositories designated by the secretary of the Treasury.

Government National Mortgage Association (GNMA): an agency of the Department of Housing and Urban Development. Its primary function is in the area of government-approved special housing programs, by offering permanent financing for low-rent housing. Nickname, Ginnie Mae. See *Ginnie Mae trusts.*

government obligations (GO): instruments of the U.S. government public debt that are fully backed by the government, as contrasted with U.S. government securities—that is, Treasury bills, notes, bonds, and savings bonds.

"governments": as used in the United States, all types of securities issued by the federal government (U.S. Treasury obligations), including, in its broad concept, securities issued by agencies of the federal government. [67]

government saving: tax receipts less government expenditures.

government securities: securities issued by U.S. government agencies for example, Federal Land Bank bonds and Federal Home Loan Bank notes. These securities are not guaranteed by the federal government.

government securities dealers: firms, including a few large banks with their own dealer units as well as nonbank dealers, that finance significant inventories of U.S. government stocks via borrowing from banks and corporations.

GPAM: see *graduated-payment adjustable mortgage.*

GPMs: see *graduated-payment mortgage.*

grace period:

(1) most contracts provide that the policy will remain in force if premiums are paid at any time within a period (the "grace period") varying from 28 to 31 days following the premium-due date.

(2) the period when a mortgage payment becomes past due, before it goes into default.

graduated payment: repayment terms calling for gradual increases in the payments on a closed-end obligation. A graduated payment loan usually involves negative amortization. [200]

graduated-payment adjustable mortgage (GPAM): a GPM with an adjustable rate; the borrower and lender share interest rate risk. See *graduated-payment mortgages, price-level-adjusted mortgage.*

graduated payment adjustable mortgage loan: a mortgage instrument that combines features of the graduated payment mortgage and the adjustable mortgage loan was authorized by the Federal Home Loan Bank Board in July 1981. Lenders are now able to offer mortgage loans where the interest rate may change to reflect changes in the market place and where the monthly payments for the first 10 years may be set at a lower amount than required to fully amortize the loan.

graduated-payment mortgage (GPM): first insured by the Federal Housing Administration in 1977, where payments are much lower at first than for traditional level-payment mortgages. Prices then rise gradually and level off after a few years. The idea is to put home ownership within reach of young people who might otherwise be forced by spiraling housing prices and high interest rates to remain renters. See also *flexible-payment mortgage, pledged-account mortgage, price-level-adjusted mortgage, reverse-annuity mortgage, rollover mortgage, variable-rate mortgage.*

grand: slang, $1000.

grandfathered activities: nonbank activities, some of which would normally be impermissible for bank holding companies, but which were acquired or engaged in before a particular date. Such activities may be continued under the "grandfather" clause of the Bank Holding Company Act—some until 1981 and some indefinitely. [1]

grant: a clause in a deed reflecting the transfer of title to real property.

grantee: an individual to whom a grant is made; the person named in a deed to receive title to property.

granter: a person who offers credit.

grantor: an individual who makes a grant; a person who executes a deed giving up title to property.

gratuitous coinage: a government policy of producing coins from metal without cost to the owner of the metal.

gratuity: a gift or donation.

gravy: money that is in excess of what is anticipated; money easily earned.

green: slang, paper money.

greenbacks:

(1) inconvertible notes used during the Civil War that were legal tender for all public and private

debts except interest on the national debt or import duties.

(2) presently, used to refer to any of the paper money issues of the Federal Reserve Banks or the U.S. Treasury.

greenlining: a response of community citizens who withdraw their accounts from lending institutions that they believe practice redlining. See *redlining.*

green power: the power of money.

Gresham's law: describes the fact that bad money tends to drive out good money. Refers to the way in which people protect themselves from loss by spending money of questionable value and holding onto money of known better value. Cf. *quantity theory. See good money.*

grift: slang, money made dishonestly, especially by swindling.

gross asset: all property in possession of a company. Gross assets are the total of the ledger and non-ledger assets. [42]

gross book value: the dollar amount at which an asset is carried on a firm's books, without making a deduction for accumulated depreciation or any other contra accounts. [105]

gross charge: the ratio between the interest charge on a discount interest loan and the discounted amount disbursed to the borrower. [59]

gross debt: all long-term credit obligations incurred and outstanding, whether backed by a government's full faith and credit or nonguaranteed, and all interest-bearing short-term credit obligations.

gross deposits: all deposits, without any exclusions or deductions. This would include all forms of demand and time deposits (i.e., those due banks and government deposits).

gross estate: all of a person's property before debts, taxes, and other expenses or liabilities have been deducted; to be distinguished from *net estate,* which is what is left after these items have been taken into account. [37]

gross income: revenues before any expenses have been deducted.

gross income multiplier: a figure by which effective gross income is multiplied to obtain an amount that indicates the capital value of property. [44]

gross lease: a lease of property under which the lessor agrees to meet all charges which would normally be incurred by the owner of that property. [62]

gross savings: the sum of capital consumption (depreciation), and personal and corporate savings.

gross spread: a banking term used to determine underwriting fees. See *underwriter.*

gross volume: total dollar amount of all merchant sales and cash advances. [105]

ground lease: a contract for the rental of land on a long-term basis. [105]

ground rent:

(1) a price paid each year, or for a term of years, for the right to occupy a parcel of real property.

(2) rent paid for vacant land. If the property is improved, ground rent is that portion attributable to the land only. [105]

group banking: a form of banking enterprise whereby a group of existing banks form a holding company. The holding company supervises and coordinates the operations of all banks in the group. A majority of the capital stock of each bank in the group is owned by the holding company.

Group of Ten: composed of the prosperous countries of the world who fix and regulate their policies in international monetary activities. Members are Belgium, Canada, France, Great Britain, Italy, Japan, the Netherlands, Portugal, Spain, Sweden, the United States, and West Germany. Switzerland is an unofficial member.

growing equity mortgage: a home mortgage with a fixed interest rate, but monthly payment may vary according to an agreed schedule or index. Synonymous with *rapid-payoff mortgage.*

GSA: see *Glass-Steagall Act of 1933.*

GSL: see *guaranteed student loans.*

guarani: monetary unit of Paraguay.

guaranteed deposits: see *Federal Deposit Insurance Corporation.*

guaranteed interest:
(1) rate of interest return specified in the policy as the rate at which reserves will be accumulated.
(2) rate of interest paid on funds deposited with the company, either for advance premium deposits or in accordance with the settlements options. [12]

guaranteed letter of credit: travelers' letters of credit or commercial letters of credit; the party requesting the credit issuance does not pay the bank in cash for the equivalent amount of the credit upon its issuance. The bank substitutes its own credit for people or firms, to encourage more domestic and foreign trade.

guaranteed mortgage: a mortgage with a guarantee of payment of principal or interest or both. The Federal Housing Administration and the Veterans Administration offer the majority of these mortgages today.

guaranteed portion: the percentage of the financed portion of a transaction guaranteed by Eximbank once the exporter retention and commercial bank retention (if any) are deducted. [198]

guaranteed residential value: a condition in capital lease where the lessee insures the lessor that the leased asset will have a specified value at the end of the lease term.

guaranteed student loans (GSL): loans primarily made by banks, savings and loan associations, and credit unions, and some colleges. The federal government pays the full 9 percent interest on loans for college students while they are enrolled.

guarantee of signature: a certificate affixed to the assignment of a stock certificate or registered bond or to other documents by a bank or stock exchange house, vouching for the genuineness of the signature of the registered holder. [37]

guarantor: one who makes a guaranty; an individual who by contract is prepared to answer for the debt, default, and miscarriage of another. See *guaranty.*

guaranty: a contract, agreement, or undertaking involving three parties. The first party (the guarantor) agrees to see that the performance of a second party (the guarantee) is fulfilled according to the terms of the contract, agreement, or undertaking. The third party is the creditor, or the party, to benefit by the performance.

guaranty fund: a fund which a mutual savings bank in certain states must create through subscriptions or out of earnings to meet possible losses resulting from decline in value of investments or from other unforeseen contingencies. In other states, such a fund is known as the *surplus fund.* [39]

guaranty savings bank: a savings bank with features of both a mutual savings bank and a stock savings bank.

guardian: an individual chosen by a court to oversee the property rights and person of minors, persons adjudged to be insane, and other incompetents.

guardian account: an account in the name of a guardian who acts on behalf of and administers the funds for the benefit of the ward. [39]

guardian ad litem: a particular guardian chosen for the single purpose of carrying on litigation and preserving a ward's interests but who has no control or power over the ward's property.

guardian de son tort: a person, though not a regularly appointed guardian, who takes possession of an infant's or an incompetent person's property and manages it as if he or she were guardian, thereby becoming accountable to the court.

guardianship account: an account in the name of a guardian who acts on behalf of and administers the funds for the benefit of the ward.

guilder: monetary unit of the Netherlands, Netherlands Antilles, and Surinam.

guillotine clause: slang, a clause that permits the lender to call a loan if the mortgage conditions are not met.

gulf riyal: monetary unit of Dubai and Qatar.

gyp 'ems: slang, for graduated-payment mortgages. See *graduated-payment mortgage.*

HA: see *house account.*

habendum clause: a deed of mortgage clause that defines the extent of the property being transferred. It reads: "To have and to hold the premises herein granted unto the party of the second party (i.e., the grantee), his heirs and the assigns forever."

half-buck: slang, a half-dollar (50 cents).

handbill: paper currency.

handling charge: see *interchange fee.*

hang-out loan: a loan lasting longer than its lease.

hard: see *hard currency.*

hard cash: metallic currency, as distinguished from paper money.

hard currency: currency whose value is expected to remain stable or increase in terms of other currencies; alternatively, a freely convertible currency may be referred to as *hard.*

hard loan: a foreign loan that must be paid in hard money.

hard money (currency):

(1) currency of a nation having stability in the country and abroad.

(2) coins, in contrast with paper currency, or soft money.

(3) describes a situation in which interest rates are high and loans are difficult to arrange. Synonymous with *dear money.*

hard stuff: slang, money.

HC: see *holding company.*

head teller: a teller in a bank who sometimes has the title of assistant cashier. The head teller is usually custodian of the reserve cash in the bank's vault. It is his or her responsibility to see that an "economical" quantity of cash is on hand at all times to meet the normal demands of the bank's customers. It is his responsibility to assemble the cash figures for all tellers at the end of the business day and prepare the cash report for the general ledger. He is also responsible for the work of all tellers in the bank, and he must recount cash for a teller who comes up with a difference at the end of the day. He must fully report any overage or shortages that may appear and assist where possible to locate the difference. [10]

heirs: people who receive(d) the title to property upon the death of an ancestor or other testator.

heirs-at-law: the persons who inherit the real property of a person who dies without a valid will disposing of his or her property. [105]

held over: see *holdovers.*

hereditament: property that can be inherited.

HHFA: see *Housing and Home Finance Agency.*

hidden amenities: desirable aspects of property that are provided but not always given attention on first inspection.

high finance:
(1) utilizing another's funds in a speculative fashion, which may re-

sult in a loss to the funds' owner.
(2) borrowing to the maximum of one's credit.
(3) extremely complicated transactions.

high posting: see *postlist.*

high-powered money: see *monetary base.*

high-ratio loan: mortgage loans in excess of 80 percent of the sales price or value, whichever is less. [105]

high-volume accounts: an account whose activity is so unusually large as to warrant special handling. [31]

H. in D.C.: see *holder in due course.*

Hinky Dinky: the name of a Nebraska supermarket chain whose employees operate in-store terminals provided by First Federal Savings & Loan of Lincoln, Nebraska, to permit First Federal customers to make deposits and withdrawals in the store. This service is significant because (a) it enables off-premises access to accounts maintained at a depository institution, and (b) the accounts bear interest. See *service counter terminals.*

historical cost: the principle requiring that all information on financial statements be presented in terms of the item's original cost to the entity. The dollar is assumed to be stable from one time period to another.

historical rate: assets such as inventories, property, plant, and equipment are translated into dollars at the rate in effect when the assets were acquired.

HKIBOR: see *Hong Kong interbank offered rate.*

hokeys: see *Home Owners' Loan Corporation Bonds.*

HOLC: Home Owner's Loan Corporation. A federal corporation organized in 1933 for the purpose of making loans to owners of small homes who were either delinquent in their payments and in danger of losing their homes or on the verge of becoming delinquent.

hold: used to indicate that a certain amount of a customer's balance is held intact by the bookkeeper until an item has been collected, or until a specific check or debit comes through for posting. [31]

holder: the bearer possessing an instrument.

holder in due course: a person who has taken an instrument under the following conditions; (a) that it is complete and regular upon its face; (b) that he or she become a holder of it before it was overdue, and without notice that it had been previously dishonored, if such was the fact; (c) that the holder took it in good faith and for value; and (d) that at the time it was negotiated to him or her, the holder had no notice of any infirmity in the instrument or defect in the title of the person negotiating it. See *endorsement.*

holding company: a corporation that owns the securities of another, in most cases with voting control. Synonymous with *parent company* and *proprietary company.* See *group banking, holding company (multiple-bank), holding company (one-bank).*

holding company (multiple-bank): a bank holding company, however defined, that owns or controls two or more banks. [74]

holding company (one-bank): at present, there is no legal definition of a one-bank holding company. A very broad definition would be any company that owns or controls a single bank. [74]

holding company affiliate: a legal term fully defined in the Banking Act of 1933. Generally, it pertains to any organization that owns or controls any one bank either through stock ownership or through any means that allows it to elect a majority of the bank's directors. [74]

holding the line: monetary or fiscal policies used to prevent or discourage prices from climbing above a current level. Measures include freezing prices, increasing bank reserves, increasing the discount rate, and restricting consumer loans.

holdovers: used, usually in large banks to describe a portion of work that has to be processed by a twilight shift or a night force. The 40-hour work-week makes it frequently necessary for the bank to employ three shifts. Since the business day starts officially at midnight, work that has not been processed by the twilight force is "held over" to the night force, which starts processing the remaining work. The work, for control purposes, is credited to the twilight force, and recharged as "holdovers" to the night force. [10]

hollow note: a $100 bill.

holographic will: a will entirely in the handwriting of the testator. [105]

home banking: a concept in banking, pioneered in 1980 by Banc One Corporation in Columbus, Ohio. By connecting a device to TV sets and telephones, customers will be able to call up information about bills and bank accounts on their TV screens and pay bills with a push of a button. Since this approach does not allow deposits and cash withdrawals, it isn't considered a branch bank.

home conversion: borrowing against your home.

home debit: a self-check; any draft or check drawn upon a bank and subsequently brought to the same institution for deposit or payment.

home financing: the providing of funds, secured by a mortgage, for the purchase or construction of a residential structure containing one, two, three, or four dwelling units. [59]

home improvement loan: an advance of funds, usually not secured by a mortgage and usually short-term, made to a property owner for the upgrading of his property, such as maintenance and repair, additions and alterations, or replacement of equipment or structural elements. [59]

Home Loan Bank Act (System): see *Federal Home Loan Bank System.*

Home Loan Bank Board: an agency that roughly parallels for the Federal Home Loan Bank System the duties of the Board of Governors of the Federal Reserve Bank System.

Home Mortgage Disclosure Act: a federal law requiring certain financial institutions to disclose information about their home mortgage activities to the public and to government officials. [105]

homeowner's insurance: a broad form of insurance coverage for real estate that combines hazard insurance with personal liability protection and other items. [59]

Home Owners' Loan Act of 1933: federal legislation establishing the Home Owners' Loan Corporation

with $200 million from the Reconstruction Finance Corporation; the corporation was authorized to release up to $2 billion in bonds to exchange for mortgages. See *Federal Savings and Loan Association.*

Home Owners' Loan Corporation Bonds: authorized by the Home Owners Loan Act of 1934, $2 billion of bonds could be sold or exchanged for mortgages by the Home Owners Loan Corporation. Nicknamed "hokeys." The Corporation is now defunct and all bonds have been recalled.

homestead association: the name used by some savings associations in the state of Louisiana. [59]

homestead estate: a type of estate ownership in land, permissible in a number of states, that protects the possession and enjoyment of the owner against the claims of creditors and from execution and sale for his or her general debts, provided that he or she has a family. [59]

homogenization: the blurring of the traditional distinctions among a nation's financial institutions, where banks, thrift institutions, and credit unions have moved onto each other's turf but increasingly are facing stiff competition from nonregulated, nonfinancial institutions.

Hon'd: see *honored.*

Hong Kong interbank offered rate (HKIBOR): the Hong Kong equivalent of LIBOR—the rate at which deposits are offered to prime banks in Hong Kong. See also *ADIBOR, SIBOR.*

honor bond: see *bond, honor.*

honored: when attributed to a draft or a note, the paper was either accepted or paid.

horizontal audit: a method of testing the practical operation of internal controls by observing the accounting procedures. This is done by a public accountant. [105]

hot card: used to describe a card being used on an account on which excessive purchasing is taking place. Usually a lost or stolen card or otherwise indicative of unauthorized purchasing. [105]

hot card list: a list of delinquent accounts or stolen plastic cards. See *restricted card list.* [105]

hot money: money that is received through means that are either illegal or of questionable legality.

"hots": in Great Britain, Treasury bills on the day they are issued, with their full term to run.

house account: any account belonging to a client that has not been nor ever may be assigned to a firm's representative.

house bill: any bill of exchange drawn by a central office against a branch or affiliate.

house of issue: an investment banking firm engaged in underwriting and distribution of security issues.

Housing Act of 1961: authorized new programs for federal involvement in housing, including subsidized rental housing for low- and moderate-income families, and Federal Housing Administration insurance of liberal term loans for repair and modernization in declining urban areas; expanded funds for Federal National Mortgage Association special assistance functions. [51]

Housing and Community Development Act of 1977: raised ceilings on single-family loan amounts for association lending, federal agency purchases, Federal Housing Administration insurance and security for Federal Home Loan Bank advances; raised ceilings on conventional and FHA home improvement loans. [51]

Housing and Home Finance Agency: a single agency created in 1977, responsible for major housing programs and activities of the federal government.

hypothecary value: the value assigned by a lender to the collateral pledged to secure a loan.

hypothecate: to promise and place property to secure a loan. The identified property is said to be hypothecated.

hypothecated account: an account that is pledged or assigned as collateral for a loan. Savings accounts and trust accounts are usually selected for purposes of hypothecation.

hypothecated asset: things pledged without transferring possession or title.

hypothecation: an agreement or contract that permits a bank or a creditor to utilize the collateral pledge to secure a loan, in case the loan is unpaid at maturity.

I: the nominal market interest rate. [81]

IA: see *inactive account.*

IADB: *Inter-American Development Bank.*

IBA:
(1) see *Independent Bankers Association of America.*
(2) see *International Banking Act of 1978.*
(3) see *Investment Bankers Association.*

IBEC: see *International Bank for Economic Cooperation.*

IBFs: see *international banking facilities.*

IBRD: see *International Bank for Reconstruction and Development.*

idemsonans: describes a legal document in which absolute accuracy in the spelling of names is not demanded (e.g., "Eliot" or "Elliott" would be acceptable as designation of a person named Elliott).

identification: the procedure by which a bank teller or other employee assures himself as far as possible (through documents, contact with another bank, and other means) that the person with whom he is dealing is the person he or she claims to be. [39]

idle money:
(1) inactive bank deposits. See *unclaimed balances.*
(2) uninvested available funds.

IF: see *insufficient funds.*

IIB: see *International Investment Bank.*

illiquid:
(1) not easily convertible into cash; the opposite of liquid. Illiquid assets can be converted into cash, but usually at a major loss in value. Fixed assets are illiquid assets.
(2) not established by any documentary evidence.

illusory: appearing false. If that which seems to be a promise is found not to be a promise, it is said to be illusory.

IMC: International Monetary Conference organized by the American Bankers' Association; holds an annual conference on financial and monetary issues. Participants are chairpersons or chief executives of the member bank.

IMF: see *International Monetary Fund.*

IMM: see *international money management.*

immediate and deferred credit: items sent to a Federal Reserve Bank are generally divided into separate cash letters which contain items for immediate credit and items for deferred credit. [31]

immediate beneficiary: a beneficiary of a trust who is entitled to receive immediate benefits from the trust property, whether or not limited to income; opposed to ultimate beneficiary. Synonymous with *primary beneficiary.* [37]

immediate credit: when a depositor draws on cash and home debit items in the form of withdrawal or check, while checks drawn on other banks are subject to "deferred availability" until they are collected, by the bank in which they have been deposited.

immediate delivery: an arrangement whereby an investor selects mortgages, generally from a mortgage banker's off-the-shelf inventory, for delivery, acceptance, and payment within a limited period, usually 30 days. [22]

immediately available funds: funds that the purchasing bank can either use or dispose of on the same business day that the transaction giving rise to the receipt or disposal of the funds is executed. [202]

Immediate Payment Zones: an area served by one of approximately 40 check-clearing facilities at Federal Reserve Banks, their branches, and various separate regional centers. Immediate payment zones were established as the result of a Federal Reserve Board (FRB) policy statement (June 1971) that directed the expansion of regional check-clearing facilities for overnight clearing of most commercial bank checks. One objective of the FRB is to expand the zones as much as possible in order to minimize the shipping and processing of checks at the local level, where most remain throughout their lifetimes. A long-range goal is to effect immediate payment from bank to bank throughout the country via FedWire. [105]

immigrant remittances: funds of immigrants that are sent out of the country.

immovable: describes real property that cannot be moved (e.g., land, trees, structures).

immunity: that which confers the ability to escape from the legal duties or penalties imposed on others (see, e.g., indemnity).

impact loan: a medium-term loan, usually five years, to a Japanese firm by a foreign bank in foreign currency.

impaired credit: the reduction of credit given to a corporation resulting from the bank's decision that its credit worthiness has weakened. See *credit, line of credit.*

impaired risk: a risk that is substandard or under average.

impair investment: a money or near-money expenditure which does not result in capital formation, being either for consumption or a transfer and acquisition of existing capital.

impersonal account: a ledger account bearing a title which is not a personal name.

implicit costs: costs originating within the business that are the responsibility of the owner (e.g., time, money).

implicit interest: synonymous with *imputed interest.*

implied contract: a contract agreement that can be assumed by the nature of the actions of two parties but which does not entail an express agreement. [105]

implied easement: infringement on property that has been left unchallenged over a period of time. The infringement is apparent from continued and lengthy use.

implied trust: a trust created by operation of law or by judicial construction, to be distinguished from an express trust, which is created by express language, oral or in writing. [37]

imprinter: device supplied to each merchant who affiliates with a bank card plan to produce an image of the embossed characters of the bank card on all copies of sales drafts and credit slips. [105]

imprinter fee: the amount charged by the bank to a merchant for use of a bank-owned imprinter. [105]

imprinting: to place on the face of a document the magnetic ink characters specified by the American Bankers Association. Synonymous with *encoding.* [31]

improvement: a change made in an asset to improve its condition with the expectation that it will also increase its value.

imputed: describes a value estimated when no cash payment is made, in order to establish that value.

imputed income: income received in some form other than money, usually stated in terms of goods or services. Imputed income includes wages paid in kind, rental value of owner-occupied homes, food and fuel produced and consumed on farms, and interest payments by financial intermediaries, which do not explicitly enter the national accounts. [105]

imputed interest: an estimate of value, charge, or interest due for using capital even though a cash payment has not been made. Synonymous with *implicit interest.*

inactive account: an account that has little or no movement. The balance may be stationary, neither deposits nor withdrawals having been posted to the account for a period of time. Cf. *idle money.* Synonymous with *dormant account.*

inactive bad debt account: an account charged off and judged to be uncollectible. [55]

inactive trust: a trust in which the trustee has no duty except to hold title to the property. [37]

inalienable: not able to be sold or transferred. Synonymous with *non assignable.*

INAS: see *Interbank National Authorization System.*

in balance: see *trial balance.*

incentive bonus: cash payments, usually made at the end of the year, based on some measurement of individual performance and not equal in percentage or amount for individuals in the group being rewarded. [105]

inchoate: newly begun or incomplete.

inchoate interest: a future interest in real estate.

in-clearing items: items received by a bank as a result of a clearinghouse exchange are commonly called incoming clearings, or shortened to "in-clearings." [31]

income account: an account in the general ledger of a bank. Expenses are listed under the assets, and the total expenses are usually deducted from the income accounts total to show the net profit to date as a portion of the undivided profits accounts.

income approach to value: a procedure for property appraisal in which the value on the net amount of income produced by the property is used. This value is determined by subtracting the total income of the property from expenses to determine net profit.

income beneficiary: a person who, by the terms of a will or a trust instrument, is entitled to receive income from property for a specified number of years or for life. [37]

income capital certificates: Federal Home Loan Bank Board Certificates that are agreements to pay back a corporation's loan, plus interest, when and if associations in financial difficulty get into a better position. Payments are installments, and are always less than the association's net income. Income capital certificates were initiated in September 1981.

income in respect of a decedent (IRD): income items and deductible obligations that would have been receivable or payable by the decedent had he or she lived and that are received or paid by his or her estate or successor to the property have the same tax consequences to the estate or successors when received or paid and retain the same character they would have had in the hands of the decedent. [105]

income interchange: sales drafts received by a cardholder bank. [105]

income property: property, usually commercial, industrial, or residential, owned or purchased for a financial return expected.

income statement:

(1) the profit and loss statement of a given concern for a particular period of time.

(2) a copy of the income cash ledger for a particular trust account.

income velocity of money: the average number of times each year that a dollar is spent on purchasing the economy's annual flow of final goods and/or services—its gross national product.

incoming clearings: see *in-clearing items.*

incoming exchanges: those checks presented by member banks to a clearinghouse for clearing purposes. See *clearinghouse.*

incoming mail: checks and drafts received through the mail for deposit from other banks and depositors. [31]

inconvertible money: irredeemable funds; circulating money that cannot be converted into the standard. United States money has been inconvertible since 1933 because it is not redeemable in gold. See *fiat money.* Synonymous with *irredeemable money.*

incorporate: to form into a corporation; become a corporation. [62]

incorporated trustee: any trust company or bank under its charter and by law that can serve as a fiduciary.

incorporation: the procedure in obtaining a state charter to form a corporation.

incorporeal property: intangible, personal property (i.e., without body); includes property rights, mortgages, and leases. See *choses in action.*

incumbrance: see *encumbrance.*

incur: to sustain or become liable for, usually in reference to a cost, expense, loss, or debt. [105]

incurably depreciated: describes damaged property that is beyond rehabilitation or property that is uneconomical to repair.

indebtedness: a debt is owed; any form of liability.

indefeasible: incapable of being annulled or rendered void; as, an indefeasible title to property. [37]

indent.: see *indenture.*

independent audit: an audit performed by an independent auditor. See also *audit report.*

independent bank: a bank that operates in one locality. The directors and officers are generally local to the community.

Independent Bankers Association of America: created in 1930, an association to promote the interest of independent banking in the United States as a vibrant, contributing force within the economy.

index:

(1) an ordered reference list of the contents of a file or document, together with keys or reference notations for identification of location of those contents.

(2) a statistical yardstick expressed in terms of percentages of a base

year or years. For example, the Federal Reserve Board's index of industrial production is based on 1967 as 100. In April 1973 the index stood at 121.7 which meant that industrial production during that month was about 22 percent higher than in the base period.

indirect compensation: incentive bonuses or cash profit sharing earned and received in cash in the same year. Indirect compensation includes all cash payments received in addition to base salary or guaranteed year-end bonuses. [105]

indirect foreign exchange standard: see *gold exchange standard.*

indirect liability: a party who endorses the note of a maker for a bank or guarantees a note as guarantor for a maker is said to have indirect liability on the note.

indirect loan: purchase by banks of loan contracts between retail merchants and customers. [105]

indirect origination: the purchase of a ready-made loan from a source other than a regular lender (such as a subdivision contractor, or a mobile home or home improvement dealer), usually as part of an on-going business relationship between the association and the seller. See also *loan origination.* [59]

indirect quotation: quotation of fixed units of domestic currency in variable units of foreign currency.

indirect standard: the monetary system that does not directly convert its currency into a standard metal such as gold or silver but allows, as a right of ownership, the exchange of the domestic currency into the currency of a nation that is on a metal standard. The ratio of

exchange is credited and held with only occasional changes.

individual account: an account in the name of one individual, as contrasted with an account or a corporation, a partnership, or an account in two or more names. [50]

individual banker: a private banker; an unincorporated bank, found in only a few states.

individual retirement accounts (IRA): originally, individual pension accounts available to anyone who was not covered at work by a qualified pension plan. Effective January 1, 1982, all wage earners, including those already in company pension plans are able to make tax-deductible contributions to IRAs. Effective 1987, restricted for some individuals covered by employer pension plans. See *Tax Reform Act of 1986.*

indorsement: see *endorsement.*

industrial bank: a financial institution originally organized to extend loans to employees. The bank derives its funds through a form of worker savings. Most industrial banks have now been merged into commercial banks. Cf. *labor banks.*

industrial banking companies: institutions chartered to extend installment credit to consumers and to accept some form of savings deposit, or sell investment certificates or certificates of deposit, as at least a partial means of financing the operation. [203]

industrialist: an individual who owns, controls, or plays a critical role in the operation of an industrial organization.

industrial loan commitments: amount of loans to industrial borrowers which have been approved but for which the funds have not yet been advanced to them. [40]

industrial loans: loans outstanding to industrial borrowers under an amendment to the Federal Reserve Act which authorized the Federal Reserve Banks to make loans to certain business firms unable to get credit from other financial institutions on reasonable terms. This authority was terminated in August 1959. [40]

industrial production: a measure issued by the Federal Reserve mid-month for the previous month, of the physical output of factories and mines.

inelastic demand (inelasticity): exists when a price increase leads to a higher total sales, revenue, or a price decrease leads to a lower sales revenue. A perfectly inelastic demand occurs when the demand for an item does not change with changes in price.

inelastic supply: a condition in which the quantity of an item produced does not alter, or changes minimally, with a price change.

ineligible bills: in Great Britain, bills not eligible for rediscount at the Bank of England.

INET: see *Interbank Network Electronic Transfer.*

infirmity: in the creation or transfer of title, any known act or visible omission in detail, that would invalidate the instrument.

inflation: an increase in the price level creating a decrease in the purchasing power of the monetary unit. Cf. *deflation, prime interest (rate).*

inflation accounting: the bookkeeping practice that shows the impact of inflation on corporate assets and profits.

inflationitis: slang for "the dollar-ain't-worth-a-hill-o'-beans blues."

infringement: encroaching on someone else's property (i.e., trespassing). Cf. *intrusion.*

ingot: a bar of metal cast from a mold.

ingress: the ability to enter property or land.

inherit: to acquire the property of a person who dies intestate. See also *devolution.*

initial issue: credit cards sent out at the inception of a credit card plan. [105]

in kind: value in goods and services as distinguished from value in money.

inland exchange: synonymous with *domestic exchange.*

in lieu tax: a substitute for property taxes in the case of public utilities. Usually, a tax based on gross earnings.

innocent purchaser: an individual who in good faith does not expect any hidden property defects to appear when he or she has gained title to real property.

in personam: a legal judgment binding the defendant to a personal liability. Cf. *in rem.*

in-plant banking: a banking service whereby facilities for banking transactions are provided to employees on the company's premises. [105]

inquiry balance: the amount of funds that will be displayed to the holder of a bank services card requesting a balance inquiry. [105]

in rem: a legal judgment that binds, affects, or determines the status of property. Cf. *in personam.*

Ins.: see *insurance.*

inscribed: government bonds such as savings bonds whose records are held by the Federal Reserve Banks rather than the U.S. Treasury.

insolvent: an individual who has ceased to pay his or her debts or is unable to pay such debts as demanded by creditors. See *bankrupt, bankruptcy.*

installment cash credit: money loans directly to an individual and repaid through periodic payments over a specified length of time. [55]

installment contract: synonymous with *contract for deed.*

installment financing: that form of financing which involves the repayment or amortization of an obligation by payments of fixed amounts at regular intervals. [55]

installment interest: the interest on a loan payable in equal amounts at regular intervals over a period of time.

installment loan: synonymous with *personal loan.*

installment payments: periodic payments made to discharge an indebtedness. Synonymous with *amortization payments.*

Installment Sale Revision Act of 1980: this legislation liberalized the rules for postponing tax on property that is sold on the deferred-payment basis.

installment sales (homes): homeowners wanting to sell their homes who act as lenders can reap a tax benefit by allowing purchasers to pay in installments. The Internal Revenue Service allows sellers to spread their gain over a number of years instead of reporting it all in the year of sale, and thus to defer most of the capital gains tax on the profit.

installment sales credit: a one-shot loan used to buy "big ticket" items, such as cars or appliances. A down payment is usually required and a contract is signed for the balance due, plus interest and service charges. The debt is repaid in equal installments over a specified period of time. Generally involves three parties: the buyer, the seller, and the lender. [78]

instant (inst.): a business term designating the present month (e.g., on the 10th inst.). Cf. *proximo.*

Institute of Financial Education: a national educational organization, affiliated with the United States League of Savings Association, dedicated to increasing the professional skills of savings association personnel through classroom courses, home study, executive training programs, seminars, workshops, clinics, and other methods. Formerly called the *American Savings and Loan Institute.* [59]

institution: an organization (e.g., bank, insurance company, investment company pension fund) holding substantial investment assets, often for others.

institutional investor: a company having substantial funds invested in securities (e.g., a bank, labor union, college).

institutional lender: a financial institution that invests in mortgages either directly or through the purchase of mortgages or mortgage-backed securities in the secondary mortgage market. [105]

institutional market: the market for short terms and commercial paper. This market is used by corporations and financial institutions needing cash or having cash to invest in large quantities for short periods of time. [105]

instrument: any written document that gives formal expression to a legal agreement or act.

instrumentality: a subordinate agency.

insufficient funds: used when a depositor's balance is inadequate for the bank to pay a check that has been presented. A service charge is often placed on the customer when the balance is not sufficient to pay the check.

insurable interest (property and liability version): any interest in or relation to property of such nature that the occurrence of an event insured against would cause financial loss to the insured.

insurance:

(1) *general:* a method whereby those concerned about some form of hazard contribute to a common fund, usually an insurance company, out of which losses sustained by the contributors are paid. See also *self-insurance.*

(2) *law:* a contractual relationship that exists when one party (the insurer), for a consideration (the premium), agrees to reimburse another party (the insured) for loss to a specified subject (the risk) caused by designated contingencies (hazards or perils), or to pay on behalf of the insured all reasonable sums for which he or she may be liable to a third party (the claimant).

insurance binder: a written evidence of temporary hazard or title coverage that runs for a limited time and must be replaced by a permanent policy. [105]

insurance company: an organization chartered under state or provincial laws to act as an insurer. In the United States,

insurance companies are usually classified as fire and marine, life, casualty, and surety companies and may write only the kinds of insurance for which they are specifically authorized by their charters.

insurance coverage: the total amount of insurance that is carried.

insurance policy: broadly, the entire written contract of insurance. More specifically, it is the basic written or printed document, as well as the coverage forms and endorsement added to it.

insurance trust: an instrument composed wholly or partially of life insurance policy contracts.

insurance trust expenditures: cash payments to beneficiaries of contributory social insurance programs (employee retirement funds, unemployment compensation, sickness insurance, etc.). Excludes cost of administration, intergovernmental expenditures for social insurance, and noncontributory payments to former employees.

insurance trust revenue: revenue from contributions required of employers and employees for financial social insurance programs operated by state and local governments, plus earnings on assets held for such systems.

insurance underwriting: see *underwriting.*

insured: the person(s) protected under an insurance contract.

insured account: a savings account, up to but not exceeding the prescribed maximum amount, that is held in an association whose accounts are insured by the Federal Savings and Loan Insurance Corporation or a bank belonging to the

Federal Deposit Insurance Corporation.

insured association: an association whose savings accounts are insured by the Federal Savings and Loan Insurance Corporation. [59]

insured bank: a bank that is a member of the Federal Deposit Insurance Corporation.

insured closing letter: a document given to the lender by a title insurance company which insures the lender against the failure of the title company's agent to perform his or her duties according to the lender's instructions. [105]

insured deposits: deposits in banks, which are guaranteed by the FDIC against loss due to bank failure. [105]

insured loan: a loan insured by FHA or a private mortgage insurance company. [105]

intangible (personal) property: rights to personal property as distinguished from the property itself (e.g., stocks, bonds, notes, and contracts).

intangible tax: a state tax levied on all deposits in a bank (stocks, bonds, notes, etc.), excluding certain exempted items. The tax is against the individual accounts.

intangible value: the value of a company's intangible assets. [105]

Inter-American Development Bank: established in 1959 to encourage economic development of 21 member nations in Latin America. Twenty representatives from Latin American countries and the United States initiated this effort.

Interbank: the New York-based originator of Master Card. Interbank is a nonprofit institution originally formed by a group of banks to combat Bank of America's credit card system.

interbank bid rate: the rate at which the clearing member purchased or made a bona fide offer to purchase U.S. dollars for immediate delivery from another financial institution in exchange for transaction currency. [105]

interbank borrowing: usually done when banks find themselves temporarily low on liquidity and approach banks that have an excess of liquidity in order to borrow funds.

interbank demand deposits: deposits held for other commercial or savings banks; the breakdown shows the amounts for domestic (United States) and foreign banks. [40]

interbank loan: a credit extended from one bank to another. [105]

Interbank National Authorization System (INAS): the national authorization network used to approve Master Card credit transactions. [36]

Interbank Network Electronic Transfer (INET): a national electronic data transfer system operated by ICS (Interbank Card Association). [105]

interbranch: a term associated with any action or function that takes place between or among the various branches of a bank. As an example, an interbranch memorandum would be sent to all branches within a banking organization to inform them of some action, function, or decision to be instituted. All branches would receive the same message, so that all would be coordinated and put the action into effect at the same time in the same manner. [10]

interchange:
(1) a concept for a national network of EFT participants that allows customers the use of EFT services outside their normal market area. For credit cards, the practice has long been done in the processing of foreign cardholder activity through local merchants (e.g., a California customer buys a hat in New Orleans). The draft settles through interchange without the actual transmission of the paper.
(2) the exchange of debit and credit transaction data between merchant banks and cardholder banks based on an agreement between the participants. [105]

interchange authorization: an amount at or below which an authorizing member may authorize transactions on behalf of an issuer and over which authorization must be obtained from such issuer. [105]

interchange fee: charge levied and collected by either the merchant bank or card-issuing bank for the processing of interchange transactions. [105]

interchange register: a listing of all transactions between a merchant bank and a cardholder bank. [105]

intercompany market: a market for borrowing and lending of funds between nonbanking firms, without any involvement of banks.

Interdistrict Settlement Fund: a U.S. Treasury gold certificate fund held for the account of and subject to the control of the Federal Reserve System to minimize the time and expense of settlement of the inter-Federal Reserve Bank transactions.

interest accrued: interest earned but not yet due or payable.

interest bearing: a debt instrument (i.e., note bond or mortgage) upon which interest is computed. This is distinguished from equities, upon which dividends are declared.

interest bearing note: a note in which the maker agrees to pay the face of the note with interest.

interest coverage: applies to the frequency with which interest charges are earned; found by dividing the sum of the fixed charges into the earnings available for such charges, either before or after deducting income taxes.

interest earned but not collected: represents interest on loans which has not been collected in advance, but is due and payable at specified times. Interest on demand loans usually comes into this class, collection being made each month, each quarter, or longer period of time, based upon bills being sent to the borrower for interest due. This is an asset (resources) account in the general ledger. Synonymous with *interest receivable.* [10]

interest equalization tax (IET): a form of foreign-exchange control established by the U.S. government in the early 1960s whereby any U.S. resident has to pay a special tax on any purchase of overseas securities.

interest expense: the expense incurred for interest on a debt.

interest on long-term debt: interest on outstanding bonds (mortgage and debenture), receivers' certificates, and miscellaneous long-term debt, notes, and so on, issued or assumed by the utility and which are due one year or more from date of issuance. [3]

interest only account: an account which in the last two calendar months has made one or more payments of which nothing was applied to principal (ledger card balance). Loans made during the last two calendar months are excluded. [55]

interest-only mortgage: where mortgage payments are smaller for a set period, with the principal paid off when the property is sold.

interest on the unpaid balance: interest charged at an agreed rate, calculated on the balance remaining on the obligation. [105]

interest payable: a liability representing accrued interest owed by a business.

interest penalty: a fee or additional charge made when the terms of a financial contract are altered. [105]

interest period: a rollover credit made available to a borrower on the understanding that he or she may select to borrow for periods varying typically between one month and one year.

interest rate: a percentage expressing the relationship between the interest for one year and the principal.

interest rate arbitrage: the movement of funds from one money market center to another through the foreign exchange market in order to obtain higher rates of interest. [105]

interest rate peg: monetary policy followed from 1942 to 1951 where the Federal Reserve System adjusted the amount of money in order to maintain a constant interest rate on Treasury securities. See *Monetary Accord of 1951*.

interest rate swap: the exchange of two financial assets (liabilities) which

have the same present value but which generate different streams of receipts (payments). See also *swap contract*. [107]

interest receivable: synonymous with *interest earned but not collected*.

interest receivable on special assessments: the amount of interest receivable on unpaid installments of special assessments. [49]

interest-sensitive assets: items on which the interest received or paid can be changed in the near future. [105]

interest short: a term describing the amount by which a payment is insufficient to pay the accrued interest on an account. [55]

interest table: a broad term given to any mechanical indexing device, or chart, permitting independent calculation of simple or compound interest, the discount or present value, and the like, on varied amounts for certain or varied times. [10]

interest waived: refers to the amount of interest due on an account which is relinquished due to certain circumstances and arrangements made for repayment of an account. [55]

interest warrant: a firm's request for payment of interest due on its notes, debts, and so on.

interfund accounts: accounts in which transactions between funds are reflected. See *interfund transfers*. [49]

interfund loans: loans made by one fund to another. [49]

interfund transfers: amounts transferred from one fund to another. [49]

interim closing: any closing of the books of account that occurs at some time other than at the end of a fiscal year and which does not involve the summarizing of the income and expense accounts. [105]

interim loan: a short-term construction loan made to finance improvements on real property. [22]

interim receiver: a court-appointed individual asked to protect a debtor's property until an official receiver is appointed.

interim statement: a financial statement prepared before the end of the current fiscal year and covering only financial transactions during the current year to date. See *statement.* [49]

interlocutory decree: issued before a final court decree; an intermediate decree that does not resolve the matter but settles some portion of it.

intermediary bank(s): bank(s) excluding ordering bank and beneficiary's bank that participate in a funds transfer. [105]

intermediary bank advice charges: information specifying who to charge for advising the intermediary bank and how to apply these charges. [105]

intermediary bank advice identifier: information used in contracting the intermediary bank in order to send an advice (e.g., phone number, cable address). [105]

intermediary bank advice instructions: additional information which pertains to notification of the intermediary bank (e.g., bank's name, hours of availability). [105]

intermediary bank advice method: a code that specifies the method to be used to notify the intermediary bank that the account has been credited or that funds are available (e.g., phone, letter, wire). [105]

intermediary bank identifier: a code that uniquely identifies the intermediary bank. [105]

intermediary bank identifier type: a code that specifies the type of identifier used for the intermediary bank. [105]

intermediary bank method of payment: specifies how payment is to be made to the intermediary bank. [105]

intermediary bank name and address: identifies the intermediary bank by name and, optionally, the intermediary bank's postal address. [105]

intermediate credit bank: one of the 12 Federal Intermediate Banks established in 1923 to provide banks and other financial institutions with a rediscounting facility for agricultural paper of an intermediate term.

intermediate-term credit: credit that is generally extended over a period of 3 to 10 years.

internal audit: a business audit carried out by the firm itself on a continuous basis. Cf. *look back.*

internal check: coordinated methods and measures adopted by an organization to check the accuracy and validity of data and to safeguard assets.

internal controls: methods and measures employed to promote efficiency, encourage acceptance of managerial procedures and policies, check the validity of management data, and protect assets.

internal debt: the debt of a nation.

internal economies of scale: factors that bring about increases or decreases to an organization's long-run average costs or scale of operations resulting from size adjustments with the company as a product unit. They occur primarily because of physical economies or diseconomies.

internal items: debit or credit memoranda prepared by or for an officer of the bank to adjust the balance in the general ledger and for a customer's account. Examples include corrections, loan proceeds, special customer charges, and certification entries. [31]

internal national debt: that part of the national debt owed to persons within the country owing the debt.

Internal Revenue Service (IRS): the federal agency empowered by Congress to administer the rules and regulations of the Department of the Treasury, which includes the collection of federal income and other taxes. It is divided into 9 regions with 64 districts and is also responsible for the investigation and prevention of tax frauds.

internal security audit: a security audit conducted by personnel responsible to the management of the bank or department being audited. [105]

International Bank for Economic Cooperation (IBEC): established in 1964 and headquartered in Moscow; responsible for the organization and execution of payments between members of Comecon and non-Comecon nations.

International Bank for Reconstruction and Development (IBRD—The World Bank): proposed at Bretton Woods in July 1944, commencing operation in June 1946. After phasing out activities of reconstruction, primary efforts are made to provide loans for economic development. The IBRD voted on April 27, 1992 to welcome Russia and the other former Soviet republics as members. See *International Monetary Fund.* See also *Development Finance Companies.*

international banking: bank operations dealing with foreign exchange, making of foreign loans or serving as investment bankers for foreign nations, provinces, municipalities, and companies.

International Banking Act of 1978: federal legislation designed to remove many of the competitive advantages that foreign banks had over their domestic counterparts. The Federal Reserve Bank is now authorized to impose reserve requirements on foreign banks, for example, and for the first time there are restrictions on their ability to take deposits nationwide. Its basic purpose is to apply the McFadden Act of 1927, which forbids branching by American banks across state lines, to foreign banks. Until passage of this new act, foreigners have been free to open branches in any state which allowed them in. See *Edge Act.*

international banking facilities (IBFs): specially designated offices in the United States, identified by the Federal Reserve Board, permitting banks to take deposits from and make loans to nonresidents, including overseas subsidiaries of U.S. companies.

international checks (cheques): traveler's checks acceptable and payable in other nations (i.e., the American Express Travelers checks).

International Development Association: an auxiliary credit agency of the World Bank to handle requests for soft loans to developing nations to be repaid over a longer time interval than traditional, and at times to be repaid in the borrowing state's own currency. See also *World Bank Group.*

international exchange: see *foreign exchange.*

international liquidity: the total for all internationally acceptable currencies in the monetary system of the world.

International Monetary Fund (IMF): to restore orderly exchange practices following World War II, the IMF was formed and became operational on March 1, 1947. Member nations can borrow foreign currencies from the fund under specified conditions. Membership in the fund is a prerequisite to membership in the International Bank for Reconstruction and Development. See *Bretton Woods Agreement of 1944, special drawing rights.*

international money management (IMM): strategies used by firms with multinational cash flows to maximize earnings from interest and exchange rate movements while reducing exposure to risk. [94]

international money order: a money order issued by a bank, express company, or post office which is payable overseas. See also *money order.*

International Organization for Standardization (ISO): the central body for the formation and dissemination of industry standards for all national bodies. ANSI is the U.S. member of ISO. [105]

international payments mechanism: the organization of markets whereby the monies of different nations are exchanged. See *swap.*

international postal money order: a money order issued by a post office which is payable overseas.

international trade: foreign trade measured by merchandise exports and imports of a country for a stated period, often one year.

international unit: a statistical device used to put data from a number of nations on a uniform base so that the different economies can be compared.

interpleader: when an individual who has an obligation to pay for services or goods does not know which of two or more claimants should receive his or her obligation, he or she brings a suit requiring the claimants to litigate between themselves.

interproduct competition (direct): firms offering products from different product classes to the same market, such as a brokerage firm's securities competing with high-interest CDs for corporate dollars. [105]

interproduct competition (indirect): firms offering products from different product classes but competing for prospects with limited purchasing power. [105]

in terrorem clause: a provision of a will or trust agreement intended or, at any rate, calculated to frighten a possible beneficiary into doing or refraining from doing something at the peril of forfeiting his possible benefits—such as a provision that would disinherit any named or potential beneficiary who contested the will. [37]

interstate branching bill: a concept that allows banks from other states to open branches with broad services in a different state, and vice-versa. In principle, interstate branch banking creates a free trade zone, but presently remains prohibited by the McFadden Act of 1927.

Interstate Land Sales Full Disclosure Act of 1968: federal legislation requiring all large land-sales promoters to furnish prospective buyers with a detailed and accurate report on the land and to spell out buyers' rights in the transaction.

intervention: a monetary agency's transaction to maneuver the exchange rate for its currency or the level of its foreign exchange reserves.

intervention currency: the foreign currency a country uses to ensure by means of official exchange transactions that the permitted exchange rate margins are observed. Intervention usually takes the form of purchases and sales of foreign currency by the central bank or exchange equalization fund in domestic dealings with commercial banks. [42]

inter vivos: "between living persons" (Latin). In the term "trust inter vivos" or "inter vivos trust," the same as living trust. See also *gift inter vivos.* [32]

intestacy: the condition resulting from a person's dying without leaving a valid will. [32]

intestate: not having a valid will; when a person dies intestate, his or her estate is presented for settlement to administrators. See *escheat.*

intestate succession: the descent and distribution of property of a person who dies without a valid will. [37]

intrabranch: used to express an action or function that is ordered to take place within an individual branch or office, and does not affect the action of other branches or offices of an organization. An example would be a personnel problem such as tardiness or absenteeism that applies only to one office or branch of an organization. An intrabranch memorandum would be sent to all departments within the one office or branch involved. [10]

intracity: an action or function taking place within one city. As an example, intracity clearings between banks within one city. This is to be distinguished from intercity clearings or collections, which means the exchange of items through transit between different cities. [10]

intraproduct competition (direct): firms offering from the same product class to the same market, such as bank ABC, Visa card, and bank XYZ's Master Charge card. [105]

intrinsic value: the market value of the material in a thing (e.g., the value of the metal in a gold tooth filling).

intrusion: forcefully taking possession of another's real property.

inventory financing: the attempt to find the necessary capital for a firm by borrowing funds with inventory used as collateral.

inventory float: the rate of use of a company's inventory. [105]

inverse demand pattern: exists when price and volume vary at the same time and more is sold at a high price than at a lower one.

investment: the use of money for the purpose of making more money, to gain income or increase capital, or both.

investment adviser: a person or firm that advises clients on investments and is required to register under the Investment Advisers Act of 1940 with the SEC.

Investment Advisers Act: federal legislation of 1940 to regulate investment advisers, in order to protect the public from misrepresentation and dishonest investment tactics, by identifying specific unlawful activities. All investment advisers are required to register with the SEC, the administrator of the Investment Advisers Act.

investment analysts: individuals whose profession is the study and comparison of securities. Investment analysts usually serve brokerage houses or investment institutions. [105]

investment bank: a bank serving as an underwriter for new issues of bonds or stocks and as part of a syndicate redistributes the issue to investors.

investment banker: the middleman between the corporation issuing new securities and the public. The usual practice is for one or more investment bankers to buy outright from a corporation a new issue of stock or bonds. The group forms a syndicate to sell the securities to individuals and institutions. The investment banker is the underwriter of the issue.

Investment Bankers Association: a national fraternity of investment bankers engaged in investment banking activities. The IBA was founded in 1912.

investment banking: the financing of the capital requirements of an enterprise rather than the current "working capital" requirements of a business.

investment banking house: one that engages in the merchandising of corporate and government securities by purchasing them in large blocks and selling them to investors. It helps to finance the capital, or long-term, credit requirements of business organizations, whereas the commercial bank finances their short-term credit requirements. [50]

investment bill: a bill of exchange purchased at a discount with the intention of holding to maturity as an investment.

investment broker: one who negotiates only cash transactions and not those on margin.

investment club: a voluntary grouping of people who pool their monies to build up an investment portfolio, which it is hoped, will give members a better return per individual than each would have expected separately.

investment company: a company or trust that uses its capital to invest in other companies. There are two principal types: the closed-end type and the open-end, or mutual fund. (a) Shares in closed-end investment companies are readily transferable in the open market and are bought and sold like other shares. Capitalization of these companies remains the same unless action is taken to change, which is seldom. (b) Open-end funds sell their own new shares to investors, stand ready to buy back their old shares, and are not listed.

Open-end funds are so called because their capitalization is not fixed; more shares are issued as people want them.

investment credit: credit given to a firm for the purchase of property, equipment, or other identified fixed assets.

investment dollar: dollars in London that are available for the purchase of dollar securities. In time of great demand these dollars are quoted at a premium, and the amount of the premium changes daily. As there are only so many dollars available in the investment pool, the rate charged to secure them changes rapidly throughout the business day, whenever there is an unusual demand for American securities. Synonymous with *security dollars.*

investment income: any income resulting from monies invested in securities or other property.

investment in default: investment in which there exists a default in the payment of principal or interest. [49]

investment in fixed assets: the book value of fixed assets. [49]

investment manager: those individuals or companies that perform the service of managing the investments of institutions or individuals. Investment managers charge a fee for performing this service. [105]

investment market:
(1) a place where securities and other investments are sold.
(2) the state of trade in investments.

investment media: any area in which capital is invested (i.e., securities, certificates, insurance, commodities, and business ownership).

investment property: real estate acquired for profit.

investment savings account: a savings account, usually represented by a certificate for each unit of savings placed in the account, on which earnings ordinarily are mailed to the account holder when payable rather than credited to the account. [59]

investment underwriting: see *underwriting.*

investors funds: actually retail (repos) or repurchase agreements that are not funds at all. Synonymous with *money funds.* See terms above.

invisible hand: a term first used by Adam Smith to describe the ability of the perfectly competitive market to bring about the greatest benefit for all, even when all merchants selfishly maximize their own profits.

invisible imports: services, financial or personal, rendered by foreigners to the natives of a given country. These may consist of freight and passenger charges, insurance and banking services, and so on.

invisible items of trade: items, such as freight and insurance charges, which, though not shown as exports or imports, are considered along with exports and imports in determining the balance of payments between two or more nations. Cf. *visible items of trade.*

invisible trade balance: as contrasted with the import and export of goods, the trade balance created by the import and export of services (i.e., consulting and advisory services).

involuntary alienation: forced sale of real estate.

involuntary bankruptcy: see *bankruptcy.*

involuntary lien: a lien on property demanded without the consent of the owner. Construction of sewers and sidewalks near an owner's property and property tax increases are examples. Synonymous with *lien in invitum.*

IOU: an informal written agreement acknowledging a cash debt (i.e., I owe you).

IRA: see *individual retirement accounts.*

iron man: slang, a silver dollar.

irredeemable: lacking any provision to repay in money or in kind or to exchange for something of equal value.

irredeemable money: synonymous with *inconvertible money.*

irregular savings account: a savings account containing a contractual variation as to time, notice, systematic buildup, additional earnings, earnings penalty, or similar provision. [59]

irreparable harm: injury or damage that is so constant and universal that no fair or reasonable redress can be achieved in court. Therefore, the plaintiff seeks resolution by injunction.

irrevocable credit: a credit that cannot, before the date it expires, be cancelled, revoked, or withdrawn without the consent of the person in whose favor the credit is given. Used mostly in foreign travel and trade, but also used in domestic business. Synonymous with *fixed credit line.*

irrevocable documentary credit: where a bank issuing credit gives an irrevocable undertaking to pay a seller provided that specific conditions are fulfilled.

irrevocable letter of credit: a contract by an issuer to accept drafts as conditioned by the contract and to charge them against his or her account. The letter is good for a given period of time.

irrevocable trust: a trust that cannot be set aside by its originator.

IRS: see *Internal Revenue Service.*

IS: see *income statement.*

ISF: see *Interdistrict Settlement Fund.*

Islamic Development Bank (IDB): founded in 1974 and headquartered in Jeddah; assists in financing the development of countries with substantial Islamic populations.

Islamic dinar: equals one special drawing right.

IS-LM model: explains the notion of policy mix, where the *IS* curve (depicts equilibrium in goods and services market) is the locus of combinations of interest rate and real economic activity consistent with equilibrium in the goods and services market. The curve is downward sloping because lower interest rates induce higher levels of investment, which increase real income through the multiplier. The *LM* curve (depicts equilibrium in money market) is the locus of combinations of interest rate and real economic activity consistent with the equilibrium in the money market. [81]

ISO: see *International Organization for Standardization.*

issuer identifier: that portion of the primary account number (PAN) which identifies the card issuer and/or primary processing endpoint, when combined with the major industry identifier. [105]

issuing bank: the bank that issues a documentary credit, on behalf of the buyer, in favor of the beneficiary.

Istituto Centrale per il Credito a Medio Termine: Italian government agency which pays interest rebates on or refinances export credits granted by Italian banks.

itemized statement: a recap of account activity for a designated period of time. [105]

items: as used in bank collections, a flexible term broad enough to include instruments payable in money generally. The term is often used in combinations such as cash items, noncash items, collection items, city items, and out-of-town items. [50]

J: see *judgment.*

JA: see *joint account.*

jack: slang, money.

JAJO: January, April, July, October (quarterly interest payments or dividends).

Japanese Long-Term Prime Rate (JLTPR): the rate charged by Japanese banks to their most creditworthy customers for loans of over one year. [168]

jawbone: slang, establishing financial credit by presenting clear, objective information.

J&D: June and December (semiannual interest payments or dividends).

J-curve: describing the expected impact of a devaluation on a nation's trade balance.

jeeps: 9.5 percent GPMs. See *graduated-payment mortgages.*

jeopardy clause: a Eurocurrency agreement clause stating that should certain events curtail a lender's activity or the operation of the Euromarkets, other designated actions (i.e., the substitution of another agreed rate of interest) will come into effect. [83]

JLTPR: see *Japanese Long-Term Prime Rate.*

Jnt. Stk.: see *joint stock company.*

JO: see *joint ownership.*

job: in foreign exchange, a bank dealing on its own behalf with other banks.

job account: an account pertaining either to an operation that occurs regularly or to a specific piece of work, showing all charges for material and labor used and other expenses incurred, together with any allowances or other credits. [49]

jogging: the procedure of recording on a storage device the occurrence of particular types of transactions or system activities. [105]

John Doe: a name given in legal proceedings to a party whose true name is unknown. [61]

joint account: an account owned by two or more people, subject to deposit or withdrawal by all signatures of all joint owners. In banks, any account owned by two or more parties is referred to as a joint account regardless of whether all parties or any one of the parties may sign checks.

joint adventure: two persons entering into a single business for their mutual benefit, as with partners.

joint and several account: when two or more persons desire to deposit in a jointly owned account, and the account is drawn against either by check or withdrawal order, the signature of any one of the owners will be honored.

joint and severally: a term frequently encountered in loan transactions when several persons sign a note for a loan. When the term "jointly and severally" is used, each person is legally obligated to become liable for the payment of the note; the group involved must also become liable.

Joint Commission on the Coinage: created by the Coinage Act of 1965, to determine whether the nation requires new coinage and if so, what form it should take.

joint contract: two or more people who make a promise to another are joint obligors to the contract and to the other party identified.

joint deposit: see *joint account.*

joint endorsement: an endorsement made by two or more payees or endorsees.

joint liability: a liability shared by two or more people. In the event of legal proceedings, persons jointly liable must be acted against as a group. [105]

jointly and severally: see *joint and severally.*

joint mortgage: any mortgage that has been signed by two or more mortgagors, being the joint obligation of all signers.

joint note: a note with more than one maker. Should there be a default, the holder sues all the makers on a joint basis as distinguished from a "joint and several" action that is against one or all the makers.

joint ownership: the interest in property of two or more people.

joint-stock banks: in England, the name for all commercial banks. This term does not apply to the Bank of England, private banks, and so on.

joint stock company: an association that is neither a partnership nor a corporation but has some of the characteristics of each.

joint tenancy: two or more people holding equal ownership of property. Upon the death of one of the parties, the decedent's interest automatically passes on to the surviving owner(s). See *undivided right.*

joint tenants by the entireties: an account held in two or more names from which either owner may withdraw funds but for which each owner is considered to own all the funds. [105]

joint tenants with right of survivorship: property (bank account, safe deposit box) held in two or more names, to which any single owner has access without notifying the others. Right of survivorship indicates that in the event of the death of one owner, the remaining tenant(s) immediately becomes owners of the property. [105]

joint venture: a commercial undertaking by two or more people, differing from a partnership by relating to the disposition of a single lot of goods or the termination of a specific project.

JOJA: July, October, January, April (quarterly interest payments or dividends).

Jour.: see *journal.*

journal: a record of original entry. This record may be written in pen and ink at the time a transaction is made, or may be created either in original printing or carbonized as the posting of the entry is made by machine. Cf. *ledger.*

journal entry: the interpretation of a business transaction, display of the bookkeeping treatment accorded the transaction, and an explanatory description of the transaction. [105]

journalize: the process of recording a transaction in an entity's records using the double-entry system. Debits, credits, and any necessary explanations are recorded in the journal.

journal voucher: a voucher provided for the recording of certain transactions or information in place of or supplementary to the journals or registers. The journal voucher usually contains an entry or entries explanations, references to documentary evidence supporting the entry or entries, and the signature or initials of one or more properly authorized officials. [49]

JSC: see *joint stock company.*

JSDM: June, September, December, March (quarterly interest payments or dividends).

judgment: a debt or other obligation, as determined by the decision or decree of a court.

judgment account: an account on which legal action has been taken and judgment obtained. [55]

judgmental system: a nonstatistical measure of evaluating credit worthiness. [78]

judgmental system of evaluating applicants: as used in the Equal Credit Opportunity Act, any system for evaluating the creditworthiness of an applicant, other than a demonstrable and statistically sound, empirically derived credit system. That system allows for the use of any pertinent element of creditworthiness, including any information about the applicant that a creditor obtains and considers and that has a demonstrable relationship to a determination of creditworthiness. [105]

judgment creditor: an individual who has proved a debt in court or has won an action for the recovery of a debt.

judgment currency clause: a clause found in a Eurocurrency credit agreement protecting lenders against any loss arising from the fact that the loan is made in one currency and judgment given by the courts in still another.

judgment debt: any debt contested in a suit at law and proved to be valid.

judgment debtor: an individual who has been ordered by the court to make a payment to another.

judgment in personam: a judgment against a person, directing a specific defendant to do or not to do something.

judgment in rem: a judgment against a thing, as contrasted with a judgment against an individual (e.g., bank account, personal property). See *judgment lien.*

judgment lien: a charge rendered in a state or federal court on a piece of land or personal property against one who owes a debt. When applied to personal property, it is generally termed an *attachment.* See *attachment.* [51]

judgment note: a note authorizing a creditor to enter a judgment against a debtor in case of nonpayment, without the need for court action.

judgment rates: rates established by the judgment of the underwriter utilizing his or her professional skills and experience, without the application of a formal set of rules or schedule.

judgments payable: amounts due to be paid by a governmental unit as the result of court decisions, including condemnation awards in payment for private property taken for public use. [49]

judicial accounting: an account of proceedings prepared for submission to a court having jurisdiction. [37]

judicial sale: synonymous with *forced sale.*

judicial settlement: the settlement of an account in accordance with the order, judgment, or decree of a proper court, the effect of which in many states is determined by statute. [32]

juice man: slang, a loaner of money at exorbitant interest rates.

jumbo CDs: certificates of deposit in minimum denominations of $100,000.

jumbo certificates: bank certificates earning in excess of 10 percent interest.

junior interest:
(1) a legal right that is subordinate to another interest.
(2) a mortgage participation junior to another participation.

junior issue: an issue whose claim for dividends or interest, or for principal value, comes following that of another issue, called a senior issue.

junior lien: a lien against a property that has a senior lien made and recorded. The rights are enforceable only after previous liens have been satisfied.

junior mortgage: a second or third mortgage that is subordinated to a prior mortgage. Cf. *equal dignity.*

jurisdiction: authority given by the Constitution to the courts to try cases and determine causes. Different courts get differing cases, based on the nature of the offense, the amount of the claim involved, and other factors.

jurisdiction risk: a risk inherent in placing funds in a center where they will fall under the jurisdiction of a foreign legal authority, which may become hostile, or which may apply biased legal procedures; can arise in any international transaction.

just compensation: a government payment for property taken under eminent domain which reflects a fair market value for the taken property and includes compensation for incidental loss of value which may result with respect to the remaining holdings of the property owner.

justified price: a fair market price that a buyer will give for property.

just title: a title that will be supported against all claims. Considered to be a proper title. Synonymous with *clear title,* and *good title.*

JV: see *joint venture.*

kale seed: slang, money.
KD: Kuwaiti dinar.
Keogh plan (HR 10): a form of tax-qualified retirement plan established by a nonincorporated

business or self-employed individual. Investment contributions and appreciation are generally tax deferred until actually received in the form of benefits. Formerly defined under the Self-Employment Individuals Tax Retirement Act of 1962. Until January 1, 1982, in each taxable year, the contributed amount could not exceed $7500 or 15 percent of annual earned income, whichever was less. Under the Tax Reform Act of 1976, for individuals with less than $15,000 of adjusted gross income, the minimum contribution would remain at the lesser of $750 or 100 percent of self-employed income. Effective January 1, 1982, a self-employed person or an individual who has outside self-employment income can put as much as $15,000 every year in a Keogh plan, double the old limit. But the 15 percent of earnings restrictions stays in effect for Keoghs. See *Economic Recovery Tax Act of 1981.*

key account: a merchant who is of particular importance to a card plan in terms of either volume or prestige or both. [105]

kick in: slang, to contribute money, to pay one's share.

kin: persons of the same blood or members of the same family. [37]

kind:
(1) monetary unit of Papua.
(2) when used in "distribution in kind" the distribution of the property itself, not its cash value.

kindred: persons related by blood. [105]

kip: monetary unit of Laos.

kite (kiting): writing a check in an amount sufficient to overdraw the account, but making up this deficiency by depositing another check, likewise in excess of deposits, and issued on some other bank. This unorthodox procedure is considered to be evidence of fraudulent intent (e.g., mailing in the rent when your account has insufficient funds, but counting on receiving and depositing some money before the landlord has a chance to present the check for collection).

koruna: monetary unit of Czechoslovakia.

KP: see *Keogh Plan.*

krona: monetary unit of Iceland and Sweden.

krone: monetary unit of Denmark and Norway.

kwacha: monetary unit of Malawi and Zambia.

kwanza: monetary unit of Angola.

kyat: monetary unit of Burma.

L: a new definition of money supply of the Federal Reserve Board: a broad measure of liquid assets, equaling M3 plus other liquid assets not included elsewhere, such as term Eurodollars held by U.S. residents other than banks; bankers' acceptances; commercial paper; Treasury bills and other liquid Treasury securities; and U.S. Savings Bonds. Cf. *M1, M1-A, M1+, M1B, M2, M3.*

LA:
(1) see *legal asset.*
(2) see *liquid assets.*

labor banks: banks whose stock is owned by labor unions and their membership. Cf. *industrial bank.*

labor-hour method of depreciation: taking the initial cost of a capital asset, deducting the expected salvage value at the time it is discarded, and spreading the difference on the basis of labor hours of use in an accounting period as a percentage of the total labor hours of use expected to constitute the life of the asset.

laches: neglect to do a thing at the proper time, such as undue delay in asserting a right or asking for a privilege. [105]

ladder: used in the control of money market and foreign exchange positions; consists of a listing, day by day, or month by month, of the outstanding maturity of money market deposits or forward exchange contracts. [136]

LAFTA: see *Latin American Free Trade Area.*

lagged reserve accounting (LRA): a Federal Reserve ruling of September 1968, changing the timing of reserve accounting by extending the one-day lag to a two-week lag. Under this system, required reserves for each settlement week (seven days ending each Wednesday) are based on deposit liabilities held two weeks earlier. Average vault cash held two weeks earlier is counted as a part of reserves in the current week, and vault cash in the current week is counted as reserves two weeks in the future.

land banks: see *Federal Land Bank.*

land certificate: a legal document indicating proof of ownership of land or property. Contains a description of property and the owner's name and address.

land contract: installment contract drawn between buyer and seller for the sale of property. Occasionally used as a substitute for a mortgage, except that ownership of the property does not pass until payment of the last installment. [78]

land development loan: an advance of funds, secured by a mortgage, for the purpose of making, installing, or constructing those improvements necessary to produce construction-ready building sites from raw land. [59]

landesbanken: state savings banks of Germany.

land freeze: government limit on the sale or transfer of land.

landlord: the owner of leased property; the lessor.

landlord's warrant: to obtain overdue rental payments, the landlord secures a court-approved warrant that permits him or her to take possession of the lessee's personal property in the leased premises until the debt is paid. Should the debt remain, the landlord can sell the personal property at public auction. See *distress for rent;* cf. *ejectment, reentry.*

land patent: a governmental document providing proof of title to land. Cf. *land warrant.*

land revenue: any form of payment derived from ownership of land. It may take various forms (farm produce, forest rights, mineral deposits, etc.).

land tax: a tax levied on the ownership of real property. An assessed valuation determines the rate of the tax. See also *cadastre.* Synonymous with *ad valorem taxes* or *property tax.*

land trust: title to land held by a trustee in the interest of the beneficiaries of a trust.

land trust certificate: an instrument granting participation in benefits of the ownership of real estate, while the title remains in a trustee.

land value tax: a governmental levy on the value of land only (i.e., not including structures or agricultural produce on it).

land warrant: a government document given as proof of ownership to anyone buying public land.

lapse:
(1) the failure of the insured to pay the cost of the premium when due, or within the days of grace allowed.
(2) the discontinuance of a right by the passage of time, as when the grace period of a mortgage ends or the date of a lease has passed.
(3) the termination of a right through disuse or failure to meet standard obligations over a fixed time period.

lapsing schedule: a form on which are recorded the costs of fixed assets or the total yearly additions to a group of fixed assets, together with the details of the distribution of their costs over accounting periods succeeding their purchase.

larceny: the unlawful taking of the personal property of another without the individual's consent and with intent to deprive him or her of the ownership and use of it. This offense is defined by statute in nearly all states and provinces, but there are some differences in the definitions.

La Salle Street: the financial center of Chicago.

last in, first out: see *LIFO.*

last will: the will last executed by an individual; all former wills are revoked by the last one.

late charge: a special fee demanded in connection with any payment on a mortgage loan or other obligation that is not made when due. [44]

late payment: a payment made after the due date on which an additional charge may be imposed. [78]

late posting payment: payment received and credited after the billing date. [105]

latifundism: the holding of land in sizable estates.

Latin American Free Trade Area (LAFTA): headquartered in Uruguay; founded in 1960 with the goals of trade liberalization and a system of reciprocal credits between members for financing payments imbalances. Members include Argentina, Bolivia, Brazil, Chile, Colombia, Ecuador, Mexico, Paraguay, Peru, Uruguay, and Venezuela.

laundered money: funds sent through numerous depositories one after another, in an attempt to conceal the source of the money. [105]

lawful money: all forms of money that are endowed by federal law with legal tender status for the payment of all debts, both public and private.

lawful reserve: banking laws establish the lawful reserves that must be maintained by banks for the protection of depositors' accounts. These reserves were established by the Federal Reserve Act of 1933 and 1935 for national banks, and by the banking laws of the various states for state-chartered banks. The Federal Reserve Board is vested by law with power to change the lawful reserve for national banks in order to control the supply of credit throughout the United States. This board may increase the reserve requirements in order to curtail the extension of credit, or it may decrease the reserve requirements in order to permit the expansion of credit. The various state laws follow a similar pattern, being more strict in some respects and less strict in others. The lawful reserves are required to be available at all times in the form of cash, and under certain conditions, government securities, either in the vaults of the bank, or in lawful bank depositories authorized by government or state officials. [10]

laws of descent: laws governing the descent of real property from ancestor to heir; to be distinguished from laws, rules, or statutes of distribution governing the disposition of personal property. [32]

lawsuit: a claim in a court of law. [61]

lay off: slang, spreading a large loan risk among others to prevent potential loss.

layoff loan: considered to be one within the legal limit of the country bank but taken by the city bank to aid a country bank that is highly loaned up.

L/C:
(1) see *letter of credit.*
(2) see *line of credit.*

LC: see *loan capital.*

L. Cr.: see *letter of credit.*

L&D: see *loans and discounts.*

leading indicators: 12 indicators, issued by the Bureau of Economic Analysis, chosen for their record in predicting turns in the business cycle, released late in the month for the previous month.

leads and lags: changes in the pattern of international payments terms. Should a devaluation of a nation's currency be feared, its importers with overseas currency obligations will rush to pay to avoid their debts becoming greater following devaluation; they *lead* payments. Conversely, exporters will benefit by not rushing to convert export receipts in foreign currency; they *lag* payments.

lease: a form of contract transferring the use or occupancy of land, space, structures, or equipment, in consideration of a payment, usually in the form of rent. Leases can be for a short period or as long as life. In a lease, the lessor gives the use of the property to a lessee.

lease (regular or commercial): agreement to occupy and use space for a definite term at a fixed monthly rental. [24]

leaseback: a seller who remains in possession as a tenant after completing the sale and delivering the deed.

lease broker: an individual in the business of securing leases for speculation and resale in areas where land plays or exploration work is being carried out.

leased fee interest: an interest of the owner in a leased property.

lease financing: a specialized area of finance dealing with renting property owned by the lender, financing the leases of a company engaged in rentals, and financing the purchase of an item to be leased out by the borrower. [105]

lease ground: a lease that provides for occupancy and use of a parcel of unimproved land often, though obviously not always, for the construction of a building. In the event the lessee is to assume all property charges, more descriptive terminology would be *net ground lease.* [6]

leasehold: an estate or interest a tenant holds for a number of years in the property he or she is leasing.

leasehold obligation: an obligation in a leasehold, to pay a specified rental for a specified number of years.

leasehold value: the market value of a lease may increase or decrease over what was originally paid.

lease-purchase agreement: an agreement providing that a portion of a tenant's rent can be applied to the price of purchase.

Led.: see *ledger.*

ledger: a record of final entry in bookkeeping. An account is established for every type of transaction, and a ledger account is posted with every transaction affecting this particular account. Cf. *journal.*

ledger asset: those assets for which accounts are maintained in the general ledger. [42]

ledger balance: the record of the balance in a customer's account, according to the bank's records. The ledger balance may not reflect all deposits if the bank has not yet received actual payment for them. [105]

ledger control card: a monthly record to date of the total debits, credits, and balances of the customer accounts it represents. In demand deposit accounting, this card is the final record of its group to be updated. [31]

ledger journal: a record that functions as both journal and ledger. [105]

ledger proof card: a record prepared daily containing total debits and credits affecting a given group of accounts. In demand deposit accounting, this card follows the customer account cards. Its reconciliation with the daily updating totals is the control for its group. [31]

left-hand side: the rate at which a bank offers a foreign currency. [105]

legacy (bequest): a gift of personal property made in a will. There are four common types of legacy: (a) *specific legacy*—a gift of a particular piece of property, as an automobile, or an investment that has been specifically described; (b) *demonstrative legacy*—one payable in cash out of a particular designated fund; (c) *general legacy*—a gift of money in a certain sum; and, (d) *residual legacy*—includes all the remaining personal property after the payment of all obligations, charges against the estate, and all other legacies.

legal asset: any property, including securities, that can be used for payment of a debt.

legal common trust fund: a common trust fund invested wholly in property that is legal for the investment of trust funds in the state in which the common trust is being administered. The term is employed most often in or with respect to common trust funds in states that have a statutory or court-approved list of authorized investment for trustees where the terms of the trust do not provide otherwise. [37]

legal entity: any individual, proprietorship, partnership, corporation, association, or other organization that has, in the eyes of the law, the capacity to make a contract or an agreement and the abilities to assume an obligation and to discharge an indebtedness. A legal entity is a responsible being in the eyes of the law and can be sued for damages if the performance of a contract or agreement is not met.

legal interest: the maximum rate of interest permitted by state law; this rate is used in contracts in which no rate has been stated. Cf. *usury.*

legal investments:
(1) investments that savings banks, insurance companies, trustees, and other fiduciaries (individual or corporate) are permitted to make by the laws of the state in which they are domiciled, or under the jurisdiction of which they operate or serve. Those investments which meet the conditions imposed by law constitute the legal investment list. (2) investments that governmental units are permitted to make by law. See *legal list.* [49]

legal list: a list of investments selected by various states in which certain institutions and fiduciaries, such as insurance companies and banks, may invest. Legal lists are often restricted to high-quality securities meeting certain specifications. [20]

legal name: an individual's personal first and last name, used as identification when entering into certain transactions. The name must be currently in use for financial purposes and must be used without fraudulent intent. [105]

legal obligations: a debt or promise to perform, that can be enforced by legal means if necessary. [28]

legal opinion: the opinion of an official authorized to render it, such as an attorney general or city attorney, as to legality.

legal ownership: an estate of interest in property which is enforceable in a court of law; to be distinguished from *equitable ownership.* [37]

legal partnership: an estate or interest in property that is enforceable in a court of law. Cf. *equitable ownership.* [105]

legal person: often applied to a corporation that is allowed to own property, to sue, to be sued, and to exercise many of the rights accorded to natural persons.

legal rate of interest: the maximum rate of interest that is permitted by the laws of the state having jurisdiction over the legality of a transaction. Interest in excess of this legal rate is termed usury. See *usury.* Cf. *usurious rate of interest.* [10]

legal reserve: part of a bank's cash assets that must be retained as protection for depositors; ruling from the Federal Deposit Insurance Act.

legal residence: where a person lives. The law does not require anyone to spend a majority of his or her time in a certain place for it to be categorized as a legal residence. However, federal law recognizes only one legal residence for an individual.

legal tender: any money that is recognized as being lawful for use by a debtor to pay a creditor, who must accept same in the discharge of a debt unless the contract between the parties specifically states that another type of money is to be used.

legal title: the claim of right to property that is recognized by law.

legatee: an individual to whom a legacy is given by will.

legend: the text on a bank note. [27]

lek: monetary unit of Albania.

lempira: monetary unit of Honduras.

lend: to give up something of personal value, for a definite or indefinite period of time, without relinquishing ownership. See *loan.*

lender: an individual or financial institution making a trade of placing an interest on money, as with a money lender, with the expectation that the money (or other item) will be returned with the interest. See *note.*

lender-dealer agreement: in mobile home lending, a document that spells out the exact conditions under which lender and dealer will do business, and the rights and responsibilities of each. [59]

lender of funds: see *promissory note.*

lender of last resort: the name given to a central bank that will lend to individual banks whenever they experience large withdrawals.

lender's agreement: the signed agreement between the bank and FmHA describing the bank loan servicing and other responsibilities. [105]

lending institution: a finance company, bank, loan or other organization that lends money and makes money by advancing funds to others. See also *personal finance company.*

lending margins: the fixed spread that borrowers agree to pay above an agreed base rate, often LIBOR, to banks providing a Eurocredit. The full rate of interest paid by the borrower is adjusted, usually every six months, reflecting changes in LIBOR.

lending rate: the interest rate charged to borrowers by lenders.

leniency clause: in a promissory note, a clause spelling out the association's willingness to adjust loan payments temporarily if a borrower is experiencing several financial difficulties through no fault of his or her own. [59]

leone: monetary unit of Sierra Leone.

lessee: a tenant.

lessor: a landlord.

let: to lease, demise, or convey, thus a sign "to let."

letter of administration: evidence of appointment issued by a court to an individual or a trust instruction to settle the estate of a decedent who failed to name an executor. [37]

letter of advice: a note giving instructions.

letter of attorney: a document showing a power of attorney.

letter of conservatorship: a certificate of authority issued by the court to an individual or corporate fiduciary to serve as conservator of the property of a person; corresponds with *letters of guardianship.* [37]

letter of credit: an instrument or document issued on behalf of a buyer by a bank on another bank or banks, or on itself. It gives a buyer the prestige and the financial backing of the issuing bank. The acceptance by the bank of drafts drawn under the letter of credit satisfies the seller and the seller's bank in the handling of the transaction. The buyer and the accepting bank also have an agreement as to payment for the drafts as they are presented. See also *circular letter of credit, confirmed letter of credit, irrevocable letter of credit, revolving letter of credit, straight letter of credit, traveler's letter of credit, unconfirmed letter of credit.*

letter of demand: see *payoff statement*.

letter of dispute: letter with a customer's signature explaining the nature of his or her dispute. [105]

letter of hypothecation: an instrument executed by the pledgor of items or the documents of title.

letter of indication: a bank's letter of identification given to a traveler who has bought a letter of credit.

letter of license: a letter by a creditor permitting a debtor to proceed as stated to avoid bankruptcy.

letter of lien: a document signed by a purchaser, stating that specific items are held by him or her in trust for the seller. As the buyer pays for the items, the agreement becomes null and void. Synonymous with *letter of trust*.

letter of moral intent (LOMI): an undertaking by a firm falling short of a legal guarantee, usually given by a parent firm in respect of a subsidiary.

letter of trust: synonymous with *letter of lien*.

letters of administration: a certificate of authority to settle a particular estate issued to an administrator by the appointing court. Cf. *letters testamentary*. [105]

letters of conservatorship: a certificate of authority issued by the court to an individual or corporate fiduciary to serve as conservator of the property of a person; corresponds with letters of guardianship. [105]

letters of guardianship: see *letters of conservatorship*.

letters patent: a government-issued instrument granting a right or conveying title to a private person or organization.

letters testamentary: a certificate of authority to settle a particular estate issued by the appointing court to the executer named in the will; to be distinguished from letters of administration. Cf. *letters of administration*. [37]

lettuce: slang, money, especially paper money.

leu: monetary unit of Romania.

lev: monetary unit of Bulgaria.

level accrual: accrual method of recognizing earned income by dividing interest balance by the number of months to maturity. [105]

level-payment plan: an amortization plan that provides for equal monthly payments covering both principal and interest during the term of the mortgage. Part of each payment is applied to interest as earned, and the rest of the payment is credited to principal. [44]

leverage ratios: relationships among balance sheet values that measure the extent to which owners, rather than creditors, finance a business. [105]

levy (writ of):
(1) placing a lien on land or other property of a defendant.
(2) the instrument authorizing the sheriff to take a defendant's property to satisfy a plaintiff's judgment.

Li.: see *liabilities*.

liabilities: the funds a bank owes. The largest liability for a bank is deposits. See *fixed liabilities, long-term liabilities reported by U.S. banks*.

liability: a debt or obligation stated in terms of money.

liability account: see *segregated account*.

liability for endorsement: a contingent liability arising from the endorsement of an obligation owing by another, and continuing until it is ascertained that the original debtor has met or failed to meet the obligation. In the case of the default of the original debtor, the contingent liability becomes a direct one of the endorser. [105]

liability hedge: a strategy for a bank to make its liabilities less sensitive to rate changes. When a bank takes in interest-sensitive deposits (e.g., six-month money market certificates) it can fix, or very nearly fix, the cost of reissuing or rolling over the certificates simply by short-selling securities for future delivery.

liability insurance: protection against the loss of property or earning power of a business or individual. Liability insurance is of various specific types: accident, health, property damage, collision, and so on. [105]

liability ledger: see *note notice.*

LIBOR: see *London Inter-Bank Offered Rate.*

license: a right to engage in certain activities for which permission is needed.

licensed lender: a consumer finance office authorized to conduct business in the state in which it is located.

licensee: a bank that has been granted the right to issue bank cards and operate a bank card plan by a licensing authority such as Visa U.S.A. or Interbank Card Association. [105]

lien: a claim on property to secure payment of a debt or the fulfillment of a contractual obligation. The law may allow the holder of the lien to enforce it by taking possession of the property.

lien affidavit: an affidavit either stating that there are no liens against a particular property or documenting and describing any existing liens. See *recordation;* cf. *no lien affidavit.*

lienee: a person possessing a right of lien on the property of another person.

lien in invitum: a lien placed on property without the owner's approval. Synonymous with *involuntary lien.*

lienor: the holder of a lien. See *voluntary conveyance or deed.*

lien placement fee: cost of recording with the secretary of state the security interest of a bank on the title of any new or used car. [78]

lien theory: a theory of real estate law which holds that a mortgage conveys to the mortgagee a claim to, or lien on, the mortgaged property. [59]

life beneficiary: a person who receives benefits from an estate, generally in the form of income, during his or her lifetime; sometimes called a life tenant if the estate consists of real property. [37]

life contingency: probability of living or dying. Tables relating to life contingency may be found in rate manuals. [12]

life cycle hypothesis: a theory of the saving decision stating that consumers save to be able to maintain a stable level of consumption in the future.

life estate: an estate in real or personal property that terminates when the owner dies. The future of the property (i.e., after the owner's death) is usually provided for when the estate for life is prepared.

life insurance: insurance providing for payment of a stipulated sum to a designated beneficiary upon the death of the insured. Various plans of life insurance are available to fit the differing needs of many classes of insureds—for example, endowment plans, which pay back the face amount of the policy to the insured if he or she survives the specified period of the policy, or annuity contracts, under which savings are accumulated and paid back in periodic payments of guaranteed lifetime income to the annuitant if he or she survives the specified period.

life interest: the estate or interest that a person has in property for his or her own life for another person's life, or for an indefinite period limited by a lifetime. [105]

lifeline programs: the Federal Reserve Board's effort to get banks to offer low-cost checking and banking services to low- and moderate-income customers.

LIFO (last in, first out): a method of determining the effect of withdrawals on savings account dividends or interest computations. With LIFO, withdrawals are made from money that was deposited last. The withdrawal penalty under this plan is loss of interest on the last money deposited. Cf. *FIFO.*

lift check: a check that is not drawn on a bank but through the bank against the maker. Many corporations issue payroll checks in the form of lift checks. The bank through which the items are drawn accumulates a group of these items and delivers them to the maker upon receipt of a regular check in payment of the total. [31]

light gold: gold coins that have been reduced in weight, either by error of the mint or as the result of usage.

light piece: slang, a silver coin, usually a 25-cent piece.

lilangeni: monetary unit of Swaziland.

limitations of actions (statutes of): the law for each state identifying the definite time limit to the period within which a law suit can be brought under law. The terms within the statutes vary by state; however, the time within which a commercial case action should be brought is usually six years.

limit control: the component of a bank card operation which has the responsibility of monitoring cardholder balances relative to credit limits and of taking appropriate action when credit limits are exceeded. [105]

limited audit: an audit in which the effectiveness of the system of internal control and the mathematical accuracy, legality, propriety, and completeness of all transactions are determined by examining only selected items. The assumption is that the transactions selected for examination are representative of the entire group from which selected, and, therefore, if no errors are found in them, the unchecked items in the group are also correct.

limited check: a check limited as to the amount. Such checks have inscribed on their face a legend that the item is void if for more than a certain amount. Limited checks are frequently used in payroll payments by check, with the maximum amount shown on the face. This is done to frustrate attempts to raise the amount of the check.

The date by which a check must be presented for payment also constitutes a limitation. [10]

limited coinage system: the U.S. Mint's program under which the right of the individual to bring bullion for purposes of being coined is limited.

limited depositary: a Federal Reserve System member bank which under stated restrictions can receive governmental deposits.

limited legal tender: moneys that formerly were legal tender in payment of debts up to a specified amount (e.g., pennies were legal tender up to 25 cents). This was changed by law on June 5, 1933.

limited open-end mortgage: an indenture under which additional bonds may be issued, but which establishes certain limits, or measures, of maximum amounts that may be issued. [37]

limited partner: a member of a partnership who is not personally liable for incurred debts of the partnership. By law, at least one partner must be fully liable.

limited partnership: see *limited partner.*

limited power of appointment: a power of the donee (the one who has the power) to pass on an interest in property that is limited in some way—as to or for whom or to the time within which he must exercise the power; also known as special power; the opposite of general power of appointment; all powers that are not general are special or limited powers. [37]

limited-reduction plan: an amortization plan that provides for only a limited amount of princi-pal reduction prior to the expiration date of the loan. [105]

limited resource agreement: an indirect lending arrangement where a dealer sells or discounts installment contracts to a bank and is liable in case of default for a limited time, a limited dollar amount, or both. [105]

limping standard: a modification of the gold monetary standard leading to the acceptance of certain silver coins as standard money to the extent that they are made unlimited legal tender and not required to be redeemed in gold.

line functions: functions that contribute directly to bank objectives (such activities as accepting and processing deposits, investing). [105]

line of credit: an agreement between a bank and a customer: the bank agrees, over a future period, to lend the customer funds up to an agreed maximum amount. The bank has the option to withdraw from the agreement if the financial status of the borrower changes, or if the borrower fails to use the line of credit for its intended use as set forth in the agreement. The customer may borrow as much of the "line" as is required and pay interest on the borrowed portion only. A line of credit is widely used by large organizations to finance future commitments and for purchases of inventory. May be "advised"—that is, the customer is officially notified of the existence of the line—or "guidance"—that is for the bank's internal use only.

line of discount: the maximum credit that a bank will extend to a retailer on the basis of his or her accounts payable, which the merchant discounts with the bank.

liquid: capable of being readily converted to cash. Usually the assets of an entity are considered to be most liquid when they are in cash or marketable securities. Synonymous with *collectible*.

liquid asset fund: see *money market fund*.

liquid assets: those assets that are easily converted into cash (e.g., government bonds). See also *flight of capital*.

liquidate:
(1) to convert (assets) into cash.
(2) to discharge or pay off an indebtedness.
(3) to settle the accounts of, by apportioning assets and debts.

liquidated claim: a claim or debt in which the amount due is fixed by law or has been ascertained and agreed upon by the parties and no bona fide dispute regarding the amount exists between the parties. [105]

liquidated damages: the payment by all parties of an agreed sum of money as damages for breaching their contract. The courts can declare the amount to be a penalty and unenforceable if the amount is excessive.

liquidating value: the anticipated value of a particular asset that will be realized in case of liquidation of a business. [10]

liquidation cost per installment: the primary costs involved in the payment of each installment, including teller time, bookkeeping, and collection expenses. [105]

liquidation cost per loan: the cost involved in removing a loan from the active file, canceling, and returning a note. [105]

liquidity: the solvency of a business, which has special reference to the speed with which assets can be converted into cash without loss.

liquid ratio: the ratio of readily available current assets to current liabilities.

liquid saving: individuals' saving consisting of, or easily and quickly convertible into, cash. These consist of currency, bank deposits, shares in savings and loan associations, and securities. Included are holdings of persons, unincorporated businesses, trusts, and not-for-profit institutions. [70]

liquid trap: the liquidity preference theory of John Maynard Keynes. The concept that at some low interest rate, the speculative desire for cash becomes infinitely elastic. Cf. *quantity theory*.

lir.: see *lira*.

lira: monetary unit of Italy, San Marino, Turkey, and Vatican City.

living trust: a voluntary trust created from the assets of a living person.

loading:
(1) the amount added to net premiums to cover a company's operating expenses and contingencies; includes the cost of securing new business, collection expenses, and general management expenses. Precisely: the excess of the gross premiums over net premiums.
(2) money added to an installment agreement to cover selling and administrative overhead, interest, risk, and so on.

loan: a business transaction between two legal entities whereby one party (the lender) agrees to "rent" funds to the second party (the borrower). The funds may be "rented" with or without a fee. This fee is called interest or discount. Loans may be demand or time loans, depending on the agreement as to maturity. Loans may also be short-term or long-term. Cf. entries under *lend.*

loanable funds theory of interest: a concept that the interest rate is determined by the demand for, and supply of, loanable funds only, as distinguished from all money.

loan application: a form used by banks to record the formal request for a loan by a borrower. The form is specially designed by each bank to incorporate the necessary information that the bank desires having on record. The loan application may be a simple form or a more complex one, containing information relative to the assets, liabilities, income, insurance, and contingent obligations of the borrower, as well as the purpose for which the loan is intended. [10]

loan bill: a bill of exchange drawn for more than the customary time period, usually over 30 days' sight.

loan capital: part of a corporation's capital formed by long- and short-term creditors (i.e., banks, noteholders).

loan-closing payments: expenses incurred when a mortgage loan is set (mortgage costs, legal fees for preparing the papers, appraisal and recording fees, etc.).

loan committee: the group of persons responsible for approving applications for loans and thereby committing the institution to making those loans, subject to the applicants' acceptance of the loan terms. [59]

loan contract: the written agreement between a borrower and lender of funds, in which terms and conditions of the loan are set forth. [105]

loan department: the department of the bank where all the paperwork as well as the actual loan transactions are handled. All notes and other negotiable instruments and all collateral securities are filed in this department, which is bailee or custodian of these instruments and securities. The "loans made register," the record of original entry for all loans, is created here. The note notice and maturity tickler are filed here for ready reference. The liability ledger containing the complete loan record of each borrower is made and kept in this department. This department is the principal source of revenue for the operations of the bank. [10]

loan fee: any charge made to the borrower in connection with an association loan, and particularly a charge made in connection with a new mortgage loan; in the latter case, also called a *loan origination fee* or *premium of initial servicing fee.* [59]

loan fund: a fund whose principal and/or interest is loaned to individuals in accordance with the legal requirements and agreements setting up the fund. Such a fund is accounted for as a trust fund. See also *trust fund.* [49]

loan guaranty certificate: a certificate issued by the Veterans Administration advising a lending institution of the percentage of a particular loan that is guaranteed. [105]

loan guarantee fee: the fee FmHA charges the bank for its guarantee.

This fee is usually 1 percent of the total loan and is nonrefundable. [105]

loan information sheet: in secondary market transactions, a listing of loans being offered for sale, showing principal balance, term, loan-to-value ratio and other items. [59]

loan-in-process account: an accounting category representing funds remaining to be disbursed on mortgage loans that have been closed. [59]

loan interest: the amount of money paid for the use of capital or borrowed funds.

loan ledger: the liability ledger.

loan loss provision: a charge for anticipated loan losses, which appear on an income statement as an operating expense.

loan loss reserve: an account established based on a bank's loss experience to compensate for expected losses from the loans extended. [105]

loan market: places, such as banks, financial institutions, and trust companies, where loans are made.

loan maturity: date when a note becomes due and payable. [105]

loan modification provision: a clause in a mortgage permitting the borrower to defer one or more payments in the event of financial difficulties.

loan note guarantee: FmHA's signed commitment setting forth the terms of its guarantee to the bank. [105]

loan note guarantee report of loss: bank's report to FmHA of a loan default. [105]

loan officer: an officer of the bank who is designated with the responsibility of interviewing customers who may become borrowers. Certain officers have the power to grant loans. Large loans are approved by a loan committee consisting of appointed officers and directors of the bank. [31]

loan origination: all the steps taken by an association up to the time a loan is placed on its books, including solicitation of applications, application processing, and loan closing. See also *indirect origination.* [59]

loan origination fee: see *loan fee.*

loan passbook: a book in which loan payments, escrow account disbursements, and other loan account transactions are entered for the customer's records. [59]

loan predicated upon a security interest in real property: a loan secured wholly or substantially by a lien on real property for which the lien is central to the extension of the credit; that is, the borrower would not have been extended credit in the same amount or on terms as favorable without the lien on real property. [202]

loan proceeds: the net amount of funds that banks disburse from the borrower's loan account.

loan processing: all the steps taken by banks from the time a loan application is received to the time it is approved, including application taking, credit investigation, evaluation of the loan terms, and other steps.

loan rate: the rate charged for borrowing money at a specific date for a stated period. Cf. *legal interest.*

loan register: a loose-leaf or bound journal in which the details of loans are entered, usually in the order in which they are granted. [10]

loan relief: when the principal walks away via a cash or an exchange deal from an encumbrance that he or she had on a particular piece of property. [62]

loan repayments: repayments of outstanding loan principal to the association, whether in the form of regular installments or prepayments; excludes payments of interest, loan fees, and similar items of income. [59]

loans adjusted: the face value of customers' notes held (including bankers' acceptances and commercial paper purchased in the market) less interbank loans and reserves for losses on loans. [40]

loans and discounts: used by banks to designate all funds outstanding on loans. [31]

loans and investments adjusted: the total of loans adjusted, U.S. government securities, and other bank eligible securities. [40]

loans and notes payable: obligations outstanding in the form of loans and notes payable or other similar evidences (except interest coupons) of indebtedness payable on demand or within a time not exceeding one year from date of issue. [18]

loans and notes receivable: obligations in the form of demand or time loans and notes receivable, or other similar evidences (except interest coupons) of money receivable within a time not exceeding one year from date of issue. [18]

loans and other long-term assets: a part of total transaction in U.S. government assets, this account includes the flow of capital abroad resulting from all loans and credits with an original maturity of more than one year made by the federal government to foreign countries. Most of these credits finance U.S. exports of goods and services. [73]

loan schedule: a listing of due date, amount of payment, balance after payment, and other information relevant to a specific loan. [105]

loan servicing: all the steps taken to maintain a loan, from the time it is made until the last payment is received and the loan instruments are canceled. [59]

loan settlement statement: a document, prepared for and presented to the borrower at a loan closing, showing all disbursements to be made from the loan proceeds. [59]

loans in process: loans on which the bank has made a definite commitment but has not disbursed the entire loan proceeds.

loans made register: see *note notice.*

loans receivable: amounts that have been loaned to persons or organizations, including notes taken as security for such loans. The account is usually found only in the trust and agency funds balance sheet. [49]

loans to nonbank financial institutions: loans outstanding to nonbank financial institutions, subdivided as follows: sales finance, personal finance, factors, business credit companies; and others, including mortgage companies, mutual savings banks, savings and loan associations, insurance companies, and federal agencies. [40]

loan teller: an employee in the loan department who handles loan transactions. This teller is the custodian of cash in the loan teller's cash till (except in larger banks), and handles all direct transactions involving loans for the loan officer, upon the officer's recommendations and approval. The teller usually computes the interest based upon the rate set by the loan officer, accepts collateral over the counter, and performs all duties of a regular teller, but dealing specifically with the functions of the loan department. [10]

loan term: the time period granted for repayment of a loan. [59]

loan to facilitate: a mortgage loan in which the association provides the borrower with funds to purchase real estate that the association has acquired in salvage of mortgage loans. [59]

loan-to-value ratio: the ratio between the amount of a given mortgage loan and the appraised value of the security for that loan, expressed as a percentage of the appraised value. [105]

loan value: the amount a lending organization will lend on property.

loan-value ratio: the ratio of a property's appraised value in proportion to the amount of the mortgage loan.

loan voucher: a document required by some state laws, itemizing, identifying, and detailing the distribution of funds covered by the face amount of the note, including such items as discount or loan charges, fees, insurance premiums, rebates, and checks issued. [55]

lobby: the main banking room of a bank where depositors and customers of the bank may transact business with the bank. The ordinary business is transacted through the teller, whereas loans, credit extensions, trust operations, and the more complex matters of finance are handled in privacy in offices away from the bank lobby. [10]

LOC: see *letter of credit.*

local clearings: *local items.*

local items: checks drawn on other banks in the same city as the bank currently holding them. Synonymous with *local clearings.* [31]

lock box: a specialized service by which a bank acts as an agent in directly receiving and collecting a customer's incoming payments.

lockup: a note or obligation that has been renewed, the time of repayment having been extended beyond the original due date.

logo: a symbol used by a particular company or individual for identification purposes, often imprinted on letterheads and checks.

Lombard loan: a central bank loan supported by collateral such as stock and bonds. Term used primarily in England and parts of Europe.

Lombard rate: German for the rate of interest charged for a loan against the security of pledged paper.

Lombard Street: the financial area in London.

LOMI: see *letter of moral intent.*

London interbank offered rate (LIBOR): a measure of what major international banks charge each other for large-volume loans of Eurodollars, or dollars on deposit outside the United States.

long and short haul clause: the provision in the Interstate Commerce Act, as amended, which prohibits carriers from charging higher rates for a short haul than for a longer haul which includes the short haul.

long draft: a draft for more than the customary time period.

longer-term loan (term loans): funds loaned to business for more than one year, usually to acquire fixed assets. [105]

long-form mortgage clause: provides for the assumption of responsibility, for the satisfaction of the mortgage by the mortgagor when he or she takes title; the mortgagor does not simply acquire the property.

long green: slang, paper money.

long of exchange: when a trader in foreign currency holds foreign bills in an amount exceeding the bills of his or her own that have been sold and remain outstanding, the trader is long of exchange.

long-term liabilities reported by U.S. banks: include long-term deposits—in excess of one year—by foreigners in U.S. banks, mainly by foreign officials or international agencies. Some of these liabilities consist of deposits used to finance U.S. imports, plant expansion, and other financial transactions which would involve U.S. banking services, such as a foreign government's line of credit to a U.S. bank. The flow in the opposite direction appears in claims reported by U.S. banks: long-term. [3]

long-term mortgage: a home mortgage running 40 or more years.

look back: the auditing of past records to locate errors that have come to the attention of a bank's auditing department. Cf. *internal audit.*

loophole certificate (CD): under present regulations, federally insured banks are permitted to pay the market interest rate—that pegged to the weekly auction of Treasury bills—only on deposits of $10,000 or more. With the loophole certificate of deposit, the saver is loaned, generally at an annual rate of 1 percent, the difference between his or her deposit sum and the $10,000. For example, if

the depositor has only $5000, the bank issues a passbook loan for the other $5000. The loan is automatic and requires no collateral. It is only a paper transaction and the consumer never touches the money. It is credited to his account at the beginning and extracted six months later.

loot: slang, money, especially large sums of it.

Lorenz curve: a graphic device for plotting the degree of inequality in the distribution of income.

Loro Account: denoting the account of a third party, for example, a London bank paying $1 million to the Chase Manhattan Bank for the credit of the Loro Account of the Dresdner Bank, which is held by the Chase Manhattan Bank.

loss payable clause: provides for payment to a party (e.g., mortgagee or lienholder) in addition to the insured, for any losses to the insured property according to the extent of that party's interest in the property at the time of the loss.

loss ratio: a percentage arrived at by dividing the amount of the losses by the amount of the insured premium. Various loss ratios are computed (e.g., earned premium to incurred losses, written premium to paid losses).

loss reserve: a part of assets retained by a bank in available form to meet expected claims (i.e., insurance coverage on a mortgage).

lost card: a bank card that has been reported to the credit card issuer as lost or misplaced by the cardholder of record. [105]

lost in transit: an item lost between the center and either the clearinghouse or community office. [105]

lost opportunity: a professional money manager's description for investments that are not earning the current available rate of interest.

lost policy release: a statement signed by the insured releasing the bank from all liability resulting from a lost or mislaid contract of insurance.

lot:
(1) any group of goods or services making up a single transaction.
(2) a parcel of land having measurable boundaries.

low grade: of inferior quality, applied to merchandise, stocks, and so on.

low interest: an account on which the rate has been reduced to 12 percent per annum simple interest or less. [55]

LR: see *loan rate.*

LRA: see *lagged reserve accounting.*

Lshld.: see *leasehold.*

LT:
(1) see *legal tender.*
(2) see *legal title.*

lucrative title: a title that is obtained by a person who pays less than the true market value of the property; title to property obtained as a gift.

lump sum purchase: a group of assets obtained for an indicated figure, without breakdown by individual assets or classes of asset.

LUXIBOR: Luxembourg Interbank Offered Rate.

M: the equilibrium nominal money stock. [81]

M1: see *M-1A.*

M-1A: recent money supply definition of the Federal Reserve Board (1980), replacing the old M1 definition; currency plus demand deposits at commercial banks. This is essentially the same as the old M1 with one exception: it excludes demand deposits held by foreign banks and official institutions. See also *L, M-1B, M2, M3, M4, M5.*

M-1B: recent money supply definition of the Federal Reserve Board (1980); equals M-1A plus other checkable deposits at all depositary institutions, including NOW accounts, automatic transfer service, credit union share drafts, and demand deposits at mutual savings banks. See also *L, M-1A, M2, M3, M4, M5.*

M2: recent money supply definition of the Federal Reserve Board (1980); equals M-1B plus savings and small-denomination time deposits at all depositary institutions, overnight repurchase agreements (RPs) at commercial banks, overnight Eurodollars held by U.S. residents other than banks at Caribbean branches of member banks, and money-market mutual fund shares. See also *L, M-1A, M-1B, M3, M4, M5.*

M3: recent money supply definition of the Federal Reserve Board (1980); equals M2 plus large-denomination time deposits at all depositary institutions and term repurchase agreements at commercial banks and savings and loan associations. See also *L, M-1A, M-1B, M2, M4, M5.*

M4: (defunct) includes M2 plus large negotiable CDs at banks. [33]

M5: (defunct) includes M3 plus large negotiable CDs at banks, savings banks, credit unions, and savings and loans. [33]

M10: U.K. term for a measure of the wide monetary base. It comprises notes and coin in circulation and at the banks, plus banks' operational balances with the Bank of England. Changes to monetary aggregates and the analysis of bank lending, Bank of England, Quarterly Bulletin, March 1984.

Macaulay duration: an attempt to adjust the maturity of a bond by the size of its coupon to provide a better estimate of its true maturity; discounts the cash flows by the prevailing average yield to maturity.

machine pay: a plan of checking account posting whereby all media, both checks and deposits, are posted to a journal only on the first "run" of the media. The old balances of all affected accounts are picked up, the media posted, and new balances extended as in any posting run. The affected accounts may or may not be offset, depending upon the using bank's preference. The machine pay journalizing mechanically shows up items to be returned for insufficient funds, or paid as overdrafts. The run also establishes totals for checks, deposits, and new balances of affected accounts. The subsequent run on the depositor's statements must then prove to the machine pay run for checks, deposits, and new balances, verifying that the items were posted correctly, checks as checks, deposits as deposits, and the right accounts selected. [10]

magic mortgage: lending method enabling buyer to purchase a house with a very low down payment but requiring a yearly interest fee to the insurer of the loan. The term derives from MGIC, Mortgage Guarantee Insurance Corporation, which promoted the idea.

mail deposit: a deposit received by the bank through the mail rather than over the counter. The bank credits the customer's account and mails a receipt back to the customer. [31]

mail order (MO): a written direction received by mail from a cardholder wishing to have the purchase amount charged to his or her account. Special authorization procedures usually govern mail orders. [105]

mail teller: this name is used to designate the teller or division that handles deposits received by mail. [31]

maint.: see *maintenance.*

maintenance:
(1) the upkeep of any form of property (land, machinery, tools, etc.).
(2) all expenditures made to preserve an asset's value.
(3) support or sustenance that a person is legally bound to give to another.
(4) interfering unlawfully in a suit between others by assisting either party (e.g., giving one party money).

maintenance margin: the amount of money required by a clearinghouse to retain a futures position. It is less than the initial margin and allows the flexibility needed to permit minor price fluctuations.

maintenance reserve: an amount reserved to cover costs of maintenance. [62]

major industry identifier: the first digit of the Primary Account Number, signifying the major industry issuing the plastic card. [105]

majority-owned subsidiary: a subsidiary for which more than 50 percent of the outstanding voting capital stock is owned by the parent company or by another of the parent's majority-owned subsidiaries. [105]

majority stockholders: those who own more than 50 percent of the voting stock corporation, thus having controlling interest.

make good: to discharge an obligation or debt.

maker: an individual, firm, or other legal entity who signs a note, check, or other negotiable form as a responsible party.

make the cash: to decide whether the funds on hand, following receipts and payments, balance with the record of sales payments of obligations.

make-up day: in Great Britain, the day of the month on which figures are compiled for reporting to the Bank of England; usually the third Wednesday of each month.

mala fides: see *bad faith.*

malfeasance: a wrong doing; a criminal act (e.g., a public official taking graft). Cf. *misfeasance.*

malicious: describes an improper act done purposefully without excuse.

maline: a state of mind that is non-caring of the law and other's rights.

managed currency: a currency whose quantity is increased or decreased according to changes in the general price level or other objectives. The

management is by the government of a country or its central bank. The management may be designed to influence the internal price level of a nation or the ratio of that price level to the price levels of other nations, or both, or to pursue other objectives.

managed money: a monetary system in which government tries to control the circulation of money to achieve a specific goal, such as the stabilization of prices.

manager: a bank involved in managing a Eurocredit or an issue of a security.

managing agency accounts: an agency account concerning which the agent has managerial duties and responsibilities appropriate to the kind of property and in conformity with the terms of the agency; to be distinguished from a safekeeping or custody account. [37]

managing agent: the service by which an agent assumes an active role in administering another's property. [105]

managing underwriter: the syndicate organizer, also referred to as the syndicate manager or the principal underwriter. [26]

mandate: a court order to an authorized agency or officer to enforce a decree, judgment, or sentence to the court's satisfaction.

mandate of protest: see *notice of dishonor.*

mandatory: obligatory; as a power of a trustee which the trustee must exercise, mandatory power, the equivalent of a direction. [37]

MANF: May, August, November, February (quarterly interest payments or dividends).

Marg.: see *margin.*

margin:
(1) the difference between the cost of sold items and the total net sales income. See *contribution margin, profit.*
(2) the difference between the market value of collateral pledged to secure a loan and the face value of the loan itself. See also *remargining.*

marginal activity: a commercial venture barely able to meet its expenses from its revenues.

marginal analysis: the analysis of economic information by examining the results of the value added when one variable is increased by a single unit of another variable.

marginal borrower: a borrower who will reject an opportunity to borrow if the interest charge is increased.

marginal land: land that will merely repay the cost of products grown on it and will not yield increased revenue.

marginal lender: a lender or investor who will refuse to lend or invest if the rate of interest is lowered.

marginal productivity theory of interest: an interest theory explaining the interest rate as tending under competitive conditions to equal the marginal addition to output by the last unit of capital when the amount of available capital is assumed fixed.

marginal risk: the risk that a customer goes bankrupt following entry into a forward contract when the bank must close its commitment in the market, thereby running the risk that the exchange rate has shifted unfavorably in the interim. The risk is confined to the marginal amount of such a movement. Cf. *capital risk.*

marginal trading: the purchase of a security or commodity by one who borrows funds for part of the purchase price rather than paying for the entire transaction with his or her own money.

margin buying: using credit given by a broker to purchase securities.

margin call: if a borrower has securities pledged as collateral for a loan, and a declining market for the securities forces the value of the securities downward, the bank is responsible for seeing that the margin requirements are maintained. The bank will request more margin from the borrower, who will either have to pledge more collateral or partially pay the loan, to meet the established margin requirements. Synonymous with *margin notice.*

margin notice: synonymous with *margin call.*

margin of safety:
(1) the balance of income left after payment of fixed charges.
(2) the difference between the total price of a bond issue and the true value of the property for which it is issued.

margins: the limits around the par value within which a spot exchange rate of a member nation's currency is allowed to move in actual exchange market dealings and public transactions.

marketability: the rapidity and ease with which a given asset can be converted into cash. Cf. *liquid.*

marketable: that which can be sold, e.g., property that can be sold to a purchaser within a reasonable period.

marketable title: title to property that is free of defects and will be accepted by a lawyer without objection. Cf. *cloud on title, perfect title.* Synonymous with *clear title, good title.*

market acceptance: the banks, bankers, business firms, and corporations involved in transactions in bank acceptance. [105]

market audit: a method for studying the marketing activities and structure of a bank or financial institution. It is designed primarily to identify areas in which improvements are necessary to boost profits.

market data approach to value: in appraising, the estimation of the market value of a property by comparing it with similar properties sold recently. [59]

market demand: the total amount of a bank service that is wanted at a specified price at a specific time.

marketing profile: resource providing information to allow bank management to assess the future intelligently with respect to problems and opportunities, areas of potential and growth, and how the market is changing. [105]

market maker: a broker or bank that is prepared to make a two-way price to purchase or sell, for a security or a currency on a continuous basis.

marketplace: a general term identifying business and trade activities.

market rate: the interest rate charged a firm in order to borrow funds.

market ratio: the power of one good to command another in exchange for itself in a free market. Often used with reference to the relative value of gold and silver.

market share: a bank's percentage of the industry's total sales.

market stabilization: attempts to stop the working of the full and free forces in a market by some agency, such as the underwriter of an issue or a sponsoring investment banker; usually prohibited by the SEC. One exception is made when an initial offering is registered with the SEC receiving authorization to "peg" or stabilize prices of an issue. Sometimes a secondary offering receives such permission.

market value: the price that property will command on the open market. The price for which an owner is prepared to sell property and the amount a purchaser is willing to pay. See *reasonable value.*

markka: monetary unit of Finland.

mark signature: when a person is unable to write his own name, a mark or other indication (e.g., an "X") is affixed to a legal instrument.

marshaling of assets: a rule for the distribution by a court of equity of a debtor's property among his or her creditors, requiring that each creditor so exhaust his or her right as to permit all others to be paid if possible.

Maryland Savings-Share Insurance Corporation: a state-chartered mutual corporation in Maryland that insures the savings deposits held by member savings associations and serves as a central credit facility. [59]

MAS: see *Monetary Authority of Singapore.*

Massachusetts trust: see *business trust.*

masse monetaire: French for *money supply.*

master budget: comprised of all the departmental budgets in a bank or financial institution.

master file: the updated record of the closing balance in each account at a bank, as produced by the combination of the previous day's tape with the daily transactions tape. [105]

master in chancery: an official appointed by a court to assist by taking testimony, calculating interest, projecting damage costs, determining liens, and so on, as requested by the court. Cf. *referee.*

master lease: an original lease.

master notes: paper issued by big credit-worthy companies. Unlike commercial paper, which may be sold to another company, these notes are issued only to banks. Cf. *commercial paper.*

master policy:
(1) a policy issued to cover the interest of a lender or lessor of property in the possession of others.
(2) a policy issued to an insured to cover property at more than one location. If locations are in more than one state, it is customary to issue underlying policies to meet the states' legal requirements.

Mat.:
(1) see *matured.*
(2) see *maturity.*

matched book: a situation where the maturity dates for a bank's or trader's liabilities match those of his or her assets.

matched sale-purchase agreements: when the Federal Reserve makes a matched sale-purchase agreement, it sells a security outright for immediate delivery to a dealer or foreign central bank, with an agreement to buy the security back on a specific date (usually within seven days) at the same price. The reverse of repurchase agreements, matched sale-purchase agreements allow the Federal Reserve to absorb reserves on a temporary basis. [1]

matched sales: Federal Reserve action to absorb reserve temporarily by selling securities with an agreement to purchase them back within a specified period (up to 15 days) at a stated price. Synonymous with *reverse repos, reverse repurchase agreements.* [90]

matching: the process of equating assets and liabilities, either by time or currency.

materialmen's lien: see *mechanic's lien.*

matured: fully paid up, fully carried out as to terms, completed as to time or as to contract. [28]

maturity: the date on which a note, time draft, bill of exchange, bond, or other negotiable instrument becomes due and payable. A note, time draft, or bill of exchange drawn for a future date has a maturity date that is set starting with the date of the loan or acceptance and runs the specified number of days from date of loan or acceptance of maturity. Presentation and request for payment of the instrument are made on the maturity date.

maturity date: the date on which a financial obligation becomes due for payment and/or an obligation or contract expires.

maturity gap exposure: the risk created by having an asset and liability of the same size and in the same currency but of different maturity.

maturity index: synonymous with *maturity tickler.*

maturity tickler: a form made and used in the loan department of a bank. The maturity tickler is usually a copy of the "note notice" and contains all information as to the amount, due date, maker, address, collateral, and so on. It is filed according to the due date of the note. This permits ready access to the number and total value of all notes maturing on any day. The maturity ticklers are generally used by bank officials and the loan committee in daily meetings when the maturing notes are under review and discussion for official reference and action. Synonymous with *maturity index.* [10]

maturity value: the money that is to be paid when a financial obligation or other contract becomes due.

MB: see *merchant bank.*

MBA: see *Mortgage Bankers Association of America.*

McFadden Act of 1927: federal statute that banned interstate banking. Recently, new legislation has been proposed to encourage competition in banking by permitting interstate banking as a way to stimulate competition for consumer loans. See also *Douglas amendment.*

McIntyre bill: legislation introduced in 1974 to establish an "Electronic Funds Transfer System Commission." The purpose of the bill was to concentrate on the need to preserve competition and maintain consumer privacy while considering all other impacts and implications of EFTS. [105]

McLean-Platt Act: superseded by the Edge Act. See *Edge Act.*

MD: see *maturity date.*

Md: the demand for nominal money. [81]

MDT: see *merchant deposit transmittal.*

measure of value: a function of money that gives the standard for identifying the results of production using the monetary unit as the common denominator.

mechanic's lien: the legal, enforceable claim of a person who has performed work on or provided materials for a given property. Such claims are permitted by law in certain states as a claim against the title to the property. A mechanics' lien may also grant the claimant a degree of preference in case of liquidation of an estate or business.

medium of exchange: any commodity (commonly money) which is widely accepted in payment for goods and services and in settlement of debts, and is accepted without reference to the standing of the person who offers it in payment. [39]

medium other than cash: checks, notes, credit.

meeting bond interest and principal: an expression indicating that payments are being made when due. [67]

megabuck: slang, $1 million dollars.

melon:
(1) slang, unusually large profits that have not been dispersed to eligible persons.
(2) slang, the profits gained from any business venture.

member: an organization that is a participant in a specific bank card plan. [105]

member bank: a commercial bank that is a member of the Federal Reserve System. All national banks are automatically members of the system, while state banks may be admitted. By law, member banks must hold reserves (consisting of their own vault cash and deposits with their Federal Reserve Bank) equal to a percentage of their customer's deposits. [7]

member-bank reserves: currency maintained by banks who are members of the Federal Reserve System, in addition to their deposits at Federal Reserve Banks.

memo entry: miscellaneous change to an individual cardholder account record. [105]

memo post: see *account inquiry.*

memorandum account: the record of an account maintained by a bank which is not included in its assets or liabilities. An example is the record of a bad debt written off, on which subsequent recoveries are anticipated. [10]

memorandum check: a check drawn by a borrower in favor of the creditor to be used to reduce a loan if the loan is not paid at the due date; the check is thus postdated.

mercantile paper: commercial paper, that is, notes, bills, and acceptances that originate from wholesalers, retailers, or jobbers.

mercantile rate of return: the ratio, expressed in percentages, between the figure showing on the contemporary income statement and the figure appearing on the contemporary balance sheet.

mercantilism: the economic policy under which nations measure their power by the amount of precious metal they have acquired.

merchant accounting: the recording by a bank of the number and dollar value of all sales drafts and credit slips submitted by each merchant. [105]

merchant affiliate: an affiliate who receives paper from a merchant. [105]

merchant agreement: a written agreement between a merchant and a bank containing their respective rights, duties, and warranties with respect to acceptance of the bank card and related matters. [105]

merchant application: a request form prepared at the time the merchant signs up with a bank card plan. The application contains basic data about the merchant, such as type of business, number of locations, and bank references. [105]

merchant bank: used in Great Britain for an organization that underwrites securities for corporations, advises such clients on mergers, and is involved in the ownership of commercial ventures (i.e., Rothschild's, Hambro's).

merchant base: total number of merchants who have signed merchant agreements with a bank card plan. May be expressed in terms of number of agreements or number of merchant locations. [105]

merchant call report: form used by bank card sales personnel to record the results of each merchant's sales or service call. [105]

merchant collusion: the situation in which a merchant has cooperated with an individual using a fraudulent bank card for the purpose of defrauding a bank credit card plan. See *merchant fraud.* [105]

merchant depository account: a demand deposit account established by a merchant with a bank for the purpose of receiving payment for sales drafts submitted to the bank card plan. [105]

merchant deposit transmittal (MDT): form used by merchants to deposit sales drafts and credit vouchers. [105]

merchant directory: a consolidated listing of all merchants participating in a bank card plan. [105]

merchant discount:

(1) the percentage of each retail sale a merchant pays when accepting a credit or debit card in lieu of cash at the time of purchase. The percentage is withheld, generally on a monthly basis from the total sales deposited by the merchant's bank. The rate of the discount is set by the merchant's bank based on (a) card processor fees and/or percentage of total sales retained, (b) competition, and (c) total relationship with the banks. Rates may vary by as much as 4 or 5 percent in different parts of the country.

(2) compensation received by a bank from a merchant for processing and accepting the credit risk on credit card sales. [105]

merchant file: a computer record of information on all merchants services by a card issuer. [105]

merchant fraud: the process by which a merchant has submitted and received payment for sales drafts imprinted with a lost, stolen, or revoked credit card, knowing that the bank card was invalid. [105]

merchant identification card: an embossed card supplied to each merchant to be used in imprinting a merchant summary slip which is included in the sales draft envelope. Minimum embossed data include merchant account number, name and location, and checking account number. [105]

merchant member: the member with which a merchant has signed an agreement to accept blue, white, and gold bank cards. [105]

merchant membership fee: the amount charged to merchants for the privilege of affiliating with a bank card plan. [105]

merchant number: a series or group of digits that numerically identify each merchant to the merchant signing bank for account and billing purposes. [105]

merchant operating guide: a document provided by the bank to each merchant location describing the basic operating procedures that merchants must observe in handling bank card transactions and deposits. [105]

merchant outlet: a merchant location. [105]

merchant penetration: the total number of merchant outlets affiliated with a bank card plan, expressed as a percentage of total merchant outlets in the market area served by the plan. [105]

merchant plastic: see *merchant identification card.*

merchant rebate: the retroactive downward adjustment of merchant discounts paid by those merchants whose volume or average ticket size exceeds a predetermined amount over a stipulated period of time. [105]

merchant solicitation: the process of calling on merchants for the purpose of seeking their affiliation in a bank card plan. [105]

merchant's rule: a rule for partial payments of delinquent interest-bearing debts under which repayments are considered to earn interest until final settlement and not considered as applied to past-due interest.

merchant statement: a summary produced and mailed at specified intervals, usually monthly. [105]

merchant summary slip: a multipart format used to total daily merchant sales, imprinted with the merchant identification card and submitted to the bank together with sales drafts. [105]

merchant volume: total amount of transactions at a bank's merchant outlet(s). [105]

merger: the combining of two or more entities through the direct acquisition by one of the net assets of the other. A merger differs from a consolidation in that no new entity is created by a merger, whereas in consolidation a new organization comes into being and acquires the new assets of all the combining units.

merger conversion: where mutual institution's depositors can vote on a merger but are not given any cash or stock by the acquirer. They do stand first to buy the acquirer's stock, in an offering equal to the mutual's market value, as appraised by, for example, an investment banker.

message: a communication containing one or more transactions. [105]

message amount: the sum of the transaction amounts of a message. [105]

message status indicators: information supplied by the sending bank or wire service defining special circumstances pertaining to the transmission of this message (e.g., suspected/possible duplicate). [105]

Michigan roll: slang, a wad of paper money, usually, smaller denomination notes wrapped by larger value ones.

milling: the corrugated edge found on a coin.

minibranch: a retail location consisting mainly of ATMs with very few desk people present. [105]

minimum balance: the amount of money required to be on deposit in a specific account in order to qualify the depositor for special services or to waive a service charge. [105]

minimum lending rate (MLR): a bank lending rate for its customers below which the financial institution will refrain from loaning money. MLRs have been popularized by the Bank of England.

minimum payment: the smallest monthly payment a cardholder can make and remain in compliance with the terms and conditions of the cardholder agreement. [105]

minimum property standards: FHA regulations establishing minimum acceptable building standards for properties to be covered by FHA mortgage insurance. [105]

minimum yield: the lesser of yield to call and yield to maturity.

minor coins: U.S. penny and 5-cent coins.

mint: where metallic money is coined or manufactured.

mintage: the charge made by a government for converting bullion into coins.

mint mark: the small letter found on a coin, or a similar device, showing at which mint the coin was produced.

mint par of exchange: the figure derived by dividing the pure gold or silver weight of the monetary unit of one country by the pure similar metal weight of the monetary unit of another country.

mint price of gold: the price for gold which the government will pay upon delivery to the mint.

mint ratio: the ratio of the weight of one metal to another, and their equivalent in terms of the national unit of currency, such as the dollar (e.g., x grains of silver $= x$ grains of gold $= \$1$).

MINTS: see *Mutual Institutions National Transfer System, Inc.*

minus asset: the amount that must be subtracted from the original value of an asset in order that the present value of the asset may be known. [73]

MIP: see *mortgage insurance premium.*

miscellaneous charges: any charges other than advice charges germane to the transfer. [105]

miscellaneous chattel mortgage: a chattel mortgage taken on items other than household goods or a licensed automobile or truck. [55]

misencoded card: a valid card on which erroneous information has been encoded or otherwise inadvertently applied (e.g., name and/or account number and/or expiration date). [105]

misfeasance: illegal or improper exercise of a legal responsibility; failure to properly perform a lawful act, or the performing of an action without proper notice of those involved. Cf. *nonfeasance.*

mismatch: when assets and liabilities in a foreign currency fail to balance, the imbalance being either in maturity or size.

misposting: an error that causes a monetary transaction to be posted to the wrong account. [105]

misrepresentation: the giving of a positive statement or the claim to an alleged fact that is not true, thus leading to a false conclusion.

missent item: an item that has been sent in error to another bank.

missing payment: payment made that has not been posted to the appropriate account. [105]

missort: generally, a check drawn by a depositor which is wrongly sorted to a "book" or bank other than that in which the account is kept. [31]

mixed account: the balance in these accounts contains both a real and a nominal element. For example, expense or income accounts requiring adjustment for deferred expenses or income; or the sales account, the real element being cost of goods sold or decrease in merchandise, and the nominal element being profit or loss on sales.

mixed currency: a currency consisting of (a) precious metals and notes, or (b) various kinds of precious metals.

mixed property: property having characteristics of both personal and real property (e.g., house fixtures).

mixing rates: used in the foreign exchange rate system, the use of varying rates of exchange for specific categories of overseas traded goods.

MJSD: March, June, September, December (quarterly interest payments or dividends).

Mkr.: see *maker.*

MLR: see *minimum lending rate.*

MM: see entries under *money market.*

MMC: see *money market certificate.*

MMDA: money market deposit accounts. See *Garnet St. Germain Depository Institutions Act of 1982.*

MMF: see *money market fund.*

M&N: May and November (semi annual interest payments or dividends).

MO:

(1) see *mail order.*

(2) see *money order.*

mobile home: a movable, portable dwelling without permanent foundation, designed for year-round living. [59]

Mobile Home Certificates: lesser known variations of the Ginnie Mae. They are fully guaranteed pass-through securities consisting of mobile home mortgages carrying shorter maturities.

mobile home loan: a nonmortgage loan to an individual for the purchase of a mobile home, secured by the lender's claim on the mobile home. [59]

modeling: the identification of the fixed and variable components in a system, assigning them numerical or economic values and relating them to one another in a logical fashion so that solutions to operational problems can be obtained.

model savings association act: a model for a code of state law providing for the organization, operation, and supervision of state thrift and home-financing institutions. [59]

modification agreement: any agreement between the association and borrower that alters permanently one or more of the terms—interest rate, number of years allowed for retirement, monthly payment amount and the like—of an existing mortgage loan. [59]

modified accrual basis: the basis of accounting under which expenditures other than accrued interest on general long-term debt are recorded at the time liabilities are incurred and revenues are recorded when received in cash, except for material and/or available revenues which should be accrued to reflect properly the taxes levied and the revenues earned. [49]

MOD 10: see *modulus 10 check digit.*

modulus 10 check digit (MOD 10): a method of proofing an account number that has been entered into a computer system. It is used on a formula that, if the number was entered correctly, will result in a number called the *check digit.* [105]

monetarism: the body of theory related to the quantity theory of money. Its basic precept is that the quantity and changes in the money supply have the primary effect on a nation's economy. [105]

monetarist: a believer in the concept that balanced economy depends on the supply of money. Cf. *archmonetarist.*

monetary: a country's currency and/or coinage.

Monetary Accord of 1951: an agreement between the Federal Reserve System and the Treasury which permitted monetary policy to react to objectives, other than the interest-rate peg. The accord terminated the interest-rate peg. See *interest-rate peg.*

Monetary and Payments System (MAPS) Planning Committee: a committee established by the American Bankers Association in 1969 to conduct extensive research and planning efforts related to the nation's payments system. The four task forces of the committee produced detailed recommendations which were consolidated into a summary report by the committee, stressing the importance of preauthorized payments and bank charge cards as building blocks in a future electronic payments system. [36]

monetary asset: money or a claim to receive a sum of money, the amount of which is fixed or determinable without reference to future prices of specific goods or services. See *monetary liability*. [80]

Monetary Authority of Singapore (MAS): supervises much of the Asian dollar market with the Central Bank of Singapore.

monetary base: a monetary aggregate composed of funds retained by banks, by the public, and including member-bank deposits at the various Federal Reserve Banks. Measures "high powered money"—bank reserves and currency, serving as a guide to potential money creation. Issued each Thursday for the week that ended the day before.

monetary commission: specialists in banking and financial matters appointed by government action to prepare an analysis and recommendation for changes in existing legislation.

Monetary Control Act: requires that all banks and all institutions that accept deposits from the public make periodic reports to the Federal Reserve System. Starting in September 1981, the Fed charged banks for a range of services that it had provided free in the past, including check clearing, wire transfer of funds, and the use of automated clearinghouse facilities. See *Depository Institutions Deregulation and Monetary Control Act*.

monetary indemnity: the specified amount benefit, as contrasted to expense reimbursement.

monetary liability: the promise to pay a claim against a specified quantity of money, the amount of which is unaffected by inflation or deflation. See *monetary asset*.

monetary multiplier: a number showing the anticipated change in income-per-unit change in the money supply.

monetary policy: a policy of the Federal Reserve System that attempts to affect the terms on which credit can be obtained in private markets; its purpose is to regulate the nation's sales level, level of employment, and prices. See *Operation Twist (Nudge)*.

monetary reform: the process of negotiating and drafting a revised international currency system.

monetary reserve: the amount of bullion held by the government or banks as security for fiduciary or credit money in circulation. See *reserve*.

monetary sovereignty: a nation's right to safeguard its fiscal system against severe deflation, unemployment, or imbalance of its foreign payments, despite pledges of cooperation which may have been given to such organizations as the International Monetary Fund.

monetary standard: the basis upon which a money is issued, that is, the principles that determine the quantity of money.

monetary system: all policies and practices affecting a nation's money.

monetary transaction: any transaction posted to an account which has a dollar value. [105]

monetary unit: the unit of money of a nation. The monetary unit may or may not be defined in terms of a commodity into which it is convertible.

monetary working capital: items that are related to operations and not, for example, liquid assets that are surplus to operating requirements. [80]

monetize:
(1) to convert assets into money.
(2) to finance the national debt by issuing new government securities which in turn increases the amount of money in circulation.

monetizing the debt: money growth induced by attempts to moderate the effects of rapidly growing government debt on interest rates. [108]

money: any denomination of coin or paper currency of legal tender that passes freely as a medium of exchange; anything that is accepted in exchange for other things (e.g., precious metals). Major characteristics of money include easy recognition, uniformity in quality, easy divisibility, and a relatively high value within a small area. Cf. *currency.*

money broker: a person or institution serving as a go-between for borrowers and lenders of money.

money-center bank: any large bank engaged in a wide range of services, primarily for corporate clients.

moneyed corporation: a financial organization such as a bank, trust company, or insurance firm and as such subject to the banking or insurance code.

money functions: there are four generally accepted functions of money: as a unit of account, a medium of exchange, a store of value, and a standard of deferred payment.

money funds: a type of mutual fund. Though they have been marketed practically as bank accounts, the individual owns shares in a fund. The value is usually $1 per share, to make the accounting simple. The purchaser doesn't actually have a cash balance. The shares owned purchased prior to March 14, 1980,

were free from new Federal Restrictions. See *mutual fund.*

money in circulation: the total amount of currency and coin outside the Treasury and the Federal Reserve Banks.

money income: the amount of money received for work performed.

money management: financial planning with the aim of gratifying long-range as well as immediate needs and of maintaining a sound relationship among income, savings, and spending. [55]

money market (brokers): all financial organizations that handle the purchase, sale, and transfer of short-term credit instruments and notes.

money market certificate (MMC): six-month Federal Home Loan Bank Board certificate at federally insured savings and loan associations.

money market deposit accounts: see *Garnet St. Germain Depository Institutions Act of 1982.*

money market fund (MMF):
(1) many investment banking firms sponsor money-market mutual funds, which invest in such short-term credit instruments as Treasury bills. Customers earn high interest rates on the accounts and can write checks against their investment. Commercial banks contend that these accounts are offering traditional commercial banking services without the restrictions that apply to commercial banks, such as reserve requirements on deposits. See *Glass-Steagall Act of 1933, reserve requirements.*
(2) an investment vehicle whose primary objective is to make

higher-interest securities available to the average investor who wants immediate income and high investment safety. This is accomplished through the purchase of high-yield money market instruments, such as U.S. government securities, bank certificates of deposit, and commercial paper. Synonymous with *liquid assets.*

money market instruments: private and government obligations with a maturity of one year or less. These include U.S. Treasury bills, bankers' acceptances, commercial paper, finance paper, and short-term tax-exempts. [105]

money market rates: current interest rates on various money market instruments. The rates reflect the relative liquidity, security of investment, size of investment, term of investment, and general economic factors. [105]

money markets: markets where short-term debt instruments are traded.

money market securities: high-quality and generally accepted senior securities whose market prices expressed on a yield basis relate more closely to the prevailing interest rate for money than to the risks in a company's operations or in general business conditions. [67]

money multiplier: see *M-1A.*

money of account: the unit in which monetary records are kept (i.e., U.S. entries in dollars and cents).

money order (MO): postal money orders and bank money orders are instruments commonly purchased for a fee by people who do not maintain checking accounts and wish to send money to others. The names of the purchaser and the payee are shown on the face of the money order. An advantage of the money order over checks is that presentation to their original place of purchase for payment, is not required. A disadvantage is that a bank or other financial institution may charge for the service of supplying a money order.

money pinch: see *pinch.*

money price: the number of money units that must be sacrificed to purchase a particular commodity.

money rates: interest rates that lenders charge their borrowers.

money stock: see *M-1A, M2, M3.*

money supply: the total sum of currency circulating in a country. See *price;* see also *money supply (Federal Reserve).*

money supply (Federal Reserve): measures several variants in the amount of money in the economy, issued each Thursday for the week that ended eight days earlier. It has been criticized as very erratic, subject to frequent revision.

money talks: slang, money is power and can therefore buy anything.

money wage: the amount of wages in money.

monometallism: a monetary system: the monetary component is defined in terms of only one metal that is accepted in unlimited quantities for producing coins. See *real money;* cf. *bimetallism.*

monthly payment bonus account: a savings account that pays bonus earnings if the customer makes a specified number of fixed monthly deposits. [59]

monthly payment loan: a consumer or mortgage loan requiring a payment each month. [105]

moral obligation: a debt or responsibility whose payment or fulfillment is not based on legal rights or action. [28]

moral suasion: Federal Reserve System pressure exerted on U.S. banking, unaccompanied by an effort to compel compliance with the suggested action.

morning loan: bank loans to stockbrokers on an unsecured basis enabling the broker to handle stock deliveries until reimbursed by the customer.

mortality: the expectancy of an asset or class of aspects to expire or depreciate by use or the passage of time.

mortgage:
(1) a written conveyance of title to property, but not possession, to obtain the payment of a debt or the performance of some obligation, under the condition that the conveyance is to be void upon final payment.
(2) property pledged as security for payment of a debt. See *chattel mortgage;* cf. *conventional loan.*

mortgage administration: the part of a mortgage banker's service involving all clerical and supervisory functions necessary to ensure prompt repayment of mortgage loans, and to protect and enforce all rights of investors thereunder. [22]

mortgage-backed certificates: several banks, notably the Bank of America, have issued certificates covering pools of conventional mortgages insured by private mortgage insurance companies. These certificates are issued in big denominations, so the market is limited mainly to institutions.

mortgage-backed securities: bond-type investment securities representing an interest in a pool of mortgages or trust deeds. Income from the underlying mortgages is used to make investor payments. [105]

mortgage banker: a banker who specializes in mortgage financing; an operator of a mortgage financing company. Mortgage financing companies are mortgagees themselves, as well as being mortgage agents for other large mortgages.

Mortgage Bankers Association of America (MBA): the professional and business organization of persons operating under the correspondency system whose major purpose is continuing improvement in the quality of service to investors. [22]

mortgage banking: the packaging of mortgage loans secured by real property to be sold to a permanent investor with servicing retained by the seller for the life of the loan in exchange for a fee. The origination, sale, and servicing of mortgage loans by a firm or individual. [105]

mortgage banking company: specialist in purchase and sale of government-backed mortgages. [105]

mortgage bond: see *bond, mortgage.*

mortgage broker: a firm or individual that brings the borrower and lender together, receiving a commission. A mortgage broker does not retain servicing. [105]

mortgage certificate: an interest in a mortgage evidenced by the instrument, generally a fractional portion of the mortgage, which certifies as to the agreement between the mortgagees who hold the certificates and the mortgagor as to such terms as principal, amount, date of payment, and place of payment. Such certificates are not obligations to pay money, as in a bond or note, but are merely a certification by the holder of the mortgage, generally a corporate depository, that he or she holds such mortgage for the beneficial and undivided interest of all the certificate holders. The certificate itself generally sets forth a full agreement between the holder and the depository, although in some cases a more lengthy document, known as a *depository agreement,* is executed. [62]

mortgage chattel: a mortgage on personal property. [105]

mortgage clause: see *mortgagee clause.*

mortgage company: mortgage financing companies are mortgages themselves, as well as being mortgage agents for other large mortgagees. Serving as mortgage agents, these mortgage bankers collect payments, maintain complete mortgage records, and make remittances to the mortgagees for a set fee or service charge. [10]

mortgage constant: synonymous with *constant ratio.*

mortgage credit: money that is owed for the acquisition of land or buildings (frequently of a home) and which is paid back over an extended period of time; hence, long-term debt. [55]

mortgaged deed: see *deed, mortgaged.*

mortgage debenture: a mortgage bond. See *bond, mortgage.*

mortgage debt: an indebtedness created by a mortgage and secured by the property mortgaged. A mortgage debt is made evident by a note or bond.

mortgage department: a department in banks, building and loan, savings and loan associations, and trust companies, where mortgage counselors, mortgage loan officers, and mortgage recording personnel handle all phases of mortgage work for mortgagors. This department may also act as "escrow agents" for mortgagors, in that they collect in the monthly payment from the mortgagor a portion of the real estate taxes, assessments on real estate, and hazard insurance. They hold these in escrow funds until payable, and then disburse the funds for the benefit of the mortgagor, and also the mortgagee, to prevent the development of liens against the property. In some states, they administer escrow funds in connection with closing mortgages, whereas in other states mortgage closings are required to be handled by attorneys-at-law. [10]

mortgagee: the creditor or lender, to whom a mortgage is made. The mortgagor retains possession and use of the property during the term of the mortgage (e.g., the bank holds the mortgage on your house).

mortgagee clause: a clause in an insurance contract making the proceeds payable to a named mortgagee, as his or her interest may appear, and stating the terms of the contract between the insurer and the mortgagee. This is preferable usage but the same as *mortgage clause.* [53]

Mortgage Guarantee Insurance Corporation: see *magic mortgage.*

mortgage guarantee policy: a policy issued on a guaranteed mortgage. [62]

mortgage in possession: a mortgagee creditor who takes over the income from the mortgaged property upon default of the mortgage by the debtor.

mortgage insurance policy: issued by a title insurance firm to a mortgage holder, resulting in a title policy.

mortgage insurance premium (MIP): the consideration paid by a mortgagor for mortgage insurance—either to FHA or to a private mortgage insurer (MIC). [105]

mortgage interest: interest charges deducted on one's taxes. Under the 1986 Tax Act, deductible for first and second homes, others are taxed. See *Tax Reform Act of 1986.*

mortgage investment trust: a specialized form of real estate investment trust that invests in long-term mortgages, usually Federal Housing Administration-insured or Veterans Administration-guaranteed, and makes short-term construction and development loans. [59]

mortgage lien: in a mortgage given as security for a debt, serving as a lien on the property after the mortgage is recorded.

mortgage life insurance: insurance on the life of the borrower that pays off a specified debt if he dies. Synonymous with *credit life insurance.* [59]

mortgage loan: a loan made by a lender, called the mortgagee, to a borrower, called the mortgagor, for the financing of a parcel of real estate. The loan is evidenced by a mortgage. The mortgage sets forth the conditions of the loan, the manner of repayment or liquidation of the loan, and reserves the right of foreclosure or repossession to the

mortgagee. In case the mortgagor defaults in the payment of interest and principal, or if he permits a lien to be placed against the real estate mortgaged due to failure to pay the taxes and assessments levied against the property, the right of foreclosure can be exercised. [10]

mortgage loan commitment: written statement by lender to grant a specific loan amount, at a given rate, for a certain term, secured by a specific property, if the real property transaction is closed before the expiration date. [78]

mortgage loan ledger record: a document that contains a complete record of all transactions—payments of principal and interest, special disbursements, fees, charges, and the like—on a particular mortgage loan. [59]

mortgage loan report: an updated report that requires the same kind of information as the full report plus a statement certifying that all Federal Housing Administration or Veterans Administration specifications, including public record items have been met. [76]

mortgage note: a note that offers a mortgage as proof of an indebtedness and describes the manner in which the mortgage is to be paid. This note is the actual amount of debt that the mortgage obtains, and it renders the mortgagor personally responsible for repayment.

mortgage origination: the part of a mortgage banker's service involving performance of all details concerned with the making of a real estate loan. [22]

mortgage pattern: the arrangement or design of payments and other terms established by a mortgage contract. [44]

mortgage portfolio: the aggregate of mortgage loans or obligations held by a bank as assets. [44]

mortgage premium: an additional bank fee charged for the giving of a mortgage when the legal interest rate is less than the prevailing mortgage market rate and there is a shortage of mortgage money.

mortgager(or): a debtor or borrower who gives or makes a mortgage to a lender, on property owned by the mortgagor.

mortgage risk: the hazard of loss of principal or of anticipated interest inherent in an advance of funds on the security of a mortgage. [44]

mortgage securities: see *Freddie Macs, Gennie Mae trusts, Government National Mortgage Association, mortgage-backed certificates.*

mortgaging future income: pledging income not yet earned. [28]

mortgagor: see *mortgager.*

Mos.: months.

MOS: see *margin of safety.*

mother hubbard clause: a mortgage provision permitting the lender, upon default of the conditions of the mortgage, to foreclose on the overdue mortgage. Courts around the country have questioned the legality of this clause.

movable exchange: instruments quoted in the currency of the nation in which payment is to be made rather than that in which the instrument is drawn.

MS:
(1) March, September (semiannual interest payments or dividends).
(2) see *money supply.*

M$: the supply of nominal money, composed of checkable deposits and currency. [81]

M&S: March and September (semiannual interest payments or dividends).

MSB: see *mutual savings bank.*

Mtg.: see *mortgage.*

Mthly.: monthly.

MTS: manned teller system.

multicompany: diverse organizations or a variety of firms under a single management.

multicurrency loan: a loan in which several currencies are involved.

multilateralism: an international policy having as its object the freeing of international trade from the restrictions involved in bilateralism in an effort to permit nations to specialize in production and exchange in accordance with the principle of comparative advantage.

multilingual notes: paper money issued with a legend in two or more languages, as in India, Belgium, or Cyprus. [27]

multiple banking: the offering of all types of banking services to a bank's customers, as distinguished from specialization in a few services as offered by savings and loan associations, and other banking institutions. Often referred to as department store banking. Cf. *full-service bank.*

multiple budget: a budget extending two or more periods of time into the future and extended as each time period elapses.

multiple-commodity reserve dollar: a scheme to maintain a constant value ratio between gold and other commodities in terms of dollars, purporting to set a reserve of selected items. Money is redeemed in either gold or in these reserve goods, and gold and the reserve goods can always be exchanged for dollars. A constant ratio should be maintained between the value of the commodities, the gold, and the dollar.

multiple currency practice: arises when two or more effective exchange rates exist simultaneously, at least one of which, as the result of official action, is more than 1 percent higher or lower than the par value. Such practices are usually to be found where a dual exchange market exists or where the monetary authorities set different exchange rates for imports, exports, current invisibles, and capital. They often result from taxes or subsidies on specified exchange transactions. [42]

multiple currency securities: securities, mostly bonds, payable in more than one currency at the election of the holder. In the event of devaluation of a currency, the holder can elect to be paid in the currency of a nation that has not devalued its currency.

multiple currency system: a means of controlling foreign exchange where domestic currency can be exchanged for foreign currency only through a government unit or controlled bank.

multiple exchange: three or more principals involved with various pieces of property. [62]

multiple expansion of bank deposits: occurs when a loan made by one bank is used to finance business transactions and becomes a deposit in another bank. A portion of this loan can be used by the second bank as a required reserve, and the remainder can be loaned out for business use, so that it is eventually deposited in a third bank.

multiple ownership: ownership by two or more parties. Synonymous with *co-ownership.* [59]

muni: a *municipal bond.*

Munic.: municipal.

municipal bond: see *bond, municipal.*

munifunds: synonymous with *mutual funds.*

muniment of title:
(1) anything that protects or enforces; written proof that enables an owner to defend his or her title to property.
(2) deeds and contracts that show conclusive proof of ownership (e.g., warranty deed).

munis: Wall Street slang for municipal bonds. See *bond, municipal.*

mutilated currency: coin and paper currency that is not in an adequate condition for further circulation and can be withdrawn. When the mutilation is less than three-fifths of the paper bill present, it is not redeemed at face value without an affidavit from the holder that he or she certifies that the missing parts have been destroyed.

mutual assent: agreement by all parties to a contract to the same thing. Each must know what the other wishes.

mutual association: a savings association that issues no capital stock, but is owned and controlled solely by its savers and borrowers, who are called members. Members do not share in profits, because a mutual institution operates in such a way that it makes no "profit," but they exercise other ownership rights. [59]

mutual company: a corporation without capital stock (e.g., mutual savings bank): the profits, after deductions, are distributed among the owner-customers in proportion to the business activity carried with the corporation.

mutual fund: an investment company which ordinarily stands ready to buy back (redeem) its shares at their current net asset value; the value of the shares depends on the market value of the fund's portfolio securities at the time. Also, mutual funds generally continuously offer new shares to investors. See also *investment company, money funds.* [23]

Mutual Institutions National Transfer System, Inc. (MINTS): an organization affiliated with the National Association of Mutual Savings Banks (NAMSB). The MINTS Money Transfer Card is intended to become part of a future nationwide Mutual Savings Bank EFT system. [36]

mutual investment fund: synonymous with *mutual fund.*

mutualism: the argument developed by Proudhon (1809–1865) that services exchanged for each other would be mutually equal if rent, interest, and profits were eliminated.

mutuality: equality of status and opportunity among members of a savings association. [59]

mutual mortgage insurance fund: one of four FHA insurance funds into which all mortgage insurance premiums and other specified revenue of the FHA are paid and from which losses are met. [105]

mutual savings bank: a banking organization without capital stock, operating under law for the mutual benefit of the depositors. The depositor is encouraged to practice thrift, and the s vings of these small depositors are invested in very high grade securities and some first-class mortgages. Dividends from these investments are mutually distributed after deduction of expenses of the association and reserves for a guaranty fund for depositors. The principal idea of a mutual savings bank is to perform a social service for small depositors who cannot invest their savings at high yield. See also *mutual company.*

Mutual Savings Foundation of America, The: based in Washington, D.C., this nonprofit organization was established in 1961 as a vehicle to enable savings bankers to promote and improve education in the field of economics. The foundation assists educational institutions with grants-in-aid, gifts and loans to support research, and also grants, scholarships, fellowships, and loans to students in the field of economics. It also provides aid to developing nations to assist them in accumulating domestic savings. Contributions to the foundation qualify as charitable contributions for federal income tax purposes. [8]

mutual wills: a common arrangement executed pursuant to an agreement in which the husband and wife leave everything to each other.

MV: see *market value.*

N: see *note*.

NA:

(1) see *net assets*.

(2) see *no account*.

(3) no approval required (full discretion).

(4) see *nostro account*.

NAC: *New American Community*.

NACHA: National Automated Clearing House Association.

NACIS: National Credit Information Service.

NACM: National Association of Credit Management.

naird: monetary unit of Nigeria.

"naked" reserve: an adjusted reserve of each of the Federal Reserve Banks showing the true reserve position of the bank. See *reserve requirements*.

name: shorthand in foreign exchange markets referring to other participants (e.g., "I can't do the name," meaning "I am not allowed to trade with that institution").

NAMSB: see *National Association of Mutual Savings Banks*.

National Advisory Council on International Monetary and Financial Problems: comprised of the Secretary of State, the Secretary of the Treasury, the Secretary of Commerce, and chairpersons of the Board of Governors of the Federal Reserve System and the Export-Import Bank. Its function is to coordinate the policies of the United States in the World Bank and the International Monetary Fund.

National Association of Mutual Savings Banks (NAMSB): exists to serve its member banks. It provides services to individual member banks which they would find impractical to provide for themselves, and it serves the savings bank industry as a whole, through national-level programs and activities to further industry goals and objectives and to meet needs common to all savings banks. [8]

national bank: a commercial bank organized with the consent and approval of the Comptroller of the Currency and operated under the supervision of the federal government. National banks are required to be members of the Federal Reserve System and must purchase stock in the Federal Reserve Bank in their district.

National Bank Act of 1863: the act of Congress providing for the incorporation of banks under federal supervision. Such national banks are now under the supervision of the Federal Reserve System.

national bank association: synonymous with *national bank*.

national bank call: the report, submitted four times each year, to the Comptroller of the Currency on the well-being of the bank's commercial department.

national bank examination: all national banks each year are subject to a minimum of two examinations by the staff of a national bank examiner to check records to make certain that the bank is fulfilling the requirements of the National Bank Act.

national bank examiner: an employee of the Comptroller of the Currency whose function is to examine or audit banks periodically. Such an examination is done to determine the strength of a bank's financial position, the security of its deposits, and to verify that procedures are maintained consistent with federal regulations. [105]

national bank note: a type of currency issued in the United States. National bank notes are backed by two types of U.S. government bonds-2 percent consols of 1930, and the 2 percent Panama Canal bonds of 1916-1936 and 1918-1938. These bonds were called for redemption by the Bank Act of 1935, and no further issuance of national bank notes was authorized. They are being retired from circulation. National bank notes are in denominations of $5, $10, $20, $50, and $100, and each has a brown seal and the issuing bank's charter number on its face. [10]

national bank report: see *national bank call.*

National Bankruptcy Act of 1898: federal law stating the conditions under which an individual or business may declare bankruptcy, and the procedures for declaration.

National Bank Surveillance System (NBSS): a computer-based data collection and monitoring system maintained by the Office of the Comptroller of the Currency. NBSS is used to detect significantly changed circumstances within a specific bank or within the national banking system as a whole. [105]

National Commission on EFT: a commission authorized by a 1974 Act of Congress to conduct a two-year investigation into electronic funds transfer system policy and planning issues, concluding with reports and recommendations for congressional action. [36]

National Consumer Cooperative Bank: federal legislation signed by President Carter in 1978 creating a national bank to provide credit for consumer cooperatives.

National Credit Union Administration (NCUA): the federal government agency that supervises, charters, and insures federal credit unions. NCUA also insures state-chartered credit unions that apply and qualify for insurance. As of October 1979, the NCUA also operates a credit facility for member credit unions. [1]

national currency: all Federal Reserve Bank notes and national bank notes that are now retired.

National Farm Loan Association: an agricultural cooperative of local operation created as a result of the Federal Farm Loan Act. Upon subscription to shares of the Federal Land Bank in its area, the association can secure financing for farm mortgages.

National Housing Act of 1934: created the Federal Housing Administration to insure home mortgage, low-income housing project, and home improvement loans made by private lenders; established the Federal Savings and Loan Insurance Corporation to insure savings accounts at member savings associations up to $5000. [51]

national income: the total of the incomes received by all the people of a country over a stated period. It is equal to the gross national product minus depreciation minus sales taxes and other small items.

nationalism (of currency): occurring when a central bank imposes restrictions on borrowing and lending of its currency by nonresidents of the nation. See also *nonresident account.*

national liquidity: a nation's monetary situation as determined by its rates of interest on all loans and deposits.

National Monetary Commission: a body of banking and financial specialists reporting to Congress on the state of the banking structure and recommends changes. The Commission was formed in 1908.

National Mortgage Association: see *Federal National Mortgage Association.*

National Numerical System: see *transit number.*

national wealth: the combined monetary value of all the material economic products owned by all the people.

nationwide loan: a conventional loan made or purchased upon improved real estate located outside the insured institution's normal lending territory but within any state of the United States.

natural business year: a 12-month period usually selected to end when inventory or business activity is at a low point.

natural capital: land that is used as a factor of production.

natural financing:
(1) a real estate transaction requiring no outside financing, as is demanded in cash sales.
(2) the selling of properties that do not call for a third party.

natural interest rate: the interest rate at which the demand for loanable funds just equals the supply of savings. The interest rate that keeps the flow of money incomes constant rather than the interest rate, which keeps the price level constant.

NBA:
(1) see *National Bank Act of 1863.*
(2) see *National Bankruptcy Act of 1898.*

NBI: National BankAmericard Incorporated, now known as Visa U.S.A., Incorporated. [105]

NBR: nonborrowed reserve, total reserve of depository institutions less depository institutions' borrowing from the Federal Reserve. [81]

NBS: National Bureau of Standards.

NBSS: see *National Bank Surveillance System.*

NC:
(1) see *net capital.*
(2) see *net cost.*

NCCB: see *National Consumer Cooperative Bank.*

NCUA: see *National Credit Union Administration.*

near money: highly liquid assets (e.g., government securities) other than official currency.

near-term: short term as opposed to long term (i.e., the near future or less than two months usually).

negative amortizer: when a home buyer gets a bank mortgage below the going rate and the difference is added to the principal. Payments are low to start but much higher later.

negative authorization list: a list of accounts requiring exception authorization handling. [105]

negative coverage: a property financed by a mortgage with a debt service that tops its earnings.

negative factor (or value): a factor (such as advanced age) given an unfavorable or negative weight in a credit decision. [105]

negative file: an authorized system file containing a simple list of accounts for which credit, check cashing, and other privileges, should be denied. Cf. *positive file.*

negative float: see *float.*

negative interest: where a depositor is required to pay interest rather than receive it. [91]

negatively sloping yield curve: a yield curve where interest rates in the shorter dates are above those in the longer dates.

negative verification: many banks have a legend printed on the statement form going to the depositor to the effect that "if no difference is reported within 10 days, the account will be considered correct." If the bank does not hear from the depositor, it assumes that the depositor finds no discrepancies between its statement and his or her records.

Negb.: see *negotiable.*

Neg. Inst.: see *negotiable instrument.*

Negl.: see *negligence.*

negligence: failure to do that which an ordinary, reasonable, prudent person would do, or the doing of some act that an ordinary, prudent person would not do. Reference is made of the situation, circumstances, and awareness of the parties involved.

negotiability: the quality of a bank check, promissory note, or other legal instrument of value that allows legal title to it to be transferred from one individual to another by endorsement and delivery, or by delivery without endorsement.

negotiable: anything that can be sold or transferred to another for money or as payment of a debt.

negotiable check: a check payable to "to order" or "to bearer." A negotiable check in order form can be made nonnegotiable by a restrictive indorsement.

negotiable instrument: the Uniform Negotiable Instruments Act states: "An instrument, to be negotiable, must conform to the following requirements: (a) it must be in writing and signed by the maker or drawer; (b) it must contain an unconditional promise or order to pay a certain sum in money; (c) it must be payable on demand, or at a fixed or determinable future time; (d) it must be payable to order or to bearer; and (e) where the instrument is addressed to a drawee, he must be named or otherwise indicated therein with reasonable certainty."

negotiable order of withdrawal: see *NOW account.*

negotiable paper: negotiable instruments that are used in the borrowing of money on a short-term period for business objectives.

negotiation: the act by which a negotiable instrument is placed into circulation, by being physically passed from the original holder to another person.

negotiation credit: a credit instrument under which the beneficiary draws his or her drafts in a foreign currency either on the opening bank or on a designated foreign bank. The beneficiary may then sell the drafts either to the local advising bank or to any other bank in his or her area that is willing to buy the drafts as foreign exchange. [105]

neoclassical economics: an economic approach developed between 1870 and 1918, utilizing mathematics in the analysis of data and models. Neoclassicists were primarily concerned with refining the concepts of price and allocation theory, marginalism, and the theory of capital.

nest egg: slang, money saved, often deposited in a savings bank in preparation for retirement.

net: that which remains after certain designated deductions have been made from the gross amount.

net assets: the property of a business, corporation, organization, or estate, remaining after all obligations have been met.

net avails: the funds given to a borrower in the discounting of a note. It is equal to the face value of the note minus the discount.

net borrowed reserves: borrowings less excess reserves.

net capital: a firm's net worth (assets minus liabilities) minus certain deductions, for assets that may not be easily converted into cash at their full value. In the securities industry, net capital is used to determine whether a brokerage house can be considered solvent and capable of operating.

net charge-offs as percent of average net loans: loan charge-offs less recoveries as percent of net average loans outstanding. Net loans are gross loans outstanding minus unearned income and the valuation portion of loan loss reserves on an average daily basis for the year. A minus sign indicates that recoveries exceeded charge-offs.

net cost:
(1) the true cost of an item. The net cost is determined by subtracting all income or financial gain from the gross cost.

(2) the total premiums paid on a policy less any dividends, and the surrender value as of the time the net cost is determined.

net current monetary assets: equals monetary assets less monetary liabilities. The main difference between net current monetary assets and working capital is that the former definition of funds excludes inventory. See *working capital*. [80]

net demand deposits: the excess of demand deposits, including deposits, due to other banks and the U.S. government, over demand balances due from other domestic banks, with the exception of Federal Reserve Banks, foreign banks or branches, foreign branches of domestic and private banks, and cash items that are in the process of being collected.

net estate: the part of an estate remaining after all expenses to manage it have been taken out.

net federal funds borrowed as percent of average net loans outstanding: net federal funds borrowed are the bank-calculated average federal funds purchased and securities sold under agreements to repurchase, less the bank-calculated average federal funds sold and securities purchased under agreements to resell. A minus sign indicates that the bank was a net seller of federal funds. See *net charge-offs as percent of average net loans.*

net free (or net borrowed) reserves: excess reserves less member-bank borrowings from Federal Reserve Banks. The resulting difference is called net free when positive and net borrowed when negative. [72]

net ground lease: see *lease ground.*

net income: the remains from earnings and profits after all costs, expenses, and allowances for depreciation and probable loss have been deducted.

net income multiplier: a figure which, times the net income of a property, produces an estimate of value of that property. It is obtained by dividing the selling price by the monthly net rent (net income). [52]

net interest: measures the excess of interest payments made by the domestic business sector over its interest receipts from other sectors, plus net interest received from abroad. Interest paid by one business firm to another business firm is a transaction within the business sector and has no effect on the overall interest payments or receipts of the sector. The same is true of interest payments within other sectors as from one individual to another, or one government agency to another. [73]

net interest cost: the average rate of interest over the life of a bond which an issuer must pay to borrow funds. [105]

net lease: a lease stating that the landlord will incur all maintenance costs, taxes, insurance, and other expenses usually paid by the owner.

net line: the amount of liability retained on a property by a company for its own account. [54]

net long-term debt: total long-term debt, less cash and investment assets of sinking funds and other reserve funds specially held for redemption of long-term debt.

net loss: the excess of expenses and losses during a specified period over revenues and gains in the same time frame.

net new savings: see *net savings inflow.*

net option: a written instrument granting the right to buy a property at a specified price to the owner.

net savings gain: synonymous with *net savings inflow.*

net savings inflow: the change in an association's savings account balances over a given period, determined by subtracting withdrawals during the period; also called net savings gain or net savings receipts. When interest credited to accounts during the period is excluded, the resulting figure is customarily referred to as *net new savings.* Synonymous with *net savings gain and net savings receipts.* [59]

net savings receipts: synonymous with *net savings inflow.*

net surplus: the earnings or profits remaining to a corporation after all operating expenses, taxes, interests, insurance, and dividends have been paid out. The surplus is determined before deducting dividends while the net surplus is determined following the deduction of dividends.

net working capital: the excess of existing assets over present liabilities.

neutral money: a system under which the dollar would be convertible into commodities at a fixed price with the object of stabilizing the price level.

never used: designates a cardholder account that has never been active. [105]

New American Community (NAC): proposed by Professor J. M. Rosenberg in 1992 as a free-trade agreement, initially by the U.S., Canada and Mexico, to later incorporate 30 other countries of Latin America and the Caribbean, thus forming a trade-bloc of 700 million people. Eventually, when fully implemented there will be an open NAC market in banking services where money would be able to move freely across borders. A single banking license would enable banks licensed in one country to establish branches and provide cross-border services throughout the NAC. [205]

new balance: the new balance owing after payments and credits have been deducted from the previous balance and the new purchases and finance charges have been added. [105]

new business department: a section within the bank that obtains new accounts.

new cedi: monetary unit of Ghana.

new credit extended: amount of new credit the center has extended to a cardholder during the past billing period. [105]

new cruzeiro: monetary unit of Brazil.

New England NOW Accounts: a 1979 federal law that expanded NOW account authority to federally chartered associations in Connecticut, Maine, Rhode Island, and Vermont. See also *NOW account.* [51]

new rupiah: monetary unit of Indonesia.

New York Clearing House: the oldest and largest check-clearing facility in the United States. See also *clearing-house.*

New York Clearing House Association (NYCHA): eleven banks of the NYCHA were the first to make use of an automated clearinghouse at the New York Federal Reserve Bank. [105]

New York Dollars: synonymous with *New York Exchange.*

New York Exchange: any check drawn on a commercial bank in New York City. Synonymous with *New York Dollars.*

New York interest: interest computed by the exact days in a month rather than by use of a 30-day month or other. Cf. *Boston interest.*

New York NOW accounts: legislation passed in 1978 permitting FSLIC-insured-institutions in New York State to offer NOW accounts. See *NOW account.* [51]

New York plan: an equipment trust arrangement using a conditional sale as the legal device. Cf. *Philadelphia plan.*

next day funds: in EFTS, significant funds available for transfer today in like funds, and available for the next business day for same-day funds transfer or withdrawal in cash subject to the settlement of the transaction through the payment mechanism used. [105]

next friend: one who, although not regularly appointed a guardian, acts for the benefit of a minor or incompetent person or, in some instances, a married woman or for any person who, for some legal reason, cannot appear for himself. [37]

next of kin: the person or persons in the nearest degree of blood relationship to the decedent. As the term is usually employed, those entitled by law to the personal property of a person who has died without leaving a valid will (such persons do not include the surviving husband and wife except where specifically so provided by statute); to be distinguished from the heirs, who take the real property. [37]

NF: see *no funds.*

NG: an expression used to designate a check as not good because of insufficient funds. [105]

NI:

(1) see *national income*.

(2) see *negotiable instrument*.

(3) see *net income*.

NIBOR: the New York interbank official rate.

night depository: a small vault located on the inside of a bank, but accessible to the streetside of the bank. To use this vault, depositors are given a pass-key to the outer door of the night depository vault. When this door is opened, the package of money properly identified by the depositor is dropped down a chute into the night depository vault. This convenience is used by merchants who do not wish the day's receipts to remain in their place of business, and so have this means of protecting their deposits after the regular business hours of the bank. The vault is opened by a bank attendant, and the deposits properly counted and credited to the depositor's account. [10]

NIL negotiable instruments law. See *negotiable instrument*.

ninety-day savings account: an account paying interest usually equivalent to that paid on 90-day deposits in savings certificates. The account is a passbook account and is subject to substantial interest penalties if funds are withdrawn prior to the end of the 90-day period. If funds are left on deposit after 90 days, the pledge is automatically renewed for an additional period. [105]

NINOW's: non-interest-bearing NOW accounts.

NL: see *net loss*.

N&M: November and May (semi-annual interest payments or dividends).

No.: number.

N/O: registered in name of.

No. AC: see *no account*.

no account: a situation when the drawer of a check fails to possess an account in the drawee bank and the drawee returns the check to the presenting bank for credit with a statement reading "no account."

no-book transactions: a transaction that is processed without being entered into the customer's passbook, but for which a temporary receipt is issued. [105]

no funds: a situation when the drawer of a check fails to possess needed funds in the drawee bank and the drawee returns the check to the presenting bank for credit with a statement reading "no funds."

no lien affidavit: a written document by a property owner that the work has been finished on an identified property and that no liens or mortgages encumber it. Cf. *lien affidavit*.

nolo contendere: "I will not contest [it]" (Latin). In a criminal case, a form of guilty plea on the basis of which a sentence may be passed. By pleading, the defendant admits to the facts of the case without admitting his formal guilt of a crime. The plea is most often used when a guilty plea would affect other interests (e.g., a contract, insurance).

nominal account: an account established to analyze the changes in the surplus account. These include expense and income accounts which are closed into surplus at the end of each fiscal period. Cf. *real accounts*.

nominal asset: an asset whose value is inconsiderable, to be questioned, or difficult to evaluate such as claims or judgments in reorganization. Accounting tradition suggests that nominal assets be written down and carried as some token value, usually one dollar. Copyrights, goodwill and other such assets can be considered nominal assets.

nominal capital: the par value of issued shares of a corporation, as differentiated from the book or market value.

nominal cost: cost measured in monetary units at the time it was incurred, that is, ignoring changes in the purchasing power of money. Cf. *real costs*.

nominal effective exchange rate: an effective exchange rate that has not been adjusted for relative inflation differentials. [103]

nominal exchange rate: the mint par of exchange.

nominal income: the dollar value of income. Shifts in nominal income arise from changes in either real income or in price levels.

nominal interest rate:
(1) the rate given on a debt instrument, usually differs from the market or effective rate.
(2) a rate of interest quoted for a year. Should the interest be compounded more often than annually, then the effective interest rate is higher than the nominal rate.

nominalist: a person who believes that money is the standard money defined by a government.

nominal rate of exchange: the post rate of exchange, allowing a person to have a sound idea of what the foreign exchange rate is and which is used for small foreign exchange transactions.

nominal value: used in the United Kingdom for face value, or par value. In the United States, this term is equivalent to par value.

nominee: an official of a bank or trust company, or an appointed agent into whose name securities or other funds are transferred by agreement. This is done to facilitate the purchase or sale of securities, when it may be inconvenient to obtain the signature of the principal to make such transfers. It also facilitates the collection and distribution of income from securities when these securities are held in the name of a nominee. Nominee arrangements also apply to custodianships. [10]

nonaccrual asset: an asset, such as a loan, that has been questioned on bank examination is known to be a "slow" or "doubtful" (of payment) loan. A reserve is set up or applied on this type of loan, and it is excluded from the earning or accrual assets.

nonassignable: synonymous with *inalienable*.

nonbank bank loophole: an interpretation of federal law allowing nonbanking companies to open banking offices and commercial banks to open limited service branches across state lines, despite the statutory ban on interstate banking. See also *Garnet St. Germain Depository Institutions Act of 1982*.

nonborrowed reserves: total reserves less member-bank borrowings from reserve banks. [72]

noncash item: any instrument that a bank declines to accept as a cash item, and therefore handles on a collection basis. The customer's account is not credited until settlement for the item takes place. [105]

noncompetitive tender: the submission to a bank when wishing to purchase Treasury bills directly from a Federal Reserve Bank, indicating the willingness to pay the average price of all the competitive offers from large institutions that buy millions of Treasury bills each week. The minimum purchase is $10,000, with multiples of $5000 above that.

noncurrent: that which is due more than one year after the date of issuance.

noncurrent liabilities: claims against the assets of an entity that will become due a year or more later.

nonexpendable disbursements: disbursements that are not chargeable as expenditures; for example, a disbursement made for the purpose of paying off an account payable previously recorded on the books. [49]

nonexpendable fund: the principal, and sometimes also the earnings, of which may not be expended. [49]

nonexpenditure disbursements: disbursements that are not chargeable as expenditures; for example, a disbursement made for the purpose of paying off an account payable previously recorded on the books. [49]

nonfeasance: failure to perform a legal duty. Cf. *malfeasance.*

nonfiling insurance: insurance purchased by a lender to protect against any loss that may result from a loan on collateral without properly filing or recording any lien on the collateral. [105]

noninstallment credit: credit granted, with payment to be made in a lump sum, at a future date.

non-interest-bearing note: a note whose maker does not have to pay any interest.

noninvestment property: property that will not yield income.

nonmarketable liabilities of U.S. government (including medium-term securities): other medium-term securities include foreign holdings of nonmarketable, medium-term U.S. government securities, payable before maturity only under special conditions. Examples of these are nonconvertible "Roosa Bonds" issued by the Treasury, and Certificates of Participation representing Export-Import Bank loans sold mainly to foreign governments and central banks. [73]

nonmember bank: U.S. Banks that are not members of the Federal Reserve System. These institutions are either state or private banks.

nonmember depository institution: a depository institution (commercial bank, mutual savings bank, savings and loan association, credit union, or U.S. agency or branch of a foreign bank) that is not a member of the Federal Reserve System. Nonmember depository institutions that offer transaction accounts or nonpersonal time deposits are subject to reserve requirements set by the Federal Reserve, and they also have access to the Federal Reserve discount window and Federal Reserve services on the same terms as member banks. [200]

nonmerchantable title: an unmarketable title that is legally unsound because it shows property defects. See *cloud on title.*

nonmonetary transactions: any transaction posted to an account which does not have a dollar value affecting the account balance. Changes to cardholder master file records, such as name changes, address changes, and changes of credit limit are nonmonetary transactions. [105]

nonmortgage loan: an advance of funds not secured by a real estate mortgage.

nonnegotiable: wanting in one of the requirements of a negotiable instrument, and as a consequence not entitled to the benefits of negotiability, such as freedom from many defenses that could otherwise be raised by the maker (e.g., fraudulent inducement). A nonnegotiable document is transferable by assignment. To prevent transfer, the label "nontransferable" should be used.

nonnegotiable title: a title that cannot be transferred by delivery or by endorsement.

nonnotification loan: a loan made by a bank or commercial finance company on the security of accounts receivable. The original debtor is not notified that the account has been pledged; the loan is made with recourse, that is, if an account receivable is not paid, the borrower still remains liable for the amount loaned against the receivable.

nonnotification plan:

(1) an indirect lending arrangement where a dealer's customer is not informed that his or her installment sales contract has been sold to the bank and the customer continues to make payments to the dealer.

(2) the act of pledging accounts receivable as loan security without notifying the account customers. [105]

nonoperating expense: the outlays and losses of a savings association that are nonrecurring in nature and that do not result from the ordinary savings and lending operations of the institution, such as the expense of maintaining real estate owned or a loss taken on the sale of a nonmortgage investment. [59]

nonoperating income: the receipts and profits of a savings association that are nonrecurring in nature and that do not result from the ordinary savings and lending operations of the institution, such as a profit on the sale of a nonmortgage investment. Synonymous with *nonrecurring income.* [59]

non-par bank: see *non-par item.*

non-par item: a check that cannot be collected at the par or face value when presented by another bank. All checks drawn on member banks of the Federal Reserve System, and nonmember banks that have met the requirements of the Federal Reserve System, are collectible at par. Some nonmember banks in certain regions of the United States levy an exchange charge against the check presented for collection and payment. These banks are called nonpar banks, and deduct the exchange charge when remitting the payment to the bank requesting collection and payment. See *par list.* [10]

nonpayment: the failure to pay as agreed. [28]

nonperformance: the failure of a contracting party to provide goods or services according to an agreement.

nonperformer: a nonperforming loan.

nonperforming loans: loans that are in trouble; loans where the lender's management judges that the borrower fails to have the ability to fulfill the original contractual terms of the loan or where payments of interest or principal are overdue by 90 days or more.

nonpossessory estate: see *future estate.*

nonrecurring charge: any cost, expense, or involuntary loss that will not, it is felt, be likely to occur again.

nonrecurring income: synonymous with *nonoperating income.*

nonrefundable debt: an issue of debt not called by the issuer prior to maturity in order to replace it with a new issue.

nonresident account: a bank account held by an individual who is defined as nonresident for the purposes of exchange control. Cf. *resident.*

nonresidential mortgage loan: a mortgage loan secured by nonresidential property such as an office building, store, factory, or church. [59]

nonrevenue receipts: collections, other than revenue, such as receipts from loans where the liability is recorded in the fund in which the proceeds are placed and receipts on account of recoverable expenditures. See also *revenue receipts.* [49]

nonsovereign public buyer:
(1) a government owned or controlled entity—such as a development bank, province, or municipality—that does not carry the full faith and credit of its government. [198]
(2) an entity whose obligations are not guaranteed by a sovereign public agency. Eximbank usually requires that the obligation of these buyers be guaranteed by the ministry of finance, the central bank, or an acceptable commercial bank. [190]

nonstarred card: generally indicates that purchases under $50 do not require an authorization. [105]

nonstock money corporation: any corporation operating either under the banking law or the insurance law which does not issue stock (e.g., mutual savings banks, credit unions, mutual insurance companies).

nonsufficient funds: a term indicating that a check or item drawn against an account is in excess of the account balance. [105]

nonvalidating stamp: the stamp that banks place on the back of domestic drafts accompanying bills of lading which removes the bank from certain liability. The stamp words state that the bank is not responsible, nor does it guaranty the documents stamped.

no-par value: having no face value.

no-passbook savings: the same as a regular passbook savings account, except that no passbook is used. Deposits and withdrawal slips are receipted by the teller, with a copy returned to the depositor for personal records. A periodic statement is rendered in place of a passbook. Withdrawals must be made by the depositor personally.

no protest: instructions given by one bank to another collecting bank not to object to items in case of nonpayment. The sending bank stamps on the face of the item the letters "NP." If the item cannot be collected, the collecting bank returns the item without objecting.

no record: the report given to a credit grantor by a credit bureau when no record exists in the bureau files regarding a particular customer. [41]

normal lending territory: synonymous with *regular lending area.*

normal return: the income on a specific investment, computed at a standard interest rate. [105]

normal sale: a transaction that pleases both the seller and buyer of property and in which no unforeseen or abnormal situations surface.

normal value: the price or a property commanded on the open market.

nostro account: "our" account; an account maintained by a bank with a bank in a foreign country. Nostro accounts are kept in foreign currencies of the country in which the monies are held, with the equivalent dollar value listed in another column. Cf. *vostro account.*

nostro overdraft: part of the bank's statement indicating that it has sold more foreign bills of exchange than it has bought, resulting in the domestic bank's owing currencies to foreign banks in the amount of the nostro (our) overdraft.

notarial acknowledgment: the acknowledgment of the due execution of a legal instrument before a notary public. The statement of the notary public as to the face and date of the acknowledgment, with the notary public's signature and seal of office and date of expiration of commission to serve as notary public. [37]

notarial certificate: the certificate of the notary public as to the due acknowledgment of the instrument. [37]

notarial protest certificate: see *notice of dishonor (protest jacket).*

notarized draft: a withdrawal order signed and acknowledged before a notary public, who affirms that the person who signed the draft personally appeared before him or her, was known to be the person indicated, and executed the draft for the purpose indicated. [39]

notary public: a person commissioned by a state for a stipulated period (with the privilege of renewal) to administer certain oaths and to attest and certify documents, thus authorizing him or her to take affidavits and depositions. A notary is also authorized to "protest" negotiable instruments for nonpayment or nonacceptance. See *notice of dishonor (protest jacket).*

note: an instrument, such as a promissory note, which is the recognized legal evidence of a debt. A note is signed by the maker, called the borrower, promising to pay a certain sum of money on a specified date at a certain place of business, to a certain business, individual, or bank, called the lender.

note broker: see *bill broker.*

note issue: the amount of bank notes issued by the issuing authority.

note liability: the liability that a Federal Reserve Bank has for the notes it has outstanding.

note loan: the classification of an unsecured loan. [55]

note notice: a form made and used by the loan department of a bank. The note notice contains all information as to the amount: due date, maker's name and address, securities pledged, if any, and so on. It is mailed to the borrower several days before the maturity of the note, as a reminder of the due date of the note. If the bank is posting the "liability ledger" by machine, the "loans made register," customer's liability ledger card, note notice, and maturity tickler are all created in one posting operation. [10]

note of hand: any promissory note.

note payable: a liability, evidenced by a formal written promise to pay a specified sum at a fixed future date. Notes may be either short (one year or less) or long term.

note payable register: a special book where detailed records of all notes and acceptances payable are recorded.

note receivable: a promissory note collected by a business from a customer.

note receivable discounted: a note assigned by the holder to another person. Should the note be assigned with recourse, it is the contingent liability of the assignor until the debt is paid. See *factoring.*

note receivable register: a special book where detailed records of all notes and acceptances receivable are recorded.

note teller: synonymous with *loan teller.*

notice account: a passbook savings account on which the customer agrees to give the association specified notice before making a withdrawal. As long as he gives the agreed notice, his funds earn at a higher interest rate than that paid on passbook accounts; insufficient notice for a withdrawal may incur a penalty. [59]

notice day: the day on which notices of intention to deliver may be issued.

notice of dishonor (protest jacket): when a "holder in due course" presents an instrument for payment or acceptance by a drawee, and the maker or drawee fails to honor the instrument, the holder in due course gives it to a notary public. The notary public also presents the instrument to the maker or drawee as a legal formality. If the maker or drawee again dishonors the instrument by refusing to pay for or to accept it, the notary public prepares a "notice of dishonor," or in the terminology of some states, a "mandate of protest" or a "notarial protest certificate." Cf. *acceptance for honor.*

notice of protest: a declaration made and witnessed by a notary public, stating that a check, bill of exchange, or note has been presented and payment has been refused. [105]

notice of withdrawal: a notice that may be required by a mutual savings bank or other recipient of savings deposits before a withdrawal of funds is permitted. The length of time required before the notice becomes effective varies in the several states. [39]

no-ticket savings plan: a variation of the "unit-savings plan" whereby the normal savings account transaction, either deposit or withdrawal, is accomplished without the use of either a deposit ticket or withdrawal slip. A deposit is recorded just as in the unit-savings plan, but the depositor is not required to make out a deposit ticket under this machine-printed entry plan. In place of a withdrawal slip, the depositor merely writes his or her signature on the same line as the machine-printed entry of withdrawal. As in the unit savings plan, the passbook, ledger card, and lock-protected audit tape are posted in original printing in one operation directly in front of the depositor, who is the "auditor" of the transaction. [10]

notification plan: the act of pledging accounts receivable as loan security, and notifying the customers maintaining the accounts receivable of such action. The payments on the accounts are then usually sent directly to the party making the loan. [105]

noting a bill: the notation on a bill of exchange by a notary public after presentation of the bill protesting its nonpayment. The notation consists of the date, notary's initials, reason for nonpayment, and the notary's charges.

novation:
(1) the replacement of a new debt or obligation for an older one. See *open-end mortgage;* cf. *renewal, standstill agreement.*
(2) the replacement of a new creditor or debtor for a former creditor (or debtor).

NOW (negotiable order of withdrawal) account: a savings account from which the account holder can withdraw funds by writing a negotiable order of withdrawal (NOW) payable to a third party. [59] Until January 1, 1980 NOW accounts were available only in New England, New York, and New Jersey. Effective with new federal regulations, all savings and loans as well as banks, for the first time nationally, are allowed to offer interest-bearing checking

accounts (NOW accounts). See also *super-NOW.*

NP:
(1) see *no protest.*
(2) see *notary public.*
(3) see *note payable.*

NR: see *note receivable.*

NS: see *net surplus.*

NSF: not sufficient funds.

NT Dollar: monetary unit of China (Taiwan).

nudge: see *Operation Twist (Nudge).*

nudum pactum: "an empty promise" (Latin); a statement for which no consideration has been given.

numbered account: a bank account where the owner is identified only by a number so as to preserve anonymity.

numerical transit system: see *American Bankers Association number.*

numismatic: pertaining to coins and the collection of coins and medals.

nursery finance: institutional loans to profitable organizations that plan to go public shortly. See *risk capital, venture capital.*

NWC: see *net working capital.*

NYBOR: New York inter-bank offered rate.

O&A: October and April (semiannual interest payments or dividends).

OA: see *open account.*

objection to title: a weakness in a title for property, requiring adjustment. See *cloud on title.*

objective indicators: an attempt to find factors affecting changes in the exchange rate—to date unsuccessful. [105]

Oblg.: see *obligation.*

Oblig.: see *obligation.*

obligation: the legal responsibility and duty of the debtor (the obligor) to pay a debt when due, and the legal right of the creditor (the obligee) to enforce payment in the event of default.

obligation bond: see *bond, obligation.*

obligator: synonymous with *obligor.*

obligatory maturity: the compulsory maturity of any bond or note, as distinguished from optional maturity dates or early redemption dates.

obligee: a creditor or promisee.

obligor: a debtor or promisor; principal.

OBU: see *offshore banking unit.*

obverse: the front or face of a note, as opposed to the reverse or back. It usually bears the value of the note, its date, and the principal vignette. [27]

OCO: see *one-cancels-the-other order.*

Od.:
(1) see *overdraft.*
(2) see *overdraw.*
(3) see *overdue.*

OD: see *on demand.*

odd-days' interest: interest earned in closed-end credit transactions which accrues with respect to days that are not part of a regular payment schedule. "Odd days" generally arise in connection with dealer paper (retail installment sales contracts assigned to the bank) when the period before the first payment is either longer or shorter than the interval between the remainder of the payments. [105]

OE: see *operating expense.*

off-balance sheet financing: financing that is not clearly displayed on the balance sheet (i.e., some leasing).

offer(ed): to present for acceptance or refusal.

offering telex: in Euromarkets, a telex sent out to banks offering participation in a bond issue or sometimes a credit.

offeror: one who makes an offer.

off-host: an operating mode in which the terminals do not have access to a positive file at the card-issuing bank. On-line/off-host implies connection to negative files stored in the front-end processor of the card-issuing bank. [105]

Office of Savings Associations (OSA): the agency of the savings and loan industry replacing the Federal Home Loan Bank Board.

Office of the Comptroller of the Currency: the office within the U.S. Treasury Department having the responsibility for overall supervision and examination of national banks. [105]

Office of Thrift Supervision: see *savings industry bill.*

officer:
(1) any principal executive of a corporation to whom authority has been delegated, usually by the board of directors.
(2) a manager of a primary bank function.

officer's check: synonymous with *cashier's check.*

official check: synonymous with *cashier's check.*

official exchange rate: the ratio that is applied by the monetary authority of one nation in exchanging its money for that of another nation.

offset:
(1) either of two equivalent entries on both sides of an account.
(2) the right accruing to a bank to take possession of any balances that a guarantor or debtor may have in the bank to cover a loan in default.
(3) a depositor who has both a deposit credit balance and a loan balance is denied the right of offset if the bank becomes insolvent and closes.

offshore banking unit (OBU): a bank in Bahrain, or any other center with similar organizations; not allowed to conduct business in the domestic market, only with other OBUs or with foreign institutions.

offshore profit centers: branches of major international banks and multinational corporations in Nassau, Bermuda, the Cayman Islands, and other low-tax banking centers as a way of lessening taxes.

of record: as shown by the record; usually employed in such entries as "attorney of record," showing that the one named is the recognized representative of the party at interest. [37]

Ohio Deposit Guarantee Fund: a state-chartered mutual institution in Ohio that insures the savings accounts held by member savings associations and serves as a central credit facility. [59]

OI:
(1) see *operating income.*
(2) see *ordinary interest.*

OJAJ: October, January, April, July (quarterly interest payments or dividends).

ok: correct.

ok packages: a list or package of checks that has been processed in a branch office, proved for accuracy, checked for date and endorsement, and considered OK by the branch office. The total on the package is used at the main office for the final consolidation of totals without the main office having to rerun the items in the package. [10]

old and new balance proof: a method of proof used in a bank, especially in savings departments, to prove the correct pickup of old balances, and to establish the net amount of increase or decrease to ledger controls. An adding machine tape, or a columnar journal sheet is used as a permanent record of this proof. All affected ledger cards are sorted by account number, and then run on an adding machine. Generally, the new balances are run in the first column. In the next column, the old balances are run so that the old balances appear opposite the new balances and the old balances must equal the difference in the totals of the deposits and the withdrawals. If these two differences agree, it is proof that the old balance was picked up correctly on every account affected in the day's business. [10]

Old Lady of Threadneedle Street: a popular name for the Bank of England.

Omnibus Banking Bill of 1984: New York State legislation designed to halt mortgage loan losses by state banks and to improve the business climate for New York banking institutions. Also repeals a 20 percent limit on out-of-state lending by state-chartered savings and loan associations.

Omnibus Reconciliation Act of 1980: federal legislation; imposed restrictions on use of mortgage subsidy bonds plus other miscellaneous tax changes.

on account:
(1) describes a payment made toward the settlement of an account.
(2) a purchase or sale made on *open account.*

on balance: the net effect or result.

on demand: describing a bill of exchange that is payable on presentation. See *demand note.*

one-bank holding company: a corporation that owns control of one commercial bank.

one-cancels-the-other order (OCO): a contingency order in which one part is automatically canceled as soon as the other part is filled.

one-day certificates: authorized by Congress in 1971, the Federal Reserve Banks buy and sell guaranteed obligations of the government directly from or to the United States. By law, these certificates cannot exceed $5 billion.

one hundred percent reserve: a banking system that can be substituted for the fractional reserve system. Commercial banks can be required to hold reserves for the full amount of their deposits and would not be able to make loans with any funds except those available from paid-in capital and surplus.

one hundred percent statement: a statement showing the conversion of all the individual items in a balance sheet to a percentage of the total assets.

one-name paper: single-name paper, straight paper. An instrument signed by only one party, individual, or firm, as contrasted with obligations having two or more obligors.

one-stop banking: provided by a bank whose clients can do all banking business at that bank. Cf. *full-service bank.*

on-host: an operating mode in which the terminals do have access to a positive file at the card-issuing bank. On-line/on-host implies connection to positive files stored in the bank's files. [105]

on-line data capture (ODC): an input system for bank card dollar entries. [105]

on-line off-host: an operating mode where financial service terminals are accessing only the front-end processor and do not have access to the central computer system containing the data base. Authorization is limited to the files contained in the processor. [105]

on-line on-host: an operating mode where financial service terminals are on-line, with the central computer system interfacing with a front-end processor. [105]

on-the-spot loan: an extension of funds on a preapproved credit line or credit card. [105]

on-us check: any depositor's check drawn on and payable at the bank wherein the account is carried is termed an "on us" check when presented for payment to the drawee bank. [10]

ooftish (offtish): slang, money, usually to be used for speculation.

open account: credit extended that is not supported by a note, mortgage, or other formal written evidence of indebtedness (e.g., merchandise for which a buyer is billed later). Synonymous with *book account.*

open book account: see *open account.*

open credit: credit that is allowed without immediate proof of a customer's credit worthiness.

open door policy: a condition where citizens and products of foreign countries receive the same treatment as domestic citizens and products.

open economy: an economy free of trade restrictions.

open-end bond: see *bond, open-end.*

open-end clause: an optional mortgage clause, used in states that recognize its validity, which provides that the pledge of real estate will cover additional advances of funds that the borrower may request and the lender agrees to grant at unknown times in the future. Under the terms of this clause, all subsequent advances represent a claim on the property dating from the time of recording of the original mortgage. [59]

open-end lease: a lease that may involve an additional payment based on the value of property when returned. [78]

open-end mortgage: a mortgage that permits the borrower to reborrow money paid on the principal up to the original amount.

open inflation: the situation wherein there is no control of prices and there is an increase in money demand for goods relative to the supply of goods. Shortages are adjusted then by a rise in prices.

opening entry:
(1) the entry made to begin a set of books; the entry debiting all existing assets and crediting liabilities, reserves, and capital accounts.
(2) the first entry in an account.

open-market committee: a committee composed of the Board of Governors of the Federal Reserve System plus the presidents of five of the Federal Reserve District Banks. See *open-market operations.*

open-market credit: short-term financing enabling commercial paper houses to purchase notes and resell them in the open market.

open-market operations: operations carried out by the Federal Reserve System, in which it buys or sells government bonds in the same market other institutional investors use.

open-market paper: bills of exchange or notes drawn by one with high credit standing, made payable to himself or herself and indorsed in blank. These are sold to financial institutions other than banks.

open-market rates: the money rates set for classes of paper in the open market, as distinguished from banks rates offered to customers, and rates for advances and rediscounts set by Federal Reserve Banks for all member banks.

open mortgage: a mortgage that can be paid off, without penalty, at any period prior to its maturity.

open position: a dealer's aggregate assets and liabilities in a currency.

open to buy: the currently unused portion of a total dollar credit line agreed upon. [28]

open trade: any transaction that has not yet been closed.

operating assets: those assets that contribute to the regular income from the operations of a business. Thus stocks and bonds owned, unused real estate, loans to officers, and so on, are excluded from operating assets.

operating capital: funds available for use in financing the day-to-day activities of a business. [105]

operating company: a company whose officers direct the business of transportation and whose books contain operating as well as financial accounts. [18]

operating costs: costs of maintenance, utilities, office equipment, salaries, and such required to keep a business operational.

operating expense:
(1) actual expense incurred in the maintenance of property (e.g., management, repairs, taxes, insurance); not included as operating expenses are mortgage payments, depreciation, and interest paid out.
(2) any expense incurred in the normal operation of a business. This is to be distinguished from expenditures, which are disbursements that are capitalized and depreciate over a period of years.

operating income:
(1) income to a business produced by its earning assets and by fees for services rendered.
(2) rental monies obtained from the operation of a business or from property.

operating lease: a lease where the asset is not wholly amortized during the obligatory period of the lease, and where the lessor does not rely for his or her profit on the rentals in the obligatory period.

operating losses: losses incurred in the normal (i.e., nonnegligent) operation of a business.

operating officer: the officer who heads up an operating department in a large bank. He or she is in complete charge of the operations of his or her department. A distinction is to be made between an operating officer and the other officials, such as the vice-presidents, who are specialists in their fields. The cashier of the bank can be considered the senior operating officer in charge of the overall operations of the bank in its routine work. The vice-presidents are specialists in the fields of loans, credits, investments, and trusts. In smaller banks, it is not uncommon for vice-presidents to be in charge of certain operations as well as being specialists in their field. Any decision regarding the operation of a department is usually left to the operating officer in charge of the department. His or her recommendations regarding personnel requirements, equipment purchases, type and quantity of supplies used, and so on, carry great weight with higher officials. [10]

operating profit: profit arising from the regular operation of an enterprise engaged in performing physical services (e.g., public utilities), excluding income from other sources and excluding expenses other than those of direct operation. [62]

operations analysis: a system of analyzing specific savings association operations in order to establish norms, appraise efficiency, improve operations, and reduce costs accrued. [59]

operations manager: individual responsible for the operational phases of a bank card plan, including accounting, sales draft auditing, and statement preparation. [105]

Operation Twist (Nudge): in 1961 the Federal Reserve and the U.S. Treasury attempted to raise short-term interest rates relative to long-term rates to harmonize domestic and foreign objectives. Bank time-deposit interest rates were increased, and funds were redirected from short- to long-term goals.

opinion of title: legal opinion stating that title to property is clear and marketable; serves the same purpose as a certificate of title. [62]

OPM: other people's money.

option:

(1) a privilege to buy or sell, receive, or deliver property, given in accordance with the terms stated, with a consideration for price. This privilege may or may not be exercised at the option holder's discretion. Failure to exercise the option leads to forfeiture.

(2) the right of an insured or a beneficiary to select the form of payment of the proceeds of an insurance contract.

option account: a charge account in which the consumer may choose either to pay at the end of 30 days or to spread payments over a longer period of time. If he or she chooses to spread payments beyond 30 days, he or she pays a service charge. [40]

optional (revolving) credit: a regular open or 30-day charge account to which the customer has requested to have the "option" added. That is, he may pay the whole balance within 15 or 20 days of receipt of his bill (when there will be no credit service charge) or may pay any portion of it that is convenient. Then on any amount not paid by the time the next bill is made out (which would be after the 15- to 20-day period following the first bill), a charge of 1 percent, of 1 1/2 percent, or the like is added. As in other revolving credit plans, this charge would not be applied to purchases or additions in the then-current month but just to the sum left unpaid from the last billing. [28]

optional date: the date at which a municipality or corporation has the right to redeem its obligations under certain conditions.

optional payment bond: see *bond, optional payment.*

optional valuation date: the date on which the size of an individual's estate is computed for purposes of tax payment. It can be set at the date of death or as of six months following death, provided the assets are not disposed of in the interim.

option contract: a contract in foreign exchange to deal in foreign exchange, wherein the date of completion of the deal, but not its existence, is at the customer's choice with a specified period.

optionee: the holder of an option; a prospective buyer.

optioner: any property owner.

order:

(1) a request to deliver, sell, receive, or purchase goods or services.

(2) identifying the one to whom payment should be made: "Made to the order of."

ordering bank: the bank that instructs the sender to execute the transaction. [105]

ordering bank identifier: a code that uniquely identifies the ordering bank. [105]

ordering bank identifier type: a code that specifies the type of ordering bank identifier used. [105]

ordering bank name and address: identifies the ordering bank by name and, optionally, the ordering bank's postal address. [105]

order instrument: a negotiable instrument containing the words "pay to the order of . . ." or "pay to (the name of payee) or order," requiring endorsement and delivery prior to negotiation.

order of distribution: an order by a probate or other court having jurisdiction of an estate directing distribution of estate property to persons or others entitled thereto. [37]

order paper: in dealing with negotiable instruments, an instrument is called *order paper* when it is in such form as to require indorsement by the payee or indorsee. *Order paper* can be converted to *bearer paper* by a blank indorsement. Cf. *bearer paper.*

order party: party instructing the sender to execute the transaction. [105]

orders: requests made for the delivery of goods or services.

ordinary asset: an asset that is bought and sold as a regular component of a continuing business activity. What may be an ordinary asset to one firm may be a capital asset to another. A real estate broker selling property would be selling an ordinary asset, whereas a retailer would be selling a capital asset if he sold land.

ordinary discount: the difference between the value at maturity and the present value which at an assumed rate of interest will accumulate to the value of maturity.

ordinary gain (or loss): gain or loss realized from the sale or exchange of property that is not a capital asset, such as inventory.

ordinary interest: interest that is calculated based on 360 days to the year.

organization certificate: in the formation of a bank, one of the statements that must be filed, usually with the Comptroller of the Currency.

organization expense: direct costs when forming a new corporation (incorporation fees, taxes, legal fees, etc.).

original balance: the beginning debt or obligation before any payment has been made on it to reduce it. [28]

original issue discount: debt instruments that are originally sold at less than par but which return par at maturity, with the interest paid being equal to the discount.

originating bank: a bank that receives paperless entries from participating business entries in an automated clearinghouse system and which forwards the entries to the Automated Clearing House. [105]

origination fee: a charge made for initiating and processing a mortgage loan.

originator: the banking house or individual investment banker who is the first to promote a proposed new issue for a corporation.

originator identifier: a code that uniquely identifies the originator to the originator's bank. [105]

originator identifier type: a code that specifies the type of identifier used in the originator identifier field. [105]

originator name and address: identifies the originator by name and, optionally, the originator's postal address. [105]

originator's bank: a bank that acts as the financial agent for the originator of a transfer. [105]

originator's reference: originator's transaction reference which identifies the original transaction in a transfer. [105]

originator to beneficiary information: information conveyed from the originator to the beneficiary. [105]

OSA: see *Office of Savings Association.*

other income: a general heading on the income statement under which are grouped revenues from miscellaneous operations, income from the lease of road and equipment, miscellaneous rent income, income from nonoperating property, profit from separately operated properties, dividend income, interest income, income from sinking and other reserve funds, release of premiums on funded debt, contributions from other companies, miscellaneous income, and delayed income credits. [18]

other liabilities and accrued dividends: miscellaneous liabilities plus dividends accrued but unpaid on Federal Reserve Bank stock owned by the member banks. [40]

other loans: mostly loans to individuals, except farmers, for consumption purposes. [40]

other loans for purchasing or carrying securities: loans to other than brokers and dealers for the purpose of purchasing or carrying securities.

other long-term debt: long-term debt other than mortgage bonds and debentures. This includes serial notes and notes payable to banks with original maturity of more than one year. [3]

other real estate: synonymous with *owned real estate.*

other securities: all securities other than U.S. government obligations—that is, state, municipal, and corporate bonds. (Member banks are generally not permitted to invest in stocks other than Federal Reserve bank stock). [40]

ouguiya: monetary unit of Mauritania.

"our" account:

(1) a term used by bank personnel in reference to their due from (nostro) account. See also *nostro account.*

(2) in EFTS, when used in funds transfer messages, the account "due to" the sending bank.

out card: a card substituted for a ledger card when the latter is removed from the file. The out card should contain the balance, the date the ledger card was removed, by whose authority, and the person in whose possession the ledger card is held. There are occasions when ledger cards must be removed from the ledger trays for reference—for example, when a borrower who is already borrowing funds from the bank requests a large loan. The ledger card is the record that must be used to review the borrower's use of credit, how the loans in the past were liquidated, and when the customer last completely liquidated his borrowings. This information supplements other available credit information held by the bank and is used by the loan committee in arriving at decisions. [10]

outgoing interchange: transactions deposited with an acquiring bank and sent to an issuing bank. [105]

outlawed: promissory note debarred by the statute of limitations of actions. [105]

outlays: any expenditures.

out-of-area card: synonymous with *foreign card*.

out of line: a stock whose price is determined to be either too low or too high. This is often determined by noting the corporation's price-earnings ratio.

out-of-plan: a bank card issued by another bank or to a transaction originating at a merchant affiliated with another bank or bank card association. [105]

out-of-plan card: synonymous with *foreign card*.

out-of-pocket expense: a cost incurred by an individual, often when on a business trip; the item or service is paid for in cash or by check or charge account, and the employee expects reimbursement from the company.

out-of-town item: see *foreign items, transit letter.*

output:
(1) the quantity yielded in any operation.
(2) the average dollar gross domestic product produced in a stated period.

outright transaction: a purchase sale or forward exchange without a corresponding transaction spot.

outside borrowing: borrowing funds from sources other than a Federal Home Loan Bank or a state-chartered central reserve institution.

outstanding: any unpaid or uncollected debt.

outstanding checks: issued checks by a depositor that have not yet been paid by the bank.

Outstg.: see *outstanding.*

overall coverage: the relationship of income available or payments on corporate obligations divided by the amount of such annual charges. The better the coverage over a time period, the sounder the issue.

overall market price coverage: the ratio of net assets to the sum of all prior obligations at liquidating value plus the issue in question taken at market price. [30]

over and short account: an account carried in the general ledger. Overages and shortages from all sources, and their nature, are posted to this account, which is also termed a "suspense" or "differences" account in banks. At the end of the fiscal period, this account is closed out to profit and loss and becomes either an increase or a decrease to the undivided profits account in the general ledger. In larger banks, a subsidiary ledger is carried on this account so that the overages and shortages of all departments are carried as separate accounts. In this way, the frequency of any differences can be localized to a department and this department brought under control. [10]

overapplied overhead: the excess of amount of overhead cost applied to a product over the amount of overhead cost incurred.

overcapitalize:
(1) to provide an excessive amount of capital to a business.
(2) to set too high a value on property.
(3) to place too high a value on the nominal capital of a company.

overcertification: a rarely used certification by the bank of a customer's check where the collected balance in the person's account is less than the amount recorded on the check.

overcheck: a check drawn against an uncollected or insufficient balances; an overdraft.

overcommitment: synonymous with *over extension.*

overdraft: when a depositor draws a check for more than the balance on deposit with a bank and the bank honors that check, he or she is said to be "overdrawn." The bank can either return the check to the bank from which it came or to the person who presented it for payment, marked "insufficient funds." The bank can also elect to render the customer a service and pay the check.

overdraft banking: a service offered to demand deposit customers whereby a line of credit is associated with an individual's account. Checks drawn on insufficient funds are not returned to the presenter but are paid from funds from the credit line. [105]

overdraft checking account: a line of credit that allows a person to write checks for more than the actual balance, with a finance charge on the overdraft. [1]

overdraw: to write a bank check for an amount exceeding the deposit in the bank on which the check is drawn. See *cushion checking (credit), kite (kiting), overdraft.*

overdue: a payment that has not been made at the time it was due.

overextension:
(1) the expansion by a business concern of buildings, equipment, and so on, in excess of the company's present or prospective future needs. Synonymous with *overcommitment.*
(2) credit received or extended beyond the debtor's ability to pay.

overflow accounts: synonymous with *sweep accounts.*

overhang: involuntary foreign official holdings of a currency, usually a generalized condition, i.e., relating to a significant number of nations and involving historically large amounts of the currency concerned net of working balances; represents temporary inconvertibility due to the inability of the reserve currency nation to convert the overhang into other forms of acceptable reserve asset.

overlay: an amount included in the tax levy on general property to cover abatements and taxes that will probably not be collected. [105]

overlimit account: an account in which the assigned dollar limit has been exceeded. [105]

overlining: under federal regulations, a bank cannot make loans to any one borrower that amounts to more than 10 percent of its capital. One way around that restriction is for a small bank to parcel out shares in proposed large loans deals to more important banks. This practice is called *overlining.*

overlying mortgage: a junior mortgage subject to the claim of a senior mortgage, which has a claim prior to the junior mortgage. Cf. *equal dignity.*

overnight Eurodollars: Eurodollars issued by Caribbean branches of U.S. members' banks to U.S. nonbank customers, net of those held by money market mutual funds. [203]

over on bill: additional freight described on the bill of lading.

overplus: synonymous with *surplus.*

overprints: official marks on a current paper money issue for the reason indicated: for purposes of revaluation, cancellation, and so on. [27]

override: a commission paid to managers that is added to their salary.

oversaving: when planned saving exceeds planned investment, oversaving is said to occur, and the quantity of cash removed from income movement exceeds the amount returned to it, resulting in the decline of income.

overshooting: the failure of an exchange rate to find its true level, but to move beyond it, owing to temporary pressures, which then are reversed as the excessive movement of the exchange rate is perceived. [182]

oversighting of foreign banks: see *Federal Reserve oversight.*

OWC: see *owner will carry.*

owe: to be obliged to pay something to someone for something received; an indebtedness.

owned real estate: real estate acquired by a bank through foreclosure of a mortgage or through a deed in lieu of foreclosure or in settlement of any other obligation to the bank. Synonymous with *other real estate.* [105]

owner: a person possessing title to property.

owner financing: a creative home-financing approach where the potential buyer bypasses the bank and borrows money directly from the person selling the house. Owners often find that this type of financing is the only way they can sell their houses because so many potential buyers cannot qualify for bank loans. The buyer, for example, might borrow half the needed money from the owner at 8 percent interest and the rest from a bank at 14 percent.

ownership: the right to services and/ or benefits provided by an asset. Ownership is usually shown by the possession of legal title or by a beneficial interest in the title. [105]

owner's paper: all forms of mortgage debt, including second mortgages, held by the seller of a house, rather than a bank.

owner will carry (OWC): mortgages at below-market rates wherein a good bargainer can knock costs down further.

PA:
(1) see *per annum.*
(2) see *power of attorney.*

pa'anga: monetary unit of the Tonga Islands.

package mortgage: a home-financing mortgage covering appliances and other household items (e.g., air conditioners, refrigerators, dryers).

paid check: a check that has been canceled and paid.

PAL: preapproved loan.

Palmer rule: the Rule of 1832 (after Palmer, governor of the Bank of England at that time) which sought to make fluctuations in English currency conform to what would occur under purely metallic currency by keeping bank-owned paper at a constant level.

PAN: see *Primary Account Number.*

P&L: profit and loss.

panic: a sudden, spreading fear of the collapse of business or the nation's economy, resulting in widespread withdrawal of bank deposits, stock sales, and similar transactions. A depression may but does not always follow a panic.

PAN-PIN pair: an account number and its corresponding secret code. [105]

PAP: prearranged payments.

paper: a loan contract; commercial paper, short-term evidence of a debt.

paper basis: indicating that a nation does not employ a metallic basis for its currency. See *paper money.*

paper gold: see *special drawing rights.*

paper hanger: slang, an individual who attempts to pass or forge worthless checks on a nonexistent bank account.

paper lease: a transaction permitted by the Treasury Department, allowing a company that faces the possibility of bankruptcy to arrange a lease as long as its secured creditors agree to honor the lease if they take possession of the leased property. Originally, the Treasury's rules called for the lease to end unless the bankruptcy trustee agreed to honor it.

paperless item processing system (PIPS): an electronic funds transit system that is capable of performing transit functions by establishing accounting transactions by which bank funds are shifted from one ledger or subledger to another.

paper money: currency on which a value is printed, although unlike coins, the bills have no value in themselves; usually represents bullion held in government vaults. Cf. *fiat money.*

paper standard: a monetary system, based on paper money, that is not convertible into gold or any other item of intrinsic value.

paper title: a written document that appears to convey proof of ownership but may not in fact show proper title. Cf. *cloud on title.*

paper truncation: the act terminating the flow of paper in a transaction-processing system. For example, in an Electronic Funds Transfer system, once pertinent data from checks or credit card sales drafts are captured electronically, the paper records would be stored and would not be required in subsequent system operations. Paper truncation mandates a descriptive statement in lieu of the return to the customer of individual records of each transaction. [36]

par: when the exchangeable value of an instrument is equal to that expressed on its face without consideration of any premium or discount. See also *face value.*

paradox of thrift: a concept of John Maynard Keynes that any effort by society to raise its savings rate can lead to a reduction in the amount it can really save.

parallel loans: see *back-to-back.*

parallel standard: a monetary standard; two or more metals are coined and authorized unconditionally as legal tender. Cf. *bimetallism.*

paramount title: the foremost title, a title that is superior to all others. Often the original title used to prepare later ones.

par clearance: any check that clears at par as contrasted with a check that is non par. See *par.*

par collection: the process of check collections as stated in the "par collection requirements" of the Federal Reserve Act. See *par*.

parent company: a controlling organization that owns or manages business properties. Synonymous with *proprietary company*.

par exchange rate: the free market price of one country's money in terms of the currency of another.

Paris Club: an informal grouping of governments meeting on an ad hoc basis to find agreement on measures to be taken when a nation is unable to repay its foreign borrowings on time. [91]

par item: any item that can be collected at its par or face value upon presentation.

parity: equality of purchase power established by law between different kinds of money at a given ratio.

parity check: a summation check in which the binary digits in a character or word are added and the sum checked against a single previously computed parity digit (i.e., a check to test whether the necessary number of ones and zeros are encoded in the computer to represent a number or word correctly). [105]

parity clause: a mortgage clause by virtue of which all notes obtained by the mortgage have "equal dignity"; that is, none has priority.

par list: a Federal Reserve System list of banks that will remit in full for items that are payable to the system.

par of exchange: the market price of money in one national currency that is exchanged at the official rate for a specific amount in another national currency, or another commodity of value (gold, silver, etc.).

partially amortized mortgage: a mortgage partly repaid by amortization during the life of the mortgage and partly repaid at the end of the term.

partial payment: a payment that is not equal to the full amount owed and is not intended to constitute the full payment.

partial release: the giving up of a claim to a portion of the property held as security for the payment of a debt. [51]

participant: a bank, brokerage house, or investment firm that has agreed to sell a stock issue to the public as part of a syndicate.

participating certificate:
(1) an instrument that specifies a partial owner interest in an instrument.
(2) a federal security sold in multiples of $5000 and guaranteed by the Federal National Mortgage Association.
(3) see also *participation certificate*.

participation: an ownership interest in a mortgage. [51]

participation agreement: an understanding, the terms of which are usually specified in writing between institutional investors, to buy or sell partial ownership interests in mortgages. [51]

participation certificate:
(1) a certificate representing a beneficial interest in a pool of federal agency mortgages or loans; a formal credit instrument carrying a contractual interest obligation on a specified principal.
(2) a document showing participation in a syndicated Eurocredit; usually in negotiable form so that it can legally be sold to another bank.
(3) see also *participating certificate*.

participation fee: in the Euromarket, a bank's fee for participating in a loan.

participation loan: a loan having two or more banks as creditors. Laws prohibit banks from lending more than a fixed percentage of their capital and surplus to any one borrower. Thus banks invite other banks to participate in making large loans.

partisan issues: paper money for limited circulation issued by partisans fighting the forces occupying their country. [27]

partner: a person who is a member of a partnership; usually for the purpose of operating a business.

partnership: a contractual relationship between two or more people in a joint enterprise, who agree to share, not necessarily equally, in the profits and losses of the organization. Cf. *joint venture.*

partnership certificate: a certificate filed with a bank showing the interest of each partner in a business enterprise operating as a partnership. This certificate also shows the limited partners (partners who specify a maximum amount for which they may be held responsible in settlement of obligations incurred by the partnership), and also "silent partners" (partners who have invested funds in the partnership, but who, for certain reasons, do not wish to be publicly known as partners). [10]

party at interest: individual or group of individuals having a vested interest in a commercial enterprise.

par value (of currency): the value of a currency in terms of gold as formally proposed to the International Monetary Fund, normally subject to fund concurrence. The fund's Articles of Agreement envisage that each member country shall have an effective par value, i.e., a unitary, fixed exchange rate for spot transactions that is established and maintained in accordance with the provisions of the Articles. Synonymous with *face value.* [42]

passbook: a book record prepared by a bank for a depositor, listing date and amount of deposits, with an initial or identifying symbol indicating the teller who received the deposit. In the case of savings accounts, the passbook lists deposits, withdrawals, interest paid by the bank, dates of all transactions, each new balance, and the initial or identifying symbol of the teller handling each transaction. The passbook shows the depositor's name or names and account number. Cf. *no-passbook savings.*

passbook account: a savings account that normally requires no minimum balance, no minimum term, no specified deposits, and no notice or penalty for withdrawals. [59]

passbook loan: see *savings account loan.*

passbook savings: a savings account that uses a passbook, in which the bank records transactions. [105]

passing title: synonymous with *closing title.* See *closing (or passing) title.*

passive trust: one whose trustee has no tasks to perform and merely retains title to the trust property.

pass-through certificates: certificates guaranteed by the Government National Mortgage Association.

past due: an account on which payment has not been made according to agreement and owes a given amount which is in arrears. [41]

past-due item: any note, acceptance, or other time instrument of indebtedness that has not been paid on the due date.

pataca: monetary unit of Macao.

pawn: the pledge to pay a debt.

pawnbroker: a business manager who lends items that are pledged as security for the loan.

pay:
(1) to pay a check in cash, as when a check is paid by the paying teller. (2) to charge a check against a customer's account, as in the case of a check coming through the clearings. [50]

payable in exchange: the requirement that a negotiable instrument be paid in the funds of the place from which it was originally issued.

payables: a bookkeeping term for any and all accounts or notes payable total. Cf. *receivables.*

pay-as-you-go accounts: a variation of "special checking accounts" or "special fee accounts." Under the pay-as-you-go plan, the special-checking-account depositor purchases a checkbook, usually at the rate of 5 or 10 cents per check. The fee or service charge is therefore prepaid to the bank, and the depositor can control the cost of his checking account by the number of checks he writes. In this plan, no service charge is posted as checks are posted against the account. [10]

pay-by-phone: a service enabling customers to instruct their financial institution via telephone to initiate one or more payments from their accounts. [33]

pay date: see *PDate.*

payee: the person or organization to whom a check or draft or note is made payable. The payee's name follows the expression "pay to the order of." [7]

payer: the party primarily responsible for the payment of the amount owed as evidenced by a given negotiable instrument.

pay-in: a monetary contribution or deposit in a fund or account, usually on a periodic basis.

paying bank: a bank upon which a check is drawn and pays a check or other draft to the holder and/or collecting bank.

paying teller: a representative of the bank who is responsible for the proper paying or cashing of checks presented at the window. See *unit teller system.* [50]

pay-in warrant: see *deposit warrant.*

pay loans: computing and counting out the currency (and/or issuing the checks) to be paid out to a customer in closing his loan. [55]

payment: total sum of money borrowed, plus all finance charges, divided by the number of months in the term of the loan. [78]

payment bill: a bill of exchange presented for payment instead of acceptance.

payment coupon: the section of the billing statement containing payment information and which should be returned by the customer with the payment. [105]

payment date: the date on which a customer has agreed to make his payment each month. Synonymous with *due date.* [55]

payment for honor: paying a bill by another other than the one on whom it is drawn, when the latter has defaulted, to save the reputation or credit of the original drawee.

payment order: an order given to a bank to pay or transfer an amount of money to a third party, for the account of the third party or the account of another. [105]

payment record: a record of a customer's past payment pattern on installment cash loans and other credit transactions. [105]

payments mechanism: systems designed for the movement of funds, payments, and money between financial institutions throughout the nation. The Federal Reserve plays a major role in the nation's payments mechanism through distribution of currency and coin, check processing, wire transfers, and automated clearinghouses. Various private associations also perform many payments mechanism operations. [1]

payments system: a system (composed of people, machines, and procedures) used to transfer value from one party to another. [36]

payment stopped: a negotiable instrument such as a check upon which a "stop payment" has been issued. See *stop payment.*

payment supra protest: payment after protest. An indorser liable on a dishonored negotiable instrument that has been protested receives a right to reimbursement from the drawer for paying the instrument.

payment voucher: usually the upper part of a customer's monthly statement presented or mailed together with remittance. Becomes the posting medium for the accounts receivable bookkeeper. [41]

payoff:
(1) the complete repayment of loan principal, interest, and any other sums due; payoff occurs either over the full term of the loan or through prepayments. [59]
(2) money given for an unethical or illegal service.

payoff statement: a formal statement prepared when a loan payoff is contemplated, showing the current status of the loan account, all sums due, and the daily rate of interest. Synonymous with *letter of demand.* [59]

payor: a person who makes, or is to make, a payment. [59]

payroll savings plan: a plan whereby an employee authorizes his employer to deduct from his wages or salary each pay period a specified amount and to forward that amount to his savings association for deposit to his savings account. [59]

Payt.: see *payment.*

pay to: indicates that the receiver should provide the specified funds to the designated payee. [105]

pay to bearer: see *bearer instrument.*

pay to order: a negotiable instrument having such words is negotiable by endorsement of the within named payee and his or her delivery to another.

Pd.: paid.

PD: see *past due.*

PDA: personal deposit account.

PDate (pay date): the date on which the beneficiary is to be credited or paid. It is conventional in the United States not to recognize any payment dates other than value date. [105]

pecuniary exchange: any trade using money.

pecuniary legacy: a gift of money by will. [37]

peer group: in the National Bank Surveillance System, national bank statistics are classified into 20 peer groups, based on asset size and other characteristics. [105]

penalty clause:
(1) a clause in a promissory note specifying a penalty for late payments.
(2) a clause in a savings certificate specifying a penalty for premature withdrawal from such an account. [59]

penalty rate: the rate charged a member bank by the Federal Reserve Bank for a deficiency in the legal reserves required to be held against the deposits of that member bank.

penny ante: slang, involving an insignificant amount of cash.

Pepper-McFadden Act: see *McFadden Act of 1927.*

PER: see *par exchange rate.*

per annum: by the year.

Per. Cap.: per capita.

percentage lease: a lease providing for payment of rent based on a percentage of the gross sales or the sales over a fixed amount. [37]

per cent per month: the method of computing loan interest in which the charge is specified as a monthly percentage of the outstanding balance, as "1 percent per month on the unpaid balance." The effective yield to the lender is 12 times the monthly rate. [59]

per centum: by the hundred.

per contra item: a balance in one account that is offset by a balance from another account.

per curiam: a full court's decision (e.g., to remand), when no opinion is given.

perfect title:
(1) property displaying total right of ownership.
(2) a title that is not open to dispute or challenge because it is complete in every detail, and has no legal defects. See also *marketable title, muniment of title, quiet title suit;* cf. *cloud on title.*

performance: the fulfillment or accomplishment of a promise, contract, or other obligation according to its terms. [105]

performance letter of credit: a letter of credit which fulfills the same functions as a performance bond. Such letters of credit may be opened by American banks in support of American companies' tenders for export contracts, as U.S. banks are not permitted to issue performance or analogous bonds. [127]

periodicity: where items of revenue and expense are to be allocated to specific periods to prepare financial statements at regular intervals.

periodic procedures: the process of making adjusting entries, closing entries, and preparing the financial statements, using trial balances and work sheets.

periodic rate: an amount of finance charge expressed as a percentage that is to be applied to an appropriate balance for a specified period, usually monthly, provided that there is a balance which is subject to a finance charge. [105]

periodic statement: the billing summary produced and mailed at specified intervals, usually monthly. [105]

period of redemption: the length of time during which a mortgagor may reclaim the title and possession of his property by paying the debt it secured. [51]

permanent accounts: see *real accounts.*

permanent asset: any fixed or capital asset.

permanent financing: a long-term mortgage, amortized over 15, 20, or more years at a fixed rate of interest.

permissible nonbank activities: financial activities closely related to banking that may be engaged in by bank holding companies, either directly or through nonbank subsidiaries. Examples are owning finance companies and engaging in mortgage banking. The Federal Reserve Board determines which activities are closely related to banking. Before making such activities permissible, the board must also determine that their performance by bank holding companies is in the public interest. [1]

perpetuity:
(1) endless; the quality of going on forever (e.g., an estate willed in perpetuity).
(2) anything that is removed from the ordinary channel of commerce by limiting its capacity to be sold for a period longer than that of a life or lives in being and 21 years thereafter, plus the period of development, is said to be *removed in perpetuity.* See *emphyteutic lease.*

per procuration: the signature of a principal made by his or her agent, who has limited authority instead of having power of attorney.

personal account: an account carried in the name of a person or firm.

personal asset: an asset that is owned for personal use. [73]

personal check: a check drawn by someone as an individual (i.e., not acting as an employer or in a fiduciary capacity).

personal consumption expenditures: the sum of money and imputed expenditures made by consumers (individuals, not-for-profit institutions such as hospitals, etc.) for goods and services. It excludes purchases of dwellings (included in gross private domestic investment) but includes rental value of owner-occupied houses.

personal credit: a credit that a person possesses as differentiated from credit of a company, corporation, or partnership.

personal estate: synonymous with *personal property.*

personal finance company: a business that lends small sums of money to people, usually for personal needs, at relatively high interest rates. Most states require these organizations to be licensed.

personal financial statement: an account of an individual's personal resources and obligations. A personal financial statement is comparable to a balance sheet for a business. [105]

personal holding company: a holding company which under income tax law derives at least 80 percent of its gross income from royalties, dividends, interest, annuities, and sale of securities, and in which over 50 percent of the outstanding stock is owned by not more than five persons.

Personal Identification Number (PIN): the PIN, generally a four-digit number or word, is the secret number given to a plastic cardholder either by selection by the cardholder (customer-selected PIN) or randomly assigned by the card processor. The PIN is to be used in conjunction with the plastic card to effect any kind of transfer, withdrawal, deposit, or inquiry. It is intended to prevent unauthorized use of the card while accessing a financial service terminal. [105]

personal income: national income less various kinds of income not actually received by individuals, nonprofit institutions, and so on (e.g., undistributed corporate profits, corporate taxes, employer contributions for social insurance), plus certain receipts that do not arise from production (i.e., transfer payments and government interest).

personal installment loan: funds, borrowed by an individual for personal needs, which are repaid in regular monthly installments over a specified period.

personalized sales draft: sales drafts that have been especially printed for a merchant to provide stronger identification than would be the case if a standard form were used. [105]

personal liability: the sum owed by a natural person.

personal line of credit: synonymous with *reserve checking/overdraft checking.*

personal loan: a type of loan generally obtained by individual borrowers in small amounts, usually less than $1000. A personal loan is often secured for the purpose of consolidating debts, or paying taxes, insurance premiums, or hospital bills.

personal property: the rights, powers, and privileges an individual has in movable things such as chattels, and choses in action. Synonymous with *personal estate.*

personal saving: the difference between disposable personal income and personal consumption expenditures; includes the changes in cash and deposits, security holdings, indebtedness, reserves of life insurance companies and mutual savings institutions, the net investment of unincorporated enterprises, and the acquisition of real property net of depreciation.

personal security: an unsecured accommodation in which the net worth and the stature of the business borrower are relied on rather than some collateral which is pledged.

personal trust: see *trust, personal.*

personalty: personal property.

pertinent element of creditworthiness: in relation to a judgmental system of evaluating applicants, any information about applicants that a creditor obtains and considers and that has a demonstrable relationship to a determination of creditworthiness. [105]

peseta: monetary unit of Andorra, Balearic Island, Canary Islands, and Spain.

peso: monetary unit of Argentina, Chile, Colombia, Cuba, Dominican Republic, Mexico, Republic of the Philippines, and Uruguay.

pet bank: applied to banks in which government deposits were made after the expiration of the second U.S. Bank in 1836.

petition in bankruptcy: the form used for declaring voluntary bankruptcy. See *bankruptcy.*

petty cash: cash kept on hand for the payment of minor items. [59]

Pfandbriefe: paper issued by German mortgage banks and traded on the

Euromarkets. Secured by lendings of at least equal amount and yielding at least equal interest.

Philadelphia plan: an equipment trust arrangement using a lease as the legal device. Cf. *New York plan.*

photo card: a bank credit card containing a picture of the cardholder. [105]

pickup card: an instruction to an authorizer or a merchant directing him or her to take possession of the cardholder bank card and return it to the issuing bank. [105]

piece-of-the-action financing: a lending arrangement in which the mortgagee receives, besides regular loan interest, a negotiated percentage of the gross income of an income property, of increases in rentals over a stated period of the life of an income property, or the gross or net profit of a commercial or industrial enterprise. [59]

piggyback item: when one document attaches itself to or overlaps another during processing, causing the item to be missing from its assigned pocket in the sorter and to be sorted "free" to an unidentified pocket. [105]

pig on port: British for *accommodation paper.*

pilgrims' receipts: currency on which an overprint indicated that the notes were for use by pilgrims in another country. Pakistan, for example, overprinted some notes "for use in Saudi Arabia by pilgrims only." [27]

PIN: see *Personal Identification Number.*

pinch:

(1) general: a bind or tight situation.

(2) finance: a sudden, unanticipated rise in prices; when money rates go up suddenly, it is called a *money pinch.*

PIPS: see *paperless item processing system.*

PITI: common abbreviation for principal, interest, taxes, and insurance, used when describing the monthly carrying charges on a mortgage.

Pittsfield Project: This EFTS project in Pittsfield, Massachusetts, involves banks, savings and loans, credit unions, and many merchants in the Pittsfield area. The system involves direct payroll depositing by the employers, and a card-activated point-of-sale retail system which records transaction data for next-day funds transfer processing. [105]

placement memorandum: a document prepared by the lead manager of a syndicate in the Eurocredit market; seeks to provide information to other potential leaders to assist them in deciding whether to participate in the credit.

placing power: the ability of a bank or broker to sell securities to investors (i.e., to place the securities).

plaintiff: a complaining party or the person who begins a legal action against another person or organization, seeking a court remedy.

PLAM: see *price-level-adjusted mortgage.*

plan manager: an individual responsible for all bank credit card activities. [105]

plastic: any type of plastic card used by a consumer as a payments mechanism. The types of cards in use are generally described as credit cards, debit cards, and cash cards. [105]

plate numbers: figures in extremely small print on the side of some notes, to identify the printing plate from which they were made. [27]

platform: that portion of a bank's lobby where officers and new accounts personnel are located. [105]

Plaza Agreement: At a meeting of leaders of the major industrial nations held at the Plaza Hotel in New York City in September 1985, the U.S. decides that the dollar was too strong and the other major economic powers agree. The central banks intervene, helping to push the dollar down rapidly and bring the Japanese yen and the German mark up.

pledge:
(1) the act of transferring personal property to a trustee or creditor as security on a debt.
(2) bailment of goods to a creditor by a pledgor (bailor) to a creditor (bailee/pledgee) as security for some debt or engagement. [105]

pledged-account mortgage: a variation on graduated-payment mortgages, where a portion of the borrower's down payment is used to fund a pledged savings account, which is drawn on to supplement the monthly payment during the first years of the loan. The net effect to the borrower is lower payments at first. Payments gradually rise to slightly above those on conventional mortgages. See also *flexible-payment mortgage, graduated-payment mortgage, reverse-annuity mortgage, rollover mortgage, variable-rate mortgage.*

pledged assets: securities owned by a bank, generally U.S. government bonds and obligations, specified by law, which must be pledged as collateral security for funds deposited by the U.S. government, or state or municipal governments.

pledged loan: a mortgage loan that has been pledged as security for a borrowing; particularly, one that has been pledged as security for a Federal Home Loan Bank advance. [59]

pledgee: the person or firm to whom the security for a loan is pledged.

pledging: the offering by a borrower of his or her assets as security for the repayment of a debt. Cf. *distrain, hypothecation.*

pledging receivables: obtaining a short-term loan with receivables as collateral.

pledgor: the person or firm that makes a pledge of real or personal property as the collateral for a loan.

plunk down: slang, to make a payment in cash.

PM:
(1) see *primary market.*
(2) see *purchase money.*

PMM: see *purchase-money mortgage.*

PN: see *promissory note.*

POA: see *power of attorney.*

POB: point of business.

Poincare franc: gold franc.

point: a loan discount, which is a one-time charge, used to adjust the yield on the loan to what market conditions demand. Each point equals one percent of the principal amount. [78]

point of sale (POS): systems that permit bank customers to effect transfers of funds from their bank accounts and other financial transactions at retail points of sale. [33]

point-of-sale terminal (POST): a communication and data capture terminal located where goods or services are paid for. POST terminals may serve merchant accounting needs and may assist in processing financial transactions. In the latter case, the terminal may operate as part of an authorization/verification system or initiate direct exchanges of value among merchants, customers, and financial institutions. [36]

polymetallism: a theoretical monetary system where more than two metals are made standard money and coined in a definite ratio one to another in the matter of weight and fineness.

pooled income fund: a fund to which several donors transfer property, retaining an income interest, and giving the remainder to a single charity. [105]

pooling of interests: a method of accounting for business combinations under which the net assets are accounted for in the combined corporation's financial statements at their book value as recorded in the combining corporations, and comparative figures are restated on a combined basis. [43]

pooling of wealth: placing together the money of different individuals so that a sufficient amount will be available for a special purpose.

poor debtor's oath: in some states, an impoverished debtor may summon a creditor before a judge, and by taking a *poor debtor's oath,* be absolved from paying that particular debt. A poor person's method of bankruptcy.

portfolio selection theory: a concept developed by Nobel laureate James Tobin, enabling economists to trace the effects of monetary policies,

interest rates, and inflation on investment decisions. Tobin showed that investors tend not just to seek a good return but to balance their holdings in accordance with the overall risks involved.

position evaluation: the process of measuring the relative internal value of each position in the bank. [105]

position sheet: an accounting statement, indicating the bank or foreign exchange firm's commitment in overseas currencies.

positive authorization: authorization procedure whereby every account on file in the computer system can be accessed to determine its status before an authorization is granted or declined. [105]

positive file: an authorization system file that contains information about every account holder and is capable of providing a variety of data to be evaluated in responding to a request for authorization of credit, check cashing, or other privileges. See *ratio of accounts payable to purchases;* cf. *negative file.*

positively sloping yield curve: a yield curve where interest rates in the shorter periods are below those in the longer.

positive verification: see *direct verification.*

post: to record onto detailed subsidiary records (ledgers) amounts that were recorded in chronological records of original entry. See also *suspense account.*

postage currency: U.S. fractional currency issued in 1862 and 1863, deriving its name from the facsimile of a postage stamp on the reverse. Not to be confused with stamp money. [27]

postal money order: a checklike instrument sold by U.S. post offices for payment of a specified sum of money to the individual or firm designated by the purchaser. [59]

postaudit: an audit made after the transactions to be audited have taken place and have been recorded or have been approved for recording by designated officials, if such approval is required. See *preaudit.* [49]

postdate: dating an instrument a time after that on which it is made. See also *posting date.*

postdated check: a check bearing a date that has not yet arrived. Such a check cannot be paid by a bank before the date shown and must be returned to the maker or to the person attempting to use it. If presented on or after the date shown, the same check will be honored if the account contains sufficient funds.

posting: the act of transferring to an account in a ledger the data, either detailed or summarized, contained in a book or document of original entry. [49]

posting date:
(1) date a transaction is charged or credited to a cardholder account.
(2) date on which entries are made on the books of the receiving bank. [105]

postlist: used generally in the bookkeeping department of banks. Many banks use a posting plan whereby the old balances are listed *after* a posting run to prove the correct pickup of old balances, and to catch any "high posting" (posting over or above the last previous balance). When this type of proof is used, the bookkeeper is said to create a postlist of the previous old balances. The total of the postlist is the total of all old balances of accounts affected by the posting run. [10]

postpurchase feelings: customer attitudes developed toward the bank and its various products based on experience and information which strongly influence future behavior. [105]

pound (pound sterling): monetary unit of Great Britain. Also the currency of Cyprus, Egypt, Gibraltar, Ireland (Republic), Lebanon, Malta, Sudan, and Syria.

pound note: British currency that ceased to be legal tender at the end of 1985.

pourover: referring to the transfer of property from an estate or trust to another estate or trust upon the happening of an event as provided in the instrument. [37]

POW: pay order of withdrawal.

power: the authority or right to do or to refrain from doing a particular act, as a trustee's power of sale or power to withhold income. [37]

power in trust: a power that the donee (the trustee) is under a duty to exercise in favor of the beneficiary of the trust. [37]

power of alienation: the power to assign, transfer, or otherwise dispose of property. [37]

power of appointment: the equivalent of total ownership of part or all of a trust, since the individual having this power can identify the ultimate recipients of the trust's assets.

power of attorney: a written statement identifying a person as the agent for another with powers stated in the document. Full power may be granted, or the authority may be limited to certain functions, such as making deposits and withdrawals from a checking account. The statement must be executed before a notary and the signature of the agent is then placed on file with the bank. [29]

power of retention: the power expressed or implied in will or trust agreement permitting the trustee to retain certain or all of the investments comprising the trust property at inception, even though they may not be of a type suitable for new investments made by the trustee. [37]

power of sale: a clause included in a mortgage giving the holder or trustee the right to seize and sell the pledged property upon default in payments or upon the occurrence of any other violation of the conditions in the mortgage. See *shortcut foreclosure.*

PP:

(1) see *partial payment.*

(2) see *purchase price.*

Pr.: see *principal.*

PR: see *pro rata.*

praecipium: in the Euromarket, the manager of a credit or bond who negotiates a fee payable by the borrower. From this the manager deducts a specified amount for itself—the praecipium before dividing the balance of the fee between the rest of the management group. [104]

pre-audit: the examination of a creditor's invoices, payrolls, claims, and expected reimbursements before actual payment, or the verification of sales transactions before delivery.

pre-authorization order (PO): an agreement that permits the cardholder to effect a transaction, after signing an authorization with a merchant for such purchases, to be made from the merchant at a future date or dates without any need for the cardholder executing the resulting sales drafts or slips. [105]

pre-authorized electronic fund transfer: an electronic funds transfer authorized in advance to recur at substantially regular intervals. [105]

pre-authorized payment: a service that enables a debtor to request funds to be transferred from the customer's deposit account to the account of a creditor.

Prec.: precedent.

precatory words: expressions in a will praying or requesting (but not directing) that a thing be done or not done. [37]

precomp: precomputation or precomputed loan. [55]

preconstruction affidavit: an affidavit, required by the lender on a construction loan, in which the borrower and contractor affirm that up to a specific date no work has been started on the lot and no materials delivered, prepared for use, or used.

preexamination: the process of analysis and review undertaken by the examiner in advance of the examination to establish objectives, determine the scope of the examination, and identify key activities of the bank. The examiner coordinates data and personnel needs with the bank during this phase, which may begin up to 60 days prior to the actual examination. [105]

preferred creditor: a creditor whose claim takes legal preference over the claim of another (such as government taxes over the amount owed to an individual). [10]

preferred debt:
(1) a first mortgage.
(2) a debt that takes precedence over others.

preferred lender banks: banks with more autonomy than other banks in approving loans.

prelegal section: the component of a bank card operation responsible for collection effort on accounts in an advanced stage of delinquency, prior to the necessity for legal action. [105]

preliminary commitment: an authorization by Eximbank detailing an advance of a particular transaction the terms and conditions under which Eximbank will provide assistance in its direct loan, financial guarantee, and engineering multiplier programs. Preliminary commitments are usually issued in the early stage of a transaction to help the U.S. supplier market its good or services more effectively. Final authorization of Eximbank funding is contained in a final commitment.

preliminary expenses: expenses incurred in the establishment of an organization (e.g., costs for developing and circulating a prospectus).

preliminary title report: the results of a title search by a title company prior to issuing a title binder or commitment to insure. [105]

prelist: used generally in bookkeeping in a bank as a part of the bank's posting plan. After offsetting the ledger sheets to be affected by a posting run, the bookkeeper makes a prelist run of the balances, thus creating a total of all balances that will be affected by the run to be made. This is the opposite of *postlist,* but has the same effect in the proof of pickup of old balances. [10]

Prem.: see *premium.*

premium:
(1) the sum paid for a policy, not to be confused with premiums. As earned premium is the portion of the written premium covering the part of the policy term that is included in the time period. The pure premium is found by dividing losses by a hazard or contingency, and to which no operating expenses of the firm has been added (e.g., commissions, taxes).
(2) the amount by which one form of funds exceeds another in buying power.

premium audit: an examination by a representative of the insurer of the insured's records, insofar as they relate to the policies or coverages under consideration. See *audit.*

premium card: a bank or credit card issued at a greater cost than that of an ordinary card but having greater buying power or associated features for its holder. Cf. *debit card.*

premium currency: see *currency.*

premium of initial servicing fee: see *loan fee.*

premium on bonds: the amount or percentage by which bonds are purchased, sold, or redeemed for more than their face value.

premium on funded debt: the excess of the actual cash value of the consideration received for funded debt securities (of whatever kind) issued or assumed over the par value of such securities and the accrued interest thereon. [18]

prepaid expense: payment for items not yet received; a charge deferred for a period of time until the benefit for which payment has been made occurs (e.g., rent paid for future months).

prepay: to pay before or in advance of receipt of goods or services.

prepayment: the payment of a debt before it actually becomes due.

prepayment clause:
(1) the privilege of repaying part or all of a loan in advance of date or dates stated in a contract.
(2) a clause in a mortgage allowing the mortgagor to pay off part or all of the unpaid debt before it becomes due. This affords a saving for the mortgagor.

prepayment fee: see *prepayment penalty.*

prepayment of taxes: the deposit of money with a governmental unit on condition that the amount deposited is to be applied against the tax liability of a designated taxpayer after the taxes have been levied and such liability has been established. [49]

prepayment penalty: a penalty placed on a mortgagor for paying the mortgage before its due date. This applies when there is no prepayment clause to offset the penalty.

prepayment privilege: an optional clause in a mortgage which gives the mortgagor the right to pay all or part of a debt prior to its maturity. [105]

prerogatives: the rights, powers, privileges (e.g., diplomatic immunity) of an individual that others do not possess.

prescription: title to property or means of obtaining title based on uninterrupted possession.

presentation: a legal term used in connection with negotiable instruments. The act of presentation technically means the actual delivery of a negotiable instrument by a holder in due course to the drawee for acceptance, or to the maker for payment. Upon presentation, the holder in due course requests acceptance of a draft, or requests payment of the instrument from the maker of a note, check, or whatever. See *negotiable.* [10]

present beneficiary: synonymous with *immediate beneficiary.* [32]

present capital: proprietorship at the conclusion of a fiscal period.

presenting bank: the bank that forwards an item to another bank for payment. [105]

presentment: synonymous with *presentation.*

prestige card: a plastic identification card issued by savings and loan associations to their customers to be used in electronic funds transfer systems.

presumptive title: possession of property that leads others to presume ownership, where in fact ownership may not exist. Cf. *cloud on title.*

previous balance: the cardholder account balances as of the last billing period. [105]

previous balance method: method used for calculating finance charges on accounts that have not converted to average daily balance. Calculated by subtracting payments and credits posted during the billing period from the previous balance. [105]

price-level-adjusted mortgage (PLAM): a unique mortgage plan in which the outstanding loan balance is indexed. The interest rate is a rate net of any inflation premium. The payments on a PLAM are based on this real rate, and at the end of each year, the then outstanding balance is adjusted by an inflation factor. The principal benefit of a PLAM is the much lower initial payment than either a GPM, GPAM, or a shared appreciation mortgage. See *graduated-payment adjustable mortgage, graduated-payment mortgage, shared-appreciation mortgage.*

price rule: requires that the monetary authority attempt to maintain a chosen price index at a particular level by varying the stock of money. The sole function of policy is to prevent the price index from deviating substantially from a predetermined level. This is equivalent to keeping the relevant inflation rate at zero. [99]

Primary Account Number (PAN): the embossed and/or encoded number, consisting of the major industry identifier, issuer identifier, individual account identifier, and check digit which identifies the card issuer to which the transaction is to be routed and the account to which the transaction is to be applied unless specific instructions, with a transaction message, indicate otherwise. [105]

primary bank reserve: the total of legal reserves plus working reserves. This total is shown on bank statements with the title "cash and due from bank."

primary beneficiary: synonymous with *immediate beneficiary.*

primary data: information obtained from original sources for the specific purpose of the study being conducted, such as a survey of corporate accounts to determine their degree of satisfaction with the bank's performance. [105]

primary dealer: a dealer in U.S. government securities with whom the Federal Reserve conducts open market operations. Following evaluation the Reserve Bank can add the dealer to its list of primary dealers.

primary deposits: cash deposits in a bank.

primary market: the initial market for any item or service.

primary money: standard money.

primary reserves: a bank's legal reserves of cash and demand deposits with the Federal Reserve Bank and other banks.

primary trend: the direction in stock values that last for many months and usually for years.

prime: a very high grade or quality.

prime bill of exchange: a draft or trade acceptance which states on the face of the instrument that it was created through a business transaction involving the movement of goods. Bankers' acceptances are considered prime bills of exchange, although smaller banks must generally have the endorsement without recourse of a large bank enjoying high financial recognition in order to give the instrument "prime status." Prime bills of exchange are acceptable for rediscount with the Federal Reserve Bank, and therefore can be construed as a "secondary reserve" for banks. [10]

prime interest (rate): the rate of interest charged by a bank for loans made to its most credit-worthy business and industrial customers; it is the lowest interest rate charged by the bank. The prime rate level is determined by how much banks have to pay for the supply of money from which they make loans. See also *discount rate.*

prime maker: the party (or parties) signing a negotiable instrument and becoming the original party responsible for its ultimate payment. See *liabilities.*

prime merchant category: a classification of merchants which historical data show are good producers of credit card volume and are most likely to affiliate with a bank card plan. [105]

prime rate: see *prime interest (rate).*

prime status: see *prime bill of exchange.*

primogeniture: under common law, the right of the eldest child to inherit all real property of the parent; the estate usually passes to the son, but daughters are increasingly inheriting under this right. Cf. *entail.*

Prin.: see *principal.*

principal:

(1) one of the major parties to a transaction; either the seller or purchaser.

(2) the original amount of a deposit, loan, or other amount of money on which interest is earned or paid. See also *billed principal.*

(3) finance: the face value of an instrument, which becomes the obligation of the maker or drawee to pay to a holder in due course. Interest is charged on the principal amount.

principal balance: the outstanding total of a mortgage or other debt, excluding interest or premium.

principal beneficiary: synonymous with *ultimate beneficiary.*

principal only: an account on which payment is being credited to principal; that is, interest is no longer being charged on remaining balance. [55]

principal underwriter: synonymous with *managing underwriter.*

prior deductions method: an improper method of determining bond interest or preferred dividend coverage: the requirements of senior obligations are first deducted from earnings and the balance is applied to the requirements of the junior issue.

prior lien: a mortgage that ranks ahead of another.

prior redemption: an obligation that a debtor has paid prior to stated maturity.

prior redemption privilege: a privilege frequently extended by a debtor to the holders of called bonds permitting them to redeem their holdings prior to the call date or maturity. There are chiefly three types of offers prior redemption: (1) with interest in full to the call date; (2) with interest in full to the call date less a bank discount (usually ¼ percent per annum) based on the period from the date of collection to the date of call; and (3) with interest to the date of collection only. [37]

private bank: a bank chartered by the state in which it operates, subject to state laws and regulations, and subject to examinations by the state banking authorities. The principal distinction between private banks and other state banks is that the private bank may arise from a partnership, in which there is no capital stock.

private debt: the monetary amount owed by the public and firms of a country and not including the amount owed by various levels of government.

private enterprise: the organization of production in which the business is owned and operated by people taking risks and motivated by the wish to make a profit.

Private Export Funding Corporation: a U.S. company owned primarily by U.S. commercial banks and industrial firms.

private lender: an individual who lends money from institutional funds (insurance companies, banks, etc.).

private mortgage insurance: insurance offered by a private company that protects an association against loss up to policy limits (customarily 20 to 25 percent of the loan amount) on a defaulted mortgage loan. Its use is usually limited to loans with a high loan-to-value ratio; the borrower pays the premiums. [59]

private notes: paper money issued by merchants, shopkeepers or anyone other than the legally authorized government agency. [27]

private remittances: represent transfers or transmissions of cash and goods by individuals and by charitable and nonprofit institutions to individuals or groups residing abroad. Personal remittances include all noncommercial transfers of funds to be sent abroad by means of customary bank drafts and money orders. [73]

private sector: the segment of the total economy composed of businesses and households, but excluding government. Cf. *public sector.*

private trust:

(1) a trust created for the benefit of a designated beneficiary or designated beneficiaries; as, a trust for the benefit of the settlor's or the testator's wife and children; opposed to a charitable (or public) trust.

(2) a trust created under a declaration of trust or under a trust agreement; as, a living trust or an insurance trust; opposed to a trust coming under the immediate supervision of a court. See *court trust.* [32]

private trust fund: a trust fund that will ordinarily revert to private individuals or will be used for private purposes. For example, a fund that consists of guarantee deposits. [49]

probate:

(1) the right or jurisdiction of hearing and determining questions or issues in matters concerning a will.

(2) the action or process of proving before a court of law that a document offered for official recognition as the last will and testament of a deceased person is genuine.

probate of will: presentation of proof before the proper officer or court that the instrument offered is the last will of the decedent. [37]

problem bank: a bank, watched by a government agency, in danger of failure or bankruptcy.

proceeding: any transaction; a measure or action taken in a business.

proceeds: the actual amount of funds given to a borrower, following deductions for interest charges, fees, and so on.

processing: the preparation of a mortgage loan application and supporting documents for consideration by a lender or insurer. [105]

processing date: the date on which the transaction is processed by the acquiring bank. [105]

procuration: the authority given to another to sign instruments and to act on behalf of the person giving the procuration.

product line: a group of products that are closely related (e.g., the entire group of savings accounts offered). [105]

profit:
(1) the excess of the selling price over all costs and expenses incurred in making a sale.
(2) the monies remaining after a business has paid all its bills.

profitability: a firm's ability to earn a profit and the potential for future earnings.

profit and loss account: an account transferred from accounts receivable to a separate ledger. An amount deducted from the accounts receivable balance. An account deemed to be uncollectable, or a certain number of months past due, becomes eligible for transfer to the "profit and loss account" ledger. [41]

promisor: a firm or person responsible in keeping a promise such as an acceptor or maker of a bill or note.

promissory note: any written promise to pay; a negotiable instrument that is evidence of a debt contracted by a borrower from a creditor, known as a lender of funds. If the instrument does not have all the qualities of a negotiable instrument, it cannot legally be transferred. See *accommodation paper, note.*

proof:
(1) an operation for testing the accuracy of a previous operation—for example, relisting the checks and adding their amounts to determine the accuracy of the total shown on a deposit slip.
(2) applied to the proof sheet, the record on which the test is made.
(3) describes the method by which a type of transaction is proved, as in transit proof. Proof is generally affected when a total agrees with another total of the same items arrived at in a different manner; it is then said to be in balance. [32]

proof department: a department of a bank charged with the duties of sorting, distributing, and proving all transactions arising from the commercial operations of the bank. The proof function involves the creation of adequate records of all transactions, showing the proper distribution of all items going to other departments for further processing, and proof of the correctness of all transactions passing through the bank. The records created by the proof department are of vital importance, since examination of these records may be made months after a transaction occurs, in order to substantiate the accuracy of deposits made by customers and to establish legally that deposits were made by certain individual depositors. [10]

proof machine: equipment that simultaneously sorts items, records the dollar amount for each sorted group, and balances the total to the original input amount. [105]

proofs: the final design of an issue prepared by a printing company as a sample for the issuing authority, but not of course intended for circulation. Proofs are always printed on a different type of paper from that used for the final issue, whereas specimen notes are always on the same paper. [27]

Prop.: see *property.*

property:
(1) the exclusive right or interest of a person in his or her belongings.
(2) that which is legally owned by a person or persons and may be used and disposed of as the owner(s) see fit.

property assessment: the valuation of real property for tax purposes. [59]

property capital: stocks, bonds, mortgages, and notes are examples, but currency and bank deposits are not.

property search report: a type of credit bureau report that deals specifically with details of real property owned by a subject of inquiry. Frequently involves a search of country courthouse records for details of purchase, title, mortgage, or other encumbrance on property. [41]

property tax: synonymous with *land tax.*

proprietary card: a plastic card designed and for the exclusive benefit of customers of the issuing institution. Some EFT systems will allow proprietary cards to access a shared system without compromising proprietary features. [105]

proprietary company: a nonfunctioning parent company of a nonfunctioning controlling company, formed for the purpose of investing in the securities of other companies, and for controlling these companies through such holdings. Synonymous with *holding company* and *parent company.*

proprietor: a person who has an exclusive right or interest in property or in a business.

proprietorship certificate: a certificate filed with a bank showing the ownership of a privately owned business enterprise.

pro rata: "according to the rate" (Latin); in proportion to a total amount. For example, if a contract is terminated prior to the end of the period for which payment has been given, a pro rata return of the payment is made, in proportion to the unused period of time remaining.

pro rata rate: a premium rate charged for a short term at the same proportion of the rate for a longer term as the short term bears to the longer term.

prospectus:
(1) a plan of a proposed enterprise.
(2) a description of property for sale or lease.

protected check: a check that is prepared in such a manner as to prevent alterations. For example, *machine protection*—perforating the paper with pressure and indelible ink. *Paper protection*—any erasure of matter written in ink, by rubber eraser, knife, or chemical eradicator will remove the sensitive color and show instantly that an alteration has been attempted. *Machine printing protection*—the machine automatically prints stars or asterisks between the dollar sign and first digit of the amount. An indelible ink ribbon is used, or a ribbon treated with a acid that eats into the paper. [10]

protectionism:
(1) the imposition of border taxes and/or customs duties on imports in order to protect a domestic industry from cheaper competitive goods.
(2) a central bank system to protect currency with restrictions in order to move the exchange rate in a direction consistent with the economic policies of the concerned government.

protective covenants: restrictions, made as part of a loan agreement, that are placed on dividend payments, capital expenditures, or other actions of firm management, designed to protect the position of lenders.

protest: a written statement by a notary public, or other authorized person, under seal for the purpose of giving formal notice to parties secondarily liable that an instrument has been dishonored, either by refusal to accept or by refusal to make payment. [50]

protest fee: a charge made by a notary public for protesting a negotiable instrument which has failed to be honored.

protest jacket: synonymous with *notice of dishonor (protest jacket).*

prove: in banking, the act of creating a record, to show by a list or run of the items, the accuracy of a list or deposit created by another person. The list shows that each item is listed correctly as to amount, and that the amounts listed add up to an exact total. The two lists, one made by the bank as a record, and the other created by another person, such as a depositor, must agree in total to be *in proof.* [10]

proving cash: determining that the cash on hand is equal to the original balance plus the receipts minus payments.

provision: a charge for an estimated expense or liability or for the diminution in the cost or value of an asset. [43]

provision for loan loss: a charge for anticipated loan losses, which appears on the bank's income statement as an operating expense.

proximate clause: defining the cause that directly produces a loss.

proximo: in the following month. Cf. *instant (inst.).*

P-Star: a Federal Reserve predictor of the nation's long-term inflation rate. The formula is $P = M2 \times V^*$ divided by Q^*, where: P^* is the general level of future prices; M2 is one of the official measures of the money in the economy; V^* is a constant, representing the velocity of M2 over the past 33 years. Velocity is the rate at which money in the economy changes hands; Q^* is an estimate for the value of the nation's gross national product in the future, assuming the economy grows at 2.5 percent a year. Fed economists believe that is the fastest the economy can grow without increasing inflation.

PT:
(1) see *paper title.*
(2) see *passing title.*
(3) see *perfect title.*

Ptas.: see *peseta.*

P. Tr.: see *private trust.*

public administrator: in many states, a county officer whose main duty is to settle the estates of persons who die intestate, when there is no member of the family, creditor, or other person having a prior right of administration who is able to administer the estate. [32]

public credit: the capacity of political units to acquire funds in return for their promise to pay. Represented by government, municipal, and other public agencies' bonds and notes.

public debt: the debt of the federal government. Sometimes includes the debt of state and local governments.

public deposits: any bank deposit made by a federal, state, or municipal government.

public domain:
(1) lands over which a government exercises proprietary rights. Synonymous with *public lands.*
(2) the condition when a copyright or patent right expires, and the process or concept identified may then be exploited by anyone.

public funds: accounts established for any government, agency, or authority of government, or political subdivision. [105]

public lands: see *public domain.*

Public Law 94-455: see *Tax Reform Act of 1976.*

public relations department: a department within a bank or other business institution created and maintained to promote and encourage better harmony and relationships between that particular institution and the general public by offering a wide variety of services—educational and other—to the public without cost to the recipient. Such departments operate under a variety of names such as "courtesy," "customer's service," "public aid," and "public service." [10]

public revenue: income received by a governmental agency (taxes, tariffs, customs, etc.).

public sector: a segment of the total economy including all levels of government and excluding businesses and households. Cf. *private sector.*

pula: monetary unit of Botswana.

pull order: a method used to withhold a card from being mailed at reissue. This usually results from the account being in a past-due or overlimit status at the time of reissue. [105]

pull statement: process whereby a cardholder's statement is segregated from regular mailing procedures and routed to the requesting department. [105]

pump priming: the theory that money incomes can be increased in a depression mostly through government expenditures, on the assumption that a given expenditure by the government will induce additional expenditures through turnover of the money. If, however, the psychological reaction of the people to the process is fear, the exact opposite result may occur; a lesser velocity of circulation.

punch card check: a check that has perforations either in the body of the check or around a portion of its border. These perforations are used to re-sort and correlate the checks after they have been canceled and returned with the bank statement. This type of check must be canceled in some special manner agreed upon by the banker and the depositor. Punch card checks are used to correlate the checks by number or some other coding; thus facilitating the reconcilement of the depositor's bank statement. [10]

punched card: a card punched with a pattern of holes to represent data.

punched tape: a tape on which a pattern of holes or cuts is used to represent data.

purchase: any and every method of acquiring property except by descent. [105]

purchase and sale statement: a statement sent by a commission merchant to a customer when his or her futures position has been reduced or closed out. It shows the amount involved, the price at which the position was acquired and reduced or closed out, respectively, the gross profits or loss, the commission charged, and the net profit or loss on the transaction. Frequently referred to as a P&S. [11]

purchase commitment: in the medium-term credit and small business credit programs, an Eximbank commitment to purchase the foreign buyer's note or draft from the bank at a discounted interest rate Eximbank retains full recourse to the bank.

purchased funds: large-denomination certificates of deposits held by banks.

purchased paper: as distinguished from paper that has been discounted, any commercial paper that has been bought outright.

purchase money: monies paid to obtain ownership of property.

purchase-money mortgage: for those who put their homes on the market and find that, to sell their property, they must act as the lender themselves. The mortgage is actually a short-term instrument, that runs no more than five years and often only a year or two. In most cases, a purchase-money mortgage is a second mortgage, supplementing the buyer's partial bank financing.

purchase price:
(1) the amount for which any item is bought.
(2) the combination of monies and mortgages given to obtain a property.

purchaser: a buyer; a person who obtains title to or an interest in property by the act of purchase.

purchasing power: the value of money measured by the items it can buy. Cf. *money, real value of money.*

pure interest: the price paid for the use of capital, not to include monies for risk and all other costs incurred because of the loan. Synonymous with *net interest* or *true interest.*

purpose clause: a clause in a Euromarket borrowing stating the purpose for which the borrowing is made. [104]

purpose statement: the signed affidavit required by Federal Reserve Regulation U. The borrower of a loan must indicate the use to which any loan secured by stock is to be put. See *Regulation U.* [105]

PY: prior year.

Q:
(1) in receivership or bankruptcy proceedings.
(2) quarterly.
(3) see *Regulation Q.*

QA: see *quick assets.*

QC: see *quasi-contract.*

Qtly.: quarterly.

Qtr.: quarter.

qualification:
(1) a statement in an auditor's report directing attention to any limitation to the examination, or any doubt concerning a reported item in a company's financial statements.
(2) the operation of inscribing data fields to prepare them for automatic sorting and processing by a MICR sorter-reader. [105]

qualified acceptance: any counteroffer.

qualified endorsement: an endorsement by which the endorser seeks to avoid the usual liabilities inherent in his act. "Without recourse" is the most common example. If the instrument is not honored, the endorser does not want to become responsible for it. Cf. *recourse.*

qualified prospect: a potential customer who is able to buy a product or service and has the authority to make a decision to purchase. This conclusion is often arrived at following a check on the individual's credit.

qualitative forecasting: predictions on the future activity of bank products or services based on human judgment. [105]

quality of estate: the form in which an estate is to be owned, including type of possession and time. No indication of property value or physical characteristics is given.

quantity theory: a theory stating that a special relationship exists between the quantity of money and money income. People spend excess money holdings irrespective of the interest rate and the manner in which the new money holdings were received. Cf. *Gresham's law, liquid trap.*

quantum meruit: "as much as he deserved" (Latin); a principle of business law providing that when a service is given without a written estimate of price, there is an implied promise by the purchaser of the service to pay for the work as much as it is worth.

Quar.: quarter.

quasi-contract: an obligation similar in character to that of a contract, but which arises not from an agreement between the parties but from some relationship between them or from a voluntary act by one or more of them—for example, the management of the affairs of another without authority or the management of a common property without authority. [37]

quasi-corporation: any political subdivision of an organization or group (e.g., an unincorporated town).

quasi-money: assets that have properties similar to those of money in the strict sense, namely notes and icon plus bank deposits payable at sight.

quasi-public company: a corporation operated privately in which the public has a special interest (e.g., eleemosynary institutions).

query: to extract, from a file, records based on requested criterion. For example, listing all the customers in a title whose balance is greater than 1000. [105]

quetzal: monetary unit of Guatemala.

queue: a line or group of items or people in a bank waiting for service.

quick assets:
(1) assets that in the ordinary course of business, will be con-

verted into cash within a reasonably short time.

(2) assets that can be readily converted into cash without appreciable loss. See *liquidity.*

quick (quickie) buck: slang, money made rapidly; a windfall.

quiet title suit: a legal action to remove a defect or any questionable claim against the title to property. Cf. *cloud on title.*

quitclaim: synonymous with *remise.*

quitclaim deed: see *deed, quitclaim.*

quit rent: the last rental payment made by a tenant before leaving the property.

quota: assigned to each member of the International Monetary Fund, determines the voting power and subscription of that member and the normal quantitative limitations on its use of the fund's reserves. [105]

quo warranto: Latin for "by what authority." A suit to test the authority of a person in office or of a corporation to its franchise or charter.

R:
(1) see *rate of interest.*
(2) see *right.*

RA: see *Revenue Act of 1962, Revenue Act of 1964, Revenue Act of 1971, Revenue Act of 1976, Revenue Act of 1978.*

rack: used to describe the "rack department," which sorts, distributes, and proves items in the commercial operations of the bank.

rack rent: an unusually high rent in an amount equal to or nearly equal to the total value of the items produced on the rented property. Cf. *economic rent.*

rag money: American term for *paper money.* [27]

raise: a fraudulent increase in the face value of a negotiable instrument.

raised bills: the denomination of paper money that has been illegally raised.

raised check: a check on which the amount has been illegally increased.

raised notes: those on which there is an overprint indicating that the denomination has been increased as a result of government revalidation. [27]

raise (raising) funds: acquiring money, financing, or credit from surplus earnings of the firm, to stockholders, the public, creditors, customers, or employees.

RAM: see *reserve adjustment magnitude.*

rand: monetary unit of Lesotho, Republic of South Africa, and South-West Africa.

RANs: see *revenue-anticipation notes.*

rapid amortization: a program that permits owners of facilities to write off all or a part of their cost for income tax purposes in a short space of time, usually five years. See also *amortization.*

rapid-payoff mortgage: synonymous with *growing equity mortgage.*

ratable distribution: the proportionate distribution of an estate according to a percentage. For example, if all the legacies cannot be paid in full and each of them is reduced by the same percentage, there is ratable distribution. [37]

rate:
(1) to categorize and rank in terms of special qualities or properties.
(2) the cost of a unit of insurance. Cf. *premium.*
(3) a charge, fee, or price.

rate of exchange (ROE): the amount of funds of one nation that can be bought, at a specific date, for a sum of currency of another country. Rates fluctuate often because of economic, political, and other forces.

rate of inflation: the average percentage rate of increase of the price of money, weighted and stated in annual terms.

rate of interest: the charge for borrowing money.

rate-sensitive assets: bank loans. See *liability hedge.*

rate-sensitive liabilities: bank deposits and borrowings. See *liability hedge.*

rate structure: the charges made to customers for their use of bank funds, specified in terms of annual percentage rates. [105]

rate variance: in accounting procedures, the difference between actual wages paid and the standard wage rate, multiplied by the total actual hours of direct labor used.

rate war: a negative form of competition; sellers drop their prices below their costs for purposes of putting the competition out of business.

rating: evaluation of the moral or other risk of an individual or company.

ratio:
(1) a number relationship between two things (i.e., ratio of births to deaths).
(2) one of the various analyses made by a money-lending or credit agency, of the financial statements of a given individual, company, or other business enterprise seeking credit, to determine the desirability of granting the requested credit.
(3) the relative values of silver and gold in a monetary system based on both. See *bimetallism.*

ratio analysis: analysis of the relationships of items in financial statements. See listings under *ratio.*

rationing of exchange: governmental control of foreign exchange through the forced surrender of exchange by exporters for domestic currency at the government rate, and the subsequent allocation of such exchange to importers according to a government ration schedule.

ratio of accounts payable to purchases: this ratio, determined for the present period and compared with a similar ratio for previous periods, indicates the trend toward or from prompt payment of current obligations.

ratio of fixed assets to fixed liabilities: this ratio tends to indicate the margin of safety to the present mortgage and bond holders, if any. Failure of the ratio to meet the minimum requirement frequently suggests that additional funds should be raised from the owners rather than by mortgaging fixed assets.

ratio of notes payable to accounts payable: three quantitative factors are frequently considered when determining whether the resulting ratio (notes payable/accounts payable) is desirable: (a) notes issued in payment of merchandise, (b) notes issued to banks and brokers, and (c) notes issued to others. If a relatively large amount of the outstanding notes was issued to merchandise creditors, this might indicate that the firm is unable to take advantage of the cash discounts offered in the trade, and, also, that other lending agencies might consider the firm's credit unfavorably.

ratio of notes receivable to accounts receivable: if a financial statement discloses a large ratio of notes receivable to accounts receivable, as compared with other firms in a similar line of business, the firm with the high ratio may have a lax credit policy, or it may be extending credit to customers whose ability to pay promptly is dubious.

ratio of owned capital to borrowed capital: this ratio is considered to be important in determining the advisability of extending additional long-term credit to an applicant. If this ratio is not considered favorable, it frequently suggests that the funds desired should be raised from the owners of the business (i.e., the applicants themselves) rather than through the additional pledging of any assets.

Ravenswood plan: the combination of a checking account with a bank repurchase agreement. A high-yielding checking account first developed by the Bank of Ravenswood on Chicago's North Side.

RC:
(1) see *recurring charges.*
(2) see *register(ed) check.*
(3) see *reserve currency.*
(4) see *risk capital.*

Rcd.: received.

RCPC: see *Regional Check Processing Center.*

Rcpt.: see *receipt.*

Rct.: see *receipt.*

RE:
(1) see *rate of exchange.*
(2) see *real estate.*

readjustment plan: a voluntary program worked out by creditors and a debtor firm outside the framework of the bankruptcy courts for the purpose of avoiding going through a formal bankruptcy.

real accounts: those accounts—asset, liability, reserve and capital—whose balances are not canceled out at the end of an accounting period but are carried over to the next period. These accounts appear on the postclosing trial balance and the statement of condition. Sometimes called *permanent accounts.* [59]

real bills doctrine: the principle that if only "real" bills (i.e., bills growing out of trade transactions) are discounted, the expansion of bank money will be in proportion to the needs of trade. Expansion and contraction would thus be automatic.

real costs:
(1) costs measured in dollars of constant purchasing power or adjusted by some index serving the same purpose. Cf. *nominal cost.*
(2) costs that involve effort or sacrifice.

real effective exchange rate: an effective exchange rate adjusted for inflation differentials between the nation whose exchange rate is being measured, and other nations making up the group against which the exchange rate is calculated. [103]

real estate: tangible land and all physical property. Includes all physical substances below, upon, or attached to land; thus houses, trees, and fences are classified as real estate. All else is personal property.

real estate bond: see *bond, real estate.*

Real Estate Investment Trust (REIT): an organization, usually corporate, established for the accumulation of funds for investing in real estate holdings, or the extension of credit to others engaged in construction. These funds are usually accumulated by the sale of share of ownership in the trust.

real estate loans: loans secured by real estate, regardless of the purpose. See *mortgage.* [40]

real estate owned: all real estate directly owned by a bank, usually not including real estate taken to satisfy a debt. [44]

Real Estate Settlement Procedures Act: federal legislation of 1974, this act provided comprehensive guidelines for loan closing costs and settlement practices; effective in June 1975. See *Real Estate Settlement Procedures Act amendments.* [51]

Real Estate Settlement Procedures Act amendments: federal legislation of 1976 which eased the requirement of the Real Estate Settlement Procedures Act by permitting lenders to disclose good faith estimates of closing costs instead of actual charges, and by tying disclosure timing to receipt of the application instead of the date of closing; also eliminated disclosure of the property's previous selling price. See *Real Estate Settlement Procedures Act.* [51]

real estate sold on contract: real estate that has been sold for which the buyer does not have sufficient down payment to warrant the seller giving title; the contract generally provides that when the contract balance is reduced to a certain amount, the buyer may refinance the contract to get title to the property. [59]

real estate tax: a pecuniary charge laid upon real property for public purposes. [62]

real income: the sum total of the purchasing power of a nation or individual.

real interest rate: the rate at which a person earns future purchasing power on monetary assets. It equals the money rate minus the rate of inflation.

realization (realize): the act or process of converting into cash an asset, or the total assets, of an individual or business.

realization account: an account established to summarize and adjust the accounts of a business being liquidated. The account reflects the item-by-item realization of the assets through reduction to cash or application to the reduction of liabilities.

realization value: the amount received from the sale of an item as differentiated from other types of value, such as par, book, and so on.

realized value: under the Consumer Leasing Act, includes (a) the price received by the lessor for the leased property at disposition, (b) the highest offer for disposition, or (c) the fair market value at the end of the lease term. [105]

realized yield: the return a bond earns over a stated time period, based on the purchase price and on the assumption that the incoming cash is reinvested at a stated rate.

realizing sale: a sale to convert a paper profit into an actual profit.

real money: money containing one or more metals having intrinsic value, as distinguished from representative money such as currency issued by a realm, and checks, drafts, and so on, issued by legal entities. See *bimetallism, monometallism;* cf. *fiat money.*

real-money balances: the amount of goods and services that can be bought from a given stock of money retained by individuals. Shifts in real-money balances are computed by adjusting changes in the amount of money held for changes in the level of prices.

real property: the property that is devised by will to a party known as the devisee; or all fixed, permanent, immovable property, such as land and tenements.

real property transaction: an extension of credit in connection with which a security interest is or will be retained or acquired in real property, as defined by the law of the state in which it is located. [105]

real spendable earnings: a U.S. Bureau of Labor Statistics measure of the economy; successor to the wholesale price index. It contains a wealth of data on prices by stage of processing, sector, industry, and commodity. This index is issued the first week of the month for the previous month.

real stock: as contrasted with stock that is sold short, any long stock.

realtor: a real estate broker or an associate holding active membership in a local real estate board affiliated with the National Association of Realtors. [105]

realty: synonymous for *real estate.*

real value of money: the price of money measured in terms of goods.

real wages: the cost of items and services that can be purchased with money wages. It is useful for comparing changes in the standard of living by eliminating the effect of changes in the general price level.

reappraisal: the term applied when property is appraised a second time.

reasonable value: a value placed on property that parallels the existing market value.

reassessment: the result of a change in the assessed value of property or reappraisal of property.

rebate: unearned interest that may be returned to a borrower if his or her loan is paid off before the maturity date.

rebated acceptance: an anticipated acceptance; an acceptance paid prior to its due date.

Rec.: see *receipt.*

recap: an abbreviated term for "recapitulation" (or assembling) of totals taken from "batch proof" sheets or from proof machines which must be assembled in proper order so as to build up control totals for the various departments charged with the items. Recap sheets may be used in all departments of the bank, and all recap sheets assembled into a final recap sheet for the settlement of the entire bank. See also *settlement clerk.* [10]

recapitalization: altering the capital structure of a firm by increasing or decreasing its capital stock.

recapitalization surplus: the surplus resulting upon a recapitalization, which usually arises from reduction in the par value of stocks and the exchange of bonds for securities of lesser value.

recapitulation: see *recap.*

recap sheet: see *settlement clerk.*

recapture clause: a clause in an agreement providing for retaking or recovering possession. As used in percentage leases, to take a portion of earnings or profits above a fixed amount of rent. [62]

recapture of depreciation: on the disposal of depreciable property, the recognition and classification of some of the gain as ordinary income as opposed to all of the gain receiving long-term capital gains treatment. Used to prevent a taxpayer from converting depreciation deductions into an eventual long-term capital gain.

recast: see *recomputation.*

recasting a mortgage: reconstructing an existing mortgage by increasing its amount, interest rate, or time period.

Recd.: received.

receipt: any written acknowledgment of value received.

receipt book: a bound book of blank receipt stubs with detachable blank receipts.

receipts outstanding for funded debt: receipts for payments on account of subscriptions to funded debt. [18]

receipts outstanding for installments paid: receipts for payments on account of subscriptions to capital stock. [18]

receivables: accounts receivable owned by a business. These may be pledged as collateral for a loan secured from a bank or other financial institution.

receivables turnover: a computation done to evaluate the quality of a company's accounts receivable. Receivables turnover is calculated as the ratio of net sales to current value of receivables. The resulting figure gives an indication of the average length of time for which the firm's receivables remain outstanding. [105]

receive (advice to): an advance notice to an account-maintaining bank that it will receive funds to be credited to the sender of the message. [105]

receiver: a court-appointed, neutral party named to handle property under litigation or the affairs of a bankrupt person. The receiver is required to maintain the property and its assets for the benefit of those having equity in it until a court decision as to its disposition is made. See also *bailee, interim receiver, remaindermen, sequestered account.*

receiver's correspondent bank: a bank with which the receiver of a transfer has an account relationship and which may act as a reimbursement bank in a transfer of funds. [105]

receivership: the state of being under the care or administration of a receiver.

receiving bank:
(1) a bank that receives paperless entries from the ACH following their entry by an originating bank.
(2) the bank to whom the service transmits the message. [105]

receiving bank identifier: a code that uniquely identifies the bank that is to receive the message. Constitutes the routing code or address by which the destination bank is known to the wire service handling the message. [105]

receiving bank name: names the bank that receives the message from the service. [105]

receiving bank output sequence number: a consecutive sequence number that allows for output message control between the service and the receiving bank. [105]

receiving bank terminal identifier: a code uniquely identifying the terminal or station within the destination bank to which the message is sent. Augments and further qualifies the address of the destination bank. [105]

receiving bank time and date: time and date that the message was delivered to the receiving bank by the service. [105]

receiving teller: a bank employee assigned to the duties of accepting deposits from depositors. This teller is responsible for counting all cash received, and for verification of the count to the customer's deposit. The teller should also see that all checks deposited are properly endorsed by the depositor. The receiving teller enters the amount of the deposit in the depositor's passbook, or issues a receipt from a teller's machine for the depositor's record. [10]

recession: a phase of the business cycle that shows a downswing or contraction of the economy.

reciprocal balances: arise when two depository institutions maintain deposit accounts with each other; that is, when a reporting bank has both a due to and a due from balance with another depository institution. [202]

reciprocal statutes: similar statutes in two or more states providing mutual provisions or reciprocal treatment within the states affected concerning the subjects treated in such statutes; for example, similar

provisions with regard to corporations or inheritance taxes, a trust institution, bank, or business in another state. [37]

recission: cancellation of a contract without penalty. [105]

reclamation: a sum of money due or owing by a bank resulting from an error in the listing of the amount of a check on a clearinghouse balance.

reclassification of stock: a change or modification of the capital structure of an organization.

recognizance: acknowledgment of a former debt upon the record. [105]

recompense: a payment or award made to anyone to make amends for a loss or damage.

recomputation: to refigure and reapply, on a simple interest basis, all payments made on a precomputed loan.

reconciliation: a process for determining the differences between two items of an account so as to bring them into agreement (e.g., a bank statement and an up-to-date checkbook). See *adjustment*.

reconditioning property: improving a property's value by repairing it or making changes to enhance it.

reconveyance: the transfer of title of property back to a former owner.

recordation: the public acknowledgment in written form that a lien exists against a specific property that is identified in a mortgage. See *lien affidavit*.

records of original entry: the general journal, the cash receipts record, and the cash disbursement record. All transactions must first be analyzed and recorded in one of these records before posting to the general ledger accounts. [59]

recourse: the rights of a holder in due course of a negotiable instrument to force prior endorsers on the instrument to meet their legal obligations by making good the payment of the instrument if dishonored by the maker or acceptor. The holder in due course must have met the legal requirements of presentation and delivery of the instrument to the maker of a note or acceptor of a draft, and must have found that this legal entity has refused to pay for, or defaulted in payment of the instrument. See also *notice of dishonor (protest jacket)*. [10]

Rect.: see *receipt*.

recurring charges: those financial obligations of a recurring nature that a potential borrower must pay or has obligated himself to pay, including taxes, debt repayments, legal obligations such as alimony, and other items. [59]

red, in the: slang, losing money from operating a business.

red clause: a clause, printed in red, on a letter of credit, authorizing a negotiating banker to make advances to a beneficiary so that he or she can buy the items, and deliver them for shipment. [85]

redeemable rent: payments of rent that can be recovered (i.e., with a rental agreement containing the option to buy the property). When such an option is exercised, the purchaser receives all or a portion of the rents, or the monies may be applied to the sales price.

redemise: to renew a lease.

redemption:
(1) the liquidation of an indebtedness, on or before maturity, such as the retirement of a bond issue prior to its maturity date.

(2) purchasing back; a debtor redeems his mortgaged property when he has paid his debt in full.

redemption agent: synonymous with *clearinghouse agent*.

redemption fund: a fund created for the purpose of retiring an obligation.

redemption period: the time in which a mortgagor may buy back property by paying the amount owed (with principal and interest) on a foreclosed mortgage. The specific time is subject to state law. [105]

redemption right: a defaulted mortgagor's right to redeem his property after default and court judgment, both before and after its sale. See also *equitable right of redemption*. [59]

redemption yield: a U.K. term, synonymous with *yield* to maturity in United States.

Redi Check Plan: the customer arranges a top credit limit with the bank. He is issued a book of special checks (usually of a type prepared for automated bookkeeping). It is his privilege to write checks as he wishes, up to the total of his line of credit, which may be for $300, $500, $1000, and at times as high as $5000. Each month he receives a statement which records all of his checks that have "cleared" the bank. A service charge may be added but usually is not if he makes a deposit to cover the statement within 10, 15, or 20 days; except perhaps 25 cents for each check that has been drawn, to cover the bookkeeping. [28]

Redisc.: see *rediscount*.

rediscount:
(1) a negotiable instrument that has been discounted by a bank and

subsequently discounted a second time by a Federal Reserve bank or another bank for the benefit of the bank that originally discounted the instrument. See *bank credit.*
(2) to discount for the second time.

rediscounting: see *bank of discount.*

rediscount rate: the rate set by the Federal Reserve Bank for discounting a second time monies offered by their district member banks; the interest rate charged for discounting a negotiable instrument that has already been discounted.

Rediskontkontingent: German for the rediscount quote available to German banks at the Bundesbank.

redlining: the alleged practice of certain lending institutions of making it almost impossible to obtain mortgages, improvement loans, and insurance by homeowners, apartment house landlords, and businesses in neighborhoods outlined in red on a map, usually areas that are deteriorating or considered by the lending institution as poor investments. Cf. *greenlining.*

redraft: when a check or other bill of exchange that has been presented for payment is dishonored and consequently protested, the instrument holder can draw a bill of exchange for the original amount of the obligation plus the cost of the notary and other protest expenses. This new instrument is called a *redraft* or *cross bill.*

reentry: a landlord's right to reacquire leased property if terms in the lease, such as the making of rent payments, are not satisfied. A reentry clause must be inserted by the landlord in the original lease. Cf. *landlord's warrant.*

reexchange: the charge by the drawer of a redraft for his or her expense due to the default on the original draft.

Ref.:
(1) see *referee.*
(2) see *refunding.*

refer authorizer: a person in a credit office with the authority to approve or disapprove credit transactions which need special attention. The person is usually a section supervisor. [41]

referee: when a case is pending in court, the presiding officer requests an individual (the referee) to receive testimony from the parties and present the information to the court. When appropriate, the referee can accept foreclosed property and make a deed. See *bankruptcy, foreclose (foreclosure);* cf. *master in chancery.*

referee's foreclosure deed: a deed made by a court official that forecloses the mortgage on a property and passes the title on to the referee.

referee's partition deed: a deed made by a referee, conveying title to property when co-owners choose to divide their interest.

reference currency: a currency used in making payments to a bondholder.

reference number:
(1) number assigned to each monetary transaction in a descriptive billing system. Each reference number is printed on the monthly statement to aid in retrieval of the document, should it be questioned by the cardholder.
(2) a numeric or other symbolic means of identifying a particular transaction. [105]

refinance:
(1) to extend existing financing or to acquire new monies. Usually done when a mortgage is withdrawn so that a larger one can be placed on the property. See *refunding mortgage*.
(2) to revise a payment timetable and, frequently, to modify interest charges on the obligation.

refinanced loan: a loan that has had an addition to the principal balance. Such increases are usually for property improvements such as an added room. Normally the term and/or payment amount is also affected.

refinancing: synonymous with *refunding*.

refreshing: synonymous with *buffering*.

refund:
(1) an amount paid back of credit allowed because of an overcollection or on account of the return of an object sold.
(2) to pay back or allow credit for an amount because of an overcollection or because of the return of an object sold.
(3) to provide for the payment of a loan through cash or credit secured by a new loan.
(4) to replace one bond issue with another, usually in order to extend the maturity, to reduce the interest rate, or to consolidate several issues. [49]

refundable interest: the unearned portion of interest previously charged that will be returned to the debtor (maker of a note) if the indebtedness is liquidated prior to maturity.

refund check:
(1) a check or other instrument of currency that is repayment of money for any reason. See *rebate*.
(2) a statement for a customer's purchase that is returned.

refunding:
(1) replacing an old bond issue with a new issue, either before or at maturity of the older one. It is often done to change the interest rate on the debt.
(2) the act of returning a portion of money to the giver from an amount already paid out. See *debt*.

refunding certificates: U.S. $10 certificates of deposit, which had an interest of 4 percent for an indefinite period of time. They were issued in 1879 and intended to induce people not to redeem them but to keep them in circulation. [27]

refunding mortgage: refinancing a mortgage with monies derived from a new loan.

refund slip: synonymous with *credit slip*.

Reg.:
(1) see *register*.
(2) see *registrar*.

regional bank: one of the 12 Federal Reserve District or Regional Banks around the United States.

Regional Check Processing Center (RCPC): a Federal Reserve facility in which check-processing operations are performed. These centers serve a group of banks located within a specified area of a Federal Reserve District. They expedite collection and settlement of checks within the area on an overnight basis. [7]

register:
(1) the making of a permanent record of events.
(2) a device capable of storing a specified amount of data (e.g., one word).

register(ed) check: the title given to a check prepared by a teller, using funds recorded and placed aside in a special register, for the convenience of members of the general public who may wish to make a payment by check, but who do not maintain a checking account. The check has two stubs: one is for the purchaser and the other is used by the bank for record keeping. It is actually a money order, prepared in the form of a check, and the bank usually charges a small fee for each registered check sold.

registered as to principal: a term applied to a coupon bond, the name of the owner of which is registered on the bond and on the books of the company. Such bonds are not negotiable and cannot be sold without an assignment. [37]

registered check: see *register(ed) check.*

registered form: an instrument that is issued in the name of the owner and payable only to the owner. [105]

registered warrant: a warrant registered by the paying officer for future payment on account of present lack of funds and which is to be paid in the order of its registration. In some cases, such warrants are registered when issued; in others, when first presented to the paying officer by the holders. See also *warrant.* [49]

register of wills: in some states (Delaware, for example), the name of the officer before whom wills are offered for probate and who grants letters testamentary and letters of administration. [32]

registrar: an agency, usually a trust company or a bank, charged with the responsibility of preventing the issuance of more stock that has been authorized by a company. The registrar's primary function is to authenticate the issuing of securities. See *Torrens certificate.*

registry: a public recording of documents or information.

regular lending area: the geographical boundaries within which a security property must be located in order for a savings association to invest in a mortgage loan secured by the property, without the loan and the association being subject to special limitations set by regulatory and supervisory agencies. Synonymous with *normal lending territory.* [59]

regular mortgage: the legal document used in most states to pledge real estate as security for the repayment of a debt. [59]

regular savings account: a savings account to which additions or withdrawals may be made in any amount at any time; earnings typically are credited directly to the account at the appropriate earnings distributions times rather than mailed to the account holder. [59]

Regulation A: establishes the conditions and means by which Federal Reserve Banks extend credit to member banks and others. Credit extended to member banks is usually in the form of an advance on the bank's promissory note secured by U.S. government and federal agency securities; eligible commercial, agricultural, or construction paper; or banker acceptances. The credit cannot be extended for speculative purposes, and paper offered as collateral must be acceptable for discount or purchase under criteria specified in the regulation. [105]

Regulation B: prohibits discrimination by lenders on the basis of age, race, color, religion, national origin, sex, marital status, or receipt of income from public assistance programs. It establishes guidelines for gathering and evaluating credit information, and requires written notification to the applicant in cases where credit is denied. [105]

Regulation C: requires depository institutions making federally related mortgage loans to make annual public disclosure of the locations of certain residential loans. This is done to carry out the Home Mortgage Disclosure Act of 1935 and applies to most commercial banks, savings and loan associations, building and loan associations, homestead associations, and credit unions that make federally related mortgage loans. [105]

Regulation D: the regulation of the Federal Reserve Board which defines and prescribes legal reserve requirements of member banks. [36]

Regulation E: for financial institutions, implementing the Electronic Fund Transfer Act, which covers the limits of consumer liability and rules on the issuance of cards; adopted in March 1979. In January 1980, the Federal Reserve Board adopted additional amendments to its Regulation E proposals to become effective in May 1980. The more recent actions deal with documentation of transfers, preauthorized credits, and procedures for processing errors. See *Electronic Fund Transfer Act*. [14]

Regulation F: a regulation issued by the Board of Governors of the Federal Reserve System under authority of Section 11(k) of the Federal Reserve Act, as amended, relating to the conduct of fiduciary business by national banks. The full title of the regulation is Regulation F—Trust Powers of National Banks. [37]

Regulation G: Federal Reserve Board rule regulating lenders other than commercial banks, brokers, or dealers who, in the ordinary course of business, extend credit to people to buy or carry securities.

Regulation H: defines membership requirements and other conditions required of state-chartered banks. It also stipulates the necessary procedures to be followed when requesting approval to establish branches, and for requesting voluntary withdrawal from membership. [105]

Regulation I: requires banks joining the Federal Reserve System to subscribe to the stock of the Federal Reserve Bank in its district. The amount of stock ownership required is a percentage of the member bank's capital plus surplus. Ownership of Federal Reserve stock must be adjusted with fluctuations in the member bank's capitalization. [105]

Regulation J: the regulation of the Federal Reserve Board containing the terms and conditions governing collection of checks and other items by Federal Reserve Banks. [36]

Regulation L: discourages noncompetitive practices among member banks by restricting the relationships a director, officer, or employee of one bank can have with another banking institution. [105]

Regulation M: governs the foreign activities of member banks. Regulation M covers the requirements for establishing a foreign branch, the reserve requirements imposed on transactions by foreign branches, and determines permissible foreign banking activities. [105]

Regulation Nine (9): a regulation issued by the Comptroller of the Currency under authority of Section 1(j) of the act of September 28, 1962 (76 Stat. 668, 12 U.S.C. 92a) relating to the conduct of fiduciary business by national banks. The full title of the regulation is Regulation 9—Fiduciary Powers of National Banks and Collective Investment Funds. [37]

Regulation O: stipulates the conditions under which a member bank may loan funds to its own executive officers. [105]

Regulation Q: as established by the Federal Reserve Board, a formula it uses to determine the maximum interest that can be paid by commercial banks to their customers on time deposits.

Regulation T: the Federal Reserve Board criterion governing the amount of credit that may be advanced by brokers and dealers to customers for the purchase of securities. See *margin.*

Regulation U: the Federal Reserve Board criterion governing the amount of credit that may be advanced by a bank to its customers for the purchase of listed stocks when the requested loan is to be secured by listed stocks.

Regulation Z: this so-called truth-in-lending regulation was adopted, effective July 1, 1969, by the Board of Governors of the Federal Reserve System to implement Title I (Truth in Lending Act) and Title V (General Provisions) of the Consumer Protection Act. Dealing with the information customers of consumer credit should be given, it specifies, among other things, that they must be told the exact dollar amount of the finance charge and the annual percentage rate computed on the unpaid balance of the loan. [33]

rehypothecate: to pledge a second time.

Reichsbank: German for "imperial bank." The central bank of Germany, which receives and disburses state funds.

reimbursement: cash or other assets received as a repayment of the cost of work or services performed or of other expenditures, made for or on behalf of another governmental unit, or department, or for an individual, firm, or corporation. [49]

reimbursement arrangement: an arrangement by which a foreign correspondent bank is reimbursed for payments made according to the instructions of the bank issuing credit. [105]

reimbursement bank: the bank providing cover as a result of a funds transfer. [105]

reimbursement letter of credit: an arrangement by which a foreign correspondent bank is reimbursed for payments made according to the instructions of the bank issuing credit by drawing on another correspondent bank. [105]

reimbursement method: instructions specifying how the receiver is to obtain reimbursement for the payment requested by the sender. With prior agreements this instruction may specify a debit party other than the sender. [105]

reissue month: the month the customer's cards are sent out. The cycle number correlates with the reissue month. [105]

reissues: issues replaced into circulation after a specific lapse of time and usually with an overprint. [27]

REIT: see *real estate investment trust.*

reject: to refuse or decline a risk. [12]

relationship banking: a strategy to attract investors, where a customer deals with just one officer who can handle all services—and who becomes a salesperson in the process.

release:
(1) the written statement of a claim's settlement.
(2) the discharge of property from a mortgage lien; a written statement that an obligation has been satisfied.
(3) the cancellation or resolution of a claim against another person. [59]

release clause: a clause in a mortgage permitting payment of a part of the debt in order that a proportionate part of the property can be freed.

release date and time: date and time the sender authorizes the service to forward the instructions to the receiver. [105]

release of liability: agreement in which a lender terminates the personal obligation of a mortgagor for the payment of a debt. [105]

release of lien: an instrument discharging secured property from a lien. [105]

release of mortgage: dropping a claim against property established by a mortgage.

Rem.: see *remittance.*

remainder: upon completion of a life estate, the property reverts to the owner or goes to an heir. If the owner does not take the property back, a remainder estate is created by the same instrument. This estate begins upon the termination of the temporary estate (i.e., the life estate) that preceded it.

remainder beneficiary: the beneficiary of a trust who is entitled to the principal outright after the prior life beneficiary or other prior beneficiary has died or his or her interest has been terminated. [32]

remainder estate: an estate in property created simultaneously with other estates by a single grant and consisting of the rights and interest contingent upon and remaining after the termination of the other estates. [58]

remainder interest: a future interest which will become an interest in possession after the termination of a prior interest created at the same time and by the same instrument as the future interest. For example, H leaves his estate in trust with income to be paid to W, and on her death the trust is to terminate and the property is to be delivered to C. C has a remainder interest. [37]

remaindermen: those persons who receive the proceeds from the final distribution of a trust or estate. [25]

remainder notes: unissued and unsigned notes of a bank which either closed down or changed its design, leaving a supply of unwanted notes. With few exceptions, these should be in absolutely perfect condition. [27]

remand: the action of an appellate court in sending a cause back to the lower court that sought the appeal, accompanied by the instructions of the higher court.

remargining: placing added margin against a loan. Remargining is one option when brokers require additional cash or collateral when their securities have lost some of their value.

Rembrandt: a domestic Dutch guilder issue by a foreign borrower.

reminder letter: the first in a series of collection letters, sent by a creditor to a debtor, where the latter has neglected to make a payment on time. [105]

remise: to give or grant back; to discharge or release. Synonymous with *quit claim.*

Remitt.: see *remittance.*

remittance: funds forwarded from one person to another as payment for bought items or services.

remittance advice: information on a check stub, or on a document attached to a check by the drawer, informing the payee why a payment is being made.

remittance letter: a transit letter containing a list of checks sent for collection and payment by a sending bank to a receiving bank. The sending bank does not maintain an account with the receiving bank, and hence requests the latter to remit payment for the items sent. The receiving bank pays for the checks by remitting a bank draft to the sending bank. This is to be distinguished from a cash letter of credit, in which case the receiving bank credits the account of the sending

bank in its "due to banks" ledger. [10]

remittance payment: payment sent by mail to center for processing. [105]

remitter: the party who is the source of funds to the receiver. [105]

remitter advice charges: information specifying who to charge for advising the remitter and how to apply these charges. [105]

remitter advice identifier: information used in contacting the remitter in order to send an advice (e.g., phone number, cable address). [105]

remitter advice instructions: additional information that pertains to notification of the remitter (e.g., bank's/person's name, hours of availability). [105]

remitter advice method: a code that specifies the method to be used to notify the remitter that the account has been credited or that funds are available (e.g., phone, letter, wire). [105]

remitter identifier: a code that uniquely identifies the remitter. [105]

remitter identifier type: a code that specifies the type of identifier used for the remitter. [105]

remitter name and address: identifies the remitter by name and, optionally, the remitter's postal address. [105]

remitting: paying, as in remitting a payment; also canceling, as in remitting a debt. [28]

remitting bank: the bank which sends, or remits, the documents for collection. [132]

remonetization: the reinstatement of a coin as standard money after it has been demonetized.

remote electronic banking: electronic funds transfer systems through which bank customers conduct banking business at a location other than a bank office, for example, point-of-sale or CBCT. [33]

remote service unit: the terminology used by savings and loan associations that corresponds to the customer-bank communication terminal (CBCT) that may be employed by banks. See *customer-bank communication terminal.* [36]

removed in perpetuity: see *perpetuity.*

renege: to go back on a promise; to pull out of an agreement.

renegotiable rate: a type of variable rate involving a renewable short-term balloon note. The interest rate on the loan is generally fixed during the term of the note, but when the balloon comes due, the lender may refinance it at a higher rate. In order for the loan to be fully amortized, periodic refinancing may be necessary. [200]

renegotiable-rate mortgage (RRM): authorized by the Federal Home Loan Bank Board, requires home buyers to renegotiate the terms of the loan every three to five years— a distinct advantage if interest rates drop but a poor hedge against inflation if they go up. Cf. *variable-rate mortgage;* sometimes called the *rollover mortgage.*

renewal: extending the maturity of an existing loan obligation, or other document of relationship. Cf. *novation.*

renounce:
(1) an act by which an individual or trust institution named under a will as executor or trustee declines to accept such appointment.

(2) the act of a surviving husband or wife under the decedent's state law declining to take the provision made for him or her under the other's will and taking his or her share of the estate had the other died without a will.

(3) any action by which the beneficiary of any interest in real or personal property therewith refuses to accept such interest. [37]

rent: income received from leasing real estate.

rentes: the annual interest payable on the bonded debt of France, Austria, Italy, and a few other countries. The term is also applied to the bonds themselves.

renunciation: giving up a right or claim, without any reservation, or without naming the person who is to assume the title.

reorganization committee: a committee representing investors or creditors which develops plans for the reorganization of a distressed corporation. The National Bankruptcy Act sets strict conditions under which such groups operate.

repayments: see *loan repayments.*

repledge: synonymous with *rehypothecate.*

replenishment deposit: a payment that increases the balance of the originator's account with the receiver maintaining correspondent balances. [105]

replevin: a statute remedy for the recovery of the possession of a chattel. The right of possession can be tried only in such action. Cf. *seisin (seizin).*

report (or certificate): the report (or certificate) of an independent accountant (or auditor) is a document in which he indicates the nature and scope of the examination (or audit) that he has made and expresses the opinion that he has formed in respect of the financial statements. [77]

reporter: person employed by a credit bureau. Makes reports on credit inquiries. [41]

representative money: paper money secured by monetary metal (i.e., gold or silver certificates) deposited in the treasury of a country.

reproduction value: the sum of money which would be required to reproduce a building less an allowance for depreciation of that building. [44]

repurchase plan: type of dealer financing plan in which the responsibility is shared between a dealer and a bank in case of consumer default, and which usually provides for the sale of contracts to a bank without recourse regarding a customer's obligation to pay; the dealer, however, agrees to repurchase, for the net unpaid balance, those goods repossessed by the bank and delivered to the dealer's place of business within a specified number of days after maturity of the oldest unpaid installment. [105]

request for conditional commitment to guarantee loan: the bank's request to FmHA to indicate its willingness to guarantee a loan on the terms spelled out by the bank in its Application for Guaranteed Loan. [105]

request for contract of guarantee: a bank's request to FmHA to issue a guarantee on the bank's loan as presented in the bank's Application for Guaranteed Loan. [105]

required reserves: liquid assets that state-chartered banks must hold in accordance with regulations of state banking agencies and Federal Reserve officials.

Res.: see *reserve.*

res: in the phrase trust res, the same as trust property. The corpus of the trust. [37]

res adjudicata: Latin; the principle according to which a controversy that has once been decided is deemed to be settled forever; that is, the courts will not hear claims to which the issue adjudicated applies.

rescheduling: the renegotiation of the terms of existing debt. [91]

rescind: see *right of rescission.*

rescission: making void or annulling (e.g., the rescission of a law or judgment). See *right of rescission.*

rescript: a duplicate of a document.

reserve:

(1) a portion of the profits allocated to various reserve accounts to protect any depreciation in asset values. The reserves are taken from profits before any declaration of dividends by the board of directors.

(2) assets in the form of cash maintained in a bank's own vault. See *reserve requirements.*

(3) funds earmarked for specific purposes. For example, reserves for unearned premiums and reserves for losses in process of adjustment. Cf. *legal reserve.*

reserve adjustment magnitude (RAM): measures the impact of changes in reserve requirements by simply subtracting the current period's required reserves from those that would have been required if some base period's reserve requirements were, instead, in effect. The purpose of a RAM is to capture in the adjusted monetary base those total reserve changes that arise from changes in reserve requirements by the Federal Reserve. [79]

reserve assets:
(1) general: assets that are held as reserves, either as part of foreign exchange reserves, or as reserves of the banking system.
(2) Great Britain: assets included in the Bank of England's reserve requirements, namely deposits at the Bank, Treasury Bills, gilt-edged stock with less than a year to maturity, money at call with the London money market, and certain other assets. [137]

reserve bank: any one of the 12 Federal Reserve Banks. See *banker's bank, Federal Reserve Bank.*

reserve bank credit: credit extended to member banks by the Federal Reserve Bank through rediscounting member bank loans, purchasing acceptances, or direct loans on various security. In addition, all deposits made by a member bank qualify.

reserve checking/overdraft checking: a combination of a checking account and a preauthorized personal loan. Synonymous with *personal line of credit.* [105]

reserve city bank: a member bank of the Federal Reserve System located in cities identified by the Federal Reserve Act as amended as reserve cities. These banks are divided for reserve requirements by the act into reserve city banks and country banks.

reserve clause: a Eurocurrency credit clause allowing a lender to pass on to a borrower any further costs resulting from the imposition on the lender of new reserve requirements. [83]

reserve currency: foreign funds retained by a nation's central bank as a vehicle for settling international financial obligations. The U.S. dollar and the pound sterling are the dominant reserve currencies today.

reserve depository: an authorized bank serving as depository for part of the legal reserves against deposits other banks must hold, under law.

reserve for encumbrances: a reserve representing the segregation of a portion of a fund balance to provide for unliquidated encumbrances. See also *reserve.* [49]

reserve ratio (requirement): see *reserve requirements.*

reserve requirements: percentage of customer deposits that banks must set aside in the form of reserves. The reserve requirement ratio determines the expansion of deposits that can be supported by each additional dollar of reserves. The Board of Governors can raise or lower reserve requirements for member banks within limits specified by law. Reserve requirements act as lending controls (lowering reserve requirements allows more bank lending; raising requirements, less lending). [1]

reserves: see *reserve.*

reserves with Federal Reserve Banks: deposits of reporting member banks with the Federal Reserve Banks. Members banks are required by law to hold an amount equal to a percentage of their deposits as reserve (a deposit) in the Reserve Banks. [40]

residence:
(1) the place where one resides, whether temporarily or permanently.
(2) as used in Regulation Z, any real property in which the customer lives or expects to live. Important in real estate transactions because when an interest to secure an obligation is taken in a customer's principal residence, notice of the right of rescission must be given to the customer. [105]

residential mortgage: a loan extended for which real estate is given as collateral. The collateral is usually a single owner-occupied home or a small number of dwelling units. [105]

residential real property: improved real property used or intended to be used for residential purposes, including single-family homes, dwellings for from two to four families, and individual units of condominiums and cooperatives. [105]

residual cost (or value): the difference between the cost of a particular asset and any amortized or expensed account.

residual legacy: see *legacy.*

residual ownership: what is left following claims.

residuary bequest: the part of a will that gives instruction for the disposal of any portion of an estate remaining after payments of debts and other obligations.

residuary clause: the provision in the will or trust agreement that disposes of all of the decedent's property remaining after the payment of all taxes, debts, expenses,

and charges and the satisfaction of all other gifts in the will or trust agreement. [37]

residuary devise: a gift by will of the real property remaining after all specific devices have been made. [37]

residuary devisee: a recipient by will of any real property after all other claimants to the estate have received payment.

residuary estate: what remains in an estate after all claims to the estate have been properly disposed of.

residuary legatee: a person to whom is given the remainder of a testator's personal property after all other legacies have been satisfied. [37]

residuary trust: a trust composed of the property of the testator that remains in the estate after the payment of all taxes, debts, expenses, charges, and the satisfaction of all other gifts under the will. [37]

residue: (rest, residue, and remainder); that portion of a decedent estate remaining after the payment of all debts, expenses, and charges and the satisfaction of all legacies and devises. [37]

Resolution Trust Corporation (RTC): its function, between August 1989 and August 1992, is to take over 400 to 500 insolvent savings associations with assets of almost $300 billion, to find buyers for the "sick" institutions and to liquidate those for which there are no buyers. Eventually RTC has to liquidate almost $150 billion in troubled assets that it cannot sell. Its charter expires in 1996. See *RTC Oversight Board.*

resources: the bank's title for assets owned. The resources of a bank are offset by the liabilities and capital accounts as listed on the daily statement of condition. The major resources of a bank are cash on hand and due from banks; investments held; loans and discounts; and buildings, furniture, fixtures, and equipment. [10]

RESPA: see *Real Estate Settlement Procedures Act.*

restitution: the enforced payment of money, or its equivalent, to its rightful owner as established by law. Cf. *replevin.*

restoration premium: the premium charged to restore a policy or bond to its original value after payment of a loss.

restraint on alienation of property: a limitation on the right of a person to transfer title to property or property rights. [37]

restricted assets: money or other resources, the use of which is restricted by legal or contractual requirements. The most common examples of restricted assets in governmental accounting are those arising out of revenue bond indentures in enterprise funds. Synonymous with *restricted funds,* but this terminology is not preferred. [49]

restricted card list: a listing of cardholder accounts, in either alphabetic or numeric sequence, on which transactions are restricted and not to be completed by merchants without authorization. See *hot card.* [105]

restricted funds: synonymous with *restricted assets.* See *restricted assets.*

restrictive covenants: written agreements limiting the use of property.

restrictive endorsement: an endorsement that limits the negotiability of an instrument, or contains a definite condition as to payment; it purports to preclude the endorsee from making any further transfer of the instrument. [59]

retail banking: banking services offered to the general public, including commercial enterprises, consumers, and small business. [105]

retail credit bureaus: a center of local consumer credit information. Its primary function is to furnish reports on consumers desiring to obtain money. [105]

retail lending: loans to individuals, including home mortgages and consumer installment loans. [105]

retail money: see *wholesale money.*

retail repo: arrangements in which a lender lends the bank cash for a flexible period—usually a week to 89 days, and the bank promises to return the principal to the lender, plus interest. They are more liquid than bank savings certificates because there are usually no penalties for early withdrawal. The interest rate is competitive with money market mutual funds and much higher than the rate on passbook savings. The minimum denomination is typically $1000. However, a retail repo is an investment, not a deposit, and the money is not insured.

retirement: the paying off of a debt prior to or at maturity.

retirement fund: monies set aside by an organization; the fund builds up value over the year to provide income for employees eligible to retire and receive income from it.

retirement income: a stipulated amount of income starting at a selected retirement age. This is derived by exercising one of the settlement options available against the policy or annuity cash value.

retiring a bill: paying a bill of exchange on its due date or beforehand, at a discount.

returned check: a check the bank refused to accept and returned unpaid. [55]

return item: a negotiable instrument, principally a check, that has been sent to one bank for collection and payment and is returned unpaid to the sending bank.

revalidated notes: paper money bearing an official overprint, stamp, or other mark to indicate its renewed status as legal tender, despite the invalidity of the original note. [27]

revaluation (revalorization): the restoration (by lowering the request for, or raising the supply of foreign currencies by restricting imports and promoting exports) of the value of a depreciated national currency that has previously been devalued.

Revenue Act of 1962: federal legislation; provided investment tax credit of 7 percent on new and used property other than buildings. See also *Revenue Act of 1964, Revenue Act of 1971, Revenue Act of 1978, Revenue Adjustment Act of 1975.*

Revenue Act of 1964: federal legislation; provided for two-stage cut in personal income tax liabilities and corporate-profits tax liabilities in 1964 and 1965. See also *Revenue Act of 1962, Revenue Act of 1971, Revenue Act of 1978.*

Revenue Act of 1971: federal legislation; accelerated by one year scheduled increases in personal exemptions and standard deduction. Repealed automobile excise tax retroactive to August 15, 1971; on

small trucks and buses to September 22, 1971. Reinstated 7 percent investment tax credit and incorporated depreciation range guidelines.

Revenue Act of 1976: much of this act was revised by the Revenue Act of 1978. See *Revenue Act of 1978.*

Revenue Act of 1978: federal legislation affecting the following areas.

(a) *Individual and corporate tax cuts:* lowers tax rates and widens brackets so that raises will not bring people so quickly into higher tax levels; the personal exemption deduction goes to $1000 beginning with 1979; the top corporate rate will be 46 percent in 1979 and after, with new graduated rates for lower income corporations.

(b) *Capital gains:* sellers of capital assets held more than a year can exclude 60 percent of the gain for sales on or after November 1, 1978. Capital gains have no adverse impact on the maximum tax on earned income on or after that date; nor are they subject to the add-on 15 percent preference tax in 1979 and later.

(c) *New alternative tax on capital gains:* the excluded portion of capital gains and adjusted itemized deductions are no longer subject to the regular add-on preference tax to be replaced by a new alternative minimum tax. If a person has heavy capital gains or itemized deductions, he or she must now figure two taxes—regular taxes and an alternative tax, which is at graduated rates (25 percent maximum) above an exclusion base of $20,000; the individual pays whichever is higher.

(d) *Homeowners:* personal residence sales will no longer produce gains subject to the old add-on minimum tax or to the new alternative minimum tax described above. There is also the right to exclude all gain up to $100,000 if the individual is 55 years of age or over. Both changes apply to home sales after July 26, 1978.

(e) *Tax shelter rules:* these are broader, causing more entities to be subject to the "at risk" rules that keep people from deducting more than their equity investment. Entertainment facilities such as hunting lodges and yachts are no longer to be accepted as business deductions. Partnerships face more stringent reporting requirements, with stiff new penalties if partnership returns are not sent in on time.

(f) *Carryover basis rules postponed:* a stepped-up basis for inherited property is back. The carryover basis rules enacted in 1976 did not apply until 1980. Refund possibilities abound for those who have reported gains using carryover basis for assets inherited from someone who died in 1977 or 1978.

(g) *Other provisions:* there are changes on deductions and credits—for example, there is a new targeted jobs credit, and the investment credit is set permanently at 10 percent. The new law also contains important changes for employee benefits. See *Tax Reform Act of 1976.*

revenue-anticipation notes (RANs): short-term municipal borrowings that fund current operations and are to be funded by revenues other than taxes, especially federal aid.

revenue application notes: short-term notes sold in anticipation of receipt of revenues and payable from the proceeds of those revenues. [105]

revenue bonds payable: a liability account which represents the face value of revenue bonds issued and outstanding. [49]

revenue receipts: a term used synonymously with "revenue" by some governmental units which account for their revenues on a "cash basis." See also *nonrevenue receipts.* [49]

reverse: the back of a note. See *observe.* [27]

reverse-annuity mortgage: designed for retirees and other fixed-income homeowners who owe little or nothing on their houses. Typically, it permits them to use some or all of the equity already in the home as supplemental income, while retaining ownership. In effect, they are borrowing against the value of the house on a monthly basis. The longer they borrow, of course, the less equity they retain in the house. The loan becomes due either on a specific date or when a specified event occurs such as the sale of the property or death of the borrower. See also *flexible-payment mortgage, graduated-payment mortgage, pledged-account mortgage, rollover mortgage, variable-rate mortgage.* Synonymous with *equity conversion.*

reverse money transfer: a debit transfer in which the credit party is the sender. [105]

reverse mortgage: a loan against the value of a house.

reverse repos: synonymous with *matched sales.*

reverse repurchase agreements: synonymous with *matched sales.*

reversing entries: an accounting procedure by which equal and opposite entries are made to an account to adjust the financial records of an association. This normally occurs after closing procedures. [59]

reversion: the interest in an estate remaining in the grantor after a particular interest, less than the whole estate, has been granted by the owner to another person; to be distinguished from remainder. The reversion remains in the grantor; the remainder goes to some grantee. [37]

reversionary interest: a claim or interest that an individual can keep to property or income that has been assigned to someone else. Cf. *estate in reversion, remainder.*

reversionary right: the right to receive possession and use of property upon termination or defeat of an estate bearing the rights of possession and use and vested in another.

reverter: the interest which the grantor retains in property in which he has conveyed an interest less than the whole to another party. If the grantor makes the conveyance subject to a condition which may or may not be broken sometime in the future, he retains a possibility of reverter. [37]

revocable beneficiary: a beneficiary whose rights in the policy are subject to the insured's right of change.

revocable letter of credit: any letter of credit that may be canceled.

revocable living trust: the income from such a trust is paid to the grantor during his or her lifetime, and to the family following the grantor's death. It can be canceled by the person granting or initiating the trust.

revocable trust with consent or approval: a trust which may be terminated by the settlor or by another person but only with the consent or approval of one or more other persons. For example, A creates for his son B a trust which may be revoked by B with C's consent (in this case C may be B's mother). To be distinguished from an *irrevocable trust.* [37]

revocation: the act of annulling or making inoperative a will or a trust instrument. [37]

revolver: see *revolving credit line.*

revolving account: a line of credit that may be used repeatedly up to a certain specified limit. [78]

revolving credit line: a guaranteed standby credit arrangement whereby the firm can borrow from the bank when needed up to a certain limit.

revolving fund: money that is renewed as it is used, either by additional appropriations or by income from the programs it finances; thus the fund retains a balance at all times.

revolving letter of credit: a letter of credit issued for a specific amount that is automatically renewed for the same amount over a given period. Usually the unused renewable portion of the credit is cumulative, as long as drafts are drawn before the expiration of the credit.

revolving loan: a loan that is automatically renewed (upon maturity) without additional negotiation.

reward account: a type of checking account that gives no-charge checking to anybody with a minimum (e.g., $2000) savings account.

RF: see *revolving fund.*

RFC: Reconstruction Finance Corporation (defunct).

Rfg.: see *refunding.*

rial: monetary unit of Iran, Oman, and Yemen.

riel: monetary unit of Cambodia and Kampuchea.

right: that which is reserved by a settlor, as the right of amendment or revocation; opposed to the power granted to the trustee. [37]

right-hand side: the rate at which a bank will buy foreign currencies. [105]

right of action: the right to enforce a claim in court.

right of curtesy: see *curtesy.*

right of dower: see *dower.*

right of election: the right of a surviving husband or wife, under the decedent's estate law, to take his or her intestate share in preference to the provision made in the deceased person's will. [37]

right of foreclosure: the right of the association to take over property and close out the mortgagor's interest in it if the mortgagor violates the provisions of the mortgage or note. [59]

right of offset: a clause in the loan contract that gives the lender the right to use the balances in any of the customer's accounts as payment for the loan in the event of default. [105]

right of redemption: the right to free a property from foreclosure by paying off all debts.

right of rescission (ROR): the privilege, guaranteed by the Truth in Lending Act to cancel a contract under certain circumstances within three business days, without penalty and with full refund of all deposits submitted. See *voidable contract.*

right of survivorship: the right establishing a surviving joint owner as holder of the title to the property jointly owned. See *tenancy by the entirety;* cf. *tenancy in common.*

right of withdrawal: the privilege of an insured or beneficiary permitting withdrawal of funds placed on deposit. [12]

ringgit: monetary unit of Malaysia.

risk assets: all bank assets, except cash and direct U.S. government obligations. [105]

risk-based capital standard: a concept requiring banks to set aside capital to buttress billions of dollars in credit obligations that do not appear on the bank's balance sheets.

risk capital:
(1) capitalization that is not secured by a lien or mortgage.
(2) long-term loans or capital invested in high-risk business activities.

risk feature: an item affecting mortgage risk. [105]

risk-free rate of interest: the interest rate on a relatively riskless asset.

risk premium: additional required rate of return due to extra risk incurred.

risk rating: a systematic process of analyzing mortgage risk that results in estimation, in precise relative terms, of the soundness of individual transactions. [105]

rivets: slang, money.

riyal: monetary unit of Oman, Saudi Arabia, and Yemen.

ROE: see *rate of exchange.*

rolled over: see *rollover mortgage.*

roll over: renewing a loan contract to extend the term. It is often used to put off payments of balloons. See *balloon, buy down.*

rollover CD: a certificate of deposit package with a maturity of three years, divided into 12 six-month periods for which CDs are issued. Synonymous with *roly-poly CD.*

rollover mortgage: a short-term mortgage where the unpaid balance is refinanced, or "rolled over," every few years; at that time, the interest rate is adjusted up or down, depending on prevailing market conditions. Before the Depression of 1929, such loans were common, but since then the fixed-rate mortgage has generally been standard. During the early 1980s, the rollover mortgage again became popular. See also *flexible-payment mortgage, graduated-payment mortgage, pledged-account mortgage, reverse-annuity mortgage, variable-rate mortgage.* Synonymous with *renegotiable-rate mortgage.*

roly-poly CD: synonymous with *rollover CD.*

Roosa Bonds: see *nonmarketable liabilities of U.S. government.*

ROR: see *right of rescission.*

Rouble: see *ruble.*

routing symbol: see *check-routing symbol.*

RR:
(1) see *rediscount rate.*
(2) see *required reserves.*

RRM: see *renegotiable-rate mortgage.*

RSU: see *remote service unit.*

Rt.: see *right.*

RTC: See *Resolution Trust Corporation.*

RTC Oversight Board: the arms of the Executive Branch responsible for setting broad policies for RTC. Is ultimately held accountable for fraud and other mismanagement problems at RTC. Oversees the work of the RTC, to set general policy guidelines for RTC management and to dispense funds for S&L closings. See *Resolution Trust Corporation.*

rubber check: slang, a check that bounces, that is returned for lack of sufficient bank funds.

ruble: monetary unit of Union of Soviet Socialist Republics.

rubricated account: any earmarked account.

rule against accumulations: the limitation imposed by common law or by statute upon the accumulation of income in the hands of a trustee. [37]

rule of 78ths: see *factor, 78th.*

Rule of 72: a means for determining how long it will take for money to double at various interest rates. By dividing the rate of return into 72, the result is the number of years required to double money at that rate of interest, assuming annual compounding.

rules of the class: the terms and conditions, established by the association's board of directors and included in the savings account contract, applicable to each savings account classification, such as time and amount of deposit, rate of interest, penalty provisions, and the account designation. [59]

run: an action of a large number of people (e.g., a run on a bank occurs when a great many customers make massive withdrawals of funds).

runaway: a cardholder account that has exceeded the excessive-number-of-purchases limitation and may have exceeded its credit limit, and on which charges continue to be received or otherwise is indicative of unauthorized use. [105]

runner: an employee of the bank who delivers items to other banks in the same community, and who in turn may receive and bring back to his bank the items that the other banks may wish delivered there. The runner's duties may involve all types of messenger service for his bank. [10]

run on a bank: see *run.*

rupee: monetary unit of India, Maldives, Mauritius, Nepal, Pakistan, Seychelles, and Sri Lanka.

rupiah: monetary unit of Indonesia.

SA: see *savings account.*

S/A: in banking, survivorship agreement. See *survivorship account.*

saddle blankets: nickname for the large-size U.S. paper money before 1929. [27]

safe deposit box: a metal container that remains under lock and key in a section of a bank vault when the person who rents it is not handling or inspecting the jewelry, stock certificates, or other valuables it contains. The boxes are kept in small compartments, each with two separate locks. A box is rented with its compartment to a customer, not necessarily a depositor, for an annual fee.

safe deposit company: any financial warehouse, retaining securities, wills, and other documents.

safe deposit privilege: a plan by which customers rent compartments in a vault to keep valuable documents and possessions.

safe deposit vault: a section of the bank's vault set aside for the use of customers who may rent space in the vault for the safekeeping of valuable securities, papers, and small objects of value. See also *safe deposit box.* [10]

safekeeping: a service rendered by banks, especially banks in large metropolitan areas, where securities and valuables of all types and descriptions are protected in the vaults of the bank for the customer for a service fee. (These valuables may include securities, precious gems, valuable paintings, collection pieces of great value, silver and gold services, etc.) Many of these items are too large to be placed in safe deposit boxes. In the case of securities, some customers "buy" security counselor services of large banks, requesting the banks to handle their securities to the best advantage. The banks will buy and sell, collect dividends and interest, and credit the depositor's account with this income. Many clients of this type are foreign citizens, and wealthy Americans who spend a good portion of their time abroad, traveling or living in foreign countries. Since they cannot have constant access to safe deposit boxes, they appoint banks to act as their fiscal agents to protect and control their holdings for them in their absence. [10]

safekeeping account: an agency account concerning which the duties of the agent are to receipt for, safekeep, and deliver the property in the account on demand of the principal or on his or her order; to be distinguished from a custody account and a managing agency account. [32]

safekeeping (deposit for): the receipt by a bank of custody of specific property to be returned, as contrasted with an ordinary deposit to be repaid in money and with a safe deposit box, rented to a customer, to which the renter rather than the bank has access. [50]

safety factor: the ratio of the interest on a funded debt to the net income following the payment of the interest.

safety fund system: a system of bank insurance used in New York in the nineteenth century. The state treasurer held the fund derived from payments of 3 percent of each bank's capital stock. The fund guaranteed the bank notes issued by bank members of the system.

SAIF: see *Savings Association Insurance Fund.*

sale:
(1) the transfer of title for a sum of money and conditions, for the change of ownership of property.
(2) the transfer of title to an item or items or the agreement to perform a service in return for cash or the expectation of cash payment.

sale and lease-back: a transaction where used equipment is bought from a firm by a lessor, with title passing from the user to the lessor. The lessor then leases the equipment back to the firm, which now becomes the lessee.

sales audit: verification of the proper preparation and acceptability of bank card sales drafts, credit slips, merchant summaries, and cash advances. [105]

sales authorization: the obtaining of approval by the merchant from the bank for sales in excess of preestablished floor limits. Authorization may also be required for reasons other than dollar amount. [105]

sales budget: an estimate of the probable dollar sales and probable expenses of selling and publicity for a specified period.

sales draft: an instrument arising from the usage of a bank card which shows an obligation on the part of the cardholder to pay money to the card issues. Synonymous with *sales slip.*

sales draft clearing: in interchange arrangements, exchange of bank card items between merchant banks and cardholder banks. [105]

sales draft envelope: see *deposit envelope.*

sales slip: synonymous with *sales draft.*

salvage: the attempt to get repayment of some portion of a loan obligation which has already been written off the bank's books. [105]

salvage value: market salvage value of an asset, net of disposal costs.

same-day funds:
(1) funds placed in an account which are immediately available for Federal Reserve transfer or withdrawal in cash.
(2) signifies funds available for transfer today in like funds or withdrawal in cash, subject to the settlement of the transaction through the payment mechanism used. [105]

same-day settlement: where banks routinely receive the equivalent of cash payments on the same day that they make payments on behalf of foreign banks.

SAN: see *Subsidiary Account Number.*

sandwich lease: a leasehold in which the interest of the sublessor is inserted between the fee owner and the user of the property. The owner A of a fee simple leases to B, who in turn leases to C. The interest of A may be called the leased fee; that of B the sandwich lease, and that of C the leasehold. [62]

satisfaction of judgment: the legal procedure followed when a debtor pays the amount of judgment, together with interest and costs. "Satisfaction of judgment" is then entered on records of the court of record. [41]

satisfaction of mortgage: a document issued by mortgagee when a mortgage is paid off. [62]

satisfaction piece: an instrument acknowledging payment of an indebtedness due under a mortgage.

satisfactory account: in credit references, indicating that the terms of the account have been met as agreed. [105]

Saturday night special: a direct tender offer, made without any forewarning, that expires in one week. Such offerings were made possible by the Williams Act of 1968, which permits tender offers to run as short as seven days and does not require the bidder to tip his hand in advance with any notification.

Sav.: see *saving.*

saver's surplus: the differences between the amount of interest that savers actually get and the amount of interest for which they would have been willing to lend if the demand for loans (quantity demanded) had been less.

saving: the amount of existing income that is not spent on consumption.

savings account: money that is deposited in a bank, usually in small amounts periodically over a long period, and not subject to withdrawal by check. Savings accounts usually bear interest and some banks levy a service charge for excess withdrawal activity on an account.

savings account contract: the contractual relationship encompassing all the terms and conditions to which the customer and the association are subject when the customer opens a savings account. [59]

savings account ledger card: the association's complete record of account transactions on a particular savings account. [59]

savings account loan: a loan secured by the pledging of savings funds on deposit with the association. [59]

savings and loan association: a mutual, cooperative quasi-public financial institution, owned by its members (depositors), and chartered by a state or by the federal government. The association receives the savings of its members and uses these funds to finance long-term amortized mortgage loans to its members and to the general public. Such an association may also be organized as a corporation owned by stockholders. See *Cincotta-Conklin Bill of 1976.*

Savings Association Insurance Fund (SAIF): formerly the Federal Savings and Loan Insurance Corporation, which insures deposits up to $100,000 at thrift institutions and has been depleted by massive failures. Higher premiums from S&L's

will be put toward replenishing this fund. SAIF replaces the now insolvent FSLIC. See *Savings industry bill.*

savings bank: a banking association whose purpose is to promote thrift and savings habits in a community. It may be either a stock organization (a bank with a capital stock structure) or a "mutual savings bank." Until passage of the Cincotta-Conklin Bill in New York State or other similar bills, a savings bank had no power to perform commercial functions, but specialized in interest-bearing savings accounts, investing these savings in long-term bonds, mortgage loans, and other investment opportunities for the benefit of all depositors. See *NOW accounts.*

Savings Bank Life Insurance (SBLI): insurance written in several states through savings banks. Characterized by having no agents selling the insurance. It is bought over the counter and is available in statutory limited amounts in the form of whole life, limited-payment life, endowment, term, and annuities on a participating basis.

Savings Bank Life Insurance Council: a voluntary association of issuing savings banks formed in 1939 in Massachusetts. It supplies mutual savings banks and their policyholders with various services.

Savings Bond: see *Bond, Savings (U.S.).*

savings certificate: evidence of the ownership of a savings account typically representing a fixed amount of funds deposited for a fixed term. [59]

savings deposits: a deposit of funds to the credit of one or more individuals or to a nonprofit institution which may be subject to 30 days written notice prior to withdrawal. In practice, commercial banks have not required this notice. [69]

savings industry bill: signed by President Bush on August 9, 1989. Under the law, hundreds of savings and loan associations will be closed or merged in a process which could effectively mean the end of the savings industry as it now exists. The independent regulatory apparatus of the Federal Home Loan Bank Board was subsumed by a new Treasury Department entity called the Office of Thrift Supervision. Responsibility for insuring the deposits of savings and loan associations moves to the Federal Deposit Insurance Corporation, and a new body called the Resolution Trust Corporation. The law calls for outlays of some $166 billion over 10 years to close and merge insolvent institutions, and many more billions after that, representing the largest Federal rescue on record. That represents $50 billion to shut the savings institutions that are now insolvent, $40 billion to cover the costs of rescues undertaken in 1988, $33 billion to cover future failures of savings institutions and $43 billion in interest payments. Over 30 years, including interest, the cost is estimated at nearly $300 billion, with taxpayers paying about $225 billion and the healthy portion of the industry paying the rest. The fund insuring savings and loan deposits, the Federal Savings and Loan Insurance Corporation, moves to the Federal Deposit Insurance Corporation. The Savings

Association Insurance Fund (SAIF) replaced the FSLIC. The Resolution Trust Corporation was created to sell more than $300 billion in real estate owned by bankrupt savings and loans. Fraud will be investigated.

savings liability: the aggregate amount of savings accounts of an association's members, including earnings credited to such accounts, less redemptions or withdrawals. [59]

savings rate: a ratio showing the portion of income saved to income earned.

SBLI: see *Savings Bank Life Insurance.*

SC: see *silver certificates.*

scarce currency: in international finance, used to describe the situation where the demand for a particular nation's currency threatens to exhaust the available supply at the usual rates of exchange. When a currency becomes "scarce" in the International Monetary Fund, members of the fund are authorized to introduce exchange restrictions against that nation.

scavenger sale: property taken over by the state as the result of nonpayment of taxes (e.g., failure of a state resident to pay state income taxes). After full notice, the state may hold a public sale of the property to recover monies entitled to it, and the excess of the sale beyond the taxes and penalties due the state are returned to the resident.

schedule demand: see *demand.*

scheduled items: an FSLIC regulatory category in which every insured association is required to include the total amount of its slow loans, real estate owned as a result of foreclosure, and real estate sold on contract or financed at a high loan-to-value ratio. [59]

scheduled payment: a payment promised at a particular time, or one of several payments scheduled as to due date. [28]

schedule of charges: a schedule showing the rate charged by an international department for handling various transactions. [105]

schedule of distribution: a form of accounting which sets forth in detail the estate property contained in each share to be distributed. [37]

schilling: monetary unit of Austria.

school savings: a plan designed to promote the lesson of thrift in children in schools. A bank representative will call at the school one day a week, and assist teachers in accepting deposits in any small amount for the account of the pupil. [10]

scratch: slang, available money.

scrivener's error: a typographical error introduced when reducing an oral agreement to writing or when an agreement is typed or printed in final form.

SCT: see *service counter terminals.*

SD: see *sight draft.*

SD. CO.: see *safe deposit company.*

SDMJ: September, December, March, June (quarterly interest payments or dividends).

SDR: see *special drawing rights.*

search: in the consideration of property transfer, the examination of records for evidence of encumbrances (unpaid taxes, mortgages, etc.) against the property. Synonymous with *title search.*

seasoned loan: a loan that has been on the association's books long enough to demonstrate that the borrower's credit is sound. [59]

seasoned mortgage: periodic payments of a mortgage that are made over a long span based on the borrower's payment structure.

secondary bank reserve: high-grade securities that are readily convertible into money.

secondary beneficiary: a beneficiary whose interest in a trust is postponed or is subordinate to that of the primary beneficiary. [37]

secondary financing: see *junior mortgage.*

secondary mortgage market: an informally constituted market that includes all activity in buying, selling and trading mortgages among originators and purchasers of whole loans and interests in blocks of loans. [59]

secondary rental: a lease determined in part by the landlord's costs. As the landlord's costs (taxes, fuel, etc.) increase, proportionate rent increases are demanded.

secondary reserves: assets other than primary reserves retained by banks and capable of being rapidly converted into cash. Government bonds are a prime example of these assets.

second lien: a lien that ranks following the first lien and is to be fulfilled next.

second mortgage: a mortgage on real property that already possesses a first mortgage.

secretary: an officer of a trust company whose signature is necessary on all official documents. In large trust companies where a secretary's duties are too numerous, the board of directors may appoint assistant secretaries to perform specific duties in connection with his official functions. [10]

secured debt: any debt for which some form of acceptable collateral has been pledged. See *hypothecation.*

secured deposits: bank deposits of state or local government funds which, under the laws of certain jurisdictions, are secured by the pledge of acceptable securities or by a surety contract (known as a depository bond) for the direct protection of these funds. [67]

secured liability: an obligation that has been guaranteed by the pledge of some asset or collateral. In the event of default or inability to liquidate the liability, title of the pledged asset will pass to the creditor. [105]

secured loan: a loan that is made safe, or backed, by marketable securities or other marketable values.

secured note: a note containing a provision that, upon default, certain pledged property may be claimed by the lender as payment of a debt. [78]

securities: any documents that identify legal ownership of a physical commodity or legal claims to another's wealth.

security audit: in operations, an examination of EDP security procedures and measures for evaluating their adequacy and compliance with established policy. [105]

security capital: low-risk capital (e.g., government bonds, mortgages).

security data: a set of characters on a bank card which controls its use and limits fund withdrawals in off-line terminals. It may also contain an enciphered form of the cardholder PIN. [105]

security department: the component of a credit card operation responsible for the investigation, apprehension, and prosecution of individuals perpetrating fraud against the bank; may also be responsible for physical security of the bank card center. [105]

security dollars: synonymous with *investment dollar.*

security element: the property that will secure a loan. [59]

security instrument: the mortgage or trust deed evidencing the pledge of real estate as security for the repayment of the mortgage note. [105]

security interest: an interest that a lender has in the borrower's property to assure repayment. [78]

security officer: a bank representative who has been given responsibility for various phases of internal controls, often including the detecting of fraud and the maintaining of alarm systems and other protective devices. [201]

security record: applied to any accounting record relative to the custody of securities, whether it be for safekeeping, collateral, or trust ownership. [10]

segmentation: a bank marketing strategy involving figuring out who the richest and biggest customers are, showering them with favors, freebies, and other inducements to open or increase their accounts and, if necessary, as it often is, raising rates and fees among the less affluent to pay for it all.

segregated account: used to describe funds segregated to meet obligations which the bank has assumed for a customer. Usually it applies to cash set aside to meet drafts

drawn under a letter of credit issued by the bank. It may also apply to funds set aside to honor checks certified by the bank. It is a *liability account.* [10]

seignorage: a government's profit from issuing coins at a face value higher than the metal's intrinsic worth. It is the difference between the bullion price and the face value of the coins made from it. See *brassage.*

seisin (seizin): taking legal possession of real estate. The rightful owner seizes the property. Cf. *disseisin, replevin.*

selection check: a check, usually automatic, to verify that the correct register or another device has been selected in the performance of an instruction. [21]

self-check: a check deposited in a bank for credit, or one presented for payment in the banking institution on which it was drawn.

Self-Employed Retirement Plan: see *Keogh plan.*

selling the intermarket spread: buying a futures contract in bank CDs and selling Treasury bill futures short.

sender's correspondent bank: a bank with which the sender of a transfer has an account, which may act as a reimbursement bank in a transfer of funds. [105]

sending bank: an entity that inputs the message to the service. [105]

sending bank identifier: a code that identifies the bank that inputs the message to the service. [105]

sending bank input sequence number: a consecutive sequence number that allows for input message control between sending bank and service. [105]

sending bank name: names the bank that inputs the message to the service. [105]

sending bank terminal identifier: a code identifying the terminal or station within the sending bank from which the message was input to the service. [105]

sending bank time and date: time and date that the sending bank message was accepted by the service. [105]

sending bank transaction reference: reference assigned by the sending bank which should uniquely identify the transaction. [105]

send money: funds set aside to commence an activity.

senior: a debt ranking ahead of other debts. Cf. *subordinated.*

sequestered account: an account that has been impounded under due process of law. Since disbursement of such an account is subject to court order, the account is usually set up in a separate control. See *frozen account, receiver.*

sequestration: legal appropriation of property by a third party until there is a settlement of a stated dispute.

serial bond issue: bonds of a single issue which mature on staggered dates rather than all at one time. The purpose of a serial bond issue is to enable the issuer to retire the bonds in small quantities over a long period. [105]

serial bonds payable: a liability account that records the face value of general obligation serial bonds issued and outstanding. [49]

serial issue: a bond issue with a staggered maturity, usually due in equal annual amounts over a period of successive years. [67]

serial letters and numbers: the system of numbering notes assists the checking of quantities put into circulation as well as guarding against counterfeits and forgeries. Misprints whereby different serial numbers appear on the same note are often collected as curiosity items, as are particular combinations of serial numbers. [27]

service charge: a payment by a financial institution against an individual or organization for services rendered or are about to be rendered.

service corporation: a corporation, owned by one or more savings associations, that performs services and engages in certain activities for its owners, such as originating, holding, selling, and servicing mortgages; performing appraisal, brokerage, clerical, escrow, research, and other services; and acquiring, developing, or renovating, and holding real estate for investment purposes. [59]

service counter terminals (SCTs): a device for handling information, located in retail stores and similar places, through which individuals can obtain access to funds and possible credit a their disposal, for purposes of making deposits and withdrawals, and for making third party payments. See *electronic funds transfer system(s), Hinky Dinky.*

service value: the difference between the ledger value of a unit of property and its salvage value. [18]

servicing: in mortgage financing, the performance by the mortgagee or his or her agent of the many services which must be taken care of while the mortgage is held by the institution, such as title search, billing, collection of interest and principal payments, reinspections and reappraisals of the real property, readjustment of the terms of the mortgage contract when necessary, and tax follow-up work.

servicing contract: in secondary-market transactions, a document that details servicing requirements and legally binds the servicing institution to perform them. Such a contract refers to the seller of mortgage participations, binding it to continue accepting loan payments. See also *loan servicing.* [59]

setback: a reversal or partial loss in an activity.

settlement:
(1) the winding up and distribution of an estate by an executor or an administrator; to be distinguished from the administration of an estate by a trustee or a guardian. (2) a property arrangement, as between a husband and wife or a parent and child, frequently involving a trust. [37]

settlement check: a memorandum issued by the manager of a clearinghouse association to settle the results of a clearinghouse exchange between the member banks. This memorandum is sent to the local Federal Reserve Bank, which adjusts the accounts of the clearinghouse banks to settle the debits and credits, or "wins and losses" in the exchange each day. The term may also be used with reference to checks and drafts received in payment of items sent for collection under remittance letters. [10]

settlement clerk: a senior clerk in the proof department of a bank who is responsible for assembling totals

obtained in the proof department. These totals, showing all credits and charges to all departments, are assembled and written on a "settlement sheet," or recap sheet of the proof department. It is from this source that the proof department shows a settlement of the day's work. The settlement sheet then becomes a subsidiary record for the general ledger, and the general ledger bookkeeper may use all final totals shown on this record. [10]

settlements bank: see *Bank for International Settlements.*

settlement sheet: see *settlement clerk.*

settlor: one who finalizes a property settlement (e.g., creator of a trust).

78th: see *factor, 78th.*

severalty: property owned by one person only. See *singular property title, sole owner.*

share: synonymous with *stock.*

share account: see *savings account.*

Sharebuilder Investment Plan (SIP): developed by Merrill Lynch and Chase Manhattan Bank, a plan whereby a depositor's account is debited automatically on a prescribed date and the money transferred to a special sharebuilder account at Chase. The broker buys stock for the depositor the next morning. Chase and Merrill Lynch split the commissions on sales of the plan. There is a three-way split if a correspondent institution makes the sale. Customers benefit from rates discounted from the standard Merrill Lynch schedule, and they can buy stock with weekly or monthly installments too small to cover investments made through normal channels.

share certificate: a certificate of deposit issued by a credit union.

shared-appreciation mortgage: a home-financing technique whereby the borrower receives a mortgage rate that is one-third lower than the prevailing level. But the borrower must agree to give the lender one-third of the profits from the eventual sale of the house. A shared-appreciation mortgage has payments that are based on a long amortization schedule, but the loan becomes due and payable no later than at the end of 10 years. It has an interest rate below that on a conventional mortgage. It has a contingent interest feature, whereby at either the sale or transfer of the property or the refinancing or maturity of the loan, the borrower must pay the lender a share of the appreciation of the property securing the loan.

share draft: an order by a credit union member to pay a third party against funds on deposit with the credit union and cleared through a commercial bank.

sharing: the establishment of EFT systems as a joint enterprise by an organization of depository institutions. Sharing allows the participating depository institutions to divide the responsibilities (risks, costs) of establishing and maintaining POS and ATM systems. The four types of sharing are mandatory sharing, permissive/nondiscriminatory sharing, permissive sharing, and pro-competitive sharing. Detailed descriptions of the four types of sharing are included in *EFT and the Public Interest: A Report of the National Commission of Electronic Fund Transfers.* [105]

shave: a charge that is higher than the accepted rate, made for the handling of a note or other instrument of low quality or when the seller will take a smaller amount for any other reason.

shekel: the official currency of Israel, resurrected from Biblical times, that replaced the pound in 1980.

shelter trust: see *spendthrift provision.*

sheriff's deed: an instrument drawn under order or court to convey title to property sold to satisfy a judgment at law. [62]

Sherman Silver Purchase Act: passed by Congress in 1890, requiring the Secretary of the Treasury to purchase $4^{1}/_{2}$ million ounces of silver monthly and issue in payment Treasury Notes redeemable in gold or silver. Repealed in 1893.

shifting loan: the act of securing funds from other lending banks for assistance at the time banks ask their borrowers to pay their loans.

shilling: monetary unit of Kenya, Somalia, Tanzania, and Uganda.

shinplaster:
(1) any money made worthless either by inflation or by inadequate security.
(2) a pre-Civil War term used to depreciate the value of paper money.
(3) paper money, usually of less than one dollar face value, once used by some private financial institutions.

shoestring: slang, a tiny amount of money.

shortcut foreclosure: a method of foreclosure in which a power of sale clause in the mortgage allows the lender to sell a property if it goes into default. The borrower must be informed, but the issuing of a public statement need not be carried out. Upon property foreclosure, the junior mortgage holders' positions are wiped out, unless the sale yields more than the outstanding first mortgage.

short dates: usually periods up to one week, but sometimes periods up to a month.

short-form mortgage clause: a mortgage clause permitting the buyer to take over the mortgage, subject to and not assuming liability for its payment.

short-funded: where banks buy short-term money at high rates of interest, in the expectation that rates would soon fall and that they subsequently could obtain lendable funds more cheaply.

short of exchange: the position of a foreign exchange trader who has sold more foreign bills than the quantity of bills he or she has in possession to cover sales.

short-term debt: an obligation that is usually due within the year.

short-term funds: money borrowed from 30 days up to one year.

short-term savings account: ordinarily, an account that is to be withdrawn within less than 24 months from the date the account is opened. [59]

short-term Treasury securities: marketable U.S. Treasury bills, bonds, and notes with remaining maturity of less than 18 months held by the nonbank public, less securities held by money market mutual funds. [203]

short-term trust: an irrevocable trust running for a period of 10 years longer, in which the income is payable to a person other than the settlor, and established under the provisions of the Revenue Act of 1954. The income from a trust of this kind is taxable to the income beneficiary and not to the settlor. The agreement may provide that on the date fixed for the termination of the trust, or on the prior death of the income beneficiary, the assets of the trust shall be returned to the settlor. [37]

shut-off rates: high mortgage rates that are designed to turn away prospective buyers.

SI: see *simple interest.*

SIBOR: Singapore Interbank Offered Rate.

side collateral: security for a loan that is less than the required margin, less than the principal amount of the loan or not to be held for the full term of the loan. A loan secured only by side collateral is classified as unsecured. [105]

Sig.: signature.

Sig. Cd.: see *signature card.*

sight draft: a draft payable upon delivery and presentation to the drawee, or *upon sight.*

sight rate: the exchange rate tied to a demand draft or check. Synonymous with *check rate.*

signature book: a book containing facsimiles of the signatures of the authorized officers of a bank who may commit that bank. Such books are exchanged by banks establishing a correspondent relationship. [105]

signature card: a card signed by each depositor and customer of the bank. The signature card is technically a contract between the bank and its customer, in that it recites the obligations of both in their relationship with each other. The principal use of the signature card is that of identification of the depositor. Signature cards are made out in at least two sets, one for the signature file department, where all signatures are kept for ready reference, and the other for the file at the teller's window where the depositor will most frequently transact his business. [10]

signature field: the individual or department within the sending bank that created the message. [105]

signature file department: this department is the custodian for all signature cards. The employees of this department issue daily reports on all accounts opened and all accounts closed. As a part of the public relations and "new business" work, the signature file department may write "thank you" letters to new depositors. [10]

signature guaranteed: a securities industry requirement to have a registered owner of a security have a brokerage firm or a bank guarantee his or her signature so that a good delivery or transfer of the stock can be made.

signature panel: a small elongated rectangular strip, affixed to either side of a bank card during manufacture, which permits the cardholder to write his or her signature on the card. [105]

signed instrument: any legal agreement, or note which is written and signed. [28]

silver certificates: U.S. paper money since 1873 issued as receipts for the stated amount of silver in the U.S. Treasury. The redemption privilege was revoked by Congress in 1968. [27]

silver dollar: coined since 1792, containing 371¼ grains of silver

(77.34 percent of an ounce) and 41¼ grains of alloy. Total weight is 412½ grains. Based on the Spanish dollar.

Silver Purchase Act of 1934: authorized and directed the Secretary of the Treasury to purchase silver at home and abroad until the proportion of silver in the combined stocks of gold and silver of the United States is one-fourth of the total monetary value of such stocks or until the price of silver is $1.29½ an ounce. No time limit is set for the achievement of a 3:1 ratio between gold and silver.

silver standard: that monetary system under which money is convertible into silver at a specified rate, and vice versa, and free shipment of silver internationally is permitted. Cf. *gold standard, paper standard.*

silver wing: slang, a half-dollar (50 cents).

simple interest: interest calculated on a principal sum and not on any interest that has been earned by that sum. Cf. *compounded interest.*

simple trust: used only in tax laws to describe a trust that is required to distribute all of its income currently and that does not provide for any charitable distribution; opposed to *complex trust.* [37]

Singapore dollar CDs: a CD denominated in Singapore dollars.

Singapore interbank offered rate: the rate of interest at which Asian currency units in Singapore are prepared to lend funds to first-class banks.

single debit reporting: normal method used by mortgage bankers for reporting the current status of its mortgages when making a regular remittance to an investor. [22]

single debt: a system of mortgage accounting by which a servicer reports current installments as a lump sum. A detailed payment analysis is given only on uncollected and unscheduled payments. [105]

single-family dwelling: a housing unit designed for ownership and occupancy by one individual or family. [59]

single-lump-sum credit: a closed-end credit arrangement whereby the total outstanding balance is due on a specified date. [78]

single-name account: an account having only one owner. [105]

single-name paper: a note for which only one legal entity—the maker—is obligated to make payment at maturity. A legal distinction exists in single-name paper, in that if the obligation is incurred for one purpose, or one common interest, the paper may have more than one maker or endorser, and still be termed single-name paper. Such a case would be two or more partners making a note for a loan to the common partnership or a subsidiary company making a note endorsed by the parent company. Single-name paper is also frequently termed *straight paper.* [10]

single-payment loan: a loan whose entire principal is due on one maturity date.

single-posting system: a plan of posting used in the bookkeeping department of a bank. Single posting generally means the posting of a depositor's statement only. The ledger record may be either a carbonized ledger created with the posting of the statement, or a photographed record of the statement (under the unit-photographic plan) made on microfilm. This posting plan is to be distinguished from the *dual plan* where the statement is posted in one run and the ledger is posted in another. [10]

single proprietorship: ownership of a business by one person.

single standard: monometallism, where one metal, usually gold, is given free and unlimited coinage.

singular property title: property title granted to only one person. See *severalty.*

situs: Latin, a place or situation where a thing is located. An owner's home is the situs of his personal property.

Sk.: see *safekeeping.*

skate: slang, avoidance of a creditor; the attempt to avoid payment.

Skg.: see *safekeeping.*

skimming: an unauthorized method of duplicating the magnetically encoded data on plastic identification cards. Skimming can be accomplished by covering the magnetic stripe of a card with a piece of recording tape and applying heat. The tape can then be applied to a blank card with another application of heat, thus transferring data from one card to another. It is possible to duplicate cards with this technique without serious degradation in information recording quality. New production methods allow for easy detection of any tampering with the magnetic stripe. [105]

skip account: a cardholder with a balance owing whose whereabouts are unknown. [105]

skip-payment privilege: a privilege provided in certain mortgage contracts that allows the borrower to skip monthly payments at any time the loan is paid ahead of schedule as long as the loan is prepaid. [59]

skunk: slang, to fail to pay a debt.

skyrocketing: slang, a sharp rise in stock prices within a relatively short time period.

S&L Assn.: see *savings and loan association.*

slide: a posting error by which an amount is wrongly recorded by a bookkeeper who unintentionally places the decimal one or more digits to the right or left of the true decimal position.

sliding parity: see *crawling peg.*

slow asset: an asset that can be converted into cash, near its book value, usually after a lengthy passage of time.

slow loan: a Federal Savings and Loan Insurance Corporation regulatory category in which every insured savings association is required to list its delinquent loans. The regulations spell out what constitutes a slow loan in terms of the loan's age and length of delinquency. Loans less than one year old are slow when 60 days delinquent, those between one and seven years old are slow when 90 days delinquent, and so on. [59]

slump: a short-lived decline in the activity of a business or economy.

slush fund: slang, monies given for political purposes with the expectation that it will influence the receiver to favor the giver.

S&M: September and March (semiannual interest payments or dividends).

SM: see *second mortgage.*

small bread: slang, a small amount of money.

small loan: sometimes used to designate a personal cash loan. [41]

small loan law: a regulatory code covering cash installment loans, administered by the state, and protecting both the borrower and the lender. [55]

small potatoes: slang, a small amount of money.

small-saver certificates: certificates issued in denominations of less than $100,000 with maturities of 2.5 years or more.

small-size notes: American paper money since 1928, characterized by new designs and a smaller size. [27]

"smart" credit cards: originally developed in France, a credit card that deducts charges from a customer's bank balance at point of sale. For banks and stores, the advantage of "smart" credit cards is increased automation and expected lower costs. A unique feature is that such cards can have information placed on them and altered with ease. See *carte à mémoire.*

Smithsonian Agreements (1971): a reassessment (upward) of the value of foreign currencies in relation to the dollar. [105]

snake system: an international agreement between Belgium, The Netherlands, Luxembourg, Denmark, Sweden, Norway, and West Germany, linking the currencies of these countries together in an exchange rate system. The signatories have agreed to limit fluctuations in exchange rates among their currencies to 2.25 percent above or below set median rates. The snake was designed to be the first stage in forming a uniform Common Market currency. Members maintain fairly even exchange rates among themselves by buying or selling their currencies when the rates threaten to drop or rise beyond the 2.25 percent limits specified.

SO: see *standing order.*

Social Security Payment Program: a cooperative effort between the Social Security Administration and the U.S. Treasury Department devoted to planning and implementing a system for direct deposits of Social Security benefit payments to individuals, initially by distributing checks directly to recipients' banks, to be followed by gradual conversion from checks to tape. [36]

Society for Worldwide Interbank Financial Telecommunications (SWIFT): an organization developing a system for the electronic transfer of funds among participating banks in Europe and North America. [36]

Society of Savings and Loan Controllers: formed in 1950 under the sponsorship of the American Savings and Loan Institute as a professional organization, the society is devoted to improving the professional status of accounting and auditing officers through the development of better accounting methods and new aids to management. The society presently exists as a separate organization closely allied to institute activities and interests. This organization consists of more than 1500 of the principal accounting and chief auditing officers in savings associations. The society's technical publications

are available on a subscription basis to nonmembers. [51]

SOE: see *short of exchange.*

soft currency: the funds of a country that are controlled by exchange procedures, thereby having limited convertibility into gold and other currencies.

soft loan: a loan whose terms of repayment are generous, at times holding a low rate of interest.

soft money: paper currency, as contrasted with coinage (hard money).

soil bank: a farm program established by the government to pay farmers for removing land from cultivation.

sol: monetary unit of Peru.

sola: any overseas bill of exchange or check made up on one document instead of a check or bill drawn together.

solde: French for *balance.*

sold loan: a mortgage loan that has been sold to another institution but is still serviced by the seller. [59]

sold-out market: a market in which liquidations of weakly held contracts has largely been completed and offerings have become scarce. [2]

sole owner: the only person holding the title to a specific property or business. See *severalty.*

sole proprietorship: a proprietorship in which all equity lies with one individual.

solicit: to offer additional credit to a customer. [55]

solvency: exists when liabilities, other than those of ownership, amount to less than the total assets; the ability to pay debts.

solvent: the condition of an individual who is able to pay his or her debts.

solvent debtor section: a part of the Bankruptcy Tax Act of 1980 whereby a company that buys back its own bonds at a discount price must pay income tax on the spread between the face value of the bonds, or the original sales price, and the discount repurchase price.

Sonnie Mae: the New York State Mortgage Authority.

So. shilling: monetary unit of Somalia.

source document: a record used by the association of the initial recording of a transaction. [59]

source of shifts analysis: a means of assessing the effects of new accounts on the monetary aggregates. [98]

sovereign risk limit: a bank's limit on the amount of money in the Euromarkets that it is prepared to lend to one government.

SP: see *stop payment.*

special administrator: an administrator appointed by the court to take over and safeguard an estate pending the appointment of an executor or administrator; sometimes known as *temporary administrator.* [37]

special bank credit plans: lines of credit extended to borrowers by banks. Based upon a prearranged limit, the borrower may use all or part of the credit by writing a check. Interest charges are based on the amount of credit used during the month and the total amount outstanding. [78]

special checking account: see *pay-as-you-go accounts.*

special depository: any bank authorized by the U.S. Treasury to receive as deposits the proceeds of sales of government bonds.

special devise: a gift, by will, of a specific parcel of real property. [32]

special drawing rights (SDRs): the amount by which each country is permitted to have its international checking account with the International Monetary Fund go negative before the nation must ask for additional loans. SDRs were established at the Rio de Janeiro conference of 1967. Cf. *collective reserve unit.*

special endorsement: an endorsement that transfers title to a negotiable instrument to a party specified in the endorsement. [59]

special fee account: see *pay-as-you-go accounts.*

special guardian: a guardian appointed by a court for a particular purpose connected with the affairs of a minor or an incompetent person; sometimes a guardian ad litem is known as a special guardian. See *guardian ad litem.* [37]

special indorsement: see *special endorsement.*

special interest account: used by commercial banks to describe a savings account. Some states do not permit a commercial bank to accept savings accounts. However, deposits may be accepted on which interest is paid and under the same interest-bearing rates as a savings bank, but another name, such as *special interest accounts,* must be used.

special issues: securities issued by the U.S. Treasury for investment of reserves of government trust funds and for certain payments to veterans.

specialized examination: examination performed twice in a two-year period between general exams, which focus on specific departments and review of directors' and committee minutes, and regulatory reports. [105]

special security: effective September 1981, banks and savings and loan associations are able to take the deposits resulting from their new tax-exempt savings certificates and reinvest the money in securities offered by the Federal National Mortgage Association. See *All-Savers certificates.*

special supervisory examination: examination of banks with problems and conditions requiring more than two reviews in one year. [105]

specie: money in coin.

specie payment: payment in coin rather than with paper money.

specifications: in foreign exchange, the conditions and terms used with bills of exchange drawn under letters of credit.

specific deposit: a deposit made for a specific purpose, for example, bond coupons deposited for collection purpose only. Not a general deposit. The bank becomes only the agent or bailee of the depositor, not the debtor. The distinction is important in the case of bankruptcy or failure to follow instructions.

specific devise: a gift, by will, of a specific parcel of real property. [37]

specific duty: a customs duty based on weight, quantity, or other physical characteristics of imported items.

spendthrift provision: a provision in a trust instrument which limits the right of the beneficiary to dispose of his interest, as by assignment, and the right of his creditors to reach it, as by attachment. [32]

spendthrift trust: see *spendthrift provision.*

spillover trust: type of trust which by its terms is merged with or added to another trust or estate upon the occurrence of a certain event. See *pourover.* [37]

split deposit: the act of simultaneously cashing a check and depositing some portion of it in a bank account. [105]

split-rate account: a passbook savings account that pays increasing rate of interest, up to regulatory maximums, for increasing account balances. [59]

split-schedule loan: a mortgage that establishes interest for only a few years and then a complete amortization schedule. The loan is usually accomplished through split amortization schedules on the loan.

sponsored nonrecourse plan: an indirect lending arrangement without recourse, but with the agreement that a dealer will repurchase from a bank either a defaulted contract or the repossessed goods. [105]

sponsorship: the banking institution holding an interest in the selling price of a specific securities issue.

spooks: see *fictitious paper.*

spot against forward: a central bank's limit to control the extent to which banks can hold net current assets in foreign currency against net forward liabilities. The purpose is to prevent a buildup of foreign currency assets outside the official reserves.

spot cash: immediate cash payment as distinguished from payment at a later date.

spot exchange rate: the price of one country's currency in terms of another country's currency that is effective for immediate (today) delivery.

spot exchange transaction: a purchase or sale of foreign currency for ready delivery. In practice, market usage normally prescribes settlement within two working days. For purposes of the International Monetary Fund's Articles of Agreement, the term excludes transactions in banknotes or coins. [42]

spot/fortnight: see *spot/next.*

spot/next: a purchase of currency on Monday for settlement on Thursday is transacted at the exchange rate for spot delivery plus an adjustment for the extra day. The adjustment is referred to as the *spot/next. Spot/week* refers to delivery a week after spot; *spot/fortnight* refers to delivery a fortnight after spot.

spot/week: see *spot/next.*

spousal IRA: an IRA for the non-working spouse.

spraying trusts: synonymous with *sprinkling trusts.*

spread:

(1) *finance:* two prices given instead of one.

(2) *finance:* the difference between two prices.

sprinkling trusts: trusts in which the income or principal is distributed among the members of a designated class in amounts and proportions as may be determined in the discretion of the trustee. Synonymous with *spraying trusts.* [37]

square: a position in a currency, security, or commodity which is balanced (i.e., neither long nor short).

squeeze: when interest rates are high and money is difficult to borrow.

stabilization fund: a 1934 fund created as a result of the dollar devaluation with $2 billion to stabilize

exchange values of the U.S. dollar for dealing in foreign exchange and gold and to invest in direct government obligations. Under the Bretton Woods Agreement much of the assets of the Fund were used to contribute to the international Bank for Reconstruction and Development and the International Monetary Fund.

stabilized dollar: a plan to provide constant purchasing power for the U.S. dollar by making it into a commodity standard by means of altering the weight of the gold content of the dollar to compensate for changing prices.

stabilizing bid: a bid that the managers of an issue make for the bonds which have been issued to prevent the price of the security from going below the issue price for a certain period after the issue.

stable money: currency that remains constant in terms of the items and services it can purchase.

stake: slang, a rather substantial amount of money.

stale: a bill of exchange payable on demand, or a check, which appears on the face of it to have been in circulation for an unreasonable time period.

stale check: any check dated 90 days prior to presentation for payment.

stamped notes: paper money issued with revenue stamps on it to add to the value.[27]

standard bullion: bullion containing the same proportions of metals and the same degree of purity as the standard gold and silver coins and, thereby, making the bullion ready for coinage without further refining.

standard money: the money or unit of money on which a particular nation's monetary system is based.

standards of practice: formulated for the guidance of commercial banks operating in the installment credit field, sets forth certain standards that should be followed at all times. [105]

standard stocks: securities of established and well-known firms.

standard underwriting: the purchase pursuant to agreement by investment banking firms of the unsold portion of an issue offered by the issuing company directly to its own security holders or some other restricted group.

standby commitment: commitment for a limited period made, for a fee, as security for a construction lender by an investor who stands ready to make or purchase the committed loan at above-market terms in the event that a take-out commitment cannot be obtained on market terms. [22]

standby contract: an optional delivery forward placement contract; obligates the seller of the contract to purchase some financial instrument at the option of the buyer of the contract. [202]

standby credit:
(1) an International Monetary Fund arrangement where a member receives assurance that, during a fixed time period, requests for drawing on the IMF will be permitted on the member's representation as to need.
(2) an arrangement with a bank or group of banks whereby they agree to make a certain amount of funds available to a borrower for a specified time period.

standby letter of credit: a letter of credit or similar arrangement that represents an obligation on the part of the issuing bank to a designated third party (the beneficiary) contingent upon the failure of the issuing bank's customer (the account party) to perform under the terms of the underlying contract with the beneficiary, or obligates the bank to guarantee or stand as surety for the benefit of a third party to the extent permitted by law or regulation. [202]

standby offering: an offering of rights by a firm where an underwriter offers to stand-by to purchase any of the rights the firm is unable to sell.

standing authorization: an authorization that is executed once between a customer and a company to cover all paperless entries generated by the company for the customer's account thereafter of the same amount and for the same purpose. This contrasts with a single-entry authorization, which covers only a single paperless entry. [105]

standing mortgage: a loan in which interest is paid at specified intervals, but no principal payments are made; the entire loan falls due at maturity.

standing order: an authority given by the customer for the bank to regularly pay funds, usually a fixed dollar amount, from his or her demand deposit account.

standstill agreement: an arrangement between a debtor and a creditor under which exist new limits and conditions for the loan. Typically, a postponement of obligation payment is the result. Cf. *novation.*

star notes: U.S. replacement notes. Also the name given to some interest-bearing notes issued in 1837 by the Treasury of Texas. [27]

starred card: generally indicates that purchases under $100 do not require an authorization. [105]

state bank: a bank that is organized according to the laws of a state and is chartered by the state in which it is located to operate as a banking business. The various states have different laws governing the operation of banks.

state banking department: the organization in each state which supervises the operations and affairs of state banking institutions. The chief officer of this department is designated superintendent of banks or commissioner of banks or is given some comparable title. [39]

state bank notes: an American term referring to issues by banks which are subject to the laws in the state, as opposed to federal laws. [27]

stateless: slang, currency deposited in banks outside the country of original issue and used by the banks like any other exchange medium.

statement:
(1) a record prepared by a bank for a depositor listing all checks drawn and deposits made together with the new balance after each posting.
(2) a summary of transactions between a creditor and his or her debts or a presentation of names and amounts of accounts to show a financial condition (e.g., an IRS statement).

statement balance: that dollar amount representing the sum of the previous balance due plus cash advances and merchandise purchases for the billing period less credit for payments and/or merchandise returns plus any appropriate finance charges and service charge. [105]

statement clerk: an employee in the bookkeeping department of a bank. This title has two different meanings as applied to the duties of the clerk. In some banks the statement clerk posts the statements for depositors' checking accounts under the dual system. In other banks this title is used in describing an employee who is responsible for verification of all paid checks listed on a depositor's statement to see that the statement is complete before it is mailed to the depositor. [10]

statement film: photocopy of the actual billing statement. [105]

statement of condition: a detailed listing of a bank's resources, liabilities, and capital accounts showing its conditions on a given date. On requests (calls) by supervisory authorities several times a year, banks are required to submit sworn statements of condition. In general accounting, this type of financial report is known as a *balance sheet*. [50]

statement of liability: an expression of a cardholder's responsibilities stated on the reverse side of credit cards, cardholder agreements, or on other printed documents. [105]

statement of loan: a statement itemizing all details of a loan transaction which must be given to the borrower at the time the loan is negotiated. [55]

statement of operations: a summary of the financial operations during a given period showing the sources of income and its allocation to the payment of operating expenses, dividends to holders of savings accounts, and allocations to reserves for the protection of savers. [51]

statement savings: a savings account in which a periodic statement replaces the passbook. [105]

statement savings account: a savings account for which the customer records his or her own balance and transactions information. A periodic balance statement is received from the bank. The balance statement is reconciled to the customer's records. [105]

statement stub: the portion of a cardholder statement which is returned with the payment. [105]

state notes: issued by an American state, now forbidden. [27]

State Street: Boston's financial area.

statewide banking: the establishment of bank branches throughout a state. [105]

statused account: a cardholder record to which a status code has been posted, indicating a condition under which the cardholder may not use his account. See *blocked accounts.* [105]

status report: a hard-copy record of the status of all cardholder accounts or group of accounts on which there has been activity. [105]

statute of frauds: a law that requires certain contracts, such as agreements of sale, to be in writing in order to be enforceable. [62]

statutes of distribution: laws, rules, or statutes governing the distribution of personal property under intestacy. [37]

statutory exemptions: specified articles of personal property and a specified amount of cash left by a decedent which are set apart for his or her immediate family and which may not be subjected to the claims of creditors. [37]

statutory fee: the administrative cost of closing a loan. [78]

sterilizing gold: a strategy for preventing newly imported gold from expanding the credit base of a nation. One method is to have the U.S. Treasury pay for the gold with a draft on a commercial bank in which it has an account rather than drawing upon the Federal Reserve System and then issuing gold certificates. Cf. *desterilizing gold.*

sterling: the currency of Great Britain. The unit is the pound sterling. May also represent bills of exchange that are drawn in terms of British currency. Sterling silver is silver of at least 222 parts out of 240 of pure silver, and no more than 18 parts of an alloy.

sterling balances: sums held in sterling by a foreign nations and private persons.

sterling bloc: those nations whose trade is heavily with England and whose monetary program and currencies were kept at parity with the English pound through monetary reserves deposited in London. The bloc included the Scandinavian countries, Uruguay, Bolivia, the countries of the British Empire, and to an extent Argentina and Japan. The bloc came into existence when England left the gold standard in 1931 and the block was replaced by the sterling area in 1939.

sterling exchange: a check or bill denominated in pounds sterling and payable through a bank in the United Kingdom.

Stg.: see *sterling.*

St. Louis equation: introduced in 1968 to investigate the relative impact of monetary and fiscal actions on economic activity. [100]

stock: the legal capital of a corporation divided into shares.

stock association: a savings association organized as a capital stock corporation, with investors providing operating capital by purchasing an ownership interest in the institution, represented by shares of stock. Their stock holdings entitle them to virtually the same rights as stockholders in any other corporation, including a share of the profits. Stock associations operate in 23 states. [59]

stock registrar: a bank, financial institution, or person permitted to serve in a fiduciary position, to certify that a corporation's issued shares have not exceeded the approved amount.

stock savings bank: a bank established under state law as a profit-making organization with customary capital stock and shareholders that can accept time deposits for the purpose of saving. Most of these banks now provide expanded services and are indistinguishable from traditional commercial banks.

stolen card: a bank card that has been stolen either through the mail or directly from the cardholder of receipt. [105]

stop: the lowest rate the central bank charges dealers who temporarily tender their government securities for cash in these operations.

stop-out price: the lowest accepted price for Treasury bills at the regular weekly auction. [88]

stop payment: the order given to a bank by a depositor who wishes to prevent payment on a check he or she has issued. The depositor requests the bank to stop payment of the item in writing, or telephones the instructions and confirms them in writing.

straight: a bond with unquestioned right to repayment of principal at a specified future date, unquestioned right to set interest payments on given dates, and no right to any additional interest, principal, or conversion privilege.

straight amortization plan: an amortization plan that provides for the payment of a fixed amount of principal at specified intervals, with interest payable on the remaining balance of the loan. [44]

straight bankruptcy: a proceeding by which an individual files for release from his debts after a court arranges for his creditors to divide whatever assets he has. [76]

straight credit: a credit instrument under which the beneficiary is paid by a bank in his or her area that has been designated by the bank opening the credit. The drafts are usually drawn in the currency of the exporter. The paying bank debits the payment to the account of the opening bank on the books of the paying bank. [105]

straight lease: a lease describing regular rental payments (e.g., monthly, quarterly). Synonymous with *flat lease.*

straight letter of credit: a letter of credit in which the insurer (e.g., a bank) recognizes only the person named (e.g., an exporter) as authorized to draw drafts under the letter for advances to the named person for whose benefit the letter is issued.

straight-line interest: a method of computing interest payments which takes a straight percentage of the unpaid balance on an annual basis. [105]

straight loan: a loan to an individual or other legal entity; the basis for granting credit is the debtor's general ability to pay, unsupported by any form of collateral security.

straight mortgage: a mortgage under which the borrower is obligated to pay interest during the term of the mortgage with the full amount of the principal to become due at the end of the mortgage term.

straight paper: all unsecured notes, bills of exchange, and acceptances.

straight-reduction plan: an amortization plan that provides for the payment of a fixed amount of principal at specified intervals, with interest payable on the remaining balance of the loan. [105]

straight-term mortgage loan: a mortgage loan granted for a fixed term of years, the entire loan becoming due at the end of that time. [44]

straight-term plan: an amortization plan that provides for the payment of a fixed amount of principal at specified intervals, with interest payable on the remaining balance of the loan. [105]

street practice: any unwritten practice used by the financial community.

stretching the payables: deferring payments on accounts payable beyond the due date.

stretch the float: keeping cash in a high-interest account as long as possible before using it to pay bills.

strict foreclosure: a legal proceeding in which the association brings court action against the borrower and the court sets a date by which the borrower must redeem his or her debt in full, or the title will pass automatically to the association without public sale. [59]

stringency: a money market condition in which it is hard to obtain credit, accompanied by an increase in the rates of interest.

string of coconuts: slang, money, especially a large number of bills.

stripped Treasury obligations: an artificial equivalent of zero-coupon bonds, featuring Treasury issues, with the safety of government debt. Represents a call on interest payments of U.S. government obligations, with maturities from three months to 29 years.

Sub.: see *subordination.*

subject bid: a bid that is negotiable, rather than firm.

subject offer: an offer that is not firm but instead exploratory, in the expectation that it might induce a bid permitting additional negotiation on price.

subject to check: any payable-on-demand check where the customer need not inform the bank of his desire to withdraw funds. All commercial checking accounts are subject to check.

subject to collection: although a bank has accepted a deposit for immediate credit to an account, funds that the bank is not able to collect for some reason will be charged back to the account. [105]

subject to count: a deposit that has been credited to an account is subject to adjustment if later counting shows a discrepancy. [105]

subject to sale: when property has been offered for sale, a "subject to sale" stipulation provides for the automatic withdrawal of the offer if the property is sold before the party to whom the stipulation was made has accepted the offer.

subject to verification: although a particular deposit has been accepted for immediate credit to an account, if mathematical verification of the amount of the deposit differs from that shown on the deposit ticket, the appropriate adjustment will be made to the account. [105]

sublease: the letting of premises to a third party with the original tenant retaining an interest in the property. All or part of the leased property may be subleased. If the tenant gives up his or her entire interest, the transaction becomes an assignment of lease. See *underlease.*

submission: mortgage banker's offering of mortgages for purchase by an investor. [22]

submittal notice: a broker's notification to a property owner stating that the owner's property has been offered for sale; offering price and prospect's name and address are included.

submortgage: the result of a pledge by a lender of a mortgage in his or her possession as collateral to obtain a loan for himself or herself.

subordinated: a promise to pay which cannot legally be fulfilled until payments on certain other obligations have been made and any other conditions, defined in the indenture, are met. Cf. *senior.*

subordinated debenture: a special debenture whose bearer has a chance for payment lower than that for other creditors. As it holds a higher yield, it is considered a risky bond.

subordinated exchangeable variable-rate note: competing with bank loans, this note has the flexibility that it offers a company to raise money at prevailing short-term rates while providing the built-in option to fix the rate for longer periods.

subordinated interest: an interest in property that is inferior to another interest (e.g., a second mortgage that is inferior to the first mortgage). Cf. *equal dignity.*

subordinated notes and debentures: a form of debt issued by a bank or a consolidated subsidiary. When issued by a bank, it is not insured by a federal agency, is subordinated to the claims of depositors, has an original weighted average maturity of seven years or more, and is not subject to federal interest rate limitations. [202]

subordination: acknowledgment by a creditor in writing that the debt due him from a specified debtor shall have a status inferior or subordinate to the debt which the debtor owes another creditor. [44]

subordination agreement: where more than one legal entity has an interest or claim upon the assets of a prospective borrower, a bank may require that the other interested parties sign subordination agreements before a loan will be granted. The subordination agreement is an agreement in which another interested party grants the bank a priority claim or preference to the assets of the borrower ahead of any claim that he or she may have. [10]

subparticipation: where a bank or group of banks make a loan to borrower and then arranges for other banks to take on part of the loan.

Subsidiary Account Number (SAN): the encoded number identifying an individual account other than the primary account. [105]

subsidiary coins: coins with a denomination of less than one dollar, including minor coins such as pennies or cents.

subsidiary ledger: individual records of mortgage loan accounts, savings accounts, loans in process, and other accounts whose total appear in the general ledger. [59]

subsidy: a sum of money granted by the state to assist in the establishment or support of an enterprise or program which is considered to be of some advantage to the public.

Substitution Account: a plan of the International Monetary Fund that would allow dollar holders to exchange them for assets denominated in a basket of currencies known as special drawing rights (SDRs). The objective of the plan is to reduce the $500 billion to $1 trillion floating around the world, and thus cut the gyrations of the international financial markets. See *special drawing rights.*

subtenant: a tenant who leases a premises from another tenant; a sublessee. See *sublease.*

subvene: a grant, such as a subsidy.

succession:
(1) following another in an office, estate, and so on.
(2) the transfer of all the rights and obligations of a deceased person to those who are entitled to inherit.

succession tax: a tax on the privilege of receiving property, either by descent or by will. It is not a burden on property.

successive beneficiaries:
(1) beneficiaries who receive one after another by succession. Thus, under a will in which property is left to A for life, then to B for life, and then to C outright, B and C are successive beneficiaries.
(2) the inheritance of property by descent or transmission to the next in a succession—as from parent to child and so on down the direct line. [37]

sucre: monetary unit of Ecuador.

Suffolk bank system: a Massachusetts plan started in 1837, under which participating banks agreed to accept only the notes of such out-of-town banks as maintained a sufficient redemption account in the system. This held the notes of participating banks at par.

sum at disposal: an amount of money held available in cash at the office of a bank for a beneficiary at the instructions of another. [105]

summarizing entry: an entry in journal form written below the footings in a columnar journal showing the debits and credits to be equal.

summary deposit ticket: a special deposit ticket used by customers with large numbers of deposit items. [105]

super-NOW: accounts offered by banks and thrifts on January 5, 1983, permitting unlimited monthly transactions with a minimum balance of $2,500. The Super-NOW pays a near-market rate of interest, with a yield somewhat lower than that on the money market deposit account because banks have to post a reserve of 12 percent against the super-NOWS.

superprime instrument: a 10-day, nonrenewable note priced only a fraction above what a bank itself pays for funds.

supervisory merger: a move in the banking industry, where an institution in serious danger is forced to merge with a stronger one. To encourage this movement, loans are provided by the government-managed Federal Savings and Loan Insurance Corporation.

supplementary special deposits: see *corset.*

support: action by a person, organization, or government agency such as the Federal Reserve Banks in buying government securities in the open market or of the Department of Agriculture in purchasing agricultural commodities in the market. This practice tends to push prices of the products or items upward.

supreme court of finance: popular name for the seven-member Federal Reserve Board.

Sur.: see *surplus.*

surcharge: an added charge to a tax or other cost or account.

surety:
(1) a bond, guaranty, or other security that protects a person, corporation, or other legal entity in cases of another's default in the payment of a given obligation, improper performance of a given contract, malfeasance of office, and so on.
(2) an individual who agrees, usually in writing, to be responsible for the performance of another on a contract, or for a certain debt or debts of another individual.

suretyship: obligations to pay the debt or default of another; the function of being a *surety.*

sur mortgage: a document that demands that a person who has defaulted on mortgage payments show cause why the mortgage should not foreclose.

surplus:
(1) anything remaining or left over.
(2) the surplus account is a part of the capital structure of a bank, and is carried in the general ledger. Before a bank can open for business as a national bank, it must have a beginning surplus equal to 20 percent of the paid-in capital stock. A state bank must conform to whatever the laws of the state require as pertaining to surplus. After a bank has opened, the surplus account is made up of all past earnings less the dividends declared and paid from the profits. National banks are required to carry a minimum of 10 percent of each previous six months' earnings to their surplus account before the Comptroller of the Currency will approve the payment of a dividend. State laws deal with surplus requirements in various ways. The surplus is a part of the net worth or ownership of the bank, and in case of liquidation, any remaining portion of surplus after all creditors have been satisfied will be divided in the same related percent as the capital stock held by the stockholders. [10]
(3) excess of assets over the total liabilities and capital.

surplus fund: see *guaranty fund.*

surrender of lease: a mutual agreement between landlord and tenant to terminate all aspects of a lease before its normal expiration date.

survivorship account: an account in the names of two or more persons, each signature alone being sufficient authority for the withdrawal of funds, the balance in the account belonging to the survivor or survivors on the death of the other or others. See *alternate account, joint account.* [50]

survivorship annuity: an annuity paid to a beneficiary following the death of the individual providing for such annuity.

suspense account: an account in the general ledger used to hold over unposted items so that the business day can be closed in a state of balance.

suspense fund: a fund established to account separately for certain receipts pending the distribution or disposal thereof. [49]

suspension: a temporary closing of a bank.

Svensk Exportkredit: a Swedish company half owned by the state, half by a consortium of commercial banks; founded in 1962 for the provision of export finance at commercial rates. [145]

Sveriges Investeringsbank: the Swedish bank (state-owned) which provides, inter alia, finance for exports on commercial terms. [145]

swap:
(1) to exchange or barter.
(2) an arrangement between the central banks of two countries for standby credit to facilitate the exchange of each other's currencies. See *credit, swap network.*

swap contract: an agreement between two parties for the exchange of a series of cash flows, one representing a fixed rate and the other a floating rate. See also *interest rate swap.*

swap credits: standby credits established on a reciprocal basis from time to time among major central banks and the Bank for International Settlements enabling the central bank of a nation to settle a debit balance in its international account with another participating nation by using the latter nation's currency in place of having to resort to foreign or gold exchange.

swap drawing: a reciprocal credit exchange between the Federal Reserve and a foreign central bank in which the foreign central bank exchanges (swaps) its own currency for dollars up to an agreed maximum amount over a limited time, normally three months. [203]

swap line: a mutual credit facility whereby a government buys a foreign currency from a foreign central bank, uses the foreign currency held by foreigners, and agrees to sell the foreign currency bank to the foreign central bank at the end of three or six months. [105]

swap network: to finance U.S. interventions in the foreign exchange market, a series of short-term reciprocal credit lines between foreign banks under which the Federal Reserve System exchanges dollars for the currencies of other nations within the group, thereby allowing the Fed to buy dollars in the foreign exchange market. See *swap.*

sweat equity: equity created by the labor of a purchaser or borrower that increases the value of the property. [62]

sweating: to lower the metallic content of gold coins so that the coin can eventually be used and the gold dust can be recovered.

sweep accounts: where banks automatically transfer checking account deposits into a money market fund once they exceed a certain, generally high threshold, and just as automatically transfers the money back into the checking account when the checking balance falls too low. Synonymous with *overflow accounts.*

SWIFT: see *Society for Worldwide Interbank Financial Telecommunications.*

swing loan: a loan extended to enable the borrower to purchase real estate where the proceeds of sale of another property will be used to repay the loan. Synonymous with *bridge loan.* [105]

syli: monetary unit of Guinea.

symmetallism:
(1) a monetary system where paper currency is redeemable in two or more metals which are paid in a fixed and proportionate combination.
(2) a standard coin combining two or more precious metals.

syndicate:
(1) the association of two or more individuals, established to carry out a business activity. Members share in all profits or losses, in proportion to their contribution to the resources of the syndicate. Cf. *joint venture, partnership.*
(2) a group of investment bankers and securities dealers who, by agreement among themselves, have joined together for the purpose of distributing a new issue of securities for a corporation.

syndicate agreement: a document used for joining together members of an underwriting or loan syndicate.

syndicated loan: a loan in which a number of banks around the world participate.

syndicate manager: synonymous with *managing underwriter.*

syndicate member: an investment banker, brokerage house, or bank which joins with others under the guidance of a syndicate manager in the underwriting and distribution of a security issue.

syndicate restrictions: contractual obligations placed on an underwriting group for a security relating to distribution; price limitations, and market transactions. See *syndicate termination.*

syndicate termination (release): the point when syndicate restrictions are terminated; occurs when a security involved in trading or expected to trade at or over its initial offering price. This does not necessarily apply in the Eurobond market.

synthetic fixed-rate loan: a concept for the financial community; for borrowers, these loans would provide the security of fixed interest costs, and for lenders, it would have all the advantages of floating rates.

TA: see *tangible assets.*

tab: slang, an unpaid bill.

tables, annual investment accumulation: shows amounts to be invested yearly at a given rate of interest which will accumulate to $1,000 in a given number of years. [12]

tales, discount: tables showing the present value of a unit of money due at the end of various periods of time, or the present value of one unit per period for various periods of time at various rates. [12]

tables, interest: see *interest table*.

tacking: a process of adding a junior claim to a senior one in order to create some gain. Used in a mortgage, as when a third mortgage holder adds the first mortgage and tacks them to assume a superior position over the second mortgage holder. Cf. *equal dignity*.

taha: monetary unit of Bangladesh.

tail: in U.S. Treasury cash auctions, the difference between the average issuing price and the stop-out price.

take: to lay hold of, seize, or have in possession. See *seisin (seizin)*.

takeout loan: permanent loan on real property which takes out the interim, construction lender. [22]

taker: a borrower.

tala: monetary unit of Samoa.

tale: contracts detailing payment of metallic monies, where there is a request *by tale,* that is, by count, as contrasted with payment based on weight.

talon:
(1) a special coupon (e.g., a voucher stub).
(2) that part of a debt instrument remaining on an unmatured bond after the interest coupons that were formerly attached have been presented.

TAN: see *tax-anticipation note*.

tandem plan: a method of keeping home financing active by the purchase of mortgages by GNMA for resale to FNMA at a discount. [105]

tangible assets: physical and material (perceptible to touch) assets, as distinguished from intangible assets, which are imperceptible to touch. Examples of tangible assets are cash, land, and buildings.

tangible net worth:
(1) ordinarily, the total capital accounts (owned capital) less miscellaneous assets (intangibles). Synonymous with *total net worth*.
(2) the difference between a company's equity and the valuation of any intangible assets. [105]

tangible property: property in physical form. It can be touched, such as a house or land.

tap: slang, to ask a person or a lending organization for money.

tap CD: a certificate of deposit issued by a bank on an as-required basis with a minimum denomination of $25,000 and for a minimum of one month in dollars.

taux d'intérêt: French for *interest rate*.

taw: slang, sufficient funds to fully finance a business venture.

taxable equivalent yield: the yield on a bond producing taxable income which would be required to match the yield on a tax-exempt bond.

taxable gifts: property transferred by giver to the extent that its value exceeds allowable exemptions, exclusions, and deductions. [105]

taxable value: an assessed value utilized for taxing property, items, or income.

tax act of 1981: see *Economic Recovery Tax Act of 1981*.

tax anticipation note (TAN): any short-term, interest-bearing obligation created to be bought by businesses with monies assembled as a reserve in order to pay taxes. These notes are sold by government agencies to increase revenue.

tax anticipation warrant: see *tax anticipation note*.

tax cost: the figure used as the starting point under which gain or loss on a sale or exchange of property is determined. In the usual case, this gain or loss is simply the difference between the amount that a taxpayer paid for property (adjusted for depreciation) and the amount received when the taxpayer sells it. [37]

tax deed: a deed issued to the buyer of property that is sold because of nonpayment of taxes.

tax exemption: a right, secured by law, permitting freedom from a charge of taxes (e.g., on income that constitutes primary support of a child).

tax foreclosure: the taking of property because of unpaid taxes.

tax-free rollover: provision whereby an individual receiving a lump-sum distribution from a qualified pension or profit sharing plan can preserve the tax-deferred status of these funds by a "rollover" into an IRA or another qualified plan if rolled over within 60 days of receipt. [105]

tax lease: a long-term lease issued to the buyer of tax-delinquent property when the law prevents an outright sale.

tax lien: a lien by the government against real property for unpaid taxes.

tax liens receivable: legal claims against property which have been exercised because of nonpayment of delinquent taxes, interest, and penalties. The account includes dlinquent taxes, interest, and penalties receivable up to the date the lien becomes effective and the cost of holding the sale. [49]

tax note: see *tax anticipation note.*

tax penalty: forfeiture of a sum because of nonpayment of taxes. [62]

Tax Reform Act of 1969: federal legislation removing major benefits from controlled corporations. Multiple surtax exemptions and multiple accumulated earnings credits were withdrawn by 1975, and the incentives for establishing additional corporations within a controlled group ceased at the end of 1974. The law provided for the accumulation of capital losses to the three preceding years prior to the loss of revenue for a corporation, with no change in the future five-year advance provision for capital losses. Restrictions are given on employee benefit plans. See *Tax Reform Act of 1976, Tax Reform Act of 1984, Tax Reform Act of 1986.*

Tax Reform Act of 1976: federal legislation affecting income, estate, and gift taxes. The holding period to qualify for long-term capital gains was increased from 6 to 12 months. Also placed new restrictions on tax shelters. See also *Tax Reform Act of 1969, Tax Reform Act of 1984, Tax Reform Act of 1986.*

Tax Reform Act of 1984: federal legislation enacted by Congress as part of the Deficit Reduction Act of 1984 to reduce the federal budget deficit without resorting to repeal of across-the-board cuts in marginal tax rates adopted in the Economic Recovery Tax Act of 1981. Two major features of the Act are: (a) shortened the minimum holding period for assets to qualify for long-term capital gains treatment from one year to six months, but only for assets acquired after June 22, 1984; (b) permitted contributions to be made to an Individual Retirement Account no later than April 15 after the tax year for which an IRA benefit is sought. See also *Economic Recovery Tax Act of 1981, Tax Reform Act of 1976, Tax Reform Act of 1969, Tax Reform Act of 1986.*

Tax Reform Act of 1986 (HR-3838): federal legislation signed by President Reagan on October 22, 1986. Among the regulations dealing with individuals the law:

(1) compressed the 14 current tax brackets (15 for single taxpayers) into only two—15 percent and 28 percent.

(2) raised the standard deduction and the personal exemption.

(3) phased out the benefits of the 15 percent rate and the personal exemption for high-income taxpayers.

(4) eliminated some deductions for contributions by wealthy individuals and families to individual retirement accounts (IRAs).

(5) ended the special tax treatment of long-term capital gains. Capital gains are taxed at the same rate as other income.

(6) eliminated many tax preferences for individuals, such as deductions for consumer interest on such items as credit cards, auto loans and student loans.

(7) retained the most popular deductions used by individuals, including the deduction for mortgage interest payments on first and second homes, for charitable contributions and for state and local income and property taxes. The sales tax deduction was repealed.

(8) prevented taxpayers from using paper losses generated by tax shelters to reduce tax liability.

(9) cut the amount of income that could be deferred under so-called 401(k) retirement savings plans provided by employers.

(10) repealed the special deduction of as much as $3,000 for married couples who both work.

Among the regulations dealing chiefly with business, the law:

(1) eliminated the top corporate tax rate to 34 percent from 46 percent, occurring in mid-1987.

(2) repealed the lower tax rate for corporate net capital gains.

(3) eliminated the 6 percent or 10 percent investment tax credits effective for property placed in service after January 1, 1986.

(4) reduced depreciation allowances somewhat.

(5) limited deductions for business meals and entertainment to 80 percent of their value.

(6) made slight reductions in oil-and-gas, mining and timber preferences.

tax roll: an official statement describing property taxed, including the names of the taxpayers and the amount of their tax.

tax sale: sale of property in default because of nonpayment of taxes. See *scavenger sale.*

tax-saving retirement plan: see *Keogh plan.*

tax search: a determination by searching official records to determine whether there are any unpaid property taxes.

tax service contract: an agreement between a title company and an association under which the title company is responsible for notifying the lender of all tax and improvement lien payments as they come due. [59]

tax title: title to property acquired by purchasing land that was sold as the result of unpaid taxes.

T bill: see *Treasury bill.*

TC: see *time certificates of deposit.*

TD:
(1) see *time deposit (open account).*
(2) *Department of the Treasury, U.S.*
(3) time and savings deposits of depository institutions. [81]

TDOA: see *time deposit (open account).*

T&E: see *travel and entertainment credit card.*

TED: see *Treasury bills and Eurodollar deposits.*

Tee.: see *trustee.*

telegraphic transfer (T/T): the use of cable or telegraph to remit funds. Physical money does not move, but instead the order is wired to the cashier of a firm to make payment to an identified person or firm.

telephone account: a deposit or account under the terms of which a depositor is permitted to make more than three preauthorized or telephone transfers per month (whether to another account of the depositor or to a third party), or an account that permits a depositor to make payments to third parties through automated teller machines or remote service units. [202]

telephone bill paying: a service that permits a customer to pay a bill(s) without writing a check. The customer gives authorization to debit his or her checking account for a specific bill payment amount. The bank extracts these paperless entries for its own customers by debiting their account. At the same time the offsetting credit may be sent through the ACH, as an originating entry, to the merchant/retailer depositing bank. The ACH processes the entries and makes settlement between the originating and receiving banks. The receiving bank posts the entries and reflects them on periodic statements to the merchant/retailer. [105]

telephone order (TO): a direction received by a merchant, by telephone from a cardholder, wishing to charge the purchase amount to his or her bank card account without executing the resulting sales draft. [105]

teller: an employee of a bank who is assigned the duty of waiting on depositors and customers of the bank. The teller's principal responsibility is to handle cash for the depositor and the bank and to serve the depositor or the customer as far as his or her duties will permit. The teller is the "personal" contact between the customer and the bank. See also *head teller, loan teller, paying teller, receiving teller.* [10]

teller proof: a system of individual teller control whereby the teller balances and settles his own cash position daily. If the teller is using a bank teller's machine, this proof is very simple, because the machine will carry totals for cash received and cash paid out. Otherwise, the teller will maintain his own cash settlement sheet, listing all cash taken in and all checks cashed. Teller proof consists of using the teller's starting cash total, adding his cash received, and subtracting his cash paid out, to arrive at his cash on hand. The cash counted must agree with this cash ending total for proof. [10]

teller's check: a check drawn by a bank on another (drawee) bank and signed by a teller or tellers of the drawer bank. Tellers' checks are used in payment of withdrawal orders and, in lieu of savings bank money orders, are sometimes sold to depositors in exchange for cash. [39]

teller's stamp: a rubber stamp, usually showing the teller's number or initials and the bank's name or transit number, which the teller uses to identify deposits, cashed checks, or other posting media that he or she handles. [10]

teller terminal: an input-output unit of a computer system that replaces the teller's window posting machine in a computerized association. [59]

temporary administrator: an individual or a trust institution appointed by a court to take over and safeguard an estate during a suit over an alleged will, or over the right of appointment of an executor or administrator, or during the period that probate is delayed for any reason, such as difficulty in finding or citing missing heirs. [32]

temporary loans: short-term obligations representing amounts borrowed for short periods of time and usually evidenced by notes payable or warrants payable. They may be unsecured, or secured by specific revenues to be collected. See *tax anticipation note.* [49]

tenancy: the holding of real property by any form of title. [37]

tenancy at sufferance: a tenancy in which the tenant comes into possession of real property under a lawful title or interest and continues to hold the property even after his title or interest has terminated. [37]

tenancy at will: that estate which may be terminated by either the lessor or the lessee at any time. [62]

tenancy by the entirety: tenancy by a husband and wife in such a manner that, except in concert with the other, neither husband nor wife has a disposable interest in the property during the lifetime of the other. Upon the death of either, the property goes to the survivor. To be distinguished from *joint tenancy* and *tenancy in common.* [37]

tenancy for years: a tenancy for a definite period of time—for example, a year or 99 years. It cannot be terminated by either party alone except at the expiration of the time agreed upon. [32]

tenancy in common: ownership of property by two or more persons, each holding a separate interest. No right of survivorship exists. See *undivided right.*

tenancy in common account:
(1) a savings account that is owned by two or more persons, each of whom has a separate interest; when one owner dies, his or her shares passes to his or her heirs, not to the remaining owner(s). [59]
(2) a type of checking account, often requiring that both parties sign checks, notes, and so on; in other words, one individual cannot act independently of the other.

tenant: one who holds or possesses real property. [37]

tenant in dower: a wife who has survived her husband and in most states receives one-third of his inherited estate for the remainder of her life.

tender: the offering of money in satisfaction of a debt by producing the money and stating to the creditor a desire to pay.

ten-forty: a U.S. bond that is redeemable after 10 years, and due and payable after 40 years.

1099: the Internal Revenue Service form for reporting the payment of interest, dividends, and miscellaneous fees to individuals.

tenor: the period between the formation of a debt and the date of expected payment.

ten-spot: slang, a $10 bill.

ten-year trust: see *Clifford trust.*

term bonds payable: a liability account which records the face value of general obligation term bonds issued and outstanding. [49]

terme sec: French term meaning *outright transaction* in forward foreign exchange.

terminable interest: an interest that will terminate or fail on the lapse of time, on the occurrence of a contingency, or on the failure to occur of a contingency. [105]

termination of offer: an offer can be ended by acceptance, counteroffer, expiration of time, insanity, or death of the offeror or offeree, refusal to accept, or revocation of the offer.

term issue: a bond issue maturing as a whole in a single future year.

term loan: usually a long-term loan running up to 10 years. Such loans are generally made by the larger commercial banks and insurance companies to large, well-established business enterprises for capital expenditures such as plant improvements and purchases of equipment.

term mortgage: a mortgage with a fixed time period, usually less than five years, in which only interest is paid. Following termination of the mortgage, the total principal is demanded.

terms: the details, specifications, and conditions of a loan.

territorial bond: see *bond, insular.*

testamentary account: a category of savings accounts recognized by the Federal Savings and Loan Insurance Corporation as separately insurable, and including funds owned by an individual and invested in a revocable trust account, tentative or Totten trust account, payable-on-death account, or similar account evidencing an intention that on his or her death the funds shall belong to a specified member of the owner's family. See *Totten trust.* [59]

testamentary disposition: the disposition of property by deed, will, or otherwise in such a manner that it shall not take effect unless or until the grantor dies. [37]

testamentary guardian: a guardian of a minor or an incompetent person named in the decedent's will. [37]

testamentary trust: see *trust under will.*

testate: having completed and left an acceptable will.

testatrix: a deceased female who left a will setting forth the disposition of her wealth (total assets).

test period: see *dry run.*

thin margin: a condition where the owner of an item, such as a security, commodity, or other property, has a very small equity. Consequently, any small drop in the price or value of the item will result in a condition in which the debtor owes more than the value of the collateral put up for the loan.

third mortgage: a mortgage that is junior to both the first and second mortgages.

third-party check: a check which is given by one party to another, the recipient of which offers it to still another (third) party. [55]

third-party credit transfers: automatic deposits, or credits, to a checking, savings, or NOW account from a third party. Examples include payroll credits, Social Security payments or other federal recurring retirement benefits. Cf. *third-party debit transfers.* See *electronic fund transfers.*

third-party debit transfers: automatic withdrawals, or debits, from a checking, savings or NOW account and payable to a third party (e.g., periodic deductions for insurance premium payments). Cf. *third-party credit transfers.* See *electronic funds transfers.*

third-party payment service: a payment plan whereby a financial institution transfers a depositor's funds to a third party or to the account of the third party upon the negotiable or nonnegotiable order of the depositor. A checking account is one type of third-party payment service. [59]

third-party transfer: a nonnegotiable order to a savings association, issued by an account holder, to pay a specified sum of money to a third party. [59]

third window: an alternative low interest source of lending to developing countries by the World Bank.

thirty days after date: an amount due for payment on a time draft 30 days following the date of the draft.

thou: slang, $1,000.

Threadneedle Street: the financial area of London.

threat monitoring: the analysis, assessment, and review of audit trails and other data collected for searching out system events which may constitute security violations. [105]

360-day year—365-day year: the base used for calculations of daily interest to be paid on certain interest-bearing accounts. The difference in income as computed by the two methods will be material when large sums of money are involved. [105]

three-party paper: sales contracts purchased from retail merchants by banks and other lenders. [105]

thrift account: synonymous with *savings account* or *special interest account.* See *savings account, special interest account, thrifts.*

thrift institution: the general term for mutual savings banks, savings and loan associations, and credit unions. See *thrifts.* [1]

thrifts: there are two types of thrifts, the savings banks and savings and loan industries. Today they are both engaged in basically the same business—taking in consumer deposits and reinvesting them in mortgages. Together they hold almost $800 billion (1981) in assets, more than any financial industry except commercial banks, whose assets amount to $1.5 trillion (1981). Savings banks, which theoretically are owned by their depositors, were established by philanthropists to promote savings among the poor. The founders gave ultimate power to self-perpetuating boards of trustees. Thus, unlike depositors in S&Ls, savings bank depositors do not have the right to elect their trustees. Several savings banks are trying to convert to federal from state charters. Under federal rules, their depositors would gain voting rights within their respective organizations. Savings and loans originally were formed by community members to finance housing, not to promote savings. Initially, they existed for limited periods, long enough for each member to buy a home. The members chipped in to raise enough money to finance home construction. Lots were drawn to determine which member would be the first to get a house. The modern version of the savings and loan association got its start in the early 1930s. The industry boomed after World War II, when 11 million returning veterans needed housing.

through the market: a situation when a new bond offering has come to market and the yield to maturity is lower than comparable bonds outstanding.

tickler: an index for maturity dates of notes, bonds, acceptances, and so on, serving as a reminder to banks and financial institutions that these instruments will at some future time period be approaching maturity.

tied loan: a foreign loan limiting the borrower to spending the proceeds only in the nation making the loan. Cf. *counterpart monies.*

tight credit: synonymous with *tight money.*

tight money: high interest rates demanded in the borrowing of money. Synonymous with *tight credit.*

tight money market: a condition when the supply of money is less than the demand for it, with a resulting tendency for a firming of interest rates. See also *easy money.*

till money: funds kept at a front desk or register, as distinguished from monies held in a bank.

time adjusted rate of return: the rate of interest at which the existing value of anticipated cash inflows from a particular project equals the present value of expected cash outflow of the same activity.

time certificates of deposit: a time deposit evidenced by a negotiable or nonnegotiable instrument specifying an amount and a maturity. Savings bonds and savings certificates are merely forms of nonnegotiable time certificates of deposits. [69]

time deposit: a deposit from which a customer has the right to withdraw funds at a specified date 30 or more days following the date of deposit, or from which, if the bank requires, the customer can withdraw funds only by giving the bank written notice 30 days or more in advance of the planned withdrawal.

time deposit (open account) (TDOA) (golden passbook): funds deposited under agreement. They bear interest from the date of deposit, although the agreement usually requires that such funds remain on deposit for at least 30 days. The agreement stipulates a fixed maturity date or number of days after which payment will be made, or it is stipulated that payment will be made after a given period following notice by the depositor of intention to withdraw. See *Regulation Q.*

time draft: a draft payable a specified number of days (30, 60, or 90 days, for example) after its date of issuance or acceptance. [10]

time loan: a loan made for a specified period. The maturity date generally is 30, 60, 90, or 120 days after the date of the loan. Interest is usually collected in advance, at the time the loan is made, as a *discount*.

time lock: a device on safes and vaults preventing the safe door from opening until a certain time has passed.

time money: funds loaned out for a specified time period.

time of the note: the number of days or months from date of issue to date of maturity.

time open accounts: a time deposit evidenced by a written contract specifying a maturity but leaving open the amount involved. [69]

time plan loans: a type of loan in which interest and payment are made in fixed regular amounts at monthly intervals. [105]

time preference theory of interest: an explanation of interest as the price people are willing to pay for immediate possession of goods as opposed to future possession.

time sale financing: a form of indirect loan. This is an arrangement where a lender (usually a bank) purchases a loan contract from a retailer. The contract is an installment loan agreement between the retailer and the purchaser of a good. The borrower makes payment to the bank or other indirect creditor. [105]

times interest earned: a common measure of the "earnings protection" of a bond. The figure is computed by dividing the net earnings per year (without deducting the interest of the specific issues but after taxes) by the interest requirements of the specific issue for that year.

time warrant: a negotiable obligation of a governmental unit having a term shorter than bonds and frequently tendered to individuals and firms in exchange for contractual services, capital acquisitions, or equipment purchases. [49]

time warrants payable: the amount of time warrants outstanding and unpaid. [49]

timing of notes: the function of calculating and marking the maturity date on notes and other evidences of debt. Also the number of days that a loan must run until maturity for interest calculations. [10]

title: proper and rightful ownership.

title company: see *title guaranty company*.

title deed: a legal document indicating proof of an individual's ownership of a piece of land.

title defect: a fact or circumstance that challenges property ownership. See *cloud on title*.

title exception: a specified item appearing in a title policy against which the title company does not insure. [105]

title guaranty company: a business firm created to examine real estate files (i.e., to conduct title searches) to determine the legal status of the property and to find any evidence of encumbrances, faults, or other title defects. Once a search has been completed and the property found sound, the company receives a fee from the property purchaser who needed to determine that his or her title was clear and good. The property purchaser receives an abstract of the prepared title, and the title is verified by an attorney of the company who gives an opinion but does not guarantee the accuracy of the title. The company agrees to indemnify the owner against any loss that may be experienced resulting from a subsequent defect. A title guaranty policy is evidence of the title insurance, with costs based on the value of the property and the risk involved as determined by the condition of the title. See also *title insurance.*

title guaranty policy: title insurance furnished by the owner, provided as an alternative for an abstract of title. Synonymous with *Torrens certificate.* See also *title guaranty company.* [62]

title insurance: an insurance contract from a title guaranty company presented to owners of property, indemnifying them against having a defective or unsalable title while they possess the property. This contract is considered to be a true indemnity for loss actually sustained by reason of the defects or encumbrances against which the insurer agrees to indemnify. Title insurance includes a thorough examination of the evidences of title by the insurer. See *title guaranty company.*

title insurance company: see *title guaranty company.*

title 1: the section of the FHA Insurance Program for home improvements and mobile homes. [105]

title report: the report issued by the title company prior to settlement of a real estate purchase. The report provides a legal description of the property and lists all restrictions and liens against the property.

title search: see *search, title guaranty company, title insurance.*

title theory: a system in which the mortgagee has legal title to the mortgaged property and the mortgagor has equitable title. [62]

TL: see *time loan.*

TMS: see *Transmatic Money Service.*

T note: see *Treasury note.*

TO:

(1) see *telephone order.*

(2) see *Treasury obligations.*

to credit: in the context of a payment order, this is an instruction to credit an account on the books of the paying bank, as distinct from actually paying or remitting. [105]

to debit: an instruction to charge an account on the books of a bank. [105]

token coin: see *token money.*

token money: an object, usually coins, whose value as money is greater than the market value of the materials of which it is composed.

tom/next: from tomorrow to the next business day.

top credit: ready credit.

Torrens certificate: a document, issued by the proper public authority called a *registrar* acting under the provision of the Torrens law, indicating in whom title resides. [62]

tort: a wrongful act committed by a person against another person or his or her property.

tortfeasor: a person committing a tort.

total debt: all long-term obligations of the government and its agencies and all interest-bearing short-term credit obligations. Long-term obligations are those repayable more than one year after issue.

total net worth: synonymous with *tangible net worth.*

total of payments: the total of all installments scheduled to be made in the repayment of a loan or sales contract; face of note; the sum of the amount financed and the finance charges. [55]

total reserves: member bank deposits with Federal Reserve Banks plus member bank vault cash. The sum of required and excess reserves. [72]

Totten trust: a trust created by the deposit of one's own money in his own name as trustee for another. Title is vested in the record owner (trustee), who during his life holds it on a revocable trust for the named beneficiary. At the death of the depositor, a presumption arises that an absolute trust was created as to the balance on hand at the death of the depositor. See *testamentary account.* [37]

touch: asking for a loan of a sum of money from an acquaintance or friend.

TPIN (True Pin): The Personal Identification Number used as reference, as opposed to the code remembered by the cardholder. (The TPIN is related to the PIN by the offset on the card.) [105]

Tr.: see *trust.*

TR:
(1) see *Treasury Receipt.*
(2) see *trust receipt.*

TRA: see *Tax Reform Act of 1969, Tax Reform Act of 1976, Tax Reform Act of 1986.*

trace:
(1) the record of a series of events.
(2) to record a policyholder's record of premium payment.

trade date: the day on which a deal is carried out or completed. The settlement date can be the same or later.

trade date accounting: where assets purchased are recorded in the appropriate asset category on the trade date and the bank's obligation to pay for those assets are reported. [202]

transaction: any agreement between two or more parties, establishing a legal obligation.

transaction amount: the stated funds transferred between two parties without consideration of charges. [105]

transaction card: see *debit card.*

transaction code: a code encoded or keypunched into a document prior to computer processing to indicate the type of transaction being entered into the system. [105]

transaction date: the date on which a transaction occurs. See *posting date.* [105]

transaction document:
(1) a form that contains information pertaining to a transaction generated by a bank card and which shows a transaction.
(2) a check guaranteed by a bank card. Sales slips, refund slips, and cash advance/withdrawal slips are transaction documents.

transaction file: a file containing relatively transient data to be processed in combination with a master file. For example, in payroll application, a transaction file indicating hours worked might be processed with a master file containing employee name and rate of pay. [105]

transaction-type code: a code that further defines the purpose of the transaction, such as deposit, federal funds sold, draw-down. [105]

transaction velocity of money: the ratio of the total of all money transactions in a time period to the quantity of money. Cf. *income velocity of money.*

transcript: a recap of account activity for a designated period of time. [105]

transferability: the ability to transfer ownership or title. Transferability can be restricted by so stating in a contract. The usual word is *nonassignable.*

transferable letter of credit: a documentary credit under which a beneficiary has the right to give instructions to the paying or accepting bank or to any bank entitled to effect negotiations, to make the credit available to one or more third parties.

transferee: the person or corporation to which property has been transferred. [37]

transfer fees: fees collected from buyers and/or sellers of property to defray governmental charges for changing and maintaining public records. [105]

transfer in contemplation of death: a transfer of property by gift made in apprehension of death arising from some existing bodily condition or impending peril and not the general expectation of eventual decease commonly held by all persons. [37]

transfer of title: the change of property title from one person to another. Synonymous with *voluntary alienation.*

transfer of value: a banking concept that offers the consumer a variety of ways to pay for what he or she wants without cash.

transferor: the person or corporation which conveys or transfers property. [37]

transfer payment: in government statistics, money transactions among people, government, and business for which no services are performed; there is no addition to the national product.

transferred account: a cardholder account that has been transferred from one processing center to another, from one area to another within a processing center, or from one associate to another in the same bank card plan. [105]

transfers (mail, wire, cable): *mail transfer* is the remittance of money by a bank to be paid to a party in another town or city. The instruction to pay such funds is transmitted by regular mail, hence the term "mail transfer." *Wire transfer* is used to designate a transfer of funds from one point to another by wire or telegraph. *Cable transfer* is used to designate a transfer of funds to a city or town located outside the United States by cable. Commissions or fees are charged for all types of transfers. When transfers are made by wire or cable, the cost of transmitting the instructions to pay by wire or cable is charged to the remitter in addition to the commission. [10]

transfer service fee: service fee for instant cash transaction. [105]

transfer voucher: a voucher authorizing transfers of cash or other resources between funds. [49]

transit department: a department of a bank whose function is the processing of all out-of-city items. The transit department writes all transit letters, both cash letters and remittance letters and forwards these letters to the Federal Reserve Bank, correspondent banks, and other banks for collection and payment. [10]

transit items: cash items payable outside the town or city of the bank receiving them for credit to customers' accounts. [50]

transit letter: a letter or form of deposit slip on which a bank lists and describes transit items. [50]

transit machine: a machine designed to write transit letters. [105]

transit number: the identification of a bank on its checks under the national numerical system. The number has three parts, the first designating the location of the bank, the second the bank's name, and the third (below the line) the Federal Reserve district and area within the district. These numbers facilitate routing out-of-town checks.

translation (of foreign currencies): the expression of an amount denominated in one currency in terms of another currency by use of an exchange rate between the two currencies. [43]

Transmatic: the trade name of a franchised, preauthorized payment system for savings associations. [59]

Transmatic Money Service (TMS): an EFTS service first offered in the winter of 1974 by First Federal Savings and Loan of Lincoln, Nebraska. [105]

travel and entertainment credit card (T&E card): a credit card issued for use primarily for the purchase of meals, lodging, and transportation. Major American cards are American Express, Carte Blanche, and Diner's Club.

travel department: a department in a bank established to render service to the bank's customers in any matter relative to travel or foreign transactions. In the larger coastal banks, all foreign transactions are handled by the foreign department of the bank. In interior banks, the travel department deals directly with their coastal bank correspondents in handling foreign transactions. The travel department will arrange accommodations for domestic or foreign travel, plan vacation trips, and handle foreign transactions for its customers. [10]

travelers check: a form of check especially designed for travelers, including persons on vacation and business trips. These checks are usually preprinted in denominations of $10, $20, $50, and $100, and can be cashed and used to purchase goods and services in places of business that accept them.

travelers cheque: see *travelers check.*

traveler's letter of credit: a letter of credit is issued by a bank to a customer preparing for an extended trip. The customer pays for the letter of credit, which is issued for a specific period of time in the amount purchased. The bank furnishes a list of correspondent banks or its own foreign branches at which drafts drawn against the letter of credit will be honored. See *guaranteed letter of credit, letter of indication.*

Tr. Co.: see *trust company.*

treasurer: the person who is responsible for the financial transactions of an organization.

treasurer's check: see *cashier's check.*

Treasury bill: a U.S. government short-term security sold to the public each week, maturing in 91 to 182 days.

Treasury bills and Eurodollar deposits (TED): dollar-denominated time deposits at banks in Europe.

Treasury bonds and notes: interest-bearing certificates showing indebtedness of the U.S. government. Notes have maturities of between one and seven years, whereas bonds are longer term. [105]

treasury cash holdings: currency and coin held by the Treasury. [40]

Treasury certificates: U.S. government short-term securities, sold to the public and maturing in one year.

Treasury currency: U.S. notes, paper money, silver certificates, silver coins, nickels, and cents issued by the U.S. Treasury Department. [105]

Treasury currency outstanding: currency such as U.S. notes and silver certificates, and coin in the hands of the public for which the Treasury is responsible. [40]

Treasury note: a U.S. government long-term security, sold to the public and having a maturity of one to five years.

Treasury obligations: see *Treasury bill; Treasury certificates; Treasury note.*

Treasury Receipt (TR): zero-coupon bonds of U.S. Treasury-backed certificates available from brokerage and investment banking concerns.

treasury securities: interest-bearing obligations of the U.S. government issued by the Treasury as a means of borrowing money to meet government expenditures not covered by tax revenues. Marketable Treasury securities fall into three categories: bills, notes, and bonds.

The Federal Reserve System holds more than $100 billion of these obligations, acquired through open market operations. [1]

treasury stock: the title to previously issued stock of a corporation that has been reacquired by that corporation by purchase, gift, donation, inheritance, or other means. The value of such stock should be considered to be a deduction from the value of outstanding stock of similar type rather than as an asset of the issuing corporation.

Treasury Tax and Loan Account (TT&LA): an account held by the Treasury with a commercial bank.

Treasury warrant: an order on the U.S. Treasury in ordinary bank check form. It is the instrument by which all treasury disbursements are made.

Trf.: transfer.

trial balance: a list of the balances of the accounts in a ledger kept by double entry with the debit and credit balances shown in separate columns. If these are equal or their net balance agrees with a controlling account, the ledger from which the figures are taken is said to be *in balance.* [49]

trick: a special low coupon at a high yield on a long maturity of a municipal bond issue, which enables a bidder to lower the net interest cost (NIC) to the issuer in the hopes of making a winning bid on the bonds. [105]

true annual rate of interest: synonymous with *annual percentage rate.*

true cost banking: an efficient way of providing money to borrowers, a policy requiring consumers and corporations to pay higher borrowing costs. See *Depository*

Institutions Deregulation and Monetary Control Act.

true discount rate: an installment finance method by which the rate is calculated on the total note, by deducting the charge at the time the loan is created.

true interest: see *pure interest.*

True PIN: see *TPIN.*

truncation: a banking industry term for check safekeeping. The electronic sorting out of charges and transmitting them back to the issuer banks, which send payment back the same way.

trust: a fiduciary relationship between persons: one holds property for the benefit and use of another.

trust, corporate: the name applied to the division of a bank that handles the trust and agency business of corporations.

trust, personal: that branch of a trust company whose function is connected with the handling of trusts for individuals. Some of the functions performed are those of executorship of estates, administration of trust funds, investment services, and guardianships. Detailed records are maintained and statements mailed to beneficiaries of every transaction affecting a trust. [10]

trust account: a general term to cover all types of accounts in a trust department, including estates, guardianships, and agencies as well as trusts proper. [37]

trust administrator: a person in the employment of a trust institution who handles trust accounts in the sense of having direct contacts and dealings with trust customers and beneficiaries. [37]

trust agreement (trust instrument): an agreement between an employer and a trustee used in connection with a pension plan. It defines the trustee's powers and duties, and tells how the funds of the pension plan shall be invested and how payments shall be made to those who benefit under the plan. A trust agreement is usually used in connection with self-administered pension plans and individual policy pension plans.

trust and agency fund: in governmental accounting, a fund established to account for assets held by the government as trustee or agent (e.g., the government is trustee of a fund bequeathed to it under a will for loaning for stated purposes, but agent of a fund to account for taxes collected for other governmental units).

trust authority: the legal right of a corporation to engage in trust business. [32]

trust business: a trust company, or a trust department of a bank, which settles estates, administers trusts, and performs agency functions for individuals, corporations, governments, associations, and public or educational or related institutions is said to engage in the trust business. [10]

trust by declaration: see *declaration of trust.*

trust by order of court: a trust created by an order of a court of competent jurisdiction. [37]

trust charges: the charges made by a trust institution for its trust and agency services.

trust committee: a committee of directors or officers or both of a trust institution charged with general or specific duties relating to its trust business. [37]

trust company: an institution, usually state supervised, that engages in the trust business, and usually in all commercial banking activities.

trust costs: the costs to a trust institution of rendering trust and agency services; opposed to trust charges, which are the costs to trust institution customers or beneficiaries for obtaining trust and agency services. [32]

trust deed: see *deed, trust.*

trust department: the department of a bank that provides trust and agency services. The trust department by regulation must have books and assets separate from those of commercial banking activities. [25]

trust deposit: a deposit made by a trustee under a trustee account agreement.

trustee: a person to whom the title to property has been conveyed for the benefit of another.

trustee deed: see *deed, trustee.*

trusteed fund: any accumulation of capital held in trust for retirement, religious, educational, research, profit-sharing, or other purposes. [22]

trustee in bankruptcy: the individual appointed by a court or by creditors to carry out the responsibilities of trust in a bankruptcy proceeding.

trust estate: an estate held in trust by one individual for the welfare of another.

trust for support: a trust which provides that the trustee shall pay or apply only so much of the income or principal as in its judgment is necessary for the support,

including education, of the beneficiary. [37]

trust function: the fiduciary capacity in which an individual or a trust institution may act, such as executor, administrator, guardian, or trustee. [37]

trust fund: the funds held by a trustee for the benefit of another person.

trust funds, federal: trust funds established to account for receipts that are held in trust by the government for use in carrying out specific purposes and programs in accordance with a trust agreement or a statute.

trust institution: a trust company, state bank, national bank, or other corporation engaged in the trust business under authority of law. A corporation is a trust institution if any of its department is engaged in trust business, although other departments may be engaged otherwise. [37]

trust instrument: see *trust agreement.*

trust inter vivos: synonymous with *living trust* and *voluntary trust.*

trust investments: the property in which trust funds are invested; a broad term that includes all kinds of property, not securities alone. [37]

trust officer: the administrative officer of a trust company, or of the trust department of a bank. He is responsible for the proper administration of trusts, the investment of trust funds, and the administration of agencies for trust clients. [10]

trustor: an individual who establishes a trust. Synonymous with *settlor.*

trust powers: as used in the Federal Reserve Act, authority to engage in the trust business; to be distinguished from the powers of a trustee. [37]

trust property: see *res.*

trust receipt: a receipt in the form of an agreement by which the party signing the receipt promises to hold the property received, in the name of the bank delivering the property. It further agrees that the property shall be maintained in a form that can be readily identified. If the property is further fabricated in a manufacturing process, it must be properly identified on the trust receipt. Trust receipts are used mostly to permit importers to obtain possession of merchandise for resale. Arrangements for this type of financing are usually completed before the issuance of letters of credit. The trust receipt is used as collateral security for the advance of funds by the bank to meet the acceptances arising out of the letter of credit. Under the terms of the agreement, the importer is required to pay to the bank proceeds from the sale of merchandise as soon as they are received. The importer is also required to keep the merchandise insured, and the bank may take possession of the merchandise at any time without due process of law. Federal Reserve Banks do not recognize trust receipts as good collateral, and the legal status of the trust receipt has not been clearly defined by the courts. [10]

trust relationship: when an individual or other legal entity takes over legal title to certain property to hold it in trust for another individual or other legal entity as specified in the trust indenture, a trust or fiduciary relationship is established. The legal entity taking possession of the property is the trustee; the legal entity who will benefit from the relationship is the beneficiary. The beneficiary has an equitable title to the property, and may bring suit in courts of equity to maintain his or her rights as set forth in the trust agreement, and to prevent mishandling of the property by the trustee. [10]

trust under agreement: a trust evidenced by an agreement between the settlor and the trustee. Synonymous with *trust inter vivos* or *living trust.* [32]

trust under decree: a trust evidenced by a decree of a court of equity. [37]

trust under deed: a trust evidenced by a deed of conveyance, as distinguished from an agreement; originally confined to real property but now frequently applied to personal property as well. [37]

trust under will: a trust created by a valid will, to become operative only on the death of the testator; opposed to a *living trust* and the same as *testamentary trust.* [37]

Truth-in-Lending Act of 1968: officially, the Consumer Credit Protection Act of 1968, it requires most categories of lenders to disclose the true annual interest rate on virtually all types of loans and credit sales as well as the total dollar cost and other terms of a loan. See *Fair Credit Billing Act, Regulation Z, right of rescission.*

T/T: see *telegraphic transfer.*

TTLA: see *Treasury Tax and Loan Account.*

tub, in the: slang, in bankruptcy.

tughrik: monetary unit of Mongolia.

twenty-four-hour banking: the availability for customer transactions that is provided by the presence of automated teller machines. Customers using these machines can access their accounts at any time. [105]

twenty percent rule: where a customer wishing to borrow funds from a bank must maintain an average deposit balance equal to at least twenty percent of the proposed borrowing.

two bits: slang, a quarter, 25 cents.

two-case note: a $2 bill.

two-name paper: a short-term negotiable instrument wherein two people guarantee payment.

two-tier gold price: a 1968 agreement among central bank members of the Gold Pool, the International Monetary Fund, and the Bank for International Settlements, to suspend the pool's sale of gold on the free market at the U.S. price of $35 per troy ounce.

two-tier markets: an exchange rate regime which insulates a nation from the balance-of-payments impact of capital flow while it maintains a stable exchange rate for current account transactions.

UCC: see *Uniform Commercial Code.*

UCCC: see *Uniform Consumer Credit Code.*

ultimate beneficiary: a beneficiary of a trust who is entitled to receive the principal of the trust property in final distribution; synonymous with *principal beneficiary;* opposed to *immediate beneficiary* and *income beneficiary.* [37]

ultimo: the month prior to the existing one.

unaccrued: income resulting when payments are received but not yet due, as in the case of one receiving a rent payment before the due date.

unallotted balance of appropriation: an appropriation balance available for allotment. [49]

unamortized bond discount: the portion of the original bond discount that has not been charged off against earnings.

unamortized discounts on bonds sold: that portion of the excess of the face value of bonds over the amount received from their sale which remains to be written off periodically over the life of the bonds. [49]

unamortized premiums on bonds sold: an account which represents that portion of the excess of bond proceeds over par value and which remains to be amortized over the remaining life of such bonds. [49]

unattended banking terminal (automated teller, cash dispenser): an electronic machine usually activated by a magnetically striped plastic card, capable of dispensing cash in stipulated amounts or performing other teller-type functions, such as the transfer of funds from checking to savings; may be remote and free standing or affixed to a banking building. [105]

unclaimed balances: the balances of the accounts for funds on deposit that have remained inactive for a period designated by the bank. Eventually these unclaimed balances are handed over to the U.S. Comptroller of the Currency.

uncollected cash items: checks in the process of collection for which payment has not yet been received from the banks on which the checks are drawn. [40]

uncollected funds: a portion of a deposit balance that has not yet been collected by the depository bank. That is, sufficient time has not elapsed to permit checks drawn on other banks to have been returned for nonpayment. See *float*.

unconditional call money: Japanese term for funds lent for an initial period of two days which can then be called for repayment upon one day's notice.

unconfirmed documentary credit: a documentary credit where an advising bank informs the beneficiary of the terms and conditions of the credit without adding its undertaking that it will honor drawings on the credited, provided that documents are presented in order and in conformity with the terms of the credit.

unconfirmed letter of credit: a letter of credit in which the issuing bank has processed all the needed documents and advised the financial organization upon which the letter is drawn but the organization has not confirmed acknowledgment and accepted the advice of the letter. See *letter of credit*.

uncovered money: irredeemable paper money; money only partially, or not at all, supported by a specie reserve.

underlease: a tenant's lease of property to a third party; a sublease.

underlying lien: a claim that has priority over another claim which is junior to it.

underlying mortgage: a mortgage senior to a larger one (e.g., a building first mortgage of $100,000 that has a prior claim over a second one of $200,000). Cf. *equal dignity*.

under protest: a payment made under compulsion with the payer using these words to negate any implication from the act of payment that he or she is waiving whatever rights he or she may have.

underwriter: an individual or organization that assumes a risk for a fee. See *underwriting*.

underwriter's spread: compensation to investment bankers for helping the firm issue securities; expressed as the difference between gross and net security sales as a percent of gross sales.

underwriting: the analysis of risk and the settling of an appropriate rate and term for a mortgage on a given property for given borrowers. [105]

underwriting fee: a percentage of the spread that accrues only to members of the syndicate, in proportion to the amount of the issue underwritten.

underwriting syndicate: a combination of underwriters joined together in a joint venture to undertake the resale of securities which are to be purchased from the corporation issuing the securities (or from an intermediary). The syndicate operates under a contract setting out the terms of their responsibilities.

undesignated city: a city not designated by the Federal Reserve System as one of its reserve cities.

undistributed net income (UNI): the amount by which the distributable net income for the year exceeds the sum of any amount of income for the year required to be distributed currently; any other amounts properly paid, credited, or required to be distributed for such year; and the amount of taxes properly allocable to the undistributed portion of the distributable net income. [105]

undistributed profit: the profit of a partnership, syndicate, or joint venture prior to division among the individuals concerned.

undivided right: a part owner's right that cannot be excluded from the other owner's rights. This right exists in tenancy in common and in joint tenancy.

undo: to reverse a transaction.

undue influence: the influence that one person exerts over another person to the point where the latter is prevented from exercising his own free will. [37]

unearned discount: interest received but not yet earned.

unearned increment: the increase in the value of property that can be attributed to changing social or economic conditions beyond the control of the title holder, as distinguished from an increase in value that can be attributed to the improvements made or additions made by the labor or investment of the title holder.

unearned interest: interest on a loan that has already been collected but has not yet been earned because the principal has not been outstanding long enough. [59]

unencumbered property: real estate free and clear of any mortgages, liens, or debts of any type. See *perfect title.*

unexpired cost: any asset.

unfunded debt: any short-term or floating debt; any indebtedness not covered by a bond.

UNI: see *undistributed net income.*

uniform accounting system: a system of accounts that is common to similar organizations. This includes those promoted by a trade association for a particular industry or those promulgated by federal and state regulatory bodies. [105]

uniform cash flows: cash flows that are the same for every year.

Uniform Commercial Code: a set of statutes purporting to provide some consistency among states' commercial laws. It includes uniform laws dealing with bills of lading, negotiable instruments, sales, stock transfers, trust receipts, and warehouse receipts.

Uniform Consumer Credit Code (UCCC): a consumer protection act which contains one uniform set of regulations for all major credit grantors.

Uniform Gifts to Minors Act: an act adopted by most states providing for a means of transferring property to a minor, wherein the designated custodian of the property has the legal right to act on behalf of the minor without the necessity of a guardianship. [105]

Uniform Negotiable Instrument Act: see *negotiable instrument.*

Uniform Small Loan Law: passed on a state level, this law specifies requirements relating to the interest rate charged, maximum size of loan, and licensing and supervision of small loan companies. [105]

uninsurable title: property that a title insurance company will not insure.

unitary: a Savings and Loan subsidiary.

unit bank: a single independent bank that conducts all its operations at one office. [50]

unit banking: the type of banking in which an individual bank is separate and distinct from every other bank with regard to operation, management, and control. [50]

United States: see entries under *U.S.*

unit of account: an artificial concept providing a consistent reference value against varying exchange rates.

unit posting plan for checking accounts: a system used in a bank's commercial bookkeeping department whereby the ledger, original statement, and original journal are posted simultaneously. [105]

unit savings plan: a plan whereby savings deposits and withdrawals are posted by machine to the depositor's passbook, the bank's ledger card, and the auditor's detailed audit tape, all in original printing in one simultaneous operation. The ledger card is posted at the teller's window by the teller in the same machine operation that posts the entry in the depositor's passbook. The entry must be identical, because of the simultaneous machine printing. This assures complete protection to the depositor (who can "audit" his or her account at the window), the bank teller, and the bank. See also *dual savings plan, no-ticket savings plan.* [10]

unit system: an accounting system in which the records of the customer and the association are posted simultaneously. [59]

unit teller: an employee of a bank who is charged with the duties of both a paying and receiving teller. This teller may receive deposits or pay out funds to depositors. His cash balance at the end of the business day will be the net of his cash received, less his cash paid out. See *paying teller, receiving teller.* [10]

unit teller system: an arrangement for the convenience of customers who wish to make deposits and withdrawals at the same time. When this system is in use, the bank representative at each window is responsible for handling both receiving and paying operations. [50]

universal numerical system: a system of numbering checks with a code showing the city, state, and bank, aiding in rapid sorting of checks.

universal teller: a teller who is capable of handling all bank transactions without being assisted or having to leave the teller window. [105]

unlimited accounts: large or reputable businesses that are eligible for any amount of credit.

unlimited liability: the right of creditors to attach and seize any assets of a debtor to the extent of the indebtedness held against a business. A characteristic of the partnership and the individual proprietorship.

unlimited mortgage: any open-end mortgage; a mortgage not limited to a fixed amount.

unliquidated claim: where debtor honestly disputes the amount owing on the claim. [105]

unliquidated encumbrances: encumbrances outstanding. See also *encumbrance.* [49]

unpaid balance: on a credit purchase, the difference between the purchase price and the down payment or the value of a trade-in. With a cash loan, it is the difference between the total loan and the amount that is still owed.

unparted bullion: bullion containing base metals in addition to the precious metal.

unsatisfactory account:
(1) an indication, for credit references, that a customer has not met the terms of his or her contract.
(2) the irregular payment of a loan or frequent overdrawing of a checking account. [105]

unsecured: see *side collateral.*

unsecured creditor: a lender whose loan or debt is not secured by any collateral or mortgage.

unsecured debt: a debt for which no collateral has been pledged.

unsecured loan: a loan made by a bank based on credit information about the borrower and his or her ability to repay the obligation. The loan is not secured by collateral but is made on the signature of the borrower. A person's spouse may be asked to sign such a note. See *co-maker.*

unsecured note: a loan granted on the basis of a borrower's credit worthiness and signature; not secured by collateral. [78]

upgrade: an increase in the credit limit. [105]

upon sight: see *sight draft.*

upset price: a previously fixed starting price in the auctioning of a piece of real estate. The prospective seller will not entertain a bid below that figure.

upstream loan: a holding company with poor credit using its subsidiaries as a source of funds. Such lending by the subsidiary to a parent will not appear on a consolidated statement of the parent and the subsidiaries.

urbank: first proposed by Professor Charles Haar, in 1968, as an urban development bank controlled by a federal agency to assist communities to build needed facilities. The urbank would be a federally financed institution, making long-term loans at favorable interest rates to employers willing to return to or upgrade plants in cities.

US: United States.

usance: the period of time allowed by law or commercial practice for the payment of a bill of exchange.

U.S. banks: U.S. and foreign branches of banks chartered and headquartered in the U.S. (including U.S.-chartered banks owned by foreigners), but excluding U.S. branches and agencies of foreign banks. [202]

use: as a noun, the beneficial ownership of property the legal title to which is in another; the forerunner of the present-day trust. [32]

use data: the set of characters in bank cards used in off-line terminals, recording the most recent use of the card. [105]

used mortgage: synonymous with *assumable mortgage.*

U.S. government deposits: all deposits in reporting member banks held for the account of the U.S. government or one of its departments or bureaus. [40]

U.S. rule: a method traditionally employed in first-mortgage real estate financing where payments are applied first to accrued interest and then to the reduction of principal. [41]

U.S. Savings Bond: see *Bond, U.S. Savings.*

usuance:
(1) interest or income.
(2) the period allowed for payment of a foreign obligation.

usufructuary right: a right to appropriate use and pleasure from property owned by another.

usurious: describing a contract when made for a loan of money at a rate of interest in excess of that authorized by the statute.

usurious rate of interest: the maximum rate of interest which the law allows. Cf. *legal rate of interest.*

usury: the rate of interest paid for the use of another's money, or for credit extended, which exceeds the legal limit allowed for that type of transaction by the state whose laws govern the legality of the transaction. See *legal interest.*

usury rate: see *usurious rate of interest.*

U/T: under trust.

utter a check: to give a check to another in payment of an obligation.

Uw.: see *underwriter.*

vacation club account: funds deposited in a financial institution to accumulate money for a vacation period. Deposits are generally made weekly in small amounts. [105]

VA guaranteed loan: see *Veterans Administration loan.*

Val.: see *value.*

valid: that which is sufficient to satisfy the requirement of the law; a fact.

validation: proof or confirmation; an instrument or other evidence to confirm or give legal support to a claim or contract (e.g., factual data from an experiment).

valid date: a date expressed as month and year before which a bank card is not valid. The valid date may appear on the face of the card in embossed characters or in a magnetic strip. [105]

valuation: the fixing of value to anything. Synonymous with *appraising.*

valuation account (or reserve): an account that relates to one or more other accounts, either partly or wholly offsetting it (e.g., reserve for depreciation, unamortized debt discount). The valuation reserve is deducted from the stated value of the asset, giving its net value. [105]

valuation reserves:

(1) reserves established to provide for a drop in the existing value of the assets to which they pertain. See *appraisal.*

(2) reserves established to provide for a reasonably probable failure to achieve full value.

value: the worth of property, goods, services, and so on. See *purchasing power.*

value compensated: describing a purchase or sale of foreign exchange to be executed by cable; the purchaser reimburses the seller for the earlier value of the data of actual payment abroad of the foreign currency, theoretically resulting in no loss of interest to either party.

value date: the date on which a bank deposit becomes effective. The date is fixed based on the time required to collect a payment on the item deposited from another bank. See *collection.*

value of money: its purchasing power. The amount of goods and services it will buy at any given time.

VA mortgage: mortgage made in conformity with requirements of the Servicemen's Readjustment Act, and guaranteed to an amount specified in the act by the Veterans Administration. [22]

variable amount note: note evidencing the amount the trust department lends to a borrower from cash held in various fiduciary accounts; the amount of the loan outstanding fluctuates depending on the amount of cash on hand. [105]

variable interest plus (VIP): an innovative certificate of deposit. First attempted by Western Savings Bank, the second largest in Philadelphia; under the plan, the interest rate on the six-month certificate would be tied to the prevailing rate at the weekly auction of six-month Treasury bills. The primary motivation behind this new variable-interest-rate certificate was to stop the flow of funds out of the bank and into higher-yielding instruments, particularly money-market mutual funds. Under terms of the VIP, a depositor also could borrow as much as $9900 against the certificate at an interest rate of 1 percent above the weekly rate being earned. Bank regulators stopped this proposal in 1981.

variable interest rate U.S Savings Bond: see *Bond, Savings (U.S.)*.

variable rate: offered by many major lenders, monthly bank payments that are tied to prevailing rates. The advantage is to the buyer when rates slide, and to the seller when they soar.

variable-rate account: a passbook savings account that pays extra earnings if the customer leaves a specified amount on deposit for a specified term. [59]

variable-rate CDs: introduced in 1975, a certificate of deposit with a normal minimum maturity of 360 days. The interest rate is pegged by an issuing bank at a specified spread over the bank's current rate on 90-day CDs and is adjusted every 90 days.

variable-rate certificate: a savings certificate on which the rate of interest payable varies, depending on the term for which the money is pledged. The interest rate is set by government regulatory agencies. [105]

variable-rate mortgage: a type of mortgage, initially available in California, and now authorized nationally, which permits the interest charges on the loan to rise or fall automatically in accordance with a predetermined index, for instance, an index of banks' cost-of-funds. The interest rate can fluctuate every six months, but cannot be raised by more than 2½ percentage points over the life of the mortgage. In addition, banks must offer customers a choice between variable-rate and conventional mortgages. See also *flexible mortgage, renegotiable-rate mortgage, Wachovia adjustable mortgage*.

vault: a large room or rooms in a bank or financial institution, where the cash on hand is stored, and safe deposit boxes are located.

vault cash: that portion of the cash on hand which is not required for immediate use and is left in the vault of the bank as an immediate reserve. The remainder of the cash on hand is carried in the cash busses and cash tills under the custodian-ship of the tellers. [10]

velocity of circulation: the rate at which money supply is spent for a stated time period, usually one year.

velocity of money: see *velocity of circulation.*

velocity shop: where mortgages are sold by banks to secondary lending markets so that it can quickly get back funds to make even more mortgages.

vendee: the party who purchases or agrees to purchase property owned by another.

vendor's lien: an unpaid seller's right to take possession of property until the purchase price has been recovered. See *general lien.*

venture: a business activity or undertaking involving some or considerable risk.

venture capital: funds invested in enterprises that do not usually have access to conventional sources of capital (banks, stock market, etc.).

verification: the auditing process by which a customer is contacted regarding the status of an account or loan, to confirm the bank's records. [105]

verification factor: a numeric factor used to prove balance pickups or account selection. [105]

vested: giving the rights of absolute ownership, although enjoyment can be postponed.

vested estate: an interest in property holding present and future rights, but with the existing interest able to be transferred.

vested interest: an immediate, fixed interest in real or personal property although the right of possession and enjoyment may be postponed until some future date or until the happening of some event; to be distinguished from a *contingent interest.* [37]

vested remainder: a fixed interest in real property, with the right of possession and enjoyment postponed until the termination of the prior estate; to be distinguished from a *contingent remainder.* [37]

Veterans Administration (VA): established as an independent agency on July 21, 1930, to coordinate and consolidate federal agencies concerned with the administration of laws providing benefits for veterans. The VA helps veterans purchase homes. See *VA mortgage.* [33]

Veterans Administration loan: loaned funds, guaranteed by the Veterans Administration. These are usually housing and education loans. [105]

Veterans Administration Mortgage Guarantees: home mortgage guarantees issued by the VA under the Servicemen's Readjustment Act, to eligible applicants for any of the following purposes: (1) the purchase or construction of an owner-occupied home by the veteran; (2) the construction of a farm residence on land owned by a veteran; (3) the repair, alteration, or improvement of an owner-occupied farm or home by the veteran. Interest is set by the Veterans Administration. [66]

VI: see *vested interest.*

VIP: see *variable interest plus.*

virtuous cycle: a concept describing the kinds of actions some bankers think governments should take to minimize the impact of currency fluctuations. The virtuous cycle approach produces a series of sound economic policies to set off a chain of events in which improved economic performance produces sound currencies, which, in turn, further improves economic performance.

visible items of trade: exports and imports of item and specie. Cf. *invisible items of trade.*

V loans: pursuant to Regulation V of the Federal Reserve System, defense production loans guaranteed by the Board of Governors.

void: that which has no legal effect.

voidable contract: an agreement that can be rescinded by either of the parties in the event of fraud, incompetence, or other sufficient cause.

voluntary bankruptcy: see *bankruptcy.*

voluntary conveyance or deed: the instrument of transfer of an owner's title to property to the lien holder. Usually such conveyance serves to bypass a legal situation of a court judgment showing insufficient security to satisfy a debt, and occurs without transfer of a valuable consideration.

voluntary trust: established by a deed of transfer of certain property made voluntarily by an individual or other legal entity to a trustee for a specified purpose.

vostro account: "your account"; used by a depository bank to describe an account maintained with it by a bank in a foreign country. Cf. *nostro account.*

voucher audit: examination and approval by administrative authority of a proposed disbursement. [105]

voucher check: a form of check to which is attached another form termed a voucher. The voucher portion of the check is used to describe or otherwise designate the purpose for which the check is drawn. When a voucher check is received from a buyer by a seller, the seller detaches the voucher from the check before presenting the check for payment. The voucher is then used as the posting medium to credit the accounts receivable ledger, thereby showing payment received from the buyer. Many businesses use copies of voucher checks as their record of invoices paid.

voucher payment plan: a method of construction loan payouts in which the contractor or borrower completes lender forms requesting each payout when a particular, prespecified stage of construction is reached. [59]

voucher register: a book of original entry in which information is accumulated as to cash payments.

voucher system: a system which calls for the preparation of vouchers for transactions involving payments and for the recording of such vouchers in a special book of original entry known as a voucher register, in the order in which payment is approved. [49]

VRM: see *variable-rate mortgage.*

Wachovia adjustable mortgage: a recent approach in mortgage lending, developed by this North Carolina bank. It works this way: a customer buys a home with a 30-year adjustable mortgage. The initial mortgage rate is tied to money market and local market rates. The interest rate is adjusted every quarter in line with bill rates. The monthly payment stays the same for five years, but the new rate determines how much will go for interest and how much for principal. Every five years the monthly payment is adjusted—up or down by up to 25 percent—so the loan will be paid off on time. After 25 years the monthly payment can be adjusted by more than 25 percent if there is a danger the loan will not be paid off on time. If after 30 years the loan has not been paid off, the borrower may refinance. See *renegotiable-rate mortgage; variable-rate mortgage.*

wad: slang, a roll of paper money.

wage assignment: an agreement permitting a lender to collect a certain portion of a borrower's salary from his or her employer if payment is not made as specified in the credit contract. [78]

waiver: the voluntary relinquishment of a right in a piece of property or to a claim against another's property that would be legally enforceable if the person waiving so elected.

waiver of citation: a document executed by an interested party in an accounting proceeding by which he relinquishes his right to the formal issue and service of a citation. [37]

waiver of demand: see *waiver of protest.*

waiver of protest: a statement, signed by the endorser of a note, indicating that he or she will remain liable even if he or she is not notified that the note has not been paid when due.

walking bankruptcy: a business concern nominally in default but practically carried on by its creditors.

Wall Street: popular name for the New York City business and financial district.

Wall Street Journal: one of America's leading newspapers, noted for its coverage of financial, corporate, and market news.

ward: the infant or incompetent person who is the beneficiary of an estate of a deceased person. The ward is under the care of a guardian who is appointed by a court of law to administer the affairs of the ward with the sanction of the court having such jurisdiction, until some time as the court finds that the ward has reached majority or has become fully competent to handle his own affairs. [10]

warehousing: hypothecation of mortgage to a commercial bank as security for repayment of short-term loans. [22]

warehousing loan: a loan made on inventory held in warehouses.

Warr.: see *warrant.*

warrant: a written order in the name of the state and signed by a magistrate directing an officer to make an arrest.

warrants payable: the amount of warrants outstanding and unpaid. [49]

warranty: a statement, either written, expressed, or implied, that a certain statement identified in a contract is presently true or will be true.

wasting trust: a trust of property that is gradually being consumed.

WD: see *withdrawal.*

weed off: slang, to take money from a roll of bank notes.

weekend arbitrage: a now defunct maneuver by which banks lowered their reserve requirements by borrowing clearing house funds overseas on Friday which they did not have to cover until Monday.

white elephant: property that is so costly to maintain that it is virtually impossible to operate it at a profit; also property with respect to which a loss is certain.

whole loan: in the secondary market to indicate that the full amount of a loan is available for sale with no portion, or participation, retained by the seller. [105]

wholesale banking: the function of providing bank services, loan security, and loans to large corporate customers with strong financial statements. [105]

wholesale money: money borrowed in large amounts from banks, large firms or financial organizations, in contrast to *retail money* which is acquired by attracting deposits from individuals and small companies.

widow's allowance: the allowance of personal property made by the court or by statute to a widow for her immediate requirements after her husband's death. [37]

widow's exemption: the amount allowed as a deduction in computing the state inheritance tax on the widow's share of her husband's estate. [37]

wildcat bank: one of the unsound banks chartered by the states during the hectic banking years between 1816 and 1863. Most of these banks failed.

wildcat money: bank notes issued by wildcat banks.

will: a document in which an individual (the testator or testatrix) having full mental faculties sets forth his or her desires and bequests regarding the disposition of his total wealth after his death.

Wilmington Plan: a plan initiated by the Wilmington Savings Funds Society, a mutual savings bank, providing individual customers with a free checking account, a savings account and an agreement to permit the savings account to serve as security for an automatic short-term advance if the checking account is overdrawn. Direct payroll deposit, automatic bill paying, a cash-dispensing machine, and a percentage credit to the customer on purchases via direct debit from the customer's checking account are also available. [36]

window: any period that offers an advantageous opportunity to do an action, especially lending or borrowing of money.

window dressing: the practice of executing transactions shortly before the end of an accounting period to change artificially the items in the accounting statements of the period.

wins and losses: see *settlement check.*

wire-fate item: check or other item sent for collection or in transit letters to out-of-town banks, accompanied by instructions to notify the sending bank by wire as to whether the item is paid or not paid. This enables the sending bank to ascertain quickly whether or not the item is paid. [10]

wire house: a member firm of an exchange maintaining a communications network either linking its own branch offices to offices of correspondent firms, or linking some combination of such offices. [20]

with all faults: without a guarantee, usually in real estate transactions; of the absence of imperfections; as is.

withdrawal: the manner in which funds on deposit in savings accounts may be paid out by the bank. The depositor must present his passbook and sign either a withdrawal slip or the ledger card (no-ticket savings plan) before the bank can pay out funds against the deposit account. The signature on the withdrawal slip or signed on the proper line of the ledger card should always agree with the signature on file in the bank to insure that the right person is receiving the withdrawn funds. [10]

withdrawal form: a source document and authorization for withdrawals from a savings account used by the customers and kept by the association for its records. [59]

withdrawal notice: the written notification of intent to remove funds from an account on or after a specified date. This is required on certain types of accounts. [105]

withdrawal ratio: withdrawals expressed as a percentage of gross savings for a given period. [59]

withdrawal value: the amount credited to the savings account of a member, less deductions as shown on the records of the savings association. [59]

with exchange: a designation on a check or draft of payable with exchange indicating that any collection or exchange charges will be against the payer in the event that it is a check, or the drawee in the event that it is a draft.

with full recourse: in lending, a term in a written agreement that gives the buyer in a sale or other transaction the right to full reimbursement from the seller for any losses resulting from the loans or other items purchased. [59]

without recourse:
(1) used in endorsing a negotiable instrument where the endorser of a note is no longer responsible, should the obligation not be paid. See *qualified endorsement.*
(2) an agreement that the purchaser accepts all risks in the transaction, and gives up all rights to any recourse.

with partial recourse: in lending, a term in a written agreement that gives the buyer in a sale or other transaction the right to reimbursement for an agreed-upon portion of any losses resulting from the loans or other items purchased. [59]

with recourse:
(1) used in endorsing a negotiable instrument where the endorser of a note continues to be responsible, should the obligation not be paid.
(2) an agreement that if the seller is unable to meet his or her obligations, the purchaser has the right to endorse a claim against the seller for sustained damages.

won: monetary unit of Korea.

working capital: the excess of current assets over current liabilities representing the capital immediately available for the continued operation of a business.

working capital acceptance: a banker's acceptance that does not finance a specific trading transaction but finances a firm's general working capital needs. It is not eligible for rediscount at the Federal Reserve.

working capital loan: a short-term loan to provide money to purchase income-generating assets, such as inventory. [105]

working capital turnover: the ratio of sales to current assets.

working fund: the amount of money made available to a teller for the handling of routine transactions. [59]

working reserve (bank): consists of cash held in the bank, cash items in process of collection, and demand deposits with other individual banks, but not deposits with a Federal Reserve Bank.

workout loan: a loan granted to a borrower in a distressed financial condition pursuant to a plan to "work out" of the difficulty. Accordingly, many restrictions are imposed to assure the achievement of the purpose.

World Bank: see *International Bank for Reconstruction and Development.*

World Bank Group: collectively, the International Bank for Reconstruction and Development (World Bank) and its affiliates, the International Finance Corporation and the International Development Association.

wraparound: a financing device that permits an existing loan to be refinanced and new money to be advanced at an interest rate between the rate charged on the old loan and the current market interest rate. The creditor combined or "wraps" the remainder of the old loan with the new loan at the intermediate rate. [200]

wraparound annuities: tax-deferral schemes allowing an individual to shelter current interest income on a bank savings certificate or shares in a mutual fund in a tax-deferred annuity administered by an insurance company.

wraparound mortgages: involves two lenders, a mortgage originator and a wraparound lender. Rather than providing an entirely new mortgage at current market rates to a home buyer, the wraparound lender agrees to continue to pay the monthly installments on the existing mortgage on the home to be bought, at the original contract interest rate of the mortgage, and also to make any additional payments needed to meet the purchase price of the home. As a result, the terms of the original mortgage continue to be satisfied, the seller is compensated for the sale of his or her investment, and the home buyer is able to purchase a home and share in the benefits of the below-market rate paid by the wraparound lender on a portion of the money financed.

wrap lease: a lease structure in which one lease is wrapped around another. Another company purchase the asset and then leases the asset from the original firm to on-lease it to the lessees.

wraps: see *wraparound.*

writ: a written instrument, under a state's seal, issued from a court directing an officer of the court to do some act, or enjoining an individual to do or refrain from doing some act.

write-down: the book value to which an asset has been reduced to adjust for the capital that has been lost on the decline of the asset's value.

write-off: an asset that has been determined to be uncollectible and therefore has been charged off as a loss. Sometimes it is the debt itself. Cf. *written-down value*.

write-up: an increase in an asset's book value not resulting from added costs or an adjustment of an asset account to correspond to an appraisal value.

writ of execution: a court order issued to an officer of law commanding him or her to take certain action. [76]

written-down value: an accounting term for the valuation or cost of any asset minus the written-off depreciation.

WS: see *Wall Street*.

WSJ: see *Wall Street Journal*.

X: see *no protest*.

X-Ch.: see *exchange*.

X loan: loan made under a law other than a small loan law. [55]

X mark signature: when an individual is unable to sign his or her name because of injury or illiteracy, provision can be made for him or her to "sign" with an X. In this situation, his or her name is inserted by another person and the notation "his mark" or "her mark" is put next to the "X" and then witnessed by a person, who in addition signs the document with the notation that he or she witnessed the "X."

Xmas Club account: see *Christmas Club account*.

Yankee bond market: issues floated in the United States, in dollars, by reign governments and corporations.

yard: slang, a $100 bill, or $100.

yardstick rates: rates of one business used as a criterion for the basic regulation of rates charged by other companies.

year-end adjustment: a modification of a ledger account at the close of a fiscal period arising from an accrual, prepayment, physical inventory, reclassification, policy change, audit adjustment, or other entry, which can be done at discrete intervals. [105]

yellow-back: slang, a bank note, specifically a gold certificate.

yen: monetary unit of Japan.

yield:
(1) the profit or income created through an investment in property.
(2) to give up possession; to pay.

yield maintenance: the adjustment upon delivery of the price of a GNMA or other mortgage security purchased under a futures contract or standby commitment to provide the same yield to the purchaser as that which was specified in the original agreement.

yield to adjusted minimum maturity: a measure designed to give the yield to the shortest possible life of a bond.

yield to average life: the yield derived when the average maturity of a bond is substituted for the final maturity date of the issue.

yield to crash: see *yield to adjusted minimum maturity.*

yield to lessor: the internal rate of return generated from a lease transaction alone.

yield to put: the return a bond earns assuming that it is retained until a certain date and put (sold) to the issuing company at a specific price (the put price).

yield to worst: see *yield to adjusted minimum maturity.*

Y loan: loan made under a law other than a small loan or X loan law. [55]

"your account": see *vostro account.*

Yr.: year.

yuan: monetary unit of China.

zaire: monetary unit of Congo (Kinshasa) and Zaire.

zero-balance account: an arrangement, agreed to in advance by a drawee bank, under which a customer issues checks on an account even though funds do not exist in that account to cover the items. When the checks are physically presented to the drawee and posted, creating a minus balance, the bank contacts the customer, reports the overdraft figure, and transfers funds from another account to eliminate it, thus restoring the account to a zero balance. Commonly used by corporations that have many disbursing points and by many agencies of government.

zero basis: the condition occurring when a convertible bond is valued so highly by investors that they buy it at a premium high enough that interest received is canceled out by the premium paid to purchase the bond. The bond is said to be trading on a zero basis. [105]

zero-coupon Eurobonds: American company issues that pay no interest but are sold at a steep discount.

zero proof: a mechanical method of posting records in a manner serving to prove that the previous balance on each line of posting was made correctly.

zero-rate and low-rate mortgage: a home mortgage appearing to be completely or almost interest free. Requires a large down payment and one-time finance charge, then the loan is repaid in fixed monthly payments over a short term.

zloty: monetary unit of Poland.

REFERENCES

[1] Federal Reserve System, Board of Governors: *Glossary.*

[2] The Association of Commodity Commission Merchants: *Trading in Commodity Futures.*

[3] Edison Electric Institute: *Glossary of Electric Utility Terms.*

[4] Dun & Bradstreet, Inc.: *How Does Your Business Compare with Others in Your Line?*

[5] American Stock Exchange, Inc.: *Introducing Puts.*

[6] Society of Residential Appraisers: *Real Estate Appraisal Terminology.*

[7] Federal Reserve Bank of New York: *The Story of Checks.*

[8] National Association of Mutual Savings Banks: *This is NAMSB.*

[9] U.S. Department of Commerce: *Selected U.S. Marketing Terms and Definitions.*

[10] National Cash Register Corp.: *Financial Terminology.*

[11] Commodity Research Publication Co.: *Understanding the Cocoa Market.*

[12] Mutual of Omaha: *Terms and Definitions.*

[13] American Marketing Association: *Report on Definitions—SBA Aids, No. 127.*

[14] National Association of Mutual Savings Banks: *Annual Report, 1980.*

[15] American Stock Exchange, Inc.: *The Versatile Option.*

[16] World Bank: *Development Finance Companies.*

[17] National Foreign Trade Council: *Revised American Foreign Trade Definitions.*

[18] Association of American Railroads: *Railway Statistics Manual.*

[19] American Insurance Association: *National Building Code.*

[20] The New York Stock Exchange, Inc.: *The Language of Investing.*

[21] U.S. Office of Management and Budget: *American National Dictionary for Information Processing.*

[22] Mortgage Bankers Association of America: *Mortgages for Retirement and Endowment Funds.*

[23] Investment Company Institute: *Mutual Fund Fact Book, 1979,* "Glossary."

[24] U.S. Postal Service: *Glossary of Postal Terms.*

[25] American Bankers Association: *Trust Fact Book.*

[26] Securities Industry Association: *A Profile of Investment Banking.*

[27] Beresiner, Y. A.: *Collector's Guide to Paper Money.* New York: Stein & Day, 1977.

[28] National Foundation for Consumer Credit: *Using Credit Intelligently.*

[29] New York State Bankers Association: *What Every Woman and Man Should Know about Consumer Banking.*

[30] Wisenberger Investment Companies Service: *Investment Companies, 1979.*

[31] Burroughs Corp.: *Glossary of Financial and Data-Processing Terms.*

[32] American Institute of Banking: *Trust Department Service.*

[33] American Bankers Association: *Bank Fact Book.*

[34] International Business Machines Corp.: *Data Processing Glossary.*

[35] Small Business Administration: *SBIC Financing for Small Business.*

[36] National Science Foundation: *Consequences of Electronic Funds Transfer.*

[37] American Bankers Association: *Glossary of Fiduciary Terms.*

[38] National Cash Register Corp.: *Industrial Accounting Terminology.*

[39] American Institute of Banking: *Savings Banking.*

[40] Federal Reserve System: *Terms.*

[41] International Consumer Credit Association: *How to Use Consumer Credit Wisely.*

[42] International Monetary Fund: *Annual Report on Exchange Arrangements and Exchange Restrictions.*

[43] American Institute of Certified Public Accountants: *Glossary for Accounting Terms.*

[44] American Institute of Banking: *Home Mortgage Lending.*

[45] UNIVAC: *Glossary of Computer Terms.*

[46] Conference Board: *Economic Almanac.*

[47] U.S. Department of Commerce, National Bureau of Standards: *Units and Systems of Weight and Measures, Their Origin, Development, and Present Status.*

[48] American Marketing Association: *A Glossary of Marketing Terms.*

[49] Municipal Finance Officers Association: *Governmental Accounting and Financial Reporting Principles.*

[50] American Institute of Banking: *Principles of Bank Operation.*

[51] United States League of Savings Associations: *Savings and Loan Fact Book.*

[52] Municipal Finance Officers Association: *Public Employee Retirement Administration—Terminology.*

[53] Chamber of Commerce of the U.S.: *Dictionary of Insurance Terms.*

[54] The Hartford: *Glossary—Terms and Phrases Commonly Used in Property, Casualty, and Life Insurance.*

[55] Household Finance Corporation: *General Glossary.*

[56] Employers Insurance of Wausau: *A Dictionary of Insurance Terms.*

[57] Federal Reserve Bank of Atlanta: *Econometric Models.*

[58] American Council of Life Insurance: *Life Insurance Fact Book.*

[59] Institute of Financial Education: *Glossary of Savings Association Terminology.*

[60] U.S. Department of Labor: *Glossary of Currently Used Wage Terms.*

[61] U.S. Department of Commerce: *A Basic Guide to Exporting.*

[62] Realtors National Marketing Institute: *Real Estate Handbook.*

[63] Retail Merchant Association: *Glossary—The Display Manual.*

[64] Association of Bank Holding Companies: *Bank Holding Companies Today.*

[65] Federal Reserve Bank of New York: *Definitions.*

[66] Federal Home Loan Bank Board: *Types of Mortgages-Fact Sheet.*

[67] American Institute of Banking: *Investments.*

[68] Pacific Coast Stock Exchange: *Directory of Securities, Options Stock Analysis.*

[69] Federal Reserve Bank of Boston: *Pandora's Box—Glossary of Terms.*

[70] Tax Foundation, Inc.: *Glossary—Facts and Figures on Government Finance,* 20th edition, 1979.

[71] Federal Reserve Bank of Cleveland: "Terms," *Economic Review,* January 1967.

[72] Federal Reserve Bank of St. Louis: "Definitions," *Review.*

[73] U.S. Department of Commerce: *Dictionary of Economical and Statistical Terms.*

[74] Federal Reserve Bank of Chicago: *Definitions.*

[75] Federal Reserve Bank of Philadelphia: *What Are Federal Funds?*

[76] Associated Credit Bureaus, Inc.: *Glossary.*

[77] American Institute of Certified Public Accountants: *Accounting Research and Terminology.*

[78] Federal Reserve Bank of New York: *Consumer Credit Terminology Handbook.*

[79] Federal Reserve Bank of St. Louis: *Review,* December 1980.

[80] Financial Accounting Standards Board: *FASB Discussion Memorandum.*

[81] Federal Reserve Bank of St. Louis: *Review,* October 1982.

[82] IMF Staff Papers, *Effects of Devaluation on a Trade Balance,* Washington, DC, 1952.

[83] *Borrowing by Developing Countries on the Euro-Currency Market,* OECD, Paris, 1977.

[84] *Exchange Control Notice EC1,* Bank of England, 1976.

[85] *Finance of International Trade,* Institute of Bankers, London, 1976.

[86] *Depository Receipts, Morgan Guaranty Trust Company,* New York, 1973.

[87] *Eurocurrency Financing,* Chase Manhattan Bank, N.A., New York, 1975.

[88] Federal Reserve Bank of Kansas City, *Monthly Review,* July–August 1977.

[89] *Spotlight on the Term Loan,* Bankers' Magazine, Boston, Summer 1976.

[90] Federal Reserve Bank of New York, *Quarterly Review,* Summer 1977.

[91] *International Monetary Relations,* Royal Institute of International Affairs, London, 1976.

[92] *Development Co-operation: 1976 Review,* OECD Development Assistance Committee, Paris, 1976.

[93] Federal Reserve Bank of Chicago, *Economic Perspectives,* March–April 1978.

[94] American Management Association, *International Money Management,* New York, 1973.

[95] International Chamber of Commerce Brochure, *Incoterms,* No. 274, Paris, 1976.

[96] IMF, *IMF Survey,* Washington, DC, March 1979.

[97] Japan Securities Research Institute, *Securities Market in Japan,* 1977.

[98] Federal Reserve Bank of St. Louis, *Review,* March 1983.

[99] Federal Reserve Bank of St. Louis, *Review,* February 1983.

[100] Federal Reserve Bank of St. Louis, *Review,* April 1983.

[101] Financing Accounting Standards Board, *Statement of Financial Accounting Standards, No. 8,* Connecticut, 1975.

[102] *Euromoney,* London, October 1976.

[103] Morgan Guaranty Trust Co., *World Financial Markets,* New York, May 1978.

[104] *Euromoney,* London, March 1977.

[105] The American Bankers Association, *Banking Terminology,* Washington, DC, 1981.

[106] Federal Reserve Bank of St. Louis, *Review,* March 1984.

[107] Federal Reserve Bank of St. Louis, *Review,* October 1984.

[108] Federal Reserve Bank of St. Louis, *Review,* December 1984.

[109] *Creative Financing in the 1980s,* Practicing Law Institute, New York, 1983.

[110] *Corporate Banking: A Practical Approach to Lending, American Banker's Association,* Washington, DC, 1981.

[111] *Finance of International Trade,* Institute of Bankers, London, 1981.

[112] *Excess Reserves and Reserve Targeting,* Federal Reserve Bank of New York Quarterly Review, Autumn 1981.

[113] *Asset/Liability and Funds Management at U.S. Commercial Banks,* Bank Administration Institute, Rollowing Meadows, Ill., 1982.

[114] *Options as a Strategic Investment,* New York Institute of Finance, New York, 1980.

[115] *Export Finance,* Euromoney Publications, London, 1981.

[116] L.M. Loss & J.G. Buckley, *The Over-the-Counter Securities Markets,* Prentice-Hall, 1981.

[117] S. Haney. *BACS: The World's First EFT System.* The Banker, London, September 1984.

[118] *The Export Credit Financing Systems in OECD Member Countries,* OECD, Paris, 1982.

[119] M. Pelzer & K. Nebendorf, *Banking in Germany,* F.K. Verlag, 1973.

[120] J. Dundas Hamilton, *Stockbroking Today,* Macmillan, London, 1979.

[121] *A Note On Money Market Arbitrage,* Bank of England Quarterly Bulletin, June 1982.

[122] D.W. French. *Black-Scholes vs. Kassouf Option Pricing,* Journal of Business Finance & Accounting, Oxford, Autumn 1983.

[123] F.J. Fabozzie & I.M. Pollack, *The Handbook of Fixed Income Securities,* Dow-Jones Irwin, Homewood, Ill., 1983.